# BASIC WORKS OF
# CICERO

THE MODERN LIBRARY *is published*
*by* Random House, Inc.

# THE
# BASIC WORKS OF
# CICERO

*Edited, with an Introduction and Notes, by*
## MOSES HADAS

THE MODERN LIBRARY · *New York*

# Acknowledgments

Book 1 of *On Moral Duties*, from George B. Gardiner's *Cicero, De Officiis*, Book 1 of *On the Character of the Orator*, from E. N. P. Moor's *Cicero, De Oratore*, and the two speeches *Against Catiline* and the *Second Philippic*, from H. E. D. Blakiston's *Select Speeches of Cicero*, are used by permission of the publisher, Methuen and Company.

All but the first four chapters of Book 1 of the *Tusculan Disputations* is a slight revision of Robert Black's *Death No Bane*. The editor has supplied the version of the introductory chapters, as well as that of *On Old Age*, and has so extensively revised Cyrus R. Edmonds' translation of *Scipio's Dream* as to claim joint authorship.

*For Caelius* was newly translated for this edition by my colleague, Dr. Richmond Y. Hathorn, to whom I express most cordial thanks. Cordial thanks are due also to Professor Arthur Patch McKinlay, of the University of California at Los Angeles, and to his publishers for generous permission to use the selections from his *Letters of a Roman Gentleman* (Houghton Mifflin Company, 1926).

In the various selections revision has been limited to an occasional gloss of a Greek or other technical expression. Uniformity (at best a questionable ideal in a collection of this sort) would have required that the British "My Lords" be assimilated to the American "Gentlemen" or vice versa; and hence it has been thought best to allow each translator his own originality of style and his own mannerisms in punctuation and spelling.

M. H.

# CONTENTS

# INTRODUCTION

*by Moses Hadas*

For no national group is it so easy to choose a single representative author as it is for Rome. Not only in the volume and scope of his work but in its form and spirit, in its strength and weakness, Cicero is the perfect embodiment of Latin literature. In that literature concern for the practical and devotion to the service of Rome are central motives; to preoccupation with beauty for its own sake and to hard speculative thinking, both characteristic of the Greek literature of which the Latin was an offshoot, the Romans were indifferent. And when Latin literature is not essentially didactic and not directly useful in the austere business of being a Roman it tends to be a frivolous ornament. The deviations of Rome's greatest poet from his Greek models are significant and revealing. Where *Iliad* and *Odyssey* represent poetic truth of universal validity, *Aeneid* glorifies the the institution which is Rome. Achilles is a free agent, and his choices make his poem a tragedy of mankind; Aeneas represents the specifically Roman ideal of disciplined service to the destiny of Rome. The most impressive intellect among Roman writers is Lucretius, yet *On the Nature of Things*, didactic as it is, is calculated not merely to increase general understanding but to liberate Romans from the oppressive fear of magisterial deities and of death. Cicero's attitude to Lucretius is revealing. In 54 B.C., a year after the poet's death, Cicero writes his brother Quintus (2.9) that the poem shows "flashes of genius and of great art." Yet in his *Tusculan Disputations* (1.3 and 2.3), written ten years later, Cicero disclaims having read any Epicurean philosophy in Latin. Because it questioned the state religion, which the nobility had always used as a potent instrument of political control, Epicureanism had come to be regarded as subversive and its most gifted exponent as dangerous to the established order. And for Cicero nothing was more important than the maintenance of the established order.

The established order of the state, indeed, and his position in it were the main concern of Cicero's career. His chief literary function and his greatest success was in the public (and characteristically Roman) capacity of orator, and the most competent of his essays deal with oratory. When, in his enforced retirement from public employment, he deigned to regard philosophy and poetry, he felt constrained to justify such un-Roman pursuits by their political usefulness, and he made them strictly utilitarian. His literary as well as his political career (for a Cicero there is virtually no distinction) was devoted to the service of the idea of Rome. Nor does he seek to refine or enlarge that idea, for he is a conformist, not a rebel. If Rome's mission was to secure order and spread civilization, as Vergil's famous *Tu Romane memento* lines at the end of the sixth *Aeneid* declare, Cicero is our best example of that mission in operation. The heart of his creed was traditional order and administration, and he is the single greatest conserver and transmitter of Roman cultural values to European posterity. His was the language which gave shape to civilized discourse in the countries of Europe, and his popularizations transmitted so much of the philosophic thought of the ancients as the Middle Ages were prepared to receive. For the centuries during which Europe was a cultural unit, its unifying force, so far as an individual could provide one, was Cicero.

Of the private life of Marcus Tullius Cicero not much

needs to be said. He was born in 106 B.C. in Arpinum, from which Marius, Rome's other great 'new man,' had derived. His father took him and his younger brother Quintus to Rome to provide a good education. He became acquainted with the doctrines of the three leading philosophical schools, preferred the Stoic to the Epicurean, and the Academic to both. He listened to the eminent orators M. Antonius (grandfather of the triumvir) and L. Crassus, and heard Apollonius Molon's lectures on rhetoric. To prepare for the practice of law he attended the legal consultations of the distinguished Q. Mucius Scaevolas. By 80 B.C. he had entered upon his legal career, and in that year, whether for reasons of health or because his defense of Roscius had offended Sulla, he went abroad for two years and heard lectures in philosophy and rhetoric in Athens and Rhodes. About 76 he married Terentia, a wealthy and strong-minded woman, who bore him a daughter, Tullia, and a son, Marcus. His work brought him considerable wealth (in the form of legacies and the like; Roman lawyers did not receive direct fees), and he possessed a number of villas and a fine city house. In 47 he divorced Terentia and married his young ward Publilia; after the death of Tullia in 45 he sent her away, and devoted himself to writing until he was recalled to public activity by the assassination of Caesar in March 44. He was proscribed by the triumvirate of Octavian, Antony, and Lepidus, and was put to death in December 43.

But Cicero's private life is only a footnote to his public career. His rise to eminence was rapid; his defeat of his principal rival Hortensius in the prosecution of Verres in 70 left him the recognized leader of the Roman bar. His official career had begun with the quaestorship in 75; in 69 he was curule aedile and in 66 praetor. In politics Cicero's natural affiliation was with his own equestrian order, which included the banking interests. At the poles of the political spectrum were the aristocratic families who held a monopoly of high public office, and the *populares,* who carried on the tradition of the Gracchi and periodically agitated for cancellation of debts, distribution of public lands, and other radical measures. The equestrian order was not truly a centrist party, but rather wished to share in the prerogatives of the virtual oligarchy. Nor were the leaders of the *populares* proletarians; usually, like Julius Caesar himself, they were "gentlemen" who espoused the popular cause for reasons of political expediency. Cicero's own program, unrealistic in view of the ruthless party and personal rivalries, was to secure harmony of the orders by the co-operation of "all good men."

Cicero's election to the consulship for 63 B.C. (unprecedented for a "new man" except for the special case of Marius) was due to the fact that as an *eques* (and so a defender of the banking interests) he was a safe man, whereas his opponent, the noble Catiline, openly advocated cancellation of debts. His suppression of the Catilinarian conspiracy Cicero himself regarded as the high point of his career, but the execution without the sanction of the people of certain conspirators who were Roman citizens antagonized the *populares.* His middle-of-the-road policy led Cicero to reject an invitation to co-operate with the triumvirs Caesar, Pompey and Crassus, and he was left without their or the senate's protection. Clodius as tribune effected Cicero's heart-breaking exile in 58, but he was recalled in 57 and resumed his legal practice. When Caesar and Pompey were estranged after the deaths of Julia (Caesar's daughter and Pompey's wife) and Crassus, Pompey, who was Cicero's patron, veered to the senate. In 51/50 Cicero was proconsul of Cilicia, from which he returned as civil war was breaking out between Caesar and Pompey. He joined Pompey, but

Caesar, after his victory, permitted him to return to Rome in 47. He remained in political retirement and had no part in the assassination of Caesar in March 44, but he applauded the deed and returned to the forum to attack Antony, who inherited Caesar's policies, in the series of speeches called *Philippics*. The virulence of his attack made his proscription and death in the following year inevitable.

The personality of Cicero as well as the facts of his public career are easy to read from the extensive body of private correspondence which he has left behind; no other figure of antiquity, and few of modern times, stands so clearly revealed. If we find him a good deal of a trimmer and inordinately vain, we might well ask how many comparable figures in history would better pass scrutiny under such merciless light. If his views of politics and society were limited, we must recognize that it was inevitable for a man of his background to identify the interests of the state and of civilization with those views. For his faltering and his compromises there is one sufficient answer: he suffered death for his views. He is the shining example of the lawyer and politician in a republic making of his lawyership an art and of his politics statesmanship. And he transcended the ordinary measure of lawyer and politician by his concern for the cultural values of the race; he was not merely a patron of learning but set his own hand to propagating the wisdom of the past and making it accessible to all.

In shaping the modes of European thought and expression the contributions of Cicero are beyond calculation. Assimilation into our own culture, it is true, has already completed the direct usefulness of much of his work. Treatises on rhetoric are caviar to the general, and only amateurs of antiquity or of forensic oratory are likely to be much concerned with the bulk of Cicero's orations. But in his philosophical essays Cicero may still be read not merely

as a record of antiquity but as a guide to thought and conduct. No one could maintain that Cicero is a giant in speculative philosophy or that he created systems of thought. He
is the first to admit that his essays are merely adaptations
from the Greek: "They are mere drafts, produced with little labor; I contribute only the words, of which I have a
great abundance" (*To Atticus* 12.52). And the Greeks from
whom he borrowed were not themselves 'first philosophers'
but adherents of the Hellenistic schools then in vogue—
Stoics, Epicureans, Academics—who were concerned not
with explaining the universe so much as with helping men
adjust themselves to it. It is in his selection and presentation that Cicero performs his great service. Not only did he
transform the knotty treatises of the Greeks into lucid and
delightful and witty essays, but by his very selection and
distribution of emphasis he informed the whole of his work
with his own characteristic outlook.

It is the personal element in Cicero's writings that gives
them peculiar relevance to ourselves. We too respect culture and ideals, are impatient of subtleties, suspicious of
certainties, think of utilities and ends. Like Cicero we are
confronted by the imperious problems of civilized existence
in a great commonwealth founded upon justice and common aspirations and threatened by revolution. Cicero's
thought is directed toward providing distinctions which
should make it possible for thoughtful men to adjust to the
greater commonwealth, yield its aspirations devoted loyalty, and yet maintain personal integrity. If he were a closet
philosopher his work would not have this relevance; and if
political vicissitudes had not interrupted his public career
he would not have written philosophy at all. He wrote the
essays only in periods of enforced retirement from public
life and as an inadequate surrogate, as he himself says, for
the more important contributions to the Roman state which

his retirement prevented him from making. The writing of philosophy was the second best service he could perform for Roman patriotism. The Romans, he explains at the beginning of the *Tusculans* and elsewhere, had no philosophic literature, though they were fully the peers of the Greeks in intellectual capacity and their superiors in morality, because they had been preoccupied with more important matters. But it would be becoming for Rome to possess the ornament of a philosophic literature also, and since no other avenue of service was open and his achievements in oratory suggested his fitness for the task, he would now undertake to supply the want. But the essays are patriotic in senses other than supplying a becoming ornament. For one thing, the Roman constitution and Roman institutions are justified, as in the *Republic;* for another, the Epicureans, who were become associated with political subversiveness, are constantly refuted. But most of all, the essays make it possible for a man of thoughtful temper to be at the same time a good Roman.

Considering the brief periods of retirement which Cicero devoted to his essays—the bulk were written between the death of Tullia in 45 and his return to political activity in 44—his output is astonishing. Here we can only list the works in chronological order. *On the Republic* and *On the Laws* are political philosophy. The *Paradoxes* sets forth Stoic tenets. *On Consolation,* inspired by the death of his daughter, and *Hortensius,* which won St. Augustine to philosophy, are both lost. *On Ends* discusses views of the highest good; the statement and refutation of the Epicurean and Stoic positions each occupy a book, and the fifth book presents the acceptable Academic view. The *Academics* is a treatise on epistemology. *Tusculan Disputations* teaches how certain classes of distractions which militate against happiness can be confronted. The fragmentary *Timaeus* is

a free translation of Plato's treatise, and marks Cicero's turn
to theology. *On the Nature of the Gods* presents Epicurean,
Academic, and Stoic views of the question, and is logically
followed by *On Divination* and *On Fate*. *On Old Age*
and *On Friendship* are charming ethical essays. More specifically didactic is Cicero's hastily written last work, *On
Moral Duties*.

Another category of Cicero's writings, in which, indeed,
he shows his greatest technical competence, deals with rhetoric. In our world rhetoric has fallen upon hard times. We
seldom use the word except in a disparaging sense, and usually with the prefix 'mere,' to denote turgid artificiality in
vocabulary and syntax. But the word and the thing have
their legitimate uses; discourse is a human product and
therefore susceptible to the refinements of art, and the rules
of the art are capable of being set down. Like other arts
which are practised socially and continuously—the art of
table manners, for example—we learn the art of discourse
by imitation, but handbooks of etiquette have their place
nevertheless. Orators may unconsciously follow the rules of
the handbooks, as poets may lisp in numbers; but somewhere in the consciousness of the lisping poet are the examples of predecessors who labored over the art, and orators
who would be offended if the word 'rhetoric' were applied
to their efforts have assimilated the end product of classical
theory and practice. Mr. Winston Churchill's periods are un-
mistakably Ciceronian, whether or not he conned Cicero's
treatises, which they would not have been if Cicero's treatises had not served as Europe's textbooks in the art of
discourse through the centuries. Cicero himself was doubtless magnificently endowed by nature, but he composed his
speeches strictly according to theory, as the studious elabo-
ration of the rhythms at the end of his periods demonstrates.
He considered himself an artist in the spoken word, and

from his earliest youth and throughout his life occupied himself with the theory of his art and its history. In this field his technical works are *On Invention, On the Best Class of Orators, Parts of Oratory, Topics.* The *Brutus* gives a complete and judicious history of Roman eloquence, and *The Orator* sketches the ideal orator. Possibly the most carefully wrought of all of Cicero's works is *On the Orator,* which deals with the training of the orator, his subject matter, and his diction and delivery.

The fullest embodiment of Cicero's theory is to be found in his own speeches, which have been universally acknowledged as models in their kind. Fifty-eight have come down to us, and forty-eight others are known to be lost. Their subjects range from commonplace litigation (but usually with some political implication) to questions of the highest statesmanship. His oratorical style is characterized by richness of vocabulary, beauty of phrasing, an amplitude verging on the redundant, and extraordinary attention to cadence. In lawsuits he was almost always on the side of the defendant, and when his side was represented by several speakers he was always chosen to give the summation. Most of his political speeches were delivered in the senate, where his own party held the majority; but he could be effective with the multitude also, as when he persuaded them to relinquish a land law which was put forward for their advantage. The best known of the speeches are in four groups: the impeachment of Verres, the peculating governor of Sicily, which established Cicero's reputation; the Catilinarian conspiracy, which marks the high point of his career; the recovery of his property confiscated at his exile; and the furious *Philippics,* which attacked Antony and caused Cicero's death. Other pieces deservedly well-known are the *For Archias,* defending the Roman citizenship of a Greek poet, which expounds the practical uses of poetry; the *For*

*Cluentius,* on a charge of poisoning, which reads like a mystery thriller; and the *For Murena,* on a charge of bribery, which shows Cicero's masterful urbanity at its best.

Seldom has a critical and pregnant juncture in history been illuminated by a participant with expert knowledge and keen perception as fully as the Roman revolution is illuminated by the private correspondence of Cicero. The letters, it is important to note, were not written for publication (as those of Pliny or Symmachus, who imitated Cicero, were); Cicero placed complete reliance in his principal correspondent, Atticus, and made no effort to spare the weaknesses of important political personages or disguise his own. The 900 letters we have are divided into 37 books: 16 *To Atticus,* 16 *To Friends,* three *To His Brother Quintus,* and two *To Brutus.* These are not all that were published, and by no means all that were written. Cicero was a diligent correspondent; he might write three letters to Atticus in a single day, and did not like to have a day go by without a letter. There being no regular postal service, a letter might be written elaborately at leisure to await the chance of a messenger, or one might be written hastily while a messenger waited at the doorstep. Some of the longer and politically significant letters may have been carefully revised; the great bulk are untouched. So frank are the letters, indeed, that scholars hostile to Cicero have been able to draw up damning bills of indictment on the basis of the information they supply, and a French scholar of standing has recently argued at length that the collections were made by an enemy of Cicero for the specific purpose of discrediting him.

But only a Don Quixote or an insulated monk could reproach Cicero for his political maneuvering in an age when ambition was not only condoned but approved. In appraising Cicero's inordinate self-conceit we must remember that

he was a 'new man' who had made headway against the entrenched exclusiveness of the aristocracy. Approbation was
meat and drink to him. A concomitant of his insatiable appetite for applause, which a modern might attribute to an
inferiority complex, was a dash of hero worship for those
who had surely arrived and of awe for aristocracy of blood
even when the individual aristocrat was contemptible. The
weak mortal who wrote the letters does sometimes fall short
of the professions of the ethical preacher; but Cicero is
surely not alone in this inconsistency, and in his day the
fault was venial. For his vacillation and opportunism the
blame is partly on the exigencies of political life and its accepted standards, but partly also, surely, on Cicero's Academic criteria in philosophy and his training as a lawyer.
He was always able to see the merit in either side of a question, and his advocate's eloquence naturally tended to heap
up arguments of probability on the side which happened to
be expedient. But even to readers unconcerned with the
personality of Cicero and with the fascinating web of contemporary politics the wide and humane range of interests
in these letters, in literature, in art, and most of all in people,
makes them one of the more attractive legacies from antiquity.

Even the briefest remarks on Cicero as a writer must include the statement that Cicero also wrote verse—and that
happily (to judge by the opinion of ancient critics) the
verse is lost. From his principal poem, *On His Own Consulship,* Juvenal quotes the unfortunate lines

> O happy fate for the Roman state
> Was the date of my great consulate!

Another poem celebrated his famous fellow-townsman
Marius, and there were a number on the usual mythological
subjects. The thinness of his poetry may suggest that even

in his distinguished prose Cicero fails to rise to the rare heights which figures of comparable reputation in other literatures occupy. Perhaps the world can learn better from a figure whose stature does not demand craning of the neck and shielding of the eyes. It is significant that literary revolutions have turned upon passionate acceptance or rejection of Ciceronianism. Silver Latin is a development of Ciceronianism, but the age of Hadrian turned its back upon Cicero. Jerome chided himself for being a Ciceronian rather than a Christian—and remained a Ciceronian nevertheless. The humanists of the Renaissance refused to countenance linguistic usage which had no sanction in the pages of Cicero. When the cult of Ciceronianism hardened to the point where a Christian prelate could not name the Holy Ghost in a sermon because Cicero had no word for it the cult defeated itself and doomed Latin as a vernacular. If the language of Cicero had been permitted to retain the viability which Erasmus for one tried to give it perhaps Europe would have been better able to achieve the ecumenical ideal of Rome.

In this volume an attempt has been made to present a series of representative selections which illustrate various aspects of Cicero's thought and manner and which can at the same time be read as substantive works. The latter consideration explains not only the preponderance of philosophy over oratory and letters but also the omission of such important treatises as On the Nature of Gods and On Ends (or the Highest Good); in these the positions of the schools and their refutations are presented in alternate books, so that no single book can fairly be regarded as a substantive entity. The orations, though more masterly in craftsmanship, do not generally possess the permanent interest and value which attaches to the essays; the specimens presented

are chosen for their illustration of significant aspects of
Roman life and thought as well as of Cicero's oratorical art.
Of all Cicero's writings the Letters are doubtless the most
generally appealing, but they involve Cicero's own life and
the contemporary political situation to such a degree that
an intelligent reading presupposes detailed knowledge and
special interest, and hence only a handful are given. These
deal with crises in Cicero's life and Roman politics, exhibit
broader interests, and are generally agreed to be among the
best. In a word, the criteria for selection and allocation of
space have been general and permanent interest and value;
they justify the title *The Basic Works of Cicero.*

# DATES IN CICERO'S LIFE

B.C.

106   Birth of Cicero and of Pompey. Marius finishes the Jugur-
      thine War.

102   Birth of Quintus Cicero and of Julius Caesar. Marius
      destroys the Teutones.

91    Cicero takes the toga of manhood, writes a poem on
      Marius, and begins a hexameter translation of Aratus'
      *Phaenomena.*

86    Begins rhetorical works, of which *On Invention* is extant:
      continues studies in philosophy, rhetoric, and law.

81    First pleading; Sulla is dictator.

79-78 Foreign travel and study. Death of Sulla.

77    Returns to Rome and marries Terentia.

5     Quaestor in Sicily. Birth of Tullia.

0     Prosecution of Verres. Birth of Vergil.

69    Aedile; purchases Tusculan estate.

66 Praetor; supports Pompey for command in Mithradatic War.

65 Birth of son Marcus and of Horace.

63 Consul; suppresses Catilinarian conspiracy.

60 Refuses participation in first triumvirate (Caesar, Pompey, Crassus); writes on his consulship in Greek and in Latin.

58 Exiled by Clodius as tribune, for having put citizens to death without authority.

57 Recalled.

55 *On the Orator.*

54 *On the Republic.*

52 *On the Best Class of Orators; On the Laws* begun. Virtual anarchy at Rome 54-52.

51 Proconsul in Cilicia.

49-48 Civil war between Pompey and Caesar; Cicero joins Pompey, who is defeated and then murdered.

47 Returns to Tusculan villa.

46 *Paradoxa, Parts of Oratory, The Orator, Brutus* and a lost panegyric on Cato. Divorces Terentia.

45 Death of Tullia. *On Ends, Academics,* and (lost) *Consolation.*

44 *Tusculan Disputations* (before 15 March); between then and end of August *On the Nature of the Gods, On Divination, On Fate, On Old Age, On Friendship, On Glory, On Moral Duties, Topics;* from September the first four *Philippics.*

43 The remaining ten *Philippics.* Cicero beheaded in December.

*Columbia University, February, 1951*

# BASIC WORKS OF
# CICERO

# ON MORAL DUTIES

CICERO's main interest in philosophy was practical ethics, and On Moral Duties is the fullest and final statement of his ethical teaching. The book was written in the last year of his life, and, aside from the later Philippics, is his last writing. It is addressed to his son, then a student at the university of Athens; the son's character is revealed in the next to last letter in the present volume. Cicero's primary sources for On Moral Duties were the Stoics Panaetius and Posidonius, but his own environment, experiences and observations are more fully reflected in this than in any other of his philosophical treatises. The demoralization of the state is as present to his mind as in the recently written Second Philippic, and gives edge to his moralizing. The first (and best) book treats of the honestum or morally good under the categories of the venerable cardinal virtues of wisdom, courage, justice, and self-control. The second book deals with the utile or useful; the bases of utility and its function in the interrelations of men are discussed, and classes of utility are balanced and compared. Conflicts between the honestum and the utile are dealt with in the third book; here Cicero claims greater independence, but this section is really the poorest. For all its brilliant style On Moral Duties shows signs of the haste with which it was written. There are repetitions and illogicalities in order, and there are misplaced rhetorical flourishes. Possibly because of its haste it gives a picture of its author as untouched as that given by his letters; sane common sense appears along

3

*with conceit; noble patriotism along with partisan politics. But there is no false posturing;* On Moral Duties *is a sincere and valuable contribution to the ethical literature of the race, and has profitably been used as a textbook by generations of students in England and France and Germany who were, like young Cicero, about to embark upon life.*

1. My dear son, now that you have studied for a full year under Cratippus and in a city like Athens, you should be well equipped with the principles and doctrines of moral philosophy. A master of such power cannot fail to enrich your mind with ethical theories, while the cultured city in which you live will offer you many models for imitation. However, I have always found it best in my own case to combine the study of Latin and Greek in oratory as well as in philosophy, and I think it would be well for you to follow my example if you wish to be equally at home in the two languages. Here I flatter myself I have rendered good service to my countrymen, and it is gratifying to find that not only persons ignorant of Greek, but even educated men admit that I have done something towards developing their minds and forming their style. You should therefore continue your studies under the first thinker of the age, and that you will certainly desire to do, so long as you are not dissatisfied with your progress. But in reading the exposition of my theories which differ little from those of the Peripatetics (for we both claim to be followers of Socrates and Plato), whatever opinion you may form on the subject-matter—and you are free to judge for yourself—I am confident you will improve your Latin style. Still I would not have you think I say this in arrogance. I profess no monopoly in philosophical science, but I fancy I am within my rights in claiming as peculiarly my own a happy, perspicuous, and ornate style—the proper field of the orator, which I have cultivated all my life. I urge you, therefore, my dear son, to read with care not only my orations but also my philosophical works which are now almost as numerous as the

others. In the orations there is greater vigour, but the un-impassioned and temperate style of my essays is no less worthy of study.

I do not find that any Greek author has yet succeeded in elaborating at once the forensic and the calm philosophical style, with the possible exception of Demetrius of Phalerum, a keen logician and an orator who, though he lacks force, has the charm that marks the disciple of Theophrastus. What degree of perfection I myself have attained in these two styles let others judge; if I have failed, it is not for want of effort. I indulge the fancy that Plato, had he chosen to practise oratory, would have made an impressive and elo-quent pleader, and that if Demosthenes had followed up and published the doctrines he learned from Plato he would have been distinguished for the elegance and splendour of his diction. I have the same opinion of Aristotle and Iso-crates, but each of them took such delight in his own pur-suit that he looked coldly on the pursuit of the other.

2. When I came to choose out of the many things on which I had it in my mind to write to you, the theme of this, my first treatise, I selected what seemed to me best suited to your age and to my position as a father. Among all the elaborate and exhaustive discussions of philosophers on serious and important subjects it appears to me that nothing is more generally useful than the principles of duty they have given to the world. All our affairs, public or private, civil or domestic, our personal conduct, our so-cial transactions, inevitably fall within the province of duty; in the observance of duty lies all that is honourable, and in the neglect of it all that is dishonourable. This is the com-mon ground of all philosophers. Would any one assume the title who had no moral precepts to offer? Yet certain schools utterly distort our conception of duty by their defi-nition of the greatest good and the greatest evil. He who

severs the highest good from virtue and measures it by interest and not by honour, if he were true to his principles and did not at times yield to his better nature, could not cultivate friendship, justice or liberality; and no one can be brave who declares pain the greatest evil, or temperate who maintains pleasure to be the highest good. I have dealt with these propositions in another place although they are so obvious as to require no discussion. Now if these sects were only consistent they would not have a word to say on the subject of duty; indeed a system of moral principles permanent, invariable, and in harmony with nature, can only be established by those who maintain that honour should exclusively or mainly be pursued for its own sake. And so we find that this ethical teaching is peculiar to the Stoics, the Academics, and the Peripatetics, since the doctrines of Aristo, Pyrrho and Erillus have long since been exploded; yet even they would be entitled to treat of this question if they had recognised a difference in the value of things and given us some clue to duty. In the present inquiry, then, I shall mainly follow the Stoics. I shall not simply echo them, but, as my custom is, I shall use them as my sources, and exercise my own discretion in deciding how and what to borrow.

As duty is the subject of the whole of this treatise, it seems proper to begin with a definition of the term, a point which Panaetius has curiously omitted. The definition of terms must in fact form the basis of every scientific exposition if the scope of the argument is to be clearly understood.

3. Every question of duty has two sides: the one relating to the sovereign good, the other to the practical rules by which we may govern our conduct in every detail. The following are examples of our first class of questions. Are all duties perfect? Is one duty more important than another? and so forth. The rules of conduct are indeed related to the

highest good, but the relation is not quite evident, because they bear more directly on the regulation of our daily life: these are the duties I purpose to expound in the present treatise. Duties may also be divided into what are called the ordinary and the perfect. Perfect duty the Greeks define as that which is right; ordinary duty as that for doing which an adequate reason can be given.

According to Panaetius, in forming a resolution we have three things to consider. Is the subject of deliberation honourable or dishonourable? This is a problem which often distracts our minds with contrary opinions. In the second place we cast about and reflect whether the thing will procure comfort and enjoyment, wealth and abundance, position and power, whereby we may profit ourselves and those who are dear to us. This second question turns entirely on expediency. The third is concerned with the conflict between the honourable and that which appears to be expedient. When interest drags us one way and honour calls us back, the mind is bewildered and distracted with doubt. In this classification two points are omitted, a serious defect in a logical division. We not only ask whether the contemplated act is honourable or dishonourable, but we seek to determine the degrees of honour and expediency. Consequently the triple division of Panaetius must be abandoned in favour of a division into five parts. I must first speak of the honourable under two heads, then similarly of the expedient, and finally of the conflict between them.

4. Animals of every species are endowed with the instinct of self-preservation which leads them to preserve life and limb, to avoid what seems hurtful, and to seek and provide the necessaries of life, such as food and shelter. The reproductive instinct and the love of offspring are also universal. But there is a wide gulf between man and beast. Swayed by sense alone, the beast lives in the present, heedless of the

past, or future. But man endowed with reason perceives the ✗ connection of things, marks their causes and effects, traces their analogies, links the future with the past, and, survey-ing without effort the whole course of life, prepares what is needful for the journey. Nature with the aid of reason like-✗ wise binds man to man, unites them by the bond of lan-guage and of social life, inspires them with a strong love of offspring, and impels them to multiply the occasions of meet-ing and consorting with their fellows. These are the motives that incite a man to procure a comfortable livelihood not only for himself but for his wife and children and all whom he cherishes and is bound to support; and this responsibility rouses his energies and braces him for work.

The distinctive faculty of man is his eager desire to investi-gate the truth. Thus, when free from pressing duties and cares, we are eager to see or hear, or learn something new, and we think our happiness incomplete unless we study the mysteries and the marvels of the universe. From this it is evident that what is true, simple, and pure, is most in har-mony with human nature. With the instinct of curiosity is allied the desire of independence; a well-constituted char-acter will bow to no authority but that of a master or a just and legitimate ruler who aims at the public good: hence arises fortitude or indifference to the accidents of fortune. How precious should we deem the gift of reason since man is the only living being that has a sense of order, decorum and moderation in word and deed. No other creature is touched by the beauty, grace and symmetry of visible ob-jects; and the human mind transferring these conceptions from the material to the moral world recognises that this beauty, harmony and order are still more to be maintained in the sphere of purpose and of action; reason shuns all that is unbecoming or unmanly, all that is wanton in thought or deed. These are the constituent elements of the conception of honour which is the subject of our inquiry: honour even when cast into the shade loses none of its beauty; honour, I say, though praised by no one, is praiseworthy in itself.

5. You have now before you, my dear Marcus, the very form, I may say, the face, of honour; and, as Plato says of Wisdom, could we but see it with our eyes, what a divine passion it would inspire! Honour springs from one of four sources. It consists in sagacity and the perception of the truth, or in the maintenance of human society, respect for the rights of others, and the faithful observance of contracts, or in the greatness and strength of a lofty and invincible spirit, or finally in that order and measure in word and deed which constitute temperance and self-command. The cardinal virtues are indeed inseparably connected, yet each of them is the source of definite classes of duties. Wisdom or prudence, for example, the first in our division, is concerned with the investigation and discovery of the truth; this is its peculiar function. He is justly considered the wisest and the most prudent of men who penetrates furthest into the truth of things and has the keenest and swiftest eye to see and unfold their principles. Truth is therefore the material on which this virtue works, the sphere in which it moves. The function of the other virtues is to provide and maintain all that is necessary for our daily life, to strengthen the bonds of human society, and to evoke that great and noble spirit which enlarges our resources and secures advantages for ourselves and our kin, but is even more conspicuous by its indifference to these objects. Order, consistency, moderation and similar qualities fall under this category and are not so much speculative as active virtues; for it is by applying measure and law to the affairs of life that we shall best observe honour and decorum.

6. Of the four parts into which we have divided the con-

ception of honour, the first, consisting in the investigation
of the truth, touches human nature most nearly. We are all
carried away by the passion for study and learning; here
we think it noble to excel and count it an evil and a shame
if we stumble or stray, if we are ignorant or credulous. In
following this natural and noble instinct there are two errors to be avoided; in the first place we must not mistake
the unknown for the known and blindly give it our assent;
to escape this error, as all must wish to do, it is necessary to
devote time and trouble to the consideration of every question. In the second place it is wrong to waste our energies on
dark, thorny, and barren studies. If we avoid these errors
and bestow our toil and care on subjects that are honourable and worthy of study, we shall deserve nothing but
praise. Thus Sulpicius was once distinguished in astronomy
as our contemporary Sextus Pompeius is in mathematics;
many have made their name in logic, more in civil law; but
though all these branches of knowledge are concerned with
the investigation of the truth, it would be wrong to be diverted from active work by any such pursuit. The worth
of virtue lies in action, yet we have many times of rest, per-
mitting us to return to our favourite pursuits: and even
without our effort, our beating, restless mind will keep us
ever at study. Now every thought and operation of the mind
is employed in deciding about things that concern our honour and happiness or in pursuing knowledge and learning.
So much for the first source of duty.

7. Of the three remaining the most extensive in its scope
is the principle which knits together human society and
cements our common interests. It has two parts—justice, the
brightest of the virtues, the touchstone of worth, and the
cognate virtue of beneficence which may also be called
kindness or liberality.

The first duty that justice enjoins is to do no violence except in self-defence, to create no privilege in public rights, and to keep for our private enjoyment only what is ours. Private property has no place in the order of nature; it originates in ancient occupation, as when people take possession of vacant land, or in the right of conquest, or in a law, a contract, an agreement, an allotment; hence we say the land of Arpinum belongs to the Arpinates, the Tusculan land to the Tusculans; and the delimitation of private estates follows the same principle. Now since by this partition the individual secures as personal property a part of that which at first belonged to all, he ought to rest content with his share: if he covets more, he breaks the laws of human society. But since our life, to quote the noble words of Plato, has not been given to us for ourselves alone (for our country claims a share, our friends another), and since, as the Stoics hold, all the products of the earth are destined for our use and we are born to help one another, we should here take nature for our guide and contribute to the public good by the interchange of acts of kindness, now giving, now receiving, and ever eager to employ our talents, industry and resources in strengthening the bonds of human society. The foundation of justice is good faith—in other words, consistency and truthfulness in regard to promises and compacts. Though it may seem rather forced, we make bold to follow the Stoics who are keen students of etymology and to assume that *fides,* faith, is so called because a promise *fiat* is fulfilled. There are two kinds of injustice; the positive injustice of the aggressor, and the negative injustice of neglecting to defend those who are wronged. To attack a man unjustly under the influence of anger or some other passion is to lay hands upon a comrade; not to defend the oppressed and shield them from injustice, is as great a crime as to desert our parents, friends, or country. Premeditated wrongs are often the result of apprehension, the aggressor fearing that he will be the victim if he does not strike the first blow. But it is chiefly for the purpose of satisfying some desire that men commit an injury; and the commonest motive is the love of money.

8. In seeking riches, our object is to procure the necessities and the luxuries of life. But men of ambition look on money as a means of acquiring influence and of attaching others to their interests. Not long ago M. Crassus asserted that no man could aspire to political eminence unless he had a fortune on the interest of which he could support a whole army. Magnificence, luxury, elegance, and plenty are no less seductive. Such is the origin of the insatiable thirst for wealth. Not that we have any fault to find with the innocent accumulation of property; it is the unjust acquisition of it of which we must beware. But the strongest temptation to forget the claims of justice is born of the passion for military and political distinction. Ennius says: "No holy bond, no faith is kept, if a kingdom is the prize," but his words have a wider application. Where the places are few and rivalry is keen the struggle often becomes so fierce that it is difficult to respect the sacred rights of society. Of this we have recently had proof in the audacity of C. Caesar who overthrew all the laws of heaven and earth to gain supreme power, the object of his mad ambition. Alas! It is just the stoutest hearts, the brightest intellects, that are fired with the passion for office and command, for power and glory. Let us then be all the more watchful not to commit the like excess. But there is a great difference between a wrong committed under the influence of some brief and transient passion and one that is wilful and premeditated. A wrong committed under a sudden impulse is not so culpable as a wrong that is planned in cold blood. But I must now leave the subject of positive injustice.

9. In neglecting the duty of defending others, men are in-

fluenced by various motives. They are reluctant to make
enemies: they grudge the trouble and expense; they are deterred by indifference, indolence, and apathy; or they are
so fettered by their own pursuits and occupations as to
abandon those whom it is their duty to protect. Perhaps
Plato does not go far enough when he says that philosophers
deserve to be called just, inasmuch as they are employed
in the investigation of the truth and profess a sovereign
contempt for those objects which most men pursue with
ardour and for which they will even draw the sword and
fight to the last. In wronging no one they doubtless realise
a negative kind of justice, but they fail in their duty when
they become so absorbed in study as to abandon those
whom they ought to defend. For the same reason he thinks
they will not, except under pressure, participate in public
affairs. It would be more natural if they came forward un-
solicited. For even an action intrinsically right is only just
in so far as it is voluntary. Some men, from excessive devotion to their private affairs, or from a sort of misanthropy,
say they prefer to mind their own business, and think that in
so doing they wrong no one. They thus escape the one kind
of injustice only to rush into the other; in fact they are traitors to society because they contribute nothing of their zeal,
their energy, or their wealth, to the public good. Having
now established the two kinds of injustice with their re-
spective causes, and having determined the constituent elements of that virtue, we can readily decide, unless we are
blinded by self-love, what is our duty in particular circumstances. For it is difficult to meddle with other people's
affairs, though our friend Chremes in Terence says:
"Nothing is indifferent to me that touches man." It is no less
true that we are most keenly alive to our own success and
our own misfortune; the good and the evil that happen to
others we see as it were across a wide gulf, and we cannot

judge of our neighbours as we judge of ourselves. It is therefore a good rule never to do a thing if we are in doubt
whether it is right or wrong; righteousness shines with a
lustre of its own; doubt is the symptom of a vicious purpose.

10. But there are many occasions when actions that appear eminently worthy of the just man or the good man, as
we commonly say, change their complexion and present a
different aspect. It may at times be just not to return what
is entrusted to our care, not to keep a promise, or to violate
the laws of veracity and honour. In such cases we should go
back to the principles which I laid down at the outset, as
the foundations of justice: do evil to no man; work for the
common good. When these principles are modified by circumstances, our duty likewise changes and is not fixed and
invariable. Thus the fulfilment of a promise or agreement
may be prejudicial either to him to whom it was made or
to him who made it. Take an instance from mythology. If
Neptune had not kept faith with Theseus, Theseus would
not have been bereft of his son Hippolytus. The third of his
three wishes, we are told, was the death of Hippolytus; this
he conceived in a fit of rage, and when it was fulfilled he was
plunged in the deepest grief. If you promise a friend something which would be hurtful to him, your promise is not
binding; or if the thing would do more harm to him than
good to you, it is no breach of duty to prefer the greater to
the lesser good. Suppose you arranged to appear in court
in support of a friend and meanwhile your son fell seriously
ill, you would not be obliged to keep your promise; nay,
your friend would be more culpable than you if he complained of being abandoned. Again it is obvious that we are
not bound to fulfil promises extorted by fear or won from us
by craft; indeed these obligations are in most cases cancelled by the decisions of the praetors, or by particular
enactments. A common form of injustice is chicanery, that

is, an over-subtle, in fact a fraudulent construction of the law. Hence the hackneyed proverb: "The greatest right is the greatest wrong." Public men are often guilty of this offence. I shall illustrate what I mean by two examples. Once a general, having concluded a truce with the enemy for thirty days, ravaged his territory by night, because, he said, the truce applied to the day but not to the night. The conduct of a countryman of ours is equally discreditable; whether it was Q. Labeo or some one else I cannot tell, for I go merely by hearsay. The story is that he was appointed by the Senate arbitrator on a boundary question between the Nolans and the Neapolitans, and on reaching the spot advised the parties separately not to be greedy or grasping and rather to retire than to push forward. They consented, and a belt of neutral land was left between them. So he fixed their frontiers in accordance with their own suggestion, the unclaimed tract he awarded to the Roman people. This surely is deceit and not arbitration. It should be a lesson to us to avoid such despicable trickery.

11. We have also our duties towards those by whom we have been wronged; for retribution and punishment have their limits. Perhaps it would suffice if the aggressor repented the injury he had done. His expression of regret would keep him from repeating the offence and would deter others from injustice. In national affairs the laws of war must be strictly observed. There are two methods of settling a dispute, discussion and force; the one is characteristic of man, the other of beasts; it is only when we cannot employ conciliation that we are justified in resorting to force. Our one object in making war should be that we may live in peace unmolested; when victory is gained we should spare those who have not been cruel or barbarous. Our forefathers enfranchised the Tusculans, the Aequians, the Volscians, the Sabines, and the Hernicans, while they razed to

the ground Carthage and Numantia. I wish they had spared Corinth, but I think they had some good reason for what they did, most probably the strength of the place which they feared might some day tempt the Corinthians to renew the war. In my opinion peace should be our constant aim if there is no danger of treachery. Had my voice been heard, we should still possess, if not the best, at least some form of government, but now we have none. It is our duty not only to be merciful to the conquered, but, even though the battering-ram has shattered their walls, to shelter those who lay down their arms and seek the protection of the commander. Justice to our enemies was so scrupulously observed among our countrymen that those who accepted the submission of states or tribes conquered in war, became their patrons by ancient usage. The laws of war are religiously recorded in the fetial code of the Roman people. International law teaches that a war is just only if it is duly declared after a formal demand for satisfaction has been made. (Popilius was governor of a province and the son of Cato was serving in his army as a recruit. Popilius having decided to disband the legion to which he belonged, discharged young Cato with the rest of the men. But he remained in the army from love of fighting; Cato then wrote to Popilius asking him to bind his son by a second military oath if he allowed him to continue in active service: because through voidance of the former oath he had no right to fight with the enemy. Such was the rigour then observed in the conduct of war.) A letter is extant which Marcus Cato the elder wrote to his son Marcus while he was serving in Macedonia in the campaign against Perses. He had heard that his son had been discharged by the consul. He therefore warned him not to engage in battle because one who was not legally a soldier had no right to draw the sword against the enemy.

12. Here I call attention to the euphemism by which the word for "stranger" has come to be substituted for "an enemy under arms." The Twelve Tables use our word for "enemy" to mean "stranger." I ask you, Could charity go further than to describe by so gentle a name the man with whom you are waging war? But the word is now so debased by usage that it has dropped the meaning of stranger and is restricted to the technical sense of an enemy under arms. In every struggle for empire and glory we must be governed by the motives which I have just mentioned as the legitimate causes of war. Still the asperity of the conflict should be tempered by the noble motive of imperial glory. As in civil strife our attitude is different to a personal enemy and to a rival—with a rival the struggle is for office and position, with an enemy for life and honour—so with the Celtiberians and Cimbrians we fought as with personal enemies, not for empire but for existence; while it was for empire that we waged war with the Carthaginians and with Pyrrhus. The Carthaginians were faithless and Hannibal was cruel, but our other enemies were more just. You may remember the noble words of Pyrrhus regarding the restoration of the prisoners of war:

> Let mercenaries truck and treat for gold;
> Honour's a thing not to be bought or sold.
> Courage and steel must end this glorious strife:
> And in the case of victory or life,
> Fortune's the judge. We'll take the chance of war:
> And what brave man soever she shall spare
> With life, depend upon't, I'll set him free:
> Let him but own the gift to the great gods and me.

—a most princely sentiment, worthy of a scion of the line of Aeacus.

13. Further, if individuals under stress of circumstances have made a promise to an enemy, even then they are

bound to keep their word. In the First Punic War Regulus
was captured by the Carthaginians and sent to Rome
on parole to negotiate the exchange of prisoners of war. On
his arrival he advised the senate not to give up the prisoners,
and despite the efforts of his kinsmen and friends to keep
him at home he preferred to return to his punishment rather
than break his word pledged to the enemy. [In the Second
Punic War, after the battle of Cannae, Hannibal sent to
Rome ten Roman soldiers who bound themselves by an oath
to come back if they did not procure the ransom of the prisoners of war, but such of them as broke their obligation
were kept disfranchised all their lives, and the like fate befell the man who had been the first to incur guilt by evad-
ing his oath. This man having quitted the camp with Hannibal's permission, returned soon after on the pretext that
he had forgotten something. When he left the camp for the
second time he fancied he was released from his oath, and
so he was in the letter but not in the spirit. In every promise
it is well to think of the meaning and not of the words. Our
forefathers have set us an admirable example of justice to
an enemy. A deserter having come from the camp of
Pyrrhus and offered to the senate to poison the king, the
senate and C. Fabricius delivered him up to Pyrrhus. In
this way they refused to countenance a criminal attempt
even on the life of a powerful aggressor.] I have said enough
on the duties of war. We should also remember that it behoves us to deal justly even with the humblest. Now there
is no lot or position meaner than that of slaves; and we are
wisely enjoined to treat them as we do hired labourers: if
we exact work from them we should give them their due.
Injustice fights with two weapons, force and fraud; fraud
suggests the mean little fox; force, the lion. Both are unworthy of man, but fraud is the more detestable. The most
criminal injustice is that of the hypocrite who hides an act

of treachery under the cloak of virtue. But I must not enlarge.

14. My next subject is beneficence or liberality, the most human of all the virtues, but one which often demands the exercise of caution. We must give heed that our bounty is not injurious either to those whom we intend to benefit or to others, that it does not exceed our means, and that in each case it is proportioned to the worth of the recipient. This last principle is the foundation of justice, the standard by which all these acts of kindness must be measured. If we offer to another under the guise of kindness what will do him harm, we are not to be accounted beneficent or liberal men but dangerous hypocrites; and if we harm one man in order to be liberal to another we are quite as unjust as if we were to appropriate our neighbour's goods. Many men, however, especially if they are ambitious of honour and glory, lavish on one the spoils of another, expecting to obtain credit as benefactors, if only they enrich their friends by fair means or by foul. Such conduct is absolutely opposed to duty. Let us therefore remember to practise that kind of liberality which will be beneficial to our friends and injurious to no one. Neither Sulla nor C. Caesar deserves to be called liberal for transferring property from its rightful owners into the hands of strangers. For without justice there is no liberality.

The second precaution of which I spoke is that our bounty should not exceed our means. Those who seek to be more generous than their circumstances permit, offend in two ways. First they wrong their kin by making over to strangers the wealth which in justice they should rather give or bequeath to those of their own blood. In the second place the passion for plunder and dishonest gain is almost inseparable from this foolish generosity which must ever replenish the source of bounty. It is also manifest that the conduct of men who are not really generous but only ambitious of the name often springs from vainglory rather than from a pure motive. Such hypocrisy, I hold, savours more of deceit than of liberality or honour.

My third rule is that we should carefully weigh the merits of those whom we intend to benefit. Let us look to the character of the recipient, his disposition towards us, our common interests and social relations, and the obligations under which we lie to him; if he unites all these claims on our kindness, we cannot look for more; if some are lacking, the number and importance of the others must turn the scale.

15. As those with whom we live are neither perfect nor ideally wise, and as we may consider ourselves fortunate if we find in them even a shadow of virtue, it is evident that we should neglect no one who exhibits the slightest trace of worth, and should respect and cherish other men in proportion as they are adorned with these gentler virtues, moderation, self-command, and this very justice of which I have spoken so much. The spirit of fortitude is generally too impetuous in the good man who has not attained moral perfection and ideal wisdom; it is the gentler virtues that seem to be more within his reach. So much for the character of the recipient of our bounty. As to the affection he may cherish towards us, our first duty is to be kindest to him who loves us best; but we should not test his love, as youths would do, by its passionate fervour but rather by its strength and constancy. If, however, we are debtors, and our duty is not to bestow but to requite a favour, it behoves us to give the greater diligence; for no duty is more imperative than gratitude. But if, as Hesiod enjoins, we ought to give back with interest, if possible, what we have borrowed, how should we answer the challenge of kindness? Must we not imitate those fertile lands which yield even more than they receive? For if we do not grudge to serve

those from whom we look for recompense, with what zeal should we not requite favours already received? Liberality is of two kinds; it gives and it returns; it is in our own power to give or not to give, but to requite a favour is for the good man a sacred obligation provided he can do so without injustice. It is necessary, however, to discriminate between benefits received; and it is clear that the greatest benefit deserves the greatest gratitude. But we must always think of the spirit, the devotion and the affection that have prompted the deed. Many blind and thoughtless men are carried away by a morbid philanthropy or by fits of generosity as sudden as the wind. But benefits conferred with judgment, deliberation, and consistency, stand upon a higher plane. Whether we bestow or requite a favour, duty requires, if other things are equal, that we should first help those who need our help most; but that is not the way of the world. For men are most eager to serve one from whom they expect the greatest reward even though he needs no help.

16. The surest means of strengthening the bonds of society is to bestow the greatest kindness on those who are nearest to us. Let us go to the root of the matter and seek in nature the first beginnings of society. The first is seen in the brotherhood of the entire human race. The bonds of connection are thought and speech, the instruments of teaching and learning, of communication, discussion, and reasoning, which unite man to man and bind them together by a kind of natural league. Nothing lifts us so far above the brutes; in some animals we recognise courage, as in the horse and the lion, yet, as animals have neither thought nor speech, we never ascribe to them justice, equity or goodness. Such is the universal brotherhood of mankind. Here the common right to all those things which nature has destined for the common use of man must be kept inviolate; and while property assigned by statute or by civil law must be held under

the conditions established by these laws, we may learn from the Greek proverb, "Among friends all things in common," how to regard all other property. The goods common to all men are, I think, defined in the words of Ennius, which though restricted by him to one instance are generally true:

> To put a wandering traveller in 's way,
> Is but to light one candle with another:
> I've ne'er the less, for what I give.

This one example teaches us to grant even to a stranger what it costs us nothing to give. Hence the common maxims: "Keep no one from a running stream"; "Let any one who pleases take a light from your fire"; "Give honest advice to a man in doubt," things which we receive with profit and give without loss. Therefore while we enjoy these blessings we must always contribute to the common weal. But since the resources of individuals are limited and the number of the needy is infinite, we must think of the standard of Ennius: "None the less it shines for him," and so regulate this general liberality that we may continue to have the means of being generous to our friends.

17. Human society may embrace a wider or a narrower circle. Apart from the tie of our common humanity, there is the closer alliance of those who belong to the same nation or tribe and speak the same language. This is a strong bond of union. A more intimate relationship subsists between members of the same state. Fellow-citizens have many things in common; the forum, the sanctuaries, colonnades and streets, laws and privileges, the courts of law, the right of suffrage, social and friendly ties, and the many reciprocal relations of commerce. Still closer is the union of kinsmen; it is human society in miniature. As all living creatures are endowed with the reproductive instinct, the first

bond of union is that between husband and wife, next that
between their children; then comes the unit of the family
and community of goods. Here we find the germ of the city,
the nursery, I may say, of the state. Next in order are the
relations of brothers and sisters and of first cousins and
their children who, cramped in the one home, go forth as
it were to found new colonies. Marriages, with their rela-
tionships, follow and kinsmen multiply. In this propagation
and its aftergrowth states have their origin. For the ties of
common blood unite men in kindness and love. It is a great
thing to have one family history, a common worship, and
a common tomb. But when good men of like character are
joined in friendship, there we find the noblest and the
strongest union. Honour, on which I love to dwell, attracts
us even in others and kindles a fellow-feeling for those
whose character it adorns. Of all the virtues justice and liberality have the greatest charm, the greatest power to excite
our love for those in whom they seem to reside; and the
strongest bond of affection is the moral sympathy which
unites the good. When two men have the same tastes and
the same desires, each loves his neighbour as himself, and
the ideal of Pythagoras is realised; the two friends become
one. Another strong bond of sympathy is the interchange
of services; so long as they are mutual and acceptable, they
bind us together in a lasting alliance.

Now if you survey in your mind all the social relations,
you will find that none is more important, none closer,
than that which links each one of us with the state. We love
our parents, we love our children, our kinsmen, and friends,
but all our loves are lost in love of country. Who would
not die for her sake if by his death he could do her good?
All the more execrable are the fiends who have mangled
her body with every outrage, who have laboured and still
are labouring to compass her ruin. But if we compare and

contrast the rival claims to our friendly offices, we must assign the first rank to our country and our parents to whom we owe so many benefits; the next to our children and our whole household, who look to us alone and have no other refuge. Next in order are those kinsmen with whom we live in harmony, and with whom we are so often united by common interests. It is they who have the strongest claim on us for material help; but close intimacy, the interchange of thought and speech, of exhortation, consolation, even of rebuke—these things thrive best in the soil of friendship, and the happiest friendship is that which is cemented by moral sympathy.

18. In apportioning all these services we shall have to consider what each man needs most and what he can or cannot procure without our aid. Thus it will often be found that the claims of necessity are stronger than the claims of kin, and that our duty to one man is more pressing than our duty to another; you would sooner help your neighbour to gather in his corn than your brother or your friend; but if a case were on trial, you would rather plead for a kinsman or a friend than for a neighbour. Such are the circumstances we must keep in view in all our moral calculations if we would be good accountants of duty, skilled in adding and subtracting, in striking a balance, and finding what is due to this one and to that. Physicians, generals and orators, however proficient in the rules of their art, achieve no great success unless they unite theory with practice; so there is no lack of precepts on duty such as I now lay down, but it is experience and practice above all that are required in a matter so important. Perhaps I have said enough to show how honour, the source of duty, originates in the rights and obligations of human society. Of the four cardinal virtues from which honour and duty are derived it is evident that the most imposing in the eyes of the world is

fortitude, that great and sublime spirit which scorns the chances of life. So, upon occasion, it is taunts like these that first come to our lips.

> Young men in show, but wenches in your hearts:
> While Cloelia plays the brave and acts your parts,
> You're for exploits that cost no sweat, nor blood.

So, when we contemplate the brave and noble deeds of some great spirit, we instinctively grow eloquent in their praise. Valour affords a field for eloquence in Marathon, Salamis, Plataeae, Thermopylae and Leuctra; valour animated our own Cocles, the Decii, Cn. and P. Scipio, M. Marcellus, and others without number, and valour has made of the Roman people a nation of heroes. The military costume which adorns almost all our statues is a further proof of our passion for glory in war.

19. But if this high spirit which shines in toil and danger is divorced from justice and fights for private ends, and not for the public good, it is anything but a virtue: it is a brutal vice, repulsive to all our finer feelings. Fortitude is therefore admirably defined by the Stoics as the virtue which fights for equity, and no one ever acquired true glory whose reputation for fortitude was founded on craft and cunning, for there can be no honour without justice.

Plato has a fine reflection on this subject: "Knowledge without justice is to be accounted cunning rather than wisdom, and even intrepidity, if prompted by personal ambition, and not by public spirit, does not deserve the name of fortitude: audacity is its name." I maintain then that fortitude or strength of character must be joined with goodness and candour, love of truth and hatred of deceit: qualities which are the very marrow of justice. Unhappily this elevation or greatness of mind is the soil in which obstinacy and the inordinate love of pre-eminence most readily take root. Plato tells us that the Lacedaemonians as a nation are consumed with the passion for victory; so it is with the man of strong character, his ambition is to rule, nay, to rule alone. But it is difficult for those who covet such pre-eminence to maintain that fair spirit which is essential to justice. Thus it happens that men of ambition neither listen to reason nor bow to public and legitimate authority, but chiefly resort to corruption and intrigue in order to obtain supreme power and to be masters by force rather than equals by law. But the greater the difficulty the greater the glory. For in every circumstance of life justice must be respected. It follows that the title of brave and magnanimous men belongs not to those who commit but to those who repel injustice. The true fortitude of the sage places honour, which above all things it instinctively pursues, not in glory but in conduct, and aspires to be first in deed rather than in name. For the slave of the capricious and ignorant mob cannot be reckoned a man of power. Yet it is the loftiest spirits that are most easily led into temptation by the passion for glory: but now we are on slippery ground, for where will you find the man who does not aspire to glory as the natural reward of the hardships he has undergone and the perils he has encountered?

20. Fortitude has two characteristics. The first is indifference to outward circumstances. It is founded on the conviction that nothing is worthy of the admiration, the desire, or the effort of man except what is honourable and decorous and that he must surrender neither to his fellow-men, to passion, nor to fortune. The second, the natural outcome of this moral temperament, is the ability to perform actions which are not only great and useful, but arduous, laborious, and fraught with danger to life and all that makes life worth living. Of the two parts of fortitude the latter is brilliant and imposing, as well as useful, but the former em-

bodies the principle which makes great men and noble spirits that laugh at fortune. To regard honour as the only good and to be free from passion are the two fruits of this virtue. It is a mark of moral courage to make light of those objects which dazzle the world, and steadily to despise them on fixed and settled principles, but it demands a character not less strong and stable to bear the bitter sorrows of life and the countless blows of fortune without departing from our natural tranquillity or sacrificing the dignity of the sage. Further, it would be inconsistent to master fear but be mastered by desire, to conquer hardship but be conquered by pleasure. Let us guard against these errors and above all shun the love of money, for there is no surer sign of a narrow, grovelling spirit, just as there is nothing more honourable or noble than to despise what fortune refuses and to devote what she bestows to beneficence and liberality. As I said above, we ought to beware of the passion for glory, for it robs us of liberty, which brave men should pursue with all their might, and we should not seek command or rather upon occasion decline it or lay it down. Again, we must put away every emotion—desire, fear, grief, joy, anger—in order that we may enjoy the tranquillity and composure of mind which brings in its train moral stability and self-respect. It is the love of this tranquillity that has led so many men in all ages to withdraw from public affairs and take refuge in a life of leisure. Among the number have been illustrious philosophers of the first rank and grave and earnest men who could not bear the ways of the people or their rulers. Some of these spent their lives in the country finding pleasure in the management of their property. They aspired to the independence of kings, who suffer no want, bow to no authority, and enjoy liberty, or the privilege of living as you please.

21. This then is the common object of ambitious states-

men and men of leisure; statesmen expect to attain it by acquiring great wealth, men of leisure by contenting themselves with their own means, however small. Neither view is to be condemned, but the life of the retired man is easier and safer for himself, less dangerous and oppressive to others, while the career of the politician who devotes himself to the conduct of important affairs is more fruitful to the world and is the highway to eminence and distinction. I should therefore be disposed to excuse the political inaction of men of genius who consecrate their lives to study and of those who through ill-health or some more serious cause withdraw from public life, leaving to others the opportunity and the credit of government. But when men without such excuse profess to scorn the commands and offices which dazzle the world, their conduct deserves nothing but censure. In so far as they despise glory and count it as naught we are bound to sympathise with their views; but it really seems as if they shrank from toil and trouble and the supposed discredit of political failure. Some men are inconsistent in opposite circumstances; they rigorously despise pleasure, in pain they are oversensitive, they scorn glory, but are crushed by disgrace, and even in their inconsistency they are inconsistent. But the born administrator should without hesitation seek for office and assume the direction of public affairs; otherwise government becomes impossible and there is no field for the display of fortitude. Now magnanimity and contempt of fortune, tranquillity and composure of mind, are not less necessary, perhaps even more necessary, to statesmen than to philosophers, if they are to be free from anxiety and to live a staid and well-balanced life. This is easier for philosophers; their life is less exposed to the blows of fortune; they have fewer wants; and in adversity they have not so far to fall. Statesmen are naturally agitated by stronger emotions than pri-

vate citizens and they are more ambitious of success. Thus
they have all the more need to exercise fortitude which frees
the mind from care. On entering political life a man should
not only consider the honourable nature of the work,
but also his ability to perform it; and in this self-examina-
tion he must guard against the groundless despair of the
coward and the excessive confidence of the man of ambition. In a word, whatever we undertake, the most thorough
preparation is necessary.

22. I wish here to correct the prevailing prejudice that
the work of the soldier is more important than the work of
the statesman. Many men seek occasions for war in order
to gratify their ambition; and the tendency is most conspicuous in men of strong character and great intellect, especially if they have a genius and a passion for warfare. But
if we weigh the matter well, we shall find that many civil
transactions have surpassed in importance and celebrity the
operations of war. Though the deeds of Themistocles are
justly extolled, though his name is more illustrious than that
of Solon, and though Salamis is cited as witness to the brilliant victory which eclipses the wisdom of Solon in found-
ing the Areopagus, yet the work of the law-giver must be
reckoned not less glorious than that of the commander. Salamis was a momentary advantage to the state, the Areopagus a benefit which will endure for ever; for it is this council
that has preserved the laws of the Athenians and their time-
honoured institutions. Themistocles can point to no instance in which he served the Areopagus, while the Areopagus can boast of rendering aid to Themistocles; for the war
was directed by the wisdom of that council which Solon
had established. The same may be said of Pausanias and
Lysander. Though they extended the limits of the Lacedaemonian empire, their exploits are nowise to be compared
with the legislation and the constitution of Lycurgus. Why,

it was to him they owed the discipline and courage of their men. To tell the truth, I never thought M. Scaurus inferior to Marius when I was a boy, nor Q. Catulus to Cn. Pompeius at the time when I was engaged in public affairs; an army in the field is nothing without wisdom at home. Scipio Africanus, who was equally remarkable as a man and as a soldier, rendered no greater service to his country by the destruction of Numantia than his contemporary P. Nasica who though not invested with official authority put to death Ti. Gracchus. The conduct of Nasica does not belong exclusively to the province of civil affairs—for an act of violence borders on warfare—still it was a political, not a military measure. That is a fine sentiment though I hear it is constantly assailed by traitors who bear me a grudge:

> Let swordsmen to the gown give place,
> And crown the orator with bays.

Not to mention other examples, when I was at the helm of state, did not the sword yield to the garb of peace? Never was our country menaced by more serious danger, never did she enjoy more profound repose: and it was through my vigilant policy that the sword slipped from the traitor's hands and fell to the ground as if by magic. When was such an exploit performed in war? Where will you find a triumph to compare with mine? I speak thus frankly, my dear son, because I know that my self-complacency will be pardoned by one who is destined to inherit my glory and follow my example. Why, the great Cn. Pompeius, a hero crowned with the laurels of victory, publicly paid me the compliment that in vain would he have won his third triumph had not my efforts preserved our city, the scene of its celebration. There is then a civic fortitude which is not inferior to the prowess of the soldier, and demands even greater energy and self-sacrifice.

23. That moral dignity, which we find in a noble and lofty spirit, depends, it is true, on force of mind, not on bodily strength; yet we must so train and school the body that it may obey our judgment and reason, whether we are discharging public functions or enduring hardships. The moral dignity, I say, which is the subject of our inquiry, consists exclusively in thought and reflection; and thus the ministers who govern the republic perform as important work as the generals who command her armies. It is by the policy of statesmen that war has often been averted, brought to a close, or even declared; the third Punic War, for instance, was undertaken on the advice of M. Cato, and even after his death it was affected by his powerful influence. Accordingly in settling a dispute the skill of the diplomatist is to be preferred to the valour of the soldier, but we should adopt this principle not through fear of war but on the ground of public expediency, and should only take up arms when it is evident that peace is the one object we pursue. Again, the strong and resolute man is not shaken by misfortune; he is never disconcerted or thrown off his balance, but at all times retains his presence of mind, his judgment, and his reason. Such are the marks of personal courage. But the man of great intellect anticipates the future, calculates the chances for good or for evil, decides how to meet every contingency, and is never reduced to the necessity of saying: "That is not what I expected." These are the features by which we recognise a great and sublime spirit, confident in its own prudence and wisdom. But to rush into battle blindfold and fight the enemy hand to hand is barbarous and brutal; nevertheless, when stress of circumstances demands it, we must draw the sword and choose death before slavery and shame.

24. To pass to the destruction and spoliation of cities we should here avoid recklessness and cruelty. In times of dis-

order, too, the brave man will punish the leaders and spare the people and in every conjuncture will cleave to what is right and honourable. I have said that some men prefer the valour of the soldier to the wisdom of the statesman, so you will find many to whom a dangerous and feverish policy is more dazzling and impressive than calm and well-considered counsels. We should never incur the imputation of cowardice by fleeing from danger, while we should avoid the other extreme of rushing into danger, which is the height of folly. It is therefore necessary in perilous enterprises to follow the practice of physicians who treat mild cases with gentle measures and only apply desperate remedies to desperate diseases. It is mad to pray for a storm when the sea is calm, but wise, when it comes, to meet it with every precaution (so it is wrong to court danger, but right to face it boldly), especially if you have more to gain by decisive action than you would lose by remaining in suspense. Now great enterprises are fraught with danger partly to those who undertake them, partly to the state, and in carrying them out some men risk their lives, others their reputation and the goodwill of their fellow-citizens. We should therefore be more willing to endanger our own interests than the welfare of our country and to stake our honour and glory more readily than other advantages. History presents many examples of men who, though ready to lavish wealth and even life for their country, turned a deaf ear to her prayers when she called for the slightest sacrifice of their glory. Callicratidas, the Lacedaemonian commander in the Peloponnesian war, performed many brilliant exploits, but at last threw away all he had won by rejecting the proposal that he should withdraw his squadron from Arginusae and not engage the Athenians. "If the Lacedaemonians lose this fleet," he replied, "they can build another, but for me flight means disgrace." The reverse at Arginusae was unimportant. But that was a fatal blow which Cleombrotus dealt to the Lacedaemonian empire when through fear of public opinion he rashly fought with Epaminondas. How much wiser the conduct of Q. Maximus of whom Ennius says:

> Fabius was slow but sure, and his delay
> Restored the tottering state. Now 'twas his way
> To mind his business, not what people said:
> He lived a great man, but he's greater dead.

Errors such as these should also be avoided in political life. There are actually men who through fear of unpopularity will not dare to express their opinions, however excellent.

25. Our statesmen will do well to remember these two precepts of Plato's. Forgetting personal interest they should aim at the public advantage and make that the object of all their efforts; again, they should care for the whole body politic and not abandon one part while protecting another. The government of a country resembles the charge of a minor. It must be conducted for the advantage of the governed, not of the governors. To promote the welfare of one section of the citizens and neglect another is to bring upon the state the curse of revolution and civil strife. What is the result? We have a democratic and an aristocratic party, but a national party hardly exists. This factious spirit it was that caused such bitter feuds at Athens and in our own republic fanned the flames of sedition and destructive civil wars. From such disasters a brave and earnest citizen worthy of supreme political power will turn with detestation. Indifferent to influence and power he will give his undivided energies to the public service and will impartially promote the interests of every class and the good of the whole nation. He will never employ false charges to expose any man to hatred or unpopularity, but will cleave to justice and hon-

our, and rather than abandon his principles will suffer the heaviest loss and brave even death itself. There is nothing more deplorable than the passion for popularity and the struggle for office. Plato has a fine simile on this subject. "Competitors for the public administration," he says, "are like sailors fighting for the helm." In another place he enjoins us not to regard our political opponents with the same hostility as men who take up arms against our country. I may cite as an example the rivalry of P. Africanus and Q. Metellus which was never embittered by personal rancour. I have no patience with those who would have us cherish bitter animosity against our rivals as if that were a mark of fortitude. No, there is nothing more praiseworthy, nothing more becoming in a great and noble character than a forgiving, forbearing spirit. In a free country, where all enjoy equal rights, if we cultivate a gracious manner it should be united with the power to disguise our feelings, for, if we are ruffled by an ill-timed visit or an impudent request, we may fall a prey to a churlish temper injurious to ourselves and offensive to others. But if the public interests are at stake this gentleness and mercy are only to be commended when they are accompanied with sternness without which government is impossible. In administering punishment and reproof it behoves us to abstain from insult and to seek the public advantage and not our personal satisfaction. Again, we should never impose a penalty disproportioned to the offence or for the same crime punish one and let another go unchallenged. Above all, when we inflict punishment, let us put away anger; he who approaches the task in an angry spirit will never observe the happy mean between excess and defect, that cardinal principle of the Peripatetics, which they would be right in preaching if they did not praise anger and tell us that nature has bestowed it for some good end. No, in all circumstances let us repudiate this passion and pray that our rulers may resemble the laws which punish not in anger but in justice.

26. Moreover when fortune smiles and everything is going to our heart's desire, it is our duty to abstain from pride,
disdain and arrogance. It is as sure a sign of weakness to be
spoiled by success as to be crushed by misfortune, and it is
a golden rule in every situation of life to keep our balance
and wear an even look and the same unruffled brow. Such
we learn from history was the character of Socrates and of
C. Laelius. Philip of Macedon, we are told, was inferior to
his son in heroism and glory but surpassed him in condescension and sympathy. The father was always noble, the
son was often mean; hence the maxim seems true: "The
higher you rise, the more lowly must you be." Panaetius records a favourite simile of his friend and pupil Africanus:
"When horses grow wild and mettlesome after constant
charges in the field of battle, their owners hand them to the
horse-breaker to make them more tractable; so presumptuous men who turn restive in prosperity should be taken to
the *manège* of reason and philosophy to learn the frailty of
human things and the fickleness of fortune." It is above
all in the height of our success that we should consult our
friends and bow to their authority. At such a season too it
is well to beware of the flatterer and close our ears to his
seductive words. We are all so well pleased with ourselves
that we accept praise as our due; hence the countless blunders of men who, puffed up with vanity, fall a prey to the
greatest delusions and bring upon themselves contempt and
ridicule. But enough of this subject. To recapitulate, the
public administration is so extensive in its range and embraces such a multitude of interests that statesmen unquestionably perform the most important work in the world and
that which demands the greatest fortitude. But it cannot be
denied that in all ages many private men of strong charac-

ter have carried on important researches or pursued great objects without quitting their own sphere. Midway between philosophers and statesmen there is another class who take delight in the management of their own affairs, never adding to their fortune by unscrupulous means nor refusing, in case of need, to aid their kinsmen, their friends, or their country. Property should be acquired by no dishonest or odious methods; it should be increased by thought, care and thrift; and it should benefit the greatest possible number provided they are worthy, and minister less to excess and luxury than to liberality and beneficence. By following these principles we may lead a lofty, dignified, and independent life, uniting candour with good faith and goodwill to all men.

27. It remains to discuss the last part of honour. This comprises considerate feeling and the virtue of self-command or moderation, which lends a sort of lustre to our life, subdues our passions and regulates our conduct. It further includes the virtue which we may call in Latin decorum; the Greeks call it *prepon*. Decorum is really inseparable from honour. Indeed the two notions are coextensive and the difference between them is more easily felt than explained. For decorum, whatever it may be, always presupposes honour. It is therefore found not only in the present division of honour, but also in the three preceding. It is decorous to think and speak wisely, to act deliberately, and in everything to see and uphold the truth; on the other hand, it is just as indecorous to be led astray and wander stumbling in the dark, as to go crazy and lose one's reason. All just acts are decorous, while unjust acts are at once dishonourable and indecorous. The same thing is true of fortitude. To act in a manly and courageous spirit is decorous and worthy of a man, to do otherwise is at once dishonourable and indecorous. The decorum of which I speak is thus

related to honour as a whole, and the relation is so manifest
that no abstruse process of reasoning is required to discover
it. In the whole of virtue we feel there is something decorous; and if we separate these two conceptions, the distinction is more theoretical than real. As bodily grace and
beauty are inseparable from health, so decorum is merged
in virtue though the two conceptions may be severed in
thought. There are two kinds of decorum; the one is general and is associated with honour as a whole, the other is
special and belongs to particular virtues. General decorum
is commonly defined as that which harmonises with the
characteristic excellence of man which distinguishes him
from all other living creatures; and special decorum as that
which so befits our nature as to invest moderation and temperance with an indefinable charm.

28. That this is the notion of decorum may be inferred
from the laws of dramatic propriety. These are fully treated
in other works, but I will here remark that poets observe
these laws when they make each personage act and speak
in accordance with his character. For example, we should
be shocked if Aeacus or Minos said, "Let them hate, so they
fear," or, "The father is the grave of his own children," because we know that they were just men: but in the mouth
of Atreus these words call forth applause, because they are
appropriate to his part. It rests with the poet to decide what
is proper to each character by the part he plays. As for man,
Nature herself has assigned to him a part far transcending
that of other living creatures. If the poet has to invest his
varied personages with their appropriate attributes, and to
clothe even vice in its peculiar garb, we, whom Nature has
placed upon the stage of life to exhibit strength of character, moderation, self-command and sympathy, we, whom
she teaches to bethink us of our duties to our fellow-men,
cannot fail to see the extent and importance of the general

decorum which is inseparable from honour as a whole, and of the special decorum which is displayed in each particular virtue. As bodily beauty attracts the eye by the symmetry of the limbs and charms us by the graceful harmony of all the parts, so the decorum which shines in our conduct engages the esteem of society by the order, consistency and restraint which it imposes on all our words and deeds. We therefore owe a certain deference to all men, especially to the good. For indifference to public opinion is a mark not only of presumption but of utter depravity. In our social relations there is a difference between justice and sympa· thy. Not to wrong our fellow-men is the function of justice: that of sympathy is not to wound their feelings; herein the power of decorum is most conspicuous. The nature of that virtue should, I think, be clear from the foregoing exposition. The duty derived from decorum conducts us in the first place to harmony with nature and the faithful observance of her laws. If we take nature for our guide we shall never go astray, but resolutely follow Prudence, that is true insight and wisdom, Justice, the principle of human society, and Fortitude or moral strength. But it is in Temperance, the division of Honour now under discussion, that the force of decorum is most conspicuous; for neither the gestures of the body nor the emotions of the mind can be called decorous unless they are in harmony with Nature. The soul is swayed by two forces: the one is appetite, called by the Greeks *horme*, which hurries us this way and that, the other reason, which teaches us what to do and what to avoid. It follows that reason must command and appetite obey.

29. Our conduct should be wholly free from thoughtless precipitation, and for every action we should be able to furnish a reasonable motive; that is as nearly as possible the definition of duty. To this end it is necessary to bring the appetites under the sway of reason; they must neither be

so impetuous as to run away from reason nor so lazy and sluggish as to lag behind her, but should be calm and free from passion: thus will consistency and moderation shine forth in all their glory. If through desire or fear the appetites run riot and become too restive to be controlled by reason, they clearly overstep the bounds of moderation. For when they cast off the yoke and revolt against their natural mistress, they not only unsettle the soul, but disfigure the body. Just look at the face of a man agitated by anger, desire, or fear, or intoxicated with pleasure; what a change in his look, his voice, his gestures and his whole aspect. To return to the conception of the duty under discussion, it is manifest that we must curb and calm our appetites and stir ourselves up to be diligent and watchful lest we grow reckless and let our lives drift without thought or care. Surely Nature never intended us for sport or jest so much as for purposes more serious and noble, and for an earnest life. Sport and jest have their own place like sleep and other kinds of repose, but we must first meet the claims of serious and important work. Wit should be neither extravagant nor immoderate but refined and elegant. As we do not allow children absolute freedom in their play but only such freedom as comports with good conduct, so even in a jest there should be some spark of virtue. Jests are of two kinds: some are low, wanton, wicked, obscene; others elegant, polished, graceful. Elegant witticisms abound not only in Plautus and the Old Attic Comedy but also in the pages of the Socratic philosophers, and we possess many happy sayings of the kind such as the *Apophthegms* collected by Cato the Elder. It is easy to distinguish the refined from the vulgar jest. At the proper season, when the mind is free, an elegant sally is worthy of a great man, but coarse thoughts expressed in coarse words are only fit for a slave. Sport as well as wit has its limits which we should never transgress lest we be carried away by passion and lapse into some deed of shame. Our "Campus" and the chase furnish examples of noble pastimes.

30. In every question of duty it is important to remember how far the nature of man transcends the nature of the brutes. The brutes are susceptible only of sensual pleasure, and at that they rush in full career; but the mind of man is nourished by study and thought, is ever seeking or doing, and is charmed with the pleasures of seeing and hearing. Why, if a man is at all prone to sensual pleasure, without descending, as some men do, to the level of the brutes, and is caught in the toils of vice, for very shame he hides and cloaks his passion. Hence it is evident that sensual pleasure is unworthy of the dignity of man and that we must scorn and cast it from us; but if we do yield to passion let us take heed that we use some measure in our indulgence. Therefore in the food we eat and the care we bestow on the body we should aim at health and strength and not at sensual pleasure. We have only to reflect on the excellence and dignity of human nature to feel how base it is to languish in luxury and pamper ourselves in voluptuous ease, and how noble it is to lead a frugal, temperate, well-disciplined life.

In the next place observe that Nature has invested us with two characters. The one is universal, inasmuch as all men participate in reason and in that excellence which lifts humanity above the brute creation. This is the one source of honour and decorum and of the very idea of right and wrong. The other character is individual. Great as are the diversities in the constitution of the body—one man is a swift runner, another a strong wrestler; one has a stately, another a graceful figure—the diversities of character are greater still. L. Crassus and L. Philippus possessed great wit, Caesar, the son of Lucius, even greater, but his was more laboured; on the other hand, their contemporaries, young

M. Drusus and M. Scaurus, were remarkable for their gravity and C. Laelius for his vivacity, while his friend Scipio united a loftier ambition with a more solemn demeanour. Among the Greeks, we are told, Socrates had a winning, playful, sprightly manner, and his discourse was full of that roguish humour which the Greeks call irony; Pythagoras and Pericles on the other hand had not a spark of gaiety and yet attained commanding influence. Among the Punic leaders Hannibal was as shrewd as Q. Maximus among our own; both had the gift of silence and the art of hiding their own stratagems and stealing a march on the enemy. For such qualities the Greeks assign the palm to Themistocles and Jason of Pherae, and we have a remarkable instance of astuteness in the artifice of Solon, who feigned madness in order to save his life and benefit his country. In contrast with these are the men of frank and open character, who love the truth, hate deceit, and set their face against craft and treachery; others again, like Sulla and M. Crassus, would stoop to anything and cringe to any man, if only they could gain their object. Thus the artful diplomacy of the Lacedaemonian Lysander formed a strong contrast with the character of Callicratidas, his immediate successor in the office of admiral. Further, we know of eminent men who were remarkable for their condescension. I may cite as examples Catulus and his son, and Q. Mucius and Mancia. Old men have told me the same thing of Nasica, but they said that his father, who punished the frantic schemes of Ti. Gracchus, had no such gracious manner and rose to greatness and celebrity for that very reason. Besides these there are countless varieties of character, none of which is to be condemned, though they all differ from one another.

31. The surest means of observing the decorum which is the object of this inquiry is to be resolute in cleaving to our own native qualities, provided they be not vicious. Without

violating the universal laws of human nature we should
follow the bent of our own character, and, leaving to other
men careers more brilliant and imposing, determine our
pursuits by the standard of our own aptitudes. It is vain to
fight against the conditions of our existence and strive after
the impossible. Thus the conception of decorum emerges
into clearer light; for, according to the adage, nothing is
decorous if it thwarts Minerva—in other words, if it is in
direct opposition to our natural genius. If there be such a
thing as decorum at all, it is nothing but the balance of the
whole conduct and of particular acts, and how can this be
maintained if we copy the nature of others to the neglect of
our own? For, as we ought to use our mother tongue which
everybody understands in order to escape the well-deserved
ridicule which some incur by foisting in Greek phrases, so
we should introduce no discord either into particular actions or into our conduct as a whole. This diversity of character is sometimes so imperious that in the same circumstances suicide is for one man a duty, for another a crime.
Was not M. Cato in the same position as those who surrendered to Caesar in Africa? Yet they might have been condemned if they had slain themselves, because their life had
been less austere, their characters more pliant; but Cato,
whom Nature had endowed with incredible resolution
which he had fortified by unswerving unity of purpose,
Cato, who had continued steadfast in every design and
every enterprise, had no choice but to die rather than behold the face of the tyrant. What miseries Ulysses suffered
in his weary wanderings! Think how he stooped to be the
slave of women (if Circe and Calypso deserve the name),
and set himself to speak pleasant things to every man he
met! Nay, in his own home he brooked the reproaches of
slaves and handmaids in order to reach at last the goal of
his desires. Ajax, on the contrary, with his proud spirit,

would have died a thousand deaths rather than suffer such indignity. These considerations teach us that every one should appraise and regulate his own character without trying if another man's will fit him: that fits a man best which is most his own. Let each one then study his own nature and be a strict judge of his merits and defects. We ought surely to have as much sense as actors who choose not the best pieces but those most suited to their powers. An actor with a fine voice appears in the Epigoni or the Medus, another will choose the Melanippe or the Clytemnaestra to exhibit his action; Rupilius, whom I remember, always played in the Antiopa, Aesop rarely in the Ajax. I ask you, if an actor observes this decorum on the stage, shall a wise man neglect it in the drama of life? Our aptitudes, I repeat, will be our best guide in choosing a career. But, if fate should ever thrust us aside into some uncongenial occupation, we should grudge no pains, thought or effort to acquit ourselves, if not with distinction, at least without discredit, and rather endeavour to avoid defects than to attain to virtues which nature has placed beyond our reach.

32. To these two characters may be added a third which fate or chance imposes on us: there is indeed a fourth which we deliberately assume. Royalty and command, rank and office, wealth and influence, and the opposite conditions, depend on fortune or on circumstances: but the part that we are to play in the world is the result of our own free choice. Thus one man turns to philosophy, another to civil law, a third to eloquence, and we have even our favourite virtues. But those whose fathers or ancestors have distinguished themselves in some particular sphere commonly strive to carry on the noble traditions of their family. Thus Q. Mucius, the son of Publius, was an eminent jurist, and Africanus, the son of Paulus, a great general. Some men superadd distinction of their own to that which they have

inherited from their fathers. The same Africanus crowned his martial glory with the renown of the orator, and Timotheus, the son of Conon, who, as a soldier, was not inferior to his father, enhanced his reputation by his ability and culture. Other men quit the beaten track and follow a path of their own, and here aspiring men of humble origin achieve the greatest success. These are the considerations we must keep in view while investigating the nature of decorum; but first of all we have to decide what we are to do and what manner of men we wish to be—the most difficult problem in the world. For it is in early youth when the judgment is most feeble that each one adopts the profession that attracts him most. He is thus committed to some definite course of life before he is fit to judge which is the best. According to Prodicus, as cited by Xenophon, Hercules in his early youth, the period set apart by nature for choosing a path of life, went out to a lonely spot and sitting down there with two paths in view, the path of Pleasure and the path of Virtue, for a long time earnestly deliberated which it was better to follow. This may have happened to Hercules "sprung from the seed of Jove," but for us it is impossible. For we all copy the models we happen to choose and feel constrained to adopt their tastes and pursuits. But for the most part we are so imbued with the principles of our parents that we naturally fall into their manners and customs. Some men are swept away by the current of popular opinion, and the ideals of the multitude are their highest ambition; others, whether through good fortune or natural ability, pursue the right path without parental instruction.

33. It rarely happens that men who possess eminent ability or extraordinary learning or culture, or even unite these two advantages, have the leisure to deliberate on the choice of a career. The question turns on the disposition and capacity of the individual. I have already said that we must

study our own nature in order to discover what is decorous in particular actions; how much more imperative is such a precaution when we are ordering our whole life, if we desire to maintain a consistent character and never falter in our duty. In this inquiry Fortune next to Nature has the most powerful influence. They both demand our attention but Nature has the stronger claim; she is in truth so much more firm and steadfast, that in conflict with Fortune she is like a goddess contending with a mortal. If, then, a man has chosen some mode of life adapted to his nature—I mean his better nature—let him persevere, for that is his duty, unless he find that he has blundered in his choice. If he has erred —and error is possible—he must change his habits and pursuits. If circumstances favour, the change will be attended with less trouble and discomfort: otherwise, he must retrace his steps with care and caution, as wise men hold that when a friend has lost his charm and forfeited our esteem the bonds of affection should be gradually untied rather than suddenly cut asunder. His career once altered, he should endeavour to show that he has acted with wisdom. I said above that we ought to follow the example of our forefathers. The rule has two exceptions. Never copy their vices; and never seek to emulate their virtues, if Nature has placed them beyond your reach. Thus the son of the elder Africanus was too infirm to rival his glory, while the son of Paulus whom he adopted walked in his father's footsteps. If then you have not the talent to become a pleader, a statesman, or a general, you should at least practise the virtues that lie within your powers, such as justice, honour, liberality, moderation, self-command; and thus your defects will be less conspicuous. The noblest heritage, the richest patrimony a father can bequeath to his children is a reputation for virtue and noble deeds. To tarnish his good name is a sin and a crime.

34. Since our duties vary at every stage of life, and some are peculiar to the young, others to the old, it is necessary to explain the distinction in a few words. It behoves a young man to respect his elders and choose the best and most trusted among them to uphold him with their counsel and authority; for the folly of youth must needs be ordered and directed by the wisdom of age. Above all the young should be restrained from passion, and their bodies and minds inured to toil and endurance, that they may be ready one day to put forth their energies in the duties of war and of peace. Even when they unbend and give themselves to enjoyment they should guard against excess and remember the dictates of modesty: and the task will be more easy if in pleasure as in business they do not shun the company of men of riper years. Old men, on the other hand, as they become less capable of physical exertion, should redouble their intellectual activity, and their principal occupation should be to assist the young, their friends, and above all their country, with their wisdom and sagacity. There is nothing they should guard against so much as languor and sloth. Luxury, which is shameful at every period of life, makes old age hideous. If it is united with sensuality, the evil is two-fold. Age thus brings disgrace on itself and aggravates the shameless licence of the young. It may not be irrelevant to speak of the duties of magistrates, of private citizens, and of foreigners. It is incumbent on the magistrate to realise that he represents the state and that he is bound to uphold its dignity and credit, to guard the constitution, and to dispense justice with an even hand, remembering that these things are sacred trusts committed to his charge. It behoves a private citizen to live on equal terms with his fellows, and not to cringe and grovel or to hold his head too high, and in public affairs to support a peaceful and honourable policy. Such are the qualities we look for in the

model citizen. As for the foreigner and the resident alien, it is his duty to mind his own affairs, and not to pry into the affairs of others or meddle in the politics of a country with which he has no concern. These are substantially the duties that we shall find to be incumbent on us when we inquire what is decorous and what is appropriate to particular characters, circumstances, and periods of life. In every purpose and in every action there is nothing more decorous than a steady and consistent demeanour.

35. The second kind of decorum is seen in our words and deeds and in the aspect of the body whether in motion or at rest. It consists of beauty, harmony, and taste, conceptions more easily understood than expressed. These three qualities again connote the desire to please those with whom we live and the wider circle of our fellow-citizens. I will therefore say a few words on this subject. In the first place, observe the care which Nature herself has bestowed on the construction of our body. She displays to view the face and all those parts the sight of which is decent, but has covered up and concealed the organs designed for the natural functions as unsightly and offensive. Here our sense of shame follows the subtle contrivance of Nature. Following her example all healthy-minded men conceal these organs and their functions, and it is even thought indecent to mention things which are not wrong provided they be done in secret. It is only the publicity of these acts and obscenity of language that constitute immodesty. I have no patience with the cynics or their Stoic rivals who sneer at modesty and scout the idea that it is right to speak of actions that are immoral, but outrageous to mention others that are innocent in themselves. Robbery, theft, adultery, are wrong, but it is not indecent to speak of them; it is right to beget children, but obscene to mention it; with these and similar arguments they attack the principle of modesty. As for us,

we ought to follow Nature and shun everything that shocks the eye or the ear. Whether we stand or walk, whether we sit or lie, our whole demeanour and all our looks and gestures should be governed by decorum. Here there are two extremes to be avoided, effeminate languor and boorish coarseness. We cannot admit that the laws of decorum are binding on the actor and the orator, but are indifferent to us. Theatrical tradition has carried the laws of modesty so far that an actor never appears on the stage without a girdle for fear of exposing his person and shocking the spectators. In our country it is not the custom for an adult son to bathe with his father or a father-in-law with a son-in-law. It is our duty, I repeat, to obey these laws of modesty especially as Nature herself is our teacher and guide.

36. There are two kinds of beauty. The first is grace, the attribute of woman; the second is dignity, the attribute of man. Therefore shun all foppery and affectation. If our manners recall the palaestra or the stage they will be offensive and ridiculous; they are only admired when they are simple and natural. The beauty of the face depends on the complexion, and the complexion is the result of exercise. The care of our person should not be carried to the extreme of obtrusive refinement; it will suffice if we are free from rough and unmannerly neglect. The same principle applies to our dress; here, as in most things, moderation is best. When we are out walking we must not be so slow and languid as to suggest a religious procession nor must we hurry so fast as to put ourselves out of breath and disturb our looks and features; for these are sure symptoms of want of balance. Still more earnestly should we endeavour to keep our emotions in their natural state of repose; and we shall succeed in the effort if we are proof against excitement and depression and intent on the maintenance of decorum. The operations of the mind are of two kinds; some are con-

nected with thought, others with appetite. Thought is employed in the discovery of truth, appetite impels to action. Let us strive then to employ our thoughts on the noblest objects and to bring our appetites under the sway of reason.

37. Speech is a great power in the world. It is of two kinds, formal discourse and conversation. Formal discourse is appropriate to judicial argument and to political and deliberative orations; conversation finds its natural place in social gatherings, learned discussions, and in friendly reunions and banquets. There is a science of rhetoric, and I am inclined to think a science of conversation possible though none exists. The demand for masters creates the supply, and though the world is full of students of rhetoric, there are neither students nor masters of conversation. Still the rules of rhetoric are equally applicable to conversation. Since the voice is the organ of speech, we should try to make it clear and pleasant. These qualities, it is true, are natural gifts, but the first may be improved by practice, the second by the imitation of calm and articulate speakers. There was nothing about the two Catuli to make you think they possessed a fine literary sense; for the culture they had was nothing extraordinary, and yet it was thought they spoke Latin with the greatest purity. Their pronunciation was agreeable, the sounds were neither mouthed nor minced, obscure nor affected; and they spoke without effort, yet without monotony or excessive modulation. The diction of L. Crassus was more copious and not less brilliant, but the eloquence of the Catuli ranked as high as his. In wit and humour Caesar, the brother of the elder Catulus, was the first speaker of his time; even at the bar his easy conversational style surpassed the laboured speeches of his rivals. If, then, we aim at decorum in everything we do, we should strive to perfect ourselves in all these qualities.

Forming our conversation on the admirable model of the disciples of Socrates, let us put forward our opinions in an easy tentative way and not without a spice of humour. Above all, we should never monopolise the conversation, but allow every one in turn to have his fair share. First of all it is necessary to consider the subject, and, whether it be grave or gay, let our language correspond. Again it is important not to betray any defect of character, such as the malice of the slanderer who delights in attacking the absent either in jest or with the serious purpose of covering them with abuse and contumely. Conversation generally turns upon family affairs, politics or learning and culture. These are the subjects to which we must endeavour to bring it back if it has drifted into another channel, but we must always study the company; for tastes differ, and nothing pleases all men at all times or to the same degree. It is well to mark the moment when the subject palls and to end as we began with tact.

38. The sound principle, that in all our conduct we should be free from passion or wild irrational feeling, ought naturally to govern our conversation. Let us betray no symptom of anger, or intense feeling, or of apathy, listlessness, or similar defects, and endeavour to exhibit respect and consideration for those with whom we converse. If at times reproof is required, it may be necessary to speak in a louder tone and in stronger language and to assume the appearance of anger. But like the cautery and the lance, that is an extreme measure which we should seldom and reluctantly employ and only as a last resource. Anger itself we must put far away, for with it we can do nothing right or well-advised. Often it will suffice to administer a gentle, but calm, reproof and to exhibit sternness without insolence. Nay more, let us show that even the severity of our censure is only intended for the good of the offender. Again,

in the quarrels we have with our bitterest enemies, it is proper to stifle our feelings and maintain our composure whatever insults may be offered to us. If we are under the dominion of excitement we lose our balance and forfeit the respect of the company. Another offence against decorum is to boast of oneself, especially without ground, and to expose oneself to derision by playing the "Braggart Captain."

39. Since I am discussing decorum in all its phases—that is at least my purpose—I must also explain what kind of house I consider appropriate for an eminent public man. As a house is built for use the plan should correspond; but at the same time comfort and elegance ought to be studied. Cn. Octavius, the first consul of that name, distinguished himself by building on the Palatine a splendid and imposing mansion. All Rome rushed to see it, and it was thought to have won for its obscure owner the votes which raised him to the consulate. Scaurus demolished the house and built with the materials a wing to his own. Thus Octavius was the first of his family to confer upon his house the honour of the consulate, while Scaurus, the son of a great and illustrious man, enlarged the house but brought to it not only political defeat but also disgrace and misfortune. The house should not constitute, though it may enhance, the dignity of the master; let the master honour the house, not the house the master; and as in all things we should think of others as well as of ourselves, a distinguished citizen must have a spacious mansion in which to receive his numerous guests and crowds of men of every condition. A palace only brings dishonour if solitude reigns in its noble halls which once were full of life in the days of another master. How grievous to hear the passers-by exclaim: "Here's the old house, but where's the old master?" and this, alas, is but too true of many houses in these times. Guard against extravagance and excessive display, especially if you are

building a house for yourself. The mere example is mischievous. For men love to copy the foibles of the great. How few have rivalled the virtue of Lucullus, how many the splendour of his mansions! Never go to excess, but let moderation be your guide not only in your house but in regard to all the necessities and comforts of life. But I must pass from this subject.

Whatever you undertake, there are three rules to be observed. In the first place, it is necessary to subject appetite to reason, for that is the surest means of fulfilling your duty; again, you must estimate the importance of the object you wish to accomplish that the effort you bestow upon it may be neither greater nor less than the case demands. Finally, observe moderation in all that concerns the aspect and dignity of a gentleman; and moderation is best attained by observing that decorum of which we have been speaking and never transgressing its limits. But the most important of these three rules is to subject appetite to reason.

40. I have next to treat of order and opportunity in our actions. These two duties are comprehended in the science which the Greeks call *eutaxia*, not that which we translate "modestia," a term connoting "modus" or moderation, but that by which we understand the observance of order. *Eutaxia* in this sense which we may also call "modestia," is defined by the Stoics as the science of accurately disposing our words and deeds. Thus order and disposition appear to have the same sense: for they define order as the disposition of things in their fit and proper places. By the place of an action they mean its fitness in point of time; it is called in Greek *eukairia*, in Latin *occasio*. Consequently "modestia" in this sense is the science of doing the right thing at the right time. Prudence, of which I spoke at the outset, may also be defined in the same way: but it is self-command, temperance, and similar virtues that concern us here. The

constituent parts of prudence were described in their proper place; here I have to state the elements of those virtues which have detained us so long, I mean the virtues which relate to sympathy and the approbation of those with whom we live. We must therefore apply such order to all our actions that they may harmonise and balance like the parts of a well-ordered discourse. How shameful and scandalous it is to interrupt a serious conversation with frivolous after-dinner talk. You may remember the happy rejoinder of Pericles. He and Sophocles, as colleagues in command, had met for the transaction of common business; just then a handsome boy passed, and Sophocles exclaimed: "What a comely youth, Pericles!" Pericles replied: "A general should control his eyes as well as his hands." Yet, if Sophocles had said this at an inspection of athletes, there would have been no fault to find. Such is the importance of time and place. If a man while travelling or taking a walk should rehearse a case he is going to plead or become absorbed in some other subject, no one would blame him, but if he did this in society he would be considered ill-bred, because ignorant of the art of timing his actions. Flagrant breaches of manners, such as singing in the forum or similar eccentricities, are so obvious as to require no special reproof or precept; but petty faults which often pass unheeded call for greater vigilance. As an expert detects in the lyre or the pipe the slightest deviation from the true tone, so in our life we should avoid discord with the greater diligence, since the harmony of our actions is more noble and more beautiful than the harmony of sounds.

41. As a musical ear detects the slightest variations of tone in the pipe, so the keen and vigilant observer of moral defects will often draw important conclusions from trifling circumstances. If we watch the glance of the eye, the expansion or contraction of the eyebrows, the marks of sorrow

or joy, laughter, speech or silence, the raising or lowering of the voice, and other things of the kind, we shall easily judge whether they are decorous or jar with duty and nature. And it will not be unprofitable to study the expression of the emotions in others, that we may ourselves avoid what we find to be indecorous in them. Alas, we see the sins of others better than our own! This is why a master most easily corrects his pupils by mimicking their defects. In a moral dilemma it is prudent to consult philosophers or even sagacious men of the world and to ask their advice on particular points of duty. For most men drift with the current of their instinct. But we must consider not only what our adviser says but also what he thinks and what are his grounds for thinking as he does. Painters, sculptors, and even poets like to submit their works to the criticism of the public in order to correct what the majority condemn, and they endeavour by themselves and with the aid of others to find where the defect lies; in like manner we must often follow the opinion of others, whether we act or refrain, alter or correct. Tradition and civil institutions are precepts in themselves, so that special precepts are unnecessary for the actions which they govern, and it would be a mistake to suppose that we may claim the right of a Socrates or an Aristippus to act or speak in defiance of usage and convention: eccentricity is the privilege of genius. As for the doctrine of the Cynics, it must be absolutely scouted as inimical to modesty, without which there can be nothing right or honourable. Further, it is our duty to respect those patriotic citizens who have proved their strength in great and noble works, and have loyally served their country, and to honour them as much as if they were invested with some public office or military command. It is our duty to reverence old age, to defer to the magistrates, and to make a distinction in our treatment of countrymen and foreigners, and in the case of foreigners to consider whether they have come in a private or a public capacity. Finally and in a word, let us respect, uphold, and maintain the great family of the human race.

42. Public opinion divides the trades and professions into the liberal and the vulgar. We condemn the odious occupation of the collector of customs and the usurer, and the base and menial work of unskilled labourers, for the very wages the labourer receives are a badge of slavery. Equally contemptible is the business of the retail dealer, for he cannot succeed unless he is dishonest, and dishonesty is the most shameful thing in the world. The work of the mechanic is also degrading; there is nothing noble about a workshop. The least respectable of all trades are those which minister to pleasure, as Terence tells us, "fishmongers, butchers, cooks, sausage-makers." Add to these, if you like, perfumers, dancers, and the actors of the *ludus talarius*. But the learned professions, such as medicine, architecture, and the higher education, from which society derives the greatest benefit, are considered honourable occupations for those to whose social position they are appropriate. Business on a small scale is despicable; but if it is extensive and imports commodities in large quantities from all the world, and distributes them honestly, it is not so very discreditable; nay, if the merchant satiated, or rather satisfied, with the fortune he has made, retires from the harbour and steps into an estate, as once he returned to harbour from the sea, he deserves, I think, the highest respect. But of all sources of wealth farming is the best, the most agreeable, the most profitable, the most noble. I have spoken of the subject at length in my Cato Major from which you may supplement this chapter.

43. I think I have said enough to show how our duties are derived from the four divisions of honour. But it is often necessary to compare and contrast two honourable courses

in order to estimate their relative importance—a point
omitted by Panaetius. Honour in its widest sense springs
from four sources: prudence, fellow-feeling, fortitude, and
temperance, and it is often necessary to compare these virtues in order to determine our duty. Now it is admitted that
the duties which are founded on the social instinct are more
in harmony with nature than those which are derived from
prudence, and this opinion may be confirmed by the following instance. If it were given to a sage to live in perfect
affluence and ease absorbed in the study of the highest
problems of philosophy, life would be a burden to him,
were he condemned to isolation and never saw the face of
man. The first of all the virtues is speculative wisdom which
the Greeks call *sophia*. We attach a different sense to *phro-
nesis* or practical wisdom, which is the science of distin-
guishing what to pursue and what to avoid. But that which
I called the highest wisdom is the science of things divine
and human, and it is concerned with the relations of men
with each other and with the gods. If that is the noblest
virtue, which it certainly is, then the duty connected with
the social instinct necessarily takes precedence of all others. Moreover the study and contemplation of the universe
would seem stunted and imperfect if it did not result in action. Action is chiefly employed in protecting the interests
of our fellow-men; it is therefore indispensable to society:
and consequently holds a higher rank than mere speculation. Such is the opinion of the noblest men and it is at-
tested by their conduct. Who, I ask, could be so rapt in the
investigation of the mysteries of the universe, so absorbed
in the contemplation of the most sublime objects, that if
suddenly apprised that his country, his father, or his friend,
was in danger or distress, he would not abandon all his
studies and fly to the rescue, even if he imagined he could
number the stars and measure the immensity of space?

From these arguments it is manifest that the duties pre-scribed by justice are superior to those which are connected with abstract studies, for they concern the welfare of humanity which should be nearest to the heart of every man.

44. Nevertheless many men have devoted their lives to speculation without renouncing the duty of promoting the interests of society. Philosophers teach men to be good citizens and benefactors of their country. Thus Epaminondas of Thebes was the pupil of Lysis the Pythagorean, and Dio of Syracuse the pupil of Plato, and I could cite many instances of the kind; and any service I myself may have rendered to my country I ascribe to those masters who trained and equipped me for public life. The influence of these great men, whether moral or intellectual, is not conveyed by the living voice alone; it is transmitted to posterity in their written works. They neglect no subject that bears on legislation, morality, or political science; indeed it may be said that it is to our affairs they devote their leisure. Thus we see that even scholars and philosophers apply their wisdom and insight principally to the advantage of their fellow-men. Hence it follows that eloquence united with wisdom is a more precious gift than the highest wisdom devoid of eloquence, because reflection is centred in itself, while eloquence embraces those with whom we are united by common interests. As bees do not swarm for the purpose of making the comb, but make the comb because they are gregarious by nature, so human beings, endowed with a still stronger social instinct, think and act in sympathy. Speculation would therefore seem forlorn and barren of useful results if it were not conjoined with the social virtue which works for the maintenance of society, that is, the great brotherhood of the human race. The same may be said of fortitude. If it had no relation to human society it would be but a brutal and savage thing. From this we

conclude that the social virtues are superior to merely speculative studies. The theory is false, that society owes its existence to necessity, or the inability of man to satisfy his
natural wants without the aid of others, that, if everything
essential to a life of comfort were supplied to us as if by a
magic wand, every man of intellect would retire from active
work and devote his undivided energies to study and learning. Far from that, he would shrink from isolation and look
for some one to join in his pursuits, his desire would be to
teach and learn, to hear and speak. Consequently every
duty tending to the preservation of society is to be preferred to that which consists in abstract study.

45. It may be necessary to inquire whether this sense of
interdependence, which is the deepest feeling in our nature,
should also be preferred in every case to moderation and
self-command. I think not. For some things are so repulsive,
others so criminal, that a wise man could never do them
even to save his country. Posidonius enumerates many
crimes of the kind, but they are either so atrocious or so
obscene that it seems wrong even to mention them. No one,
I repeat, will commit such crimes for the sake of his country; nor will his country demand such a sacrifice. But the
case is simplified by the fact that circumstances cannot arise
in which the state will profit by the dishonour of a wise
man. We may therefore regard it as settled, that in discrim-
inating between several duties we should give the preference to those which are connected with the social instinct.
Moreover, knowledge and prudence will result in deliberate
action. Consequently deliberate action stands on a higher
plane than prudence without action. So much for this subject. I have now cleared the ground so that it should not be
difficult to discover which duty is to be preferred in particular circumstances. Even in our social relations some duties
are more important than others. We are beholden first to

the immortal gods, next to our country, then to our parents, and finally to the rest of men in a descending scale. This short discussion may suffice to show that men are often in doubt not only whether an action is right or wrong, but which of two honourable courses has the higher moral worth. This subject, as I said, has been omitted by Panaetius. But I must now proceed to what remains.

WHAT remains, as has been indicated in the prefatory paragraph, is first a parallel discussion of the expedient (Book 2), and then a balancing of the expedient against the honorable (Book 3). For the first, expediences are to be weighed one against the other by much the same calculus as is urged in the case of competing honorable actions. For the second, the honorable and the expedient are proven incompatible; where the incompatibility is absolute there can be no compromise between them, and only the honorable is admissible.

# TUSCULAN
# DISPUTATIONS

Tusculan Disputations, *which also belongs to the last year of Cicero's life, is a work of ethical edification, teaching how various disconcerting emotions which militate against happiness may best be overcome. The material is more susceptible to logical argument than that of the parallel and contemporary* on old age, *and had frequently been treated by Greek writers on ethical philosophy. As always Cicero uses his Greek authorities freely, but as always it is on persuasive appeals to ordinary human sentiment rather than on strict logic that Cicero depends. The style is that of a free and fluent discourse with numerous and apt quotations from the poets, both Greek (in Cicero's own translations, of course) and Latin, and with many Roman examples. Who the "A" and "M" of the dialogue may be is not clear; the simplest supposition is that one is an Auditor and the other Marcus Cicero. But the setting and persons of a dialogue are not as important in Cicero as they are in Plato; questions are posed merely to elicit answers, and not to exhibit the construction of a philosophical position. The subjects of the five books of the* tusculans *are On Despising Death, On Enduring Pain, On Alleviating Distress, On Other Disorders of the Soul, and On Virtue as of Itself Sufficient for a Happy Life. Of the five the first is the most attractive. With a wealth of literary and historical allusion Cicero argues that death is either extinction, and hence not* an evil because the dead have no awareness, or else a transition to immortality, and hence a positive good. Socrates' argument to the same effect is quoted at length from the APOLOGY. Cicero does not consider the possibility of punishment in a future existence, and indeed immortality seems rather to mean a survival of reputation than any kind of persistence of personality. Of Plato's PHAEDO an interlocutor significantly says that he agrees with the book while reading it, "yet when I have laid the book aside and begin to reflect in my own mind upon the immortality of souls, all my previous sense of agreement slips away."

Now that I have at last secured a complete or at least a considerable release from the labours of the advocate's life and from my senatorial duties, I have once more—chiefly, Brutus, on your encouragement—returned to those studies which, though stored in memory, had been put aside through circumstances, and are now revived after a long interval of neglect. My view was that, inasmuch as the system and method of all arts which relate to right conduct of life depend on the study of wisdom styled 'philosophy,' it was incumbent on me to throw light on that study in a Latin work—not that philosophy could not be learned from Greek writers and teachers, but it has always been my opinion that our people have been wiser originators than the Greeks or have improved what they received from Greece, in such subjects as they regarded worthy of their efforts. In morality, rules of life, family and household economy, our standards are surely superior and more elegant. In the matter of government, there can be no question that our ancestors instituted better procedures and laws. Of the art of war it is needless to speak; here our people have proved their superiority in valour and even more in discipline. In natural gifts, apart from book-learning, our people are above comparison with Greeks or any other nation. Where has any nation shown gravity, steadfastness, greatness of soul, probity, faith, outstanding virtue in every department, to justify comparison with our ancestors' merits? In learning, indeed, and in all branches of literature, Greece did surpass us, and it was easy to do so where there was no competition. For while among the Greeks the poets are the oldest literary class—Homer and Hesiod lived before Rome was founded, and Archilochus was a contemporary of Romulus—poetry came to us much later. About 510 years after Rome was founded Livius Andronicus produced a play in the consulship of Claudius son of Caecus and M. Tuditanus, in the year before the birth of Ennius, who was senior to Plautus and Naevius.

2. It was late, then, before poets were either known or welcomed among us. Cato's *Origines* does state that at entertainments guests used to sing the praises of famous men to the accompaniment of a flute, but a speech of Cato's shows that this kind of talent was not highly regarded. He censures M. Nobilior for taking poets in his suite to his province, and we know that Nobilior did in fact take Ennius with him to Aetolia. The lighter then the esteem in which poetry was held, the less was it pursued. And yet those whose talents proved them poets have not failed to match the glory of the Greeks. A highly placed Roman like Fabius did paint; but if his doing so had been considered a commendable thing there would surely have been many Roman Polyclituses and Parrhasiuses. Honour nurtures art and glory is the spur to all pursuits; what is looked upon disparagingly is neglected in any nation. The Greeks held skill in vocal and instrumental music a very important accomplishment. Epaminondas (whom I count the greatest of the Greeks) was an accomplished flautist; and Themistocles, some years earlier, was despised as a boor because he declined the lyre when it was offered him at an entertainment. Accordingly musicians flourished in Greece; music was a general study, and those ignorant of it were regarded as uncultured. Geometry too was highly regarded, and mathematicians much esteemed; we have confined the art to bare measuring and calculating.

3. But we, on the other hand, early entertained esteem for the orator. At first the orator was not a scholar but only

a ready speaker. Later he was scholarly also, for we hear that Galba, Africanus, and Laelius were scholars, and that even Cato, who was much earlier, was a studious man. Then came the Lepidi, Carbo, the Gracchi, and their successors down to our own time, so that we are little if at all inferior to the Greeks. But even to our own time philosophy has been at low ebb and has not been fostered in Latin. I have now undertaken to raise and illustrate it, so that, as I have been of service to my countrymen when employed on public affairs, I may if possible be so likewise in my retirement. My enterprise will require great pains, for the existing books on the subject in Latin are said to be inaccurate; their authors were worthy men, but insufficiently trained. A man may reason well and yet be unable to express his thoughts properly; but to publish thoughts not skillfully arranged or agreeably expressed is an unpardonable abuse of letters and retirement. And so, if my efforts have added to the dignity of oratory, I shall take the more pains to uncover the fountains of philosophy, from which all my eloquence has taken its rise.

4. The fame of the rhetorician Isocrates spurred that versatile genius Aristotle to teach young men to speak and to join philosophy with eloquence. My design, similarly, is not to lay aside my habitual devotion to oratory but to give myself at the same time to this greater and more fruitful art; I have always thought that ability to speak copiously and elegantly on important questions was the most perfect philosophy. I have applied myself to this pursuit so seriously that I have already ventured upon a school after the Greek fashion. I made the attempt at my Tusculan villa, after you left us and when I had many friends about me. My assiduity and persistence in the practice of declamation has yielded to no man's; this is to be the declamation of my old age. I invited questions which anyone wished discussed, and then

argued them out, either sitting or strolling. The disputations of five days I have compiled in as many books. The procedure was that, after the would-be listener had expressed his view, I opposed it. This, as you know, is the old Socratic method of arguing against your adversary's position, for Socrates thought the highest probability could be discovered in this way. But to make the course of our discussions easier to follow I shall put them before you in the form of a debate and not in narrative form. This, then, will be the fashion of its opening:

5. *A.* Death I certainly consider a bane.

*M.* For those who are dead, or for those who have to die?

*A.* For both.

*M.* And if a bane, then a form of misery?

*A.* Undoubtedly.

*M.* And therefore both they whose lot it has already been, and they whose lot it will some day be, to die, are miserable.

*A.* That is how it seems to me.

*M.* There is none, then, who is not miserable?

*A.* Not one.

*M.* And in fact—if you mean to be consistent—all who ever have been or will be born are not only miserable, but everlastingly miserable. For if you were to confine yourself to the statement that they only are miserable who have to die, you would even then except nobody who has ever lived (for all must die); still there would be an end of the misery at the hour of death. If, however, the dead also are miserable, we are born to misery everlasting; for they who were born a hundred thousand years ago, nay, all who have ever been born, must continue in their misery.

*A.* Quite so.

*M.* Tell me, now, is there for you anything terrible in the legendary three-headed Cerberus of the Lower World? In

the roar of Cocytus? In the transportation over the Acheron? In the picture of

Tantalus who dies o' thirst, with water reaching to his chin?

or in that of

Sisyphus who rolls—
Rolls the stone and sweats and struggles, ever rolling it in vain?

or peradventure you stand in awe of those inexorable
judges, Minos and Rhadamanthus, before whom you will
have neither Lucius Licinius Crassus, nor Marcus Antonius to defend you, nor—for it is before Greek Judges that
the trial will take place—be able to retain Demosthenes to
plead your cause, but will have to be your own advocate,
in the presence of a crowded court; peradventure, I say,
you dread all this, and for that reason consider death to be
an everlasting bane.

6. *A.* Do you really believe me dotard enough to suppose
that such things are?

*M.* Do you not?

*A.* Of course not.

*M.* That is most unfortunate.

*A.* How so?

*M.* Because I could have waxed quite eloquent in refutation of them.

*A.* As who could not? Or what possible difficulty is there
in refuting such monstrosities of painters and poets?

*M.* And yet there are whole volumes teeming with arguments against them—by philosophers, too.

*A.* More fools they, then; for who could be stupid enough
to be impressed by such nonsense?

*M.* Well, then; if there is none of your miserables in the
Lower World, there is not in the Lower World any one at
all.

*A.* Just so.

*M.* Where then are your so-called miserables, and what spot do they inhabit? For if they *are*, they cannot be no-where.

*A.* Nay, but that is exactly my notion—that they are no-where.

*M.* And consequently that they *are* not?

*A.* Certainly; and miserable therein that they are nul-lities.

*M.* Now would I rather that you dreaded Cerberus than talked thus recklessly. For, observe now, in the very same breath you assert the existence which you deny. Where are your wits? For when you say *"is* miserable," you assert that who *is* not *is.*

*A.* Nay, I am not quite so dull as that.

*M.* Then what it is that you *do* say?

*A.* That Marcus Licinius Crassus, for example, is miser-able in having lost by death that colossal fortune of his; that Cneius Pompeius Magnus, again, is miserable in being deprived of all his glory; that everybody, in fact, is miser-able when lacking the light of life.

*M.* You come round to the same point. For whosoever *is* miserable, must *be.* But just now you said the dead *are not;* if, then, they *are not,* nothing can they *be*—not even miserable.

*A.* Perhaps I do not express quite clearly what I have in my head: for it is that very fact of *not being,* after you *have been,* that I consider so miserable.

*M.* What! More so than never to have been at all? Then the yet unborn are miserable already, because they *are not* (if *not being* is miserable); and we ourselves—you and I—if we are to be miserable after death (in consequence of *not being*), were miserable even before we were born (for the same reason). I, however, have no recollection of being miserable before I was born; but, if your memory, as regards yourself, be better, I should be glad to hear what you remember about yourself.

7. *A.* You are pleased to be merry; as if my words had been that they are miserable who have not been born, and not—as I really did say—"who have died."

*M.* Still you assert that they *are.*

*A.* Nay, but because they *are not,* that therefore they are miserable.

*M.* Cannot you see that you are talking contradictions? For what can be a greater contradiction than that whoever *is not* should *be*—I do not say miserable merely—but anything at all? When you pass out of the city by the Capene Gate, and mark the tombs of Calatinus, of the Scipios, of the Servilii, and of the Metelli, do you think of them as being miserable?

*A.* Since you drive me into a corner about a single word, I will not speak of them as *being* miserable, but simply as miserable—and on that very account, that they *are not.*

*M.* Oh! then you do not mean to speak of M. Crassus as *being* miserable, but of "poor M. Crassus" or of M. Crassus as miserable?

*A.* Exactly.

*M.* Just as if whatever you propound in that way must not either *be* or *not be.* Have you not mastered the veriest rudiments of dialectics? Why one of the very first principles laid down is, that every proposition (for thus it occurs to me to render the Greek word αξίωμα just at present—I will employ a better term hereafter if I can find one) is a predication of something which is either false or true. When, therefore, you speak of "poor M. Crassus," you either mean to say that M. Crassus *is* "poor" (in the sense of "miserable,") so that we may judge of the truth or falsehood of the proposition, or you mean nothing at all.

*A.* Very well, then; I will grant that the dead are not miserable, since you have forced me to confess that they who *are* not cannot *be miserable*. But how then? Are not we, who live, miserable, seeing that we must die? For what pleasure can there be in life when, night and day, the thought cannot fail to haunt us, that at any moment we must die?

8. *M.* Still, cannot you see how great a load of evil you have thus removed from humanity?

*A.* How so?

*M.* Because if for the dead also to die were miserable, we should have in this life of ours a limitless and everlasting sort of evil. But now I can see a terminus, to the which when we have run our course, there can be nothing further to be dreaded. You seem to me, however, to believe in the apophthegm of Epicharmus, a man of considerable shrewdness, and not without wits, for a Sicilian.

*A.* What is that, pray? I do not know.

*M.* I will tell you, then, and in Latin—if I can: for you are aware that I am not given to quoting Greek in a Latin lecture any more than Latin in a Greek.

*A.* And quite right too: but pray what *is* that apophthegm of Epicharmus?

*M.* "Verily I shrink from dying; little reck of being dead."

*A.* Ah! now I recall the Greek. Since, however, I have allowed, as you observe, that the dead are not miserable, bring me to think, if you can, that not even the necessity of dying is miserable.

*M.* That is not very difficult; I meditate much greater things than that.

*A.* How say you? Not difficult? And what, pray, are the greater things that you meditate?

*M.* Why, you see, since there is no bane after death, even death itself is no bane; for to it succeeds the after-death, in which you allow that there is no bane. Consequently, not even the necessity of dying is a bane, for it is but the necessity of arriving at that which you allow to be no bane.

*A.* Be a little more copious, I beg. These subtle points, so sharply and closely pressed, force me to admit rather than to assent. But what are those greater things which you contemplate?

*M.* To show that death is so far from being a bane that it is positively a blessing.

*A.* That I do not require; still I am dying to hear. For, though you may not establish all that you wish, you will establish that death is no bane. As for me, I will offer no interruption; I should prefer to hear a continuous lecture.

*M.* But suppose I ask a question; will you refuse to answer?

*A.* Nay, that were sheer insolence. But, unless it be absolutely necessary, I would rather that you did not.

9. *M.* You shall be humoured: and the exposition that you desire, I will give you to the best of my ability; not, however, in the vein of Pythian Apollo, as if all that I said were unerring and unalterable; but as one mannikin among many, tracking out probabilities by conjecture. For beyond the discernment of what is truth-like I have no power to go: the utterance of certainties I will leave to them who say that such things as certainties are possible, and who set up for being wise.

*A.* As you please; and now to listen.

*M.* The first point for consideration, then, is, what death, which seems to be a thing perfectly well understood, really is. For, notwithstanding that it seems to be perfectly well understood, there are some who think that death is the departure of soul from body; others, that no departure at all takes place, but that soul and body succumb together, and that the soul is extinguished in the body. Of those who hold that the soul departs, there are some who think that it is instantly dispersed; others, that it endures for a while; others, that it endures for ever. Moreover, as regards soul itself, there is a great variety of opinion as to what, where, and whence it is. Some have an idea that the heart is the actual soul, and so we get the words "without heart," "wanting heart," and "of one heart," meaning "senseless," "feebleminded," and "of one mind"; and the wise statesman Nasica, twice consul, got the name of "Goodheart" or "Sagacious," and so too "the man of matchless heart, Aelius Sextus." According to Empedocles the blood suffusing the heart is the soul. Others fancy that the sovereignty which we attribute to the soul is vested in a portion of the brain. Others again do not like the idea which makes the heart absolutely, or a part of the brain absolutely, the soul; but have maintained, some of them, that the soul's abiding-place is *in* the heart, others *in* the brain. Others again, as our own people pretty generally do, consider the breath of life to be the soul. The word speaks for itself; for we talk of *giving up the ghost,* and *breathing out the breath of life;* and so on in other instances. In fact the actual word for "soul" in Latin has come from the word for "breath." Zeno, the Stoic, considers soul to be fire.

10. Now what I have just mentioned, the heart, the blood, the brain, the breath of life, and fire, these are the commonly received theories. The rest are confined pretty nearly to single individuals. As many of the ancients had done before him, Aristoxenus, a musician as well as a philosopher, held, and was the most recent instance of so holding, that the soul is a sort of attunement (or *intension*) of the body itself: that, just as in vocal and instrumental music what is called harmony is produced, so by the nature and conformation of the whole body various vibrations are caused, like sounds in music. He clung to his own art; and

yet what he maintained was almost identical with what
had been noticed in all its bearings, and exploded, long
before, by Plato in the *Phaedo*. Xenocrates denied that there
was any form or substance, as it were, of the soul, asserting
that it was number, whereof, as Pythagoras had previously
declared, the power was the greatest in the whole range of
nature. His master, Plato, propounded a tri-partite soul,
whereof he placed the dominant part, reason, to wit, in the
head, as in a citadel; and the other two parts, passion and
appetite, he made subordinate, and located them in two
separate spots, placing passion in the breast, and appetite
below the midriff. Dicaearchus, on the contrary, in that debate between sundry learned persons which he represents
to have taken place at Corinth, and which he published in
three books, having in the first book introduced several
speakers, in the other two puts forward one Pherecrates,
an elder of Phthia or Phthiotis, and a descendant, he says,
of Deucalion, who argues that there is no such thing at all
as soul, that it is but an empty term, and that *animal* and
*animate* are vain appellations; that there is neither in men
nor brute any *living soul* (*animus*) or *breath of life* (*ani-
ma*), and that all that influence whereby we do or perceive
anything is equally diffused among all bodies that are quick;
and that it is not separable from the body, inasmuch as it
*is* not at all, and there *is* not anything but body, one and
uncompounded, with such conformation as to derive vitality
and perception from its own natural organization. Aristotle,
who far excels all others (Plato always excepted) in genius
and research, whilst admitting those four commonly received
elements—first propounded by Empedocles—whence everything was supposed to spring, suggests a fifth natural essence, to which belongs the mind or soul (*mens*). For thinking and foreseeing and learning and teaching and inventing
and ever so many other properties—such as remembering,

for instance, and loving and hating and desiring and fearing and feeling joy and anguish—these and others like them he considers inherent in none of those four elements; he therefore adds a fifth, which has no name, and so he calls the soul continuance—"uninterrupted and perennial movement."

11. These, unless there be some which have accidentally escaped my notice, are pretty nearly the opinions held about the soul. For we may pass by Democritus, who—great man as he certainly was—makes up his soul of smooth, round corpuscles on the theory of a fortuitous concurrence. Indeed, with this school, there is nothing for which a concourse of atoms does not account. As to which of these opinions is absolutely true, let some god see to that. Which is most truth-*like* is the main question. Which would you prefer, then? To decide between these conflicting opinions, or to return to our original argument?

A. If it were possible, I should like both; but it is difficult to fuse the two. If, therefore, without discussing these theories, we can be delivered from fear of death, let us get on with that at once. But, if that be impossible without clearing up this question about souls and their nature, let us, if you please, have that now, and the other anon.

M. The course which I understand you to prefer, is, I think, the more convenient. For, no matter which—if any —of the opinions I have set before you be correct, reason will show that death either is not a bane, or—better still— is a blessing. For, if heart, or blood, or brain, be the soul, undoubtedly—being body—it will perish with the rest of the body. But, if it be breath, peradventure it will be dispersed; if fire, quenched; if the harmony of Aristoxenus, distuned. As for Dicaearchus, who says that there is absolutely no soul, why mention him at all? According to every one of these said opinions, there is not, after death, anything whatever to concern anybody. For simultaneously with life consciousness is lost; and nothing can make any difference to the unconscious. As for the other opinions, they give hope that souls, after their departure from the body, may make their way to heaven as their own proper abode, if peradventure that idea causes you any delight.

A. Yes, indeed; and that it may be really so is my foremost wish; my next is that, even if it be not really so, yet I may be made to entertain a conviction that it is.

M. What need, then, of such aid as *ours?* Can we surpass Plato in eloquence? Peruse with care that work of his which relates to the soul, and you will require nothing beyond.

A. I have done so, I assure you, and pretty frequently too. But, somehow, as I read I assent, but when I lay the book aside and begin reflecting by myself upon the immortality of souls, all that assent slips gradually away.

M. How is that? Do you admit that souls either endure after death, or perish at the moment of death?

A. I do.

M. Suppose that they endure?

A. I admit that they are happy.

M. Suppose that they perish?

A. They are not miserable, since they *are* not at all: so much you just now compelled me to conclude.

M. How or why, then, say you that death appears to you an evil, since it will either make us happy, if souls endure, or not miserable, because unconscious?

12. A. Then, if it be not too much trouble, make it quite clear to me first—if you can—that souls do endure; next, if you do not completely establish that (for it certainly is difficult), you shall prove to me that death is devoid of bane. For what I have my fears about, is just this: whether it be not a bane, I will not say to *be* without consciousness, but to be obliged to lack it.

*M.* As regards the opinion which you desire to have established, we can make use of the very best authorities; a fact which ought always to have and generally has the greatest weight. And first of all we have the support of all antiquity, which, in proportion as it was fewer removes from the beginning of things and from the race of heaven, peradventure was better able to discern the true state of the case. Accordingly, we find that this was the one idea implanted in those ancients whom Ennius calls Casci—that in death there is consciousness, and that, at their departure from life, men are not destroyed to the extent of perishing utterly. And this may be inferred as well from many other circumstances, as especially from the pontifical laws and the religious rites in connection with tombs, which men endowed with the highest powers of mind would never have made so great an object of care, or have expressly hallowed by making the violation of them an unpardonable sin, unless their minds had cherished a fixed belief that death was not a destruction which removed and obliterated everything, but only a migration, as it were, and an exchange of one life for another; a something which in the case of illustrious men and women, would conduct them to Heaven, whilst the ruck would be detained earthward, but yet would abide continually. Hence in the opinion of our own people, "Romulus for ever lives in Heaven among the gods," and Hercules, among the Greeks (whence his worship was transferred to us, and even as far as the Ocean), is regarded as so mighty and so present a deity. Hence, too, Liber, son of Semele; and the brother-Tyndarids, of equal celebrity and fame, who are said to have been not helpers only of the Roman people in battle, but also the reporters of victory won. What of Ino, daughter of Cadmus? Does not she, who was called of the Greeks Leucothea, take rank with us as the goddess Matuta? What! Is not nearly the whole Heaven—not to hunt up more single examples—filled full of the children of men?

13. Nay, were I to undertake the exploration of antiquity, and ferret out the traditions of Greek writers, even they who are regarded as gods of the Upper House would be found to have proceeded hence, from our midst, to Heaven. Inquire whose tombs are they which are shown in Greece; bethink you (for you are initiated) of the traditions delivered at the mysteries; and then you will understand how wide is this field of evidence. But they (the men of old), not having learnt those physical sciences which did not begin to engage attention until many years afterwards, had convinced themselves of only so much as they had gathered from the indications of nature herself; of reasons and causes they had no conception. They were often induced by visions which they saw, chiefly by night, to fancy that they who had departed this life were existing, somewhere, still.

A very strong reason, moreover, which can be adduced for a belief in the existence of gods, seems to be this: that there has never been any race so wild, any human being so brutish, as not to be pervaded by some sort of notion of gods. (Many have perverted ideas upon the subject, arising from the moral obliquity of their lives; but all are of opinion that there *is* a divine power and a divine nature.) Nor is this belief the outcome of a conference of mankind; it is not an opinion which rests for its confirmation upon enactments and laws; though, of course, in every case, the common consent of all people must be regarded as a law of nature. Who, then, I would ask, is there who, under the influence of that common consent, which infers a future for the dead as well as the existence of gods, does not mourn for dead friends on this account chiefly, that he fancies them to be deprived of the blessings which life confers? Remove this apprehension, and you remove all cause of mourning. For one does not *mourn* over one's own discomfort; one is pained, no doubt, and one undergoes anguish; but all that lamentation and mourning and woe is because we fancy that those whom we loved lack the blessings of life, and are conscious of the fact. And this fancy arises from the promptings of nature; not from reasoning, not from teaching.

14. But the most cogent argument is this: that nature herself pronounces a silent verdict in favour of the immortality of souls, inasmuch as all feel an interest and a very great interest in what shall be after their death. "He planteth trees t' enrich a future age," sings the poet in the *Synephebi*. Why plants he them, and on what ground, but that he feels some link between himself and posterity? So then the thrifty husbandman shall plant trees of which himself will never see the fruit; and shall not a great man plant laws and institutions, and governments? The procreation of children, the extension of a family name, the adoption of sons, the care in testamentary dispositions, and even the decorations and inscriptions on tombs—what is the meaning of all these, but that the future also shares our thoughts? And what then? Can you doubt but that the beau-ideal of a nature should be formed upon the lines of the best natures? Now amongst mankind, what nature is superior to theirs who consider themselves born to aid, protect, and preserve their fellowmen? Hercules went up to join the gods in Heaven: but this he never would have done, but that, whilst he was in the world, he secured for himself a way thither. Such legends are of olden date, and hallowed by the religious belief of all.

15. Take the case of this Republic. What must we suppose to have been the reflections of those many, those mighty men, who laid down their lives for the common-

wealth? That their fame would be bounded by the same limits as their life? Nobody, without great hopes of immortality, would ever court death for the sake of his country. Themistocles, Epaminondas, I myself—not to seek for examples in antiquity and foreign lands—might all have lived at ease; but, somehow or other, there is inherent in the mind a forecast of times to come, and this is especially the case and most readily exhibits itself in the highest characters and the loftiest souls. But were this withdrawn, who would be such a simpleton as to live continually amidst toil and danger? I refer now to active leaders of men. But what of poets? Do they not yearn to be famous after death? Else what mean lines like these:

> Look on this form—here agèd Ennius stands,
> Who sang the deeds wrought by your fathers' hands?

He demands his meed of glory from them whose fathers he had covered with glory. And again:

> Mourn not for me—no tearful tribute give,
> For on the lips of living men I live!

But why confine myself to poets? Artists (which word includes sculptors) yearn to be famous after death: else, why did Pheidias insert a likeness of himself on the shield of his Minerva, when he was not permitted to place an inscription? What! Do not our philosophers inscribe their names upon those very books which they write about despising glory? But if universal consent be the voice of nature, and all without exception agree that there is something still appertaining to those who have departed this life; we must needs think the same. And if we may suppose that they whose souls are pre-eminent for genius or virtue see farthest into nature's properties, inasmuch as they possess the most perfect natures, it is likely to be true—as all the best men are the most zealous to serve posterity—that there is a something of which they will be conscious after death.

16. To proceed. As by natural instinct, we believe that there are gods, and by process of reasoning infer what nature they are of, so by the common consent of all nations we are led to suppose that souls endure; but in what resting-place they endure, and of what quality they are, we must infer by process of reasoning. Ignorance of this process led to the invention of the Lower World, and to those terrors which you seem—not without reason—to hold in contempt. For from the fact of bodies dropping to the ground, and then being covered with earth (*humo* whence the term *in-hume*), they imagined that the rest of a dead man's existence was spent underground. And on the heels of this belief followed great extravagances, fostered by the poets. For a close-packed audience at a theatre, with womankind and children among them, are vastly affected by such high-flown verse as this:

Lo! I come from Acheron with travail up the steep ascent,
Through caverns roofed with rugged, overhanging, giant rocks;
Where the darkness, thick and rigid, standeth like a wall in Hell.

And so deep-seated was the error (which appears to me to have been removed by this time) that, though they were perfectly aware of the burning of the bodies, they supposed that in the Lower World there took place such things as, without bodies, could neither take place nor be comprehended. They could not realize the idea of a soul with a life of its own; they demanded some sort of form and shape. Hence the Dead Scene in Homer; hence the Necromancies which my friend Appius compiled; and hence, in our own immediate neighbourhood, all the stories about the Lake of Avenus—

Whence from darkness, from the open mouth of Acheron profound—
Rise evoked the unsubstantial spirits, phantoms of the dead.

And they will have it that these phantoms speak, which,
without tongue or palate, or the properties and configura-
tion of the jaws, the sides, and the lungs, is an impossibility.
They could not perceive with the mind's eye; they referred
everything to the ocular sense. Now it is an attribute of
great genius to distract the mind from the senses, and to
withdraw the thoughts from every-day associations. And so
I dare say that during so many ages, there were others also
who did the same thing; but certainly Pherecydes of Syros,
according to written tradition, was the first to declare that
the souls of men are immortal. That was a pretty long while
ago, for he lived in the reign of the founder of my family.
This opinion was mainly supported by Pythagoras, his pupil, who, when he came to Italy in the reign of Superbus,
held under his spell the whole of what was called Magna
Graecia both by the force of his doctrines, and by his personal prestige. And for many generations afterwards so high
was the fame of the Pythagoreans that none else seemed to
have any learning.

17. But to return to the ancients. They did not for the
most part vouchsafe any reason for their opinions, unless
so far as they might be explained by numbers or diagrams.
It is said that Plato came to Italy to make the acquaintance
of the Pythagoreans, and, having learnt all about the Pythagorean system, was the first who, besides holding the
same opinions as Pythagoras touching the immortality of
the soul, also offered an explanation. This, if you have no
objection, we will pretermit, and renounce all hope of immortality.

A. How say you? Having wrought me to this pitch of
expectation, leave me in the lurch! I would rather, so help

me Hercules! be wrong with Plato, for whom I know how high is your regard, and whom you have taught me to admire, than be right with all the rest of them.

*M.* Well said! I were not unwilling myself to be wrong with him.

Have we any doubt, then—or have we a doubt in this as in most matters, but surely least of all in this, for we have mathematics to convince us?—that the earth is situated in the middle of the universe, and has, in reference to the circumference of the whole system, the semblance of a sort of point, which is called a *centre;* and that, moreover, the nature of the four elements whence everything is generated is such that, they having, as it were, all motive tendencies partitioned out and divided among them, the earthy and humid pair thereof are, by their own inclination and weight, borne vertically downwards towards earth and sea, whilst the other pair, one igneous and the other aërial—just as the former pair, by their weight and gravity, move towards the centre—tend upwards on the contrary towards the heavenly area, either because their very nature affects the higher regions, or because the lighter are naturally repelled by the heavier? Now, this being admitted, it should be clear that souls, on departure from the body, whether they be aërial or igneous, will ascend. If, however, the soul be some number or other—an idea conceived with more subtlety than lucidity—or if it be that fifth natural element, lacking name rather than intelligibility, of which I have spoken, we have to deal with something still more unique and pure—with a disposition to ascend to the highest elevation from earth. Some one of these, then, the soul assuredly is; and there is no need to leave so lively an intelligence to lie swamped in the heart, or in the brain, or in the blood of Empedocles.

18. As for Dicaearchus, with his fellow-disciple Aristox-

enus, though they were certainly men of great learning, we may, for our present purpose, leave them out of the question; for the former of them can never have felt serious grief, if he is not conscious of having a soul, and the other is so wedded to his melodies that he must needs introduce them into such matters as these. Now we may get an idea of what is meant by harmony from intervals of sounds, whereof different combinations produce several corresponding harmonies; but how position of limbs and conformation of body, without an inner soul, can produce harmony, I cannot see. However learned he be, and he certainly is learned, let him leave such matters to his master, Aristotle, and for his own part let him go and teach music; for there is excellent doctrine in that adage of the Greeks: "Let each man ply the trade that he has learnt." But reject we altogether the theory of a fortuitous concourse of smooth, round, indivisible corpuscles, which Democritus nevertheless maintained was charged with heat, and "expirable," that is, charged with air. That soul, I repeat, which, if it belong to any of the four elements of which everything is said to consist, consists of inflammated air—as was the opinion held especially, I observe, by Panaetius—must necessarily tend upward. For these two elements have in them nothing of a downward tendency, and always tend towards the heights. Thus, if they be dispersed, that process takes place far away from earth; and if they endure and preserve their constitution, *a fortiori* must they move heavenward, and *a fortiori* must this gross and concrete atmosphere, which is nearest to earth be burst through and cloven by them. For the soul is warmer, more fiery, rather, than this atmosphere which I have just termed gross and concrete, as may be inferred from the fact that our bodies, which are of the earthy element, grow warm with the fire of the soul within.

19. An aid to the escape of the soul from this atmos-

phere, as I have already repeatedly called it, and to easier
passage through it, is apparent from the further consideration that nothing is swifter than soul; there is no velocity
which can compare with the velocity of soul. If then it endures, incorrupt, and in its own likeness, it must proceed
in such wise as to penetrate and cleave all this atmosphere
in which clouds, and showers, and winds are conglomerate,
which is dank and dark by reason of exhalations from the
earth. But when the soul has surmounted this region, and
reached and recognized a nature like unto itself, it comes
to a stand-still at those fires (the stars), which are a combination of rarefied air, and tempered sun-heat, and there
puts an end to further ascent. For then, having attained a
lightness, as well as a heat assimilated to itself—being
poised, as it were, in equilibrium, it moves no whither; and
there at length is its natural habitation, when it has penetrated to what is assimilated to itself, and to where, lacking
naught, it will be nourished and sustained by the same ali-
ment whereby the stars are sustained and nourished. And
whereas we are wont to be inflamed by the calorics of the
body to almost all desires, and to be the more excited, because we strive emulously with them who possess what we
desire to have—we shall then, doubtless, be happy when,
having left our bodies behind, we shall be free from both
desires and rivalries. And, as we do now, when freed from
anxieties—namely, desire to get hold of something for inspection and examination—so then shall we do with far
greater freedom, and give up ourselves wholly to contemplation and examination: because, whilst there is naturally
implanted in all minds an insatiable desire of being face to
face with what is true, the very range of the regions whither
we shall have arrived, in proportion as they make easier our
knowledge of the celestial world, will inspire us with a still
greater longing to acquire the knowledge. For the beauty

of that world it was, as seen even here on earth, which fanned into flame what Theophrastus calls "hereditary philosophy," whereof the germ is the desire of making closer acquaintance therewith. But they above all will reap enjoyment therefrom, who, even when they were denizens of this world, surrounded as they were by its mists and obscurity, were most anxious to pierce through them with the eye of the mind.

20. For indeed, if in this life men think it an achievement to have seen the mouth of the Euxine, and the narrows of the Hellespont, through which penetrated the ship called "Argo" (for the reason that "from Argos chosen men sailed forth in quest of Phrixus' golden fleece"), or of having seen those Straits of Ocean where "Europe from Afric the swift wave divides," how grand a spectacle do we suppose that it will be, when we shall be able to take in at a glance the whole earth, and not merely its site, and shape, and compass, but its tracts also—the habitable as well as those which, by reason of cold or heat, are destitute of cultivation? For even now it is not with the eye that we discern the things which we see; nor, indeed, is there in the body any power of perception at all, but—as not only natural philosophers, but surgeons also who have seen the organs dissected and laid bare, assure us—there are channels, as it were, pierced from the seat of the soul to the eye, and the ear, and the nostril. And thus it often happens that under the obstructive influence of abstraction or disease, though both eyes and ears be perfectly open and free from injury, we neither see nor hear: whence it may be readily concluded that it is the soul (mind) which both sees and hears, and not those organs, which are but windows, as it were, of the soul (mind) and through which the intelligence can perceive nothing, unless it be heedful and on the alert. What conclusion, again, do you arrive at from the consideration

that by means of the self-same intelligence we apprehend things very dissimilar, such as colour, flavour, heat, scent, and sound? The soul certainly would never know one from another by the medium of the five passages (or messengers), unless everything were referred to it, and itself were constituted judge of everything. And such things will doubtless be discerned with far greater distinctness and clearness, when the soul has arrived—unimpeded—at the place towards which its nature tends. For now, though nature has fashioned with exquisite skill those avenues which open into the soul from the body, they are somehow clogged by earthy, material substances. But when there is nothing left but soul, there will be nothing obstructive to hinder it from discerning the true quality of everything.

21. We might discourse, if it were requisite, to any extent upon the multitude, the variety, and the magnitude of the subjects of contemplation which the soul would encounter in the celestial regions. And when I reflect thereon I am often astounded at the absolute preposterousness of a certain set of philosophers who parade their admiration of natural philosophy, and express, with effusion, their gratitude towards the first great founder and professor of it, and even revere him as a god. For they say that they were delivered by him from the most oppressive tyrants—incessant terror —and nightly and daily apprehension. What terror? What apprehension? What old woman is there so far gone in dotage as to fear what you, if you had not learnt natural philosophy, I suppose, would fear—

> The realms of Acheron and Hell profound:
> Pale haunts of Death, where darkness broods around?

Is it not shame for a philosopher to make his boast herein, that he fears not such stuff as that, and has discovered that it is all falsehood? From this one may gather how great

is their natural acumen, when—but for the instruction they
have received—they would have believed in such rubbish.
And a fine assurance, truly, do they owe to their learning;
namely, that when their hour of death arrives, they will perish altogether! And if so it be (for I say nothing to the contrary), what reason is there for joy or exultation? For my
own part, however, I cannot for the life of me see why the
opinion of Pythagoras and Plato should not be correct. For,
though Plato should advance no argument (you see what
respect I pay that great master), he would overbear me by
the mere weight of his authority. So many arguments, however, has he advanced, that he seems to have desired to convince everybody else, and to have certainly convinced himself.

22. Still, there are very many who pull in the opposite
direction, and condemn the soul—as if it had been capitally
convicted—to death. And yet there is no other reason why
the immortality of the soul appears to them incredible, but
that "they are unable to understand and to mentally grasp
the idea of what a soul is like without a body." As if they
could do so even with a body, as regards its conformation,
its size, and its site, so as to say whether, if everything that
is now hidden in a living being, could be exposed, the soul
would probably be revealed to the sight; or whether, such
is its unsubstantiality, it would escape the notice of the eye.
Let them who say that they cannot understand soul without
body reflect upon this; they will then perceive what sort of
an idea they can have of it even in conjunction with body.
For my part, when I inquire into the nature of soul, it occurs
to me that there is far more difficulty and far more obscurity
attending the effort to imagine the quality of a soul within
a body—in a strange house, as it were—than when it has
departed thence, and has arrived at the far expanse of
Heaven, its own proper dwelling-place. For, unless we are

altogether powerless to understand the nature or quality of that which we have never seen, we can assuredly conceive an idea both of deity itself and of divine soul enfranchised from body. Dicaearchus, however, and Aristoxenus—because there was a difficulty in the conception of soul, its quiddity and quality—maintained that there was no such thing as soul at all.

Indisputably the very height of attainment is to see soul with the soul alone; and doubtless this is the meaning of that precept of Apollo which admonishes every one to know himself. For the precept does not mean, I take it, that we should know our limbs, or height, or shape. Nor are we in reality bodies; nor do I, who am now addressing you, address your body. The saying, therefore, "Know thyself," means, "Know thy soul." For the body is, as it were, a mere vessel or receptacle for the soul; whatever is done by your soul, that it is which is done by yourself. Unless, then, there were something divine in "knowing it," that precept delivered by some superior mind would never have been attributed to a deity.

But if it be beyond even soul itself to know the nature and quality of soul, may it not know, pray, so much as that it *is*, that it *moves*? This is the question out of which arose that argument which is set forth by Socrates in Plato's *Phaedrus*, and is cited by me in the sixth book of my *Republic*. The substance of it is on this wise: "That which is ever moving is immortal. But that which communicates motion to other, and is itself moved of other, when it cometh to an end of movement, must necessarily come to an end of life. That alone, therefore, which is self-moved, inasmuch as it is never quitted by itself, never ceaseth to move. Nay, further; to everything else that moves this is the source, this is the first principle of motion. Now of first principle there is no beginning; for from first principle proceed all things, but itself cannot commence from any other source. Indeed, that would not be first principle which was generated elsewhence. But if it have not ever a beginning, neither hath it ever an end. For first principle once extinguished can neither itself be regenerated from other, nor from itself generate other, inasmuch as everything must commence from first principle. So, then, the first principle of motion resides in that which is self-moved. And that, again, can have neither beginning nor end, neither generation nor death: else all heaven must collapse, and all creation come to a stand-still, having no means of recovering a primary motive impulse. It being evident, then, that that is immortal which is self-moved, who would deny that this is the natural attribute of souls? For soul-less (inanimate), is all that is moved from without; soul-ful (animate), all that is stirred from within: for that is the peculiarity and innate property of soul. And if it is the only thing in the world which is self-moved continually, it certainly is not generated, and certainly is immortal."

Though all the lower order of philosophers (for such seems to be the proper term to apply to those who dissent from Plato and Socrates and that school), should put their heads together, they will not only never give so elegant an exposition of anything, but they will never even understand how ingeniously the conclusion is wrought out. The soul, then, is conscious that it moves, and together with this consciousness, it is simultaneously conscious that it moves of its own and no external impulse, and that it cannot possibly be quitted by itself. From which premises the conclusion of its immortality is arrived at—unless you have any objection to offer.

A. Not I indeed; I have been well content, not to let any objection so much as enter into my head: so much do I incline to your way of thinking.

24. *M.* Well, and pray do you think that less importance attaches to those other considerations which go to prove that there are in the souls of men certain elements of divinity? As to which, could I see how they might be generated, I might be able to see how they could perish. For, as regards the blood, bile, phlegm, nerves, and veins—the whole conformation of the limbs, and the entire body in fact—of these I fancy that I might perhaps predicate whence they may have been compounded and how they may be made up. And as regards the soul itself, if there were nothing in it beyond the fact that through it we have life, I could fancy the life of man to be supported as that of a vine or a tree; for we speak of such things as having life. Or again, if the soul of man had no properties beyond inclination and aversion, them it would share with the brutes also.

But in the first place, it has memory (illimitable, embracing things innumerable), which Plato maintained was recollection from a former existence. For in the *Meno* Socrates asks a youngster some geometrical questions about the mensuration of a square, to which the youngster replies as a child would; but so easy are the questions, that he gradually gets as far as if he had learnt geometry. Whence Socrates would have it to be inferred that learning is no more than recollection. And this position he develops still more elaborately in the discourse he held on the very day on which he died—the *Phaedo;* for he shows that anybody whatever, though apparently ignorant of every mortal thing, demonstrates by the answers he returns to a clever questioner, that he is not then learning for the first time, but by process of memory recollecting; and that it is not by any means possible that we should have implanted in us from childhood, and as it were stamped upon our souls, conceptions of so many important matters, unless the soul, before it entered the body, had been well grounded in general knowledge.

And inasmuch as nothing *really is*—as Plato always argues, (for, according to him, nothing *really is,* which has beginning and end, and that alone *really is,* which is always one and the same, and which they term *idea*)—the soul could not—when shut up in the body—take in such things, but brought them with it, ready apprehended. And so all cause for wonder at the knowledge of so many things is removed. But the soul does not discern them distinctly upon the sudden changing of its abode to so strange and so bewildering a habitation; when, however, it has collected and recovered itself, then it recognizes them by dint of reminiscence. And so learning is no more than remembering.

But, for my part, I am somehow even more astounded at the faculty of Memory. For what is that whereby we remember? What is the exact power it possesses? Whence is the origin of that power? It is no question here of the prodigious memory attributed to Simonides, to Theodectes, to him who was sent by Pyrrhus on an embassy to our Senate (I mean Cineas, of course), to Charmides (not so very long ago), to Metrodorus of Scepsis (who lived but yesterday), and to my friend Hortensius; I speak of the ordinary memory of men, and theirs chiefly who are engaged in some one of the more than usually important pursuits or professions—the greatness of whose mental capacity it is difficult to conceive, so many things do they remember.

25. Now what is the drift of all this talking? Why, it seems to me that we may thus obtain some idea of what and whence is the mysterious power which we are discussing. It certainly is not of a piece with the heart or the brain, or the blood, or atoms. Be it of air or fire, I know not; nor am I ashamed—as some whom you wot of—to confess that I do not know what I do not know. Of this, however—if I might be positive on any point that is obscure—I would be positive: whether the soul be of air or of fire, I would swear that

it is divine. For, I pray you, consider: can you conceive that so great a power as that of memory could proceed from or be composed of the earth, or this foggy and gloomy atmosphere? If you see not what it is, yet you see its quality; if not so much as that, still you see its capacity. What then? Are we to suppose that there is in the soul, a sort of "hold," for the pouring in of what we remember as into some kind of vessel? That would indeed be absurd. For such a soul, what bottom or what shape could one conceive? Or what capacity sufficiently large? Or are we to suppose that the soul receives impressions, just as wax, and that memory is but the imprints stamped upon the mental faculty? What imprints can there be of words, or even of facts? What extent of surface sufficiently boundless to exhibit so many?

That wondrous power, again, which explores what is hidden, and which is called invention and discovery: what, pray, is that? Does that appear to you to belong to this earthly, mortal, perishable element? Either in his case, who was the first to give names to all things, which Pythagoras considered the height of wisdom? Or in his who assembled scattered men, and formed them into social communities? Or in his who reduced the vocal sounds, which seemed infinite, to representation by a few letters? Or in his who noted the courses of the planet-stars, their progression, and their (apparent) halting? They all were great; even those of the earliest times, who introduced the fruits of the earth, and clothing, and covered habitations, and the decencies of life, and safeguards against wild beasts, since our domestication and civilization by whom we have gone on (and down) with the stream, from the necessary to the more luxurious arts. Our ears have gained great delectation from the discovery and regulation of the nature and variety of sounds, and we have lifted the eye of science to the stars, not those only which are fixed to certain spots, but those

also which—not in fact, but in name—are *planet* (*errant*).
Whereof whoever was the first to observe the revolutions
and movements showed that his soul was like unto Him who
had fashioned them in Heaven. For when Archimedes made
his globe with its representation of the motions of the sun,
the moon, and the five planets, he did exactly what Plato's
god—who in the *Timaeus* is represented to have constructed
the world—did, making one revolution regulate movements
very dissimilar in point of slowness and rapidity. Now, if
in the case of our world, such work demands the operation
of a god, Archimedes certainly could not have represented
the same movements on his globe without a genius partak-
ing of divinity.

26. For my part, not even your more popular and more
showy talents appear to me to be so wanting in divine properties that I could suppose a poet to pour forth his solemn,
full-toned verse, without some touch of inspiration from
Heaven, or that—without some more than human power—
the stream of eloquence rushes along, brimful of sonorous
words and flowing periods. But as for philosophy, mother
of all the arts, what is that but, as Plato says, a gift—as I say,
an invention—of the gods? It was that which trained us up,
first of all, to the worship of those aforesaid gods, and in
the next place to natural justice which has its foundation
in the association of mankind together, and lastly to moderation and greatness of mind. It was that, likewise, which
dispelled the mist from the soul, as it had been dust from
the eyes, to the end that we might discern everything, above
and below, first and last and intermediate. Thoroughly divine seems to me to be this power which brings to pass so
many and so great results. For what is memory of things and
words? And what, again, is invention? Assuredly a something than which nothing greater can be imagined, even
in a god. For *I* indeed do not suppose the gods to find

pleasure in ambrosia or nectar, or in having Youth to hand the cups; nor give I heed to Homer, who says that Ganymed, for his beauty, was carried off by the gods to be cupbearer to Jove. There was no reasonable cause for doing Laomedon so great a wrong. Homer invented these stories, and transferred to gods the characteristics of men. Of gods to men were a transference more to my taste. And what are *they*? Vitality, wisdom, invention, memory. The soul, then, is, as *I* say, divine; as Euripides dares to say, a god: and truly, if a god is either of air or fire, so also is the soul of man. For just as the heavenly nature is free from the earthy and the humid, so also the soul of man is without a particle of either. If, again, there be a fifth kind of natural element, as was first advanced by Aristotle, then this is common to both gods and souls. 27. In pursuance of which idea we have expressed ourselves as follows in the *Consolation*, in these terms precisely:

"Of souls the origin cannot be traced to anything on the earth; for in souls there is nothing mixed, or concrete, or that has the appearance of being sprung from or made of earth. There is not even anything that is either humid or breathly (*flabile*), or igneous. For in such elements there is nothing that possesses the power of memory, of intuition, of thought, that can retain the past, foresee the future, grasp the present, which are properties of that which is divine only. There is, therefore, a unique nature and power inherent in the soul, quite distinct from the ordinary, familiar, natural properties. And so, whatever that may be which possesses thought, wisdom, life, vitality—it must be of Heaven and divine, and therefore immortal. Nor can deity, as the term is understood by us, be otherwise understood than as an intelligence unhampered, free, dissociated from mortal matter, perceiving all things, moving all things and itself with the property of continual motion." Of this genus and of this same nature is the intelligence of man. Where then, or of what quality is that intelligence? Where, and of what quality is your own? Granted that I have not all that I could wish to assist me to an understanding; am I not, therefore, to be allowed to employ even what I have? Well, then, the soul, we will admit, has not the power of seeing itself; still, as the eye does, so does the soul—though it see not itself—discern other things. It does not see, which is of very little consequence, its own form (though, perhaps, it may even do that; but we will omit that point): still it assuredly discerns its power, its sagacity, its memory, its mobility, its rapidity. And these are the properties which are great, divine, everlasting. What its appearance may be, or what and where may be its precise dwelling-place, is a question which it is not worth our while to discuss.

28. Just as, when we observe, first of all, the beauty and brightness of the heavens; then that swiftness of revolution which passes comprehension; then the alternations of day and night, and the fourfold changes of the seasons, adapted to the ripening of fruits, and to the keeping of bodies in healthy order (with the sun for the regulator and the leader of it all, and with the moon, by its waxings and wanings, noting and indicating the days, as if upon a calendar); then, in the same circle, with its twelve divisions, the five planets moving along, keeping the same courses with the utmost regularity, but with different rates of motion, and the firmament everywhere studded at night with stars: then the sphere of the earth, emergent from the sea, fixed in the centre of the Universe, inhabited and cultivated in two opposite regions, whereof one, in which we dwell,

Lies seven-stars-ward 'neath the Northern pole
Whence chilly blasts drive forth the ice and snow,

and the other is Southern, unknown to us, and by the Greeks called Antipodes, and with the rest of its regions uncultivated, because either they are frozen with cold or parched with heat (whereas here, where we dwell, without fail at the proper season—

> Bright grows the sky, the trees put forth their leaves,
> The joy-producing vines with tendrils sprout,
> With load of fruits the very boughs are bent,
> The crops are thick with corn, and all is bloom;
> The fountains bubble and the meads are green:)

then the multitude of cattle, partly for food, partly for field-labour, partly for draught, partly for clothing; and, lastly, man himself, the contemplator, so to speak, of Heaven and the gods (and the worshipper of the latter), and all lands and seas subserving the good of man:—as, I say, when we observe all these things, we cannot doubt, can we? but that there presides over them either some Creator (if they were created, as Plato thinks), or, if they have been from ever-lasting (as Aristotle is pleased to suppose), some Manager of so mighty a work, so magnificent a spectacle; so is it with the intelligence of man: though you see it not (just as you see not the Deity), still, as you recognize Deity by his works, so by memory, by invention, by swiftness of movement, by all the beauty that belongs to virtue, behold and acknowledge the divine power of the soul!

29. Where, then, is it located? *I* think, in the head; and for so thinking I can adduce reasons. But of that, another time; for the present rest assured that the soul, wherever it may be, is within you. But what is its nature? Peculiar to itself, I think; but, be it igneous, or be it aërial, that is of no consequence for our purpose. Only bear this in mind: that, just as you may recognize a Deity, though you be ignorant of his whereabouts and appearance; so it behoves

you to recognize the soul which is within you, though you be ignorant of its whereabouts and its form. Now, as to knowledge of the soul, we cannot doubt, unless we be dullards in the study of natural philosophy, that in souls there is nothing composite, concrete, conglomerate, joint, or duplex. And if that be so, it certainly cannot be separated, divided, dismembered, sundered; and, therefore, it cannot perish. For perishing is, as it were, a separation, division, sundering of what before the perishing was held together by some sort of junction.

It was under the influence of such and similar considerations that Socrates did not look about him for any advocate to defend him on his capital trial, or ask any mercy of the Court which tried him. He displayed a noble independence, arising not from pride, but from magnanimity. On the last day of his life he argued freely upon this subject; and only a few days previously, when he might, without difficulty, have secured his escape from prison, he declined; and, when he all but held in his hand the deadly cup, he talked in such a strain that it seemed as if he were not being forced into his grave, but set upon his road to Heaven. 30. For thus he thought, and thus he argued: There are two routes and two corresponding courses to be followed by souls on their departure from the body. Whoever in their mortal bodies have polluted themselves, and surrendered themselves wholly to their lusts—whereby being blinded, they have contaminated themselves by personal vices and iniquities—or by compassing the ruin of their country have committed inexpiable offences, these take a devious route, shut out from the assemblage of the gods; but whoever have kept themselves pure and chaste, and have had the least possible to do with the body—have indeed always shrunk from it, and have even in their mortal bodies taken for example the life of the gods—for such there lies open an easy way of returning to them from whom they came. And so he reminds his hearers that, as the swans— the birds considered sacred to Apollo (not without reason, but because from him they appear to have received the prophetic gift of foreseeing what gain there is in Death)—are wont to die with song and joyousness, so every good and well-instructed man should do. Nor, indeed, could anybody feel a doubt about the matter, were it not that, in our earnest meditations about the soul, the same sort of thing happens to us which frequently befalls those who intently watch an eclipse of the sun; namely, that they lose the sense of sight altogether. So the eye of the soul, from incessant self-contemplation, grows dim; and thus we lose the power of concentrated observation, and what with doubts and distractions and hesitations and apprehensions of the many breakers ahead, our reason is tossed about and endangered, as if at sea on a boundless ocean.

But all this that I have been referring to is of ancient date and is borrowed from the Greeks. There is the example, however, of Cato, who departed life under such circumstances, that he could congratulate himself upon having obtained an occasion for dying. For the Deity which rules within us, forbids our departure without orders; but when the Deity has himself provided the occasion, as formerly in the case of Socrates, and more recently in that of Cato, and often in many other cases, then verily will the man who is wise depart with joy and thankfulness from the darkness here to the brightness yonder. Not that he will break out of his prison (for that were wrong); but, as if he had obtained an order from a magistrate or some constituted authority, he, feeling himself discharged by the aforesaid Deity, will depart and get him gone. For the whole life of philosophers, as the same Plato tells us, is simply a preparation for death.

31. For what else is it that we do, when we have withdrawn our soul from thoughts of pleasure (that is, of the body), and of filthy lucre (which ministers to, and is the handmaid of the body), and of State affairs, and all manner of business; what, I say, do we else but summon the soul to self-communion, compel it to be alone with itself, and isolate it completely from the body? Now to separate soul from body—what is that but to die? Wherefore, let this be our study; believe me, it is worth while; and let us disconnect ourselves from the body, that is, let us grow familiar with death. Then, as long as we be on earth, shall we have a semblance of life in Heaven; and when, released from these bonds of ours, we find ourselves on the way thither, the course of our soul will be the less retarded. For they who have lived constantly in the shackles of the body, even when released, proceed but slowly, as is the case with them who have been for many years in irons. And when we have arrived there, then, and not till then, shall we have life. For the life here is naught but death: I could give you a lamentation over it, if you wished.

A. You have done that sufficiently in the *Consolation;* when I read it I desire nothing better than to leave this world: but now still greater is my desire, having heard what I have heard.

M. Your hour will come, and that speedily, and whether you hang back or press forward: for time flies. So far, however, is death from being the bane it just now seemed to you to be, that I am very much afraid mankind have nothing else which is so certainly not a bane; nay, nothing else which is a greater blessing.

A. What matter which? Why, there are some who will not admit so much as that.

M. Yes, but now that we have broached the subject, I will never let you go in such a frame of mind that you can

by any process of reasoning be led to regard death as a
bane.

*A.* How can I, after what you have said?

*M.* How can you, do you ask? Why there occur to me
hosts of gainsayers; and not merely the Epicureans, whom
I, for my part, do not despise, although all men of learning
somehow seem to do so, but my favourite Dicaearchus argued most fiercely against this notion of immortality. For
he wrote three books (entitled *Lesbiacs*, because the scene
of the discussion is Mitylene), wherein he would make out
that souls are mortal. The Stoics, again, merely grant us a
long lease of life—like crows; they admit that the soul endures for a while, but not for ever. 32. Would you not like
to hear, then, why, even if it be so, death is not to be classed
among banes?

*A.* As you please; but nobody shall oust me from this
position of immortality.

*M.* That is right: it does not do, though, to be over-con-
fident about anything. For we are often affected by an ingenious argument; we waver, and change our opinion even
on tolerably clear points. Now, in our subject, there is considerable obscurity. Wherefore, for fear of accidents, let us
be armed.

*A.* By all means; but I will take care that there shall be
none.

*M.* Then there is no reason, I suppose, why we should
not at once dismiss our friends the Stoics? Those, I mean,
who admit that souls, after their departure from the body,
endure a long while but not for ever?

*A.* Oh! dismiss them, by all means; for they accept the
most difficult point in the whole case, that the soul can endure when parted from the body; but that which is not only
easy of belief, but, when what they maintain is granted, a
natural consequence thereof, they actually refuse to allow:

namely, that when it has endured a long while, it is hardly likely to perish.

*M.* Your censure is just: that is exactly the state of the case. Well, then, should we pin our faith to Panaetius (who wrote against Plato's *Phaedo*), when he differs from his beloved Plato, whom he everywhere calls divine, wisest of the wise, holiest of the holy, the Homer of philosophers, and with whom it is only on this subject of the immortality of the soul that he does not coincide in opinion? Now he insists, what nobody denies, that whatever is begotten perishes; and he further argues that souls are begotten, as is demonstrated by the resemblance of the procreated to the procreator, which resemblance is apparent in the character also, and not only in the body. Another argument which he adduces is that nothing feels pain but what is liable to disease; and that what is liable to disease will likewise perish: that souls feel pain, *ergo* that they perish.

33. These arguments admit of refutation. For they exhibit an ignorance of the fact that, when one speaks of the immortality of souls, one speaks of the intelligence, which is always free from all manner of disturbing emotion, and not of those parts in which sorrows, passions, and lusts have play, and which they, against whom the arguments are urged, consider to be separate from the intelligence and shut-up apart. Now, as regards resemblance, it is more striking in the case of brutes, which have no reasonable souls. Among mankind, again, it exhibits itself more prominently in the similarity of bodily parts; for as regards the souls, it makes a great difference in what sort of body they happen to be lodged. For many things appertaining to the body contribute to sharpen the intelligence, many to blunt it. Aristotle says that all men of genius are melancholic; so that, for my part, I am not sorry to be of rather a dull temperament. He enumerates several cases, and, as if the fact

were indisputable, adduces various reasons for it. But if so great influence over habit of mind resides in things engendered of the body (and those are they, whatever they may be, whence resemblance is produced), resemblance is no clinching argument that souls are engendered. I now take leave of the subject of resemblances; though I wish that Panaetius could be present. For he belonged to the social circle of Africanus (Minor); and I would ask him which of the family Africanus's brother's grandson resembled (in face he actually resembled his father), inasmuch as in his life he so far resembled all profligates, that he was an easy worst; and whom, again, the grandson of Publius Crassus—Crassus the wise, the eloquent, the prince of men—resembled; and so on, taking the grandsons and sons of many illustrious men, whose names there is no use in mentioning.

But where are we? Have we forgotten that, having already said enough about immortality, our present point was to show that, even if souls did perish, yet death was no bane?

*A.* I remembered all that: but I was nothing loath to have you wander from the point, whilst you discoursed of immortality.

34. *M.* I see that you fix your eyes above, and desire a move to Heaven. And I have hopes that such will be our lot. But suppose—as they whom you wot of maintain—that souls do not endure after death: then evidently, if so it be, we are deprived of our hope of a happier existence. Still, what bane does that opinion entail? For, suppose that the soul does perish, just like the body: is there any sense of pain or any feeling at all remaining in the body? Nobody asserts *that*, though Epicurus charges Democritus with asserting it; a charge which the followers of Democritus deny. And so in the soul likewise there remains no consciousness, for itself has become null and nowhere. Where,

then, is the bane? For there is no intermediate condition between existence and non-existence. Is it in the fact that the actual severance of soul and body does not take place without pain? Even if it be so, how insignificant is it! Moreover, I do not think that it is so generally; it generally takes place unconsciously, sometimes even pleasurably. In point of fact, whatever the true state of the case may be, it is a perfectly unimportant matter, for it takes place in the twinkling of an eye. What causes pain, or rather torture, is severance from all the blessings which life bestows; if it would not be more correct to say, from all the banes. But why should I now mourn over the life of man? I could do so, with truth and justice; but what need is there—when my object is to prevent us from supposing that we shall be miserable after death—to make even life more miserable than it is by lamentation? I have done all that in the book in which, so far as I could, I endeavoured to find consolation. It is from banes then, and not from blessings, that death removes us, if we would but have the truth. And, indeed, so stoutly maintained is this by Hegesias the Cyrenaic, that he is said to have been forbidden by King Ptolemy to urge his arguments in the schools, because, after hearing them, so many committed suicide. Callimachus too has an epigram upon Cleombrotus of Ambracia who, he says, threw himself from a parapet into the sea after reading one of Plato's *Dialogues*. The work of the said Hegesias is entitled, *Fasting to Death*, because the hero of it is starving himself to death, and being remonstrated with by his friends, replies to their questions as to his reasons, by enumerating the troubles of human life. I might do the same; though not going quite so far as he, who thought life not worth having at all. I will not answer for others; but for ourselves is it still worth having? Bereaved as we are of the solace of our private life and the honours of our public career, had we died before then, assuredly death had taken us away from the evil and not from the good.

35. Now, picture to yourself the case of somebody who has had no cross to bear, a Metellus (let us say), with his four "right honourable" sons. Picture to yourself, again, the case of Priam, with his fifty sons, seventeen of them born in lawful wedlock. In either case Fortune had the same power; she exercised it only in one. For a multitude of sons and daughters, and grandsons, and granddaughters, laid Metellus upon his pyre; Priam, bereaved of that numerous offspring, and a fugitive at the altar, fell by his enemy's hand. Had he died with sons still living and kingdom still safe,

> In the days of Phrygian glory,
> 'Neath his ceilings carved and fretted,

would he have departed from bane or blessing? From blessing, to judge by appearances; but it would undoubtedly have been a better fate for him, nor would there have been sung, in such mournful wise, the lines:

> Flames on all sides see I gleaming,
> Priam's life-blood, life-less streaming,
> Jove's high altar slaughter-teeming!

As if anything better could have happened to him *then!* But had he died before, he would have escaped the catastrophe altogether; and when it did happen, he was rid of the consciousness of his troubles. My friend Pompey, after a severe illness at Neapolis, had a turn for the better, and the people of the place went about crowned with garlands: so, of course, did they of Puteoli; the inhabitants flocked out from the towns to offer their congratulations. A silly business, just like your Greeklings; but, nevertheless, a sign of good fortune. Now, had he died at that time, would he have gone away from the good or from the evil? Doubtless from misery. For he would never have waged war with his father-in-law; he would never, unprepared as he was, have taken up arms; he would never have left his home, never have fled from Italy, never—after losing his army—have fallen defenceless among slaves with arms in their hands, never have had to weep over his children's prospects, nor would his possessions have fallen a prey to his conquerors. Had he then met his death, his star would have set in the plenitude of his fortunes. Through the prolongation of his life, how many, how great, how incredible were the misfortunes whereof he had to drain the cup! 36. Such things are escaped by death, even though they do not happen—because they might happen; but men do not reflect that such things may befall them. Everybody hopes for the good fortune of Metellus; just as if the fortunate were more numerous than the unfortunate, or there were anything certain in the affairs of mankind, or it were more reasonable to hope than to fear.

But even if it be granted that men are deprived by death of good fortune, does it follow that the dead *lack* the blessings of life, and that this is misery? Yet such must be the argument. But *can* he who *is* not, "lack" anything at all? For a pathetic term is this same "lack," because there is at the bottom of it an idea of "having not, after having had," of "missing," of "wanting back again," of "needing." These, to my mind, are the grievances of him who "lacks." One would "lack" eyes, for instance, for blindness is decidedly grievous; or children, for so is bereavement. This is applicable enough in the case of the quick; but of the dead none "lacks," not only the advantages of life, but even life itself. I am speaking now of the dead, who *are not*. As for us, who *are*, do we "lack" either horns or wings? Would anybody use such an expression? Certainly not; and why? Because from not having that which is neither by your habits nor your nature adapted for you, you would feel no "lack," though perfectly conscious that you have it not. This argument must be urged again and again, when we have once established the point (as to which there can be no doubt, if souls be mortal) that in death there is so thorough a perishing that there is not left the very faintest suspicion of consciousness. When, then, this point is once properly and thoroughly fixed, the other must be discussed, in order to perfectly understand what is meant by "lack," that there may be no mistake about terms. To "lack," then, means this: to be without that which you would wish to have. For there is a notion of wishing in "lack," unless when it is used in quite a different fashion, as in the case of fever (when you say that a patient "lacks," that is, "is free from," fever. For, in common parlance, "lack" is sometimes used in this other sense; when you "have not" something or other, and are perfectly conscious of not having it, though you are quite content to be without it). In the case of death, you cannot so use the word "lack," properly speaking, for it would not indicate any possible grievance. Properly, you "lack" what is a blessing; which lack is a bane. Not even the quick, however, "lack" even a blessing which they do not want. Nevertheless, in the case of the quick, the expression would no doubt be intelligible; as, for instance, that you yourself "lack" a kingdom: though it cannot be so accurately predicated in your case as it could have been in that of Tarquinius, when he was driven from his dominions. But in the case of the dead it is quite unintelligible; for "lack" is said of the conscious, and, as there is no consciousness in the dead, there is consequently no "lack" at all in the case of the dead.

37. However, what need to philosophize on this point, when we see that the matter does not require very much assistance from philosophy? How often, among ourselves.

have, not leaders only, but whole armies, rushed forward to certain death? But if there were any fear about it, neither would L. Brutus have fallen in the field to hinder the return of the tyrant whom he had himself expelled, nor would the Decii—the father in the obstinate battle with the Latins, the son in that with the Etruscans, and the grandson in that with Pyrrhus—have exposed themselves to the missiles of the foe; nor in one single war in their country's cause would Spain have witnessed the fall of the two Scipios, Cannae that of Paullus and Geminus, Venusia that of Marcellus, Litana that of Albinus, and Lucania that of Gracchus. Is any one of them miserable at this date? Or was he, even then, after the last gasp? Indeed, it is impossible to be miserable after loss of consciousness. Oh! but perhaps that is the very grievance, the remaining without consciousness. It were verily a grievance, if it meant to "lack." But as there can evidently *be* nothing at all in the case of one who *is* not, what grievance can there be in the case of one who neither lacks, nor is conscious? However, somewhat too much of this: but my reason for it all was that herein is the source of any shrinking of the soul for fear of death. For whosoever sees clearly —and it is plainer than daylight—that if body and soul be annihilated, the whole animate being obliterated, and complete destruction effected, the living thing which was has become nothing at all, he will at once perceive that there is then no difference between a Hippocentaur (which never existed) and King Agamemnon, and that M. Camillus now takes no more account of the civil wars than I, in his lifetime, took of the sack of Rome. Why then would Camillus have been pained, had he foreseen that some 350 years after his time there would be such a state of things as there now is; and why should I be pained, if I supposed that, in the course of ten thousand years, some other people would possess our city? Because love of country is measured, not by the standard of our consciousness, but by that of the importance attaching to its welfare.

38. Wherefore the wise man is not deterred by thoughts of death (which, because of accidents, is ever impending over us, and, because of the shortness of life, can never be very far off) from studying to promote, to all futurity, the welfare of the State and of his own people, and from feeling that between posterity—though he may be unconscious of it—and himself there is some sort of connecting link. Therefore, even he who opines that the soul is mortal may act with an eye to eternity; not from a passion for glory, of which he will not be conscious, but of virtue—in the wake whereof glory, though you heed not *that*, inevitably follows.

If then the course of nature is on this wise: that, as birth introduces us to the beginning of things, so does death to the end, it follows that, as before death there was nothing which concerned us, so there will be nothing that concerns us after death. What bane, then, can there be in this, inasmuch as death concerns neither living nor dead? The latter *are not;* the former it appertains not to. Now they who would fain modify this conclusion, maintain that it is just like sleep. As if any one could entertain the notion of living ninety years on the condition that, when sixty were completed, the rest should be taken out in sleep. Why, the very swine would scorn the idea; much more would you and I. (And yet, as a comparison, it is just enough.) Once upon a time, if we believe the story-books, Endymion fell into a deep sleep upon Latmos, a mountain of Caria, and, I suppose, has not to this day been awakened. Think you, then, that he cares one jot when eclipse comes upon Luna, by whom he is fabled to have been buried in slumber that she might kiss him as he slept? How could he, having no consciousness? Now, in sleep we have a semblance of death; and this semblance we daily assume. Have you, then, any doubt that there is no consciousness in death, when you see that in its semblance there is no consciousness?

39. Away, then, with all that almost old-womanish twaddle about untimely death being a miserable thing. What *time* pray? Nature's? But she gives life on loan, as one might lend money—without fixing beforehand a day of repayment. What ground is there for complaint, then, if she ask for it back whenever she pleases? That was the condition on which you received it. Yet the same persons hold, that if a mere child die, it should be borne with equanimity; if a babe in the cradle, that it is no matter for wailing at all. And yet in this case, Nature has been still more rigorous in demanding back what she gave. Ah! but—it is urged—he had not yet tasted the sweets of life; whereas the other had already begun to conceive great hopes and even to enjoy them. But this is exactly what, in other matters, is considered the better: to obtain half a loaf rather than no bread. Why should it be different in respect of life? Anyhow Callimachus was right in saying:

"Old Priam shed more tears than Troïlus."

On the other hand, the good fortune of such as die at the close of their *prime* has been extolled. But why? For, in my opinion, if a further lease of life were granted, a man could have nothing more delightful; inasmuch as life contains nothing more pleasant than wisdom, and that is what old age, though it take away everything else, brings with it. But what life ever is long? Or what is there at all—with which mortal man has to do at least—of long duration? Hath not old age

Them who but to-day were children, but to-day were in their
    prime
Followed up and overtaken?

But, because we have nothing beyond, we call this sort of
thing long. Such things are termed long or short, in propor=
tion to the average in every case. Aristotle says that on the
banks of the river Hypanis, which falls into the Euxine from
a part of Europe, there is an order of beasties which live one
day. Of these, therefore, any that dies at the eighth hour has
died at an advanced age, but any that dies at sunset, in positive senility, especially if it be the solstice. Compare, now,
our longest life with eternity, and we shall be found to be
in much the same category as these ephemerals.

40. Despise we, therefore, all such trash, (for by what
softer term can I describe such soft-headedness?) and consider we the essentials of a satisfactory life to be comprised
in strong-mindedness and magnanimity, and disregard and
contempt of all earthly things, and the practice of every virtue. For in these days we are emasculated by the most
effeminate theories, to such an extent that, should death
arrive ere we have realized the promises of the Chaldeans
(the drawers of horoscopes), we seem to be robbed of some
great blessing, to be cheated and left in the lurch. But if—
what with expectations and regrets—we now live in mental
suspense, torture, and anguish; ye gods of Heaven! how
welcome should that journey be, at the end of which there
will remain no more trouble, no more anxiety! How delighted I am with Theramenes: what loftiness of spirit he
displays! For, although the tears flow from us as we read,
that noble soul does not die in a manner calling for pity.
Thrown into prison by order of the Thirty Tyrants, after
quaffing his poison as if he were a-thirst, he hurled the heel-
taps from the cup so that it clinked again, and when the
sound rang in his ears, "I drink," quoth he, with a smile, "to

the noble Critias," who was his bitterest foe. For it is the wont of the Greeks at their banquets to name him to whom they are going to pass the cup. That glorious spirit was sportive with his latest breath; and when he had death already conceived within his midriff, he prophesied to the man whom he had pledged in the poison—unerringly—the death which soon afterwards overtook him. Yet who would commend *such* equanimity (which would then be culpable levity) at the hour of death—in the case of the greatest man—if he considered death to be a bane? To the same prison and to the same cup a few years later went Socrates, by just such an iniquitous sentence of his judges as Theramenes received from the Thirty Tyrants. Now what is the language which Plato represents him to have made use of before the judges, when he had been condemned to death?

41. "I have great hopes, my lords," said he, "that it is a blessed thing for me to be sent to my death. For one of two things must necessarily be: either death removes consciousness altogether, or there is, at death, a migration from these regions to some other region. If, therefore, consciousness be extinguished, and death be like that sleep which sometimes brings us rest so placid that it is free even from visions of dreams, ye good gods! what gain it is to die! Or how many days can life bring us, which are preferable to one such night? And if all the time to come is to be like this, who is there more blessed than I? But if there be truth in what is sometimes said, that death is but a migration to those realms which they who have departed this life inhabit; a far more blessed belief is that! That, having escaped from them who would fain be accounted judges, you should appear before them who are rightly called judges, before Minos and Rhadamanthus, and Aeacus and Triptolemus, and foregather with them who have lived justly and honourably! Seemeth this to you but a common-place pilgrimage? To

have the privilege of conversing with Orpheus and Musaeus, and Hesiod and Homer, at how much, pray, do ye value that? For my part I were fain to die often, if that were possible, to realize what I say. With what delight, again, should I be moved at the idea of joining the company of Palamedes and Ajax, and others who have been victims of unjust judgment! I would test the wisdom of that king of men who led the mightiest of hosts to Troy, and of Ulysses, and of Sisyphus; and, whilst I was prosecuting my inquiries, just as I was doing here, I should not be condemned to death for it. And ye, too, my lords, or those of ye who were for acquitting me, have ye no fear of death. For indeed nothing that is evil can happen to any good man, either living or dead; nor will the care of him ever be neglected by the immortal gods. Nor hath this, which hath happened to me come to pass fortuitously. Nor, indeed, have I any reason why I should be wrath either with them by whom I was accused, or with them by whom I have been condemned, save only that they believed that they were doing me hurt." And so on, all in the same fashion. But there is nothing finer than the conclusion: "It is time," said he, "that I go hence to die, ye to continue your life. Which of the two is preferable, the immortal gods know; of men, I trow, there knows not one."

42. Verily, I would rather be of this spirit, than enjoy the fortune of all those who passed sentence upon him. Though as to what he says about that which, in his own words, no one knows save the immortal gods, he knew himself which was preferable, for he had said so previously; but he held to the last to that maxim of his about never being positive as to anything. And let us also, for our own part, cling with equal stedfastness to the opinion that nothing can be a bane which has been assigned by Nature to all mankind; and make up our minds that, if death be really a bane, then it must be an everlasting one. For death appears to be the end

of a miserable life; and if death also be miserable, it is misery for ever and ever. But why cite Socrates and Theramenes, men who stood in the first rank of those who have been famous for virtue and wisdom; when a fellow of Lacedaemon, whose very name even has not come down to us, thought so little of death, that, when he was on his way thereto by sentence of the Ephors, and looked so bright and joyous, that an enemy said to him, "Mockest thou at the laws of Lycurgus?" he replied, "Nay, but I am much bounden to the gentleman, for he hath amerced me in such fine as I can pay without loan or usury." Verily a worthy son of Sparta! So much so indeed, that, methinks, a fellow of such lofty spirit must have been condemned unjustly. Our own land has produced numberless examples of the like spirit. But why recount the names of generals and captains, when M. Cato has recorded that whole legions often marched cheerfully to positions whence they did not believe that they would ever return? With the like spirit fell the Lacedaemonians at Thermopylae, on whom Simonides wrote the epitaph:

> Go, stranger, go; this news to Sparta tell—
> We kept her honoured laws; we fought and fell.

What says their famous leader Leonidas? "Forward, with stout hearts, my men of Lacedaemon; to-day, peradventure, we shall sup in Hades!" Ah! that was a stout-hearted race, so long as the laws of Lycurgus were in force. It was one of them, who, when an enemy, a Persian, remarked boastfully in conversation, "You will not be able to see the sun for the multitude of arrows and javelins," replied quietly, "We shall fight in the shade, then." But those whom I have mentioned were *men*. Of what stuff, then, was the *woman* of Lacedaemon, who. having sent her son forth to battle, and having learned that he was slain, exclaimed, "To that end had I borne him; that there might at any rate be one who would not hesitate to die for his country."

43. Yes, the Spartans were a stout and hardy race. Great is the influence of State-training. Well, and do we not admire Theodorus of Cyrene, no mean philosopher, who, when King Lysimachus threatened him with crucifixion, said, "Threaten those fellows in plush with horrors of that kind; to Theodorus it make no odds whether he rot aground or aloft." Now, by this remark of his, I am reminded to say somewhat about interment and burial, a question attended with little or no difficulty, especially after what was said just now as to having no consciousness. What Socrates thought about the matter is apparent from the Dialogue which is concerned with his death, and about which so much has already been said. For—when he had finished his argument touching the immortality of the soul, and the hour of his death drew near—being asked by Crito how he would be buried, "Verily, my friends," said he, "I have spent much labour in vain. For I have not convinced our friend Crito that I shall soar away hence and leave nothing of me behind. Howbeit, Crito, if you can overtake me, or if you find me anywhere about, then bury me as may seem to you good. But, believe me, when I am gone, none of you will be able to overtake me." This was finely said by him; leaving the matter to his friend, and at the same time showing that he himself had no anxiety about anything of the kind. Diogenes, in rougher style, but still in the same strain, only—as a Cynic—with more bitterness, ordered that he should be cast forth unburied. "What!" said his friends, "to the birds and beasts?" "By no manner of means," said he, "but lay ye beside me a staff wherewith to beat them off." "But how will you be able?" rejoined they, "for you will not be conscious." "What hurt, then," replied he, "shall the rending by the

beasts do me, being unconscious?" It was nobly said, too, by Anaxagoras, when he lay at Lampsacus a-dying and his friends asked him whether, should anything happen, he would like to be removed to Clazomenae, his native town: "No need," he replied; "the distance to Hades is the same from everywhere." In fact, as regards the whole subject of interment, one thing must be constantly kept in view, that it is entirely an affair of the body: whether the soul perish or retain vitality. Now it is quite clear that, whether the soul be annihilated or make its escape, there is no consciousness left in the body.

44. Everything, however, connected with this subject, teems with error. Achilles drags Hector at his chariot-wheels; under the impression, apparently, that the latter is being lacerated, and is conscious of it. And thus, in imagination, takes vengeance upon him; whilst poor woman mourns over this as the bitterest drop in her cup of sorrow:

> I saw, and most I grieved at that I saw,
> My Hector dragged behind the victor's car!

What Hector? Or how long will he be Hector? In better strain sing Attius and Achilles (wise for once):

> Ay, the corpse I gave to Priam—Hector's self I took away.

So it was not Hector that you dragged about, but the body which had been Hector's. See! there starts up from underground another who will not let his mother sleep:

> Mother mine, 'tis I who call thee, while thou sleep'st thy cares
>     away
> And on me hast no compassion: rise and bury me thy son.

When you hear this sort of thing chanted to low and mournful measures, which produce sadness among whole audiences, ít is hard not to believe that the unburied are miserable.

And again:

> Before
> The beasts and birds devour. . . .

He is afraid, apparently, that he will have a difficulty in using his limbs if they are mangled, but not if they are burnt to ashes:

Leave thou not my relics thus, with bones denuded of the flesh,
Thus with ugly gore bespattered, foully to be torn to shreds.

For my part, I do not see what he has to be afraid of, when he pours forth his unexceptionable verses to the accompaniment of the pipe. We should bear in mind, then, that there is nothing at all to be concerned about after death; though many (especially on the stage), are for wreaking vengeance upon their enemies, even when those enemies are dead. Thus, in Ennius, Thyestes, in some remarkably telling lines, invokes curses upon the head of Atreus; in the first place, praying that he may perish by shipwreck. That is really hard upon him: for such a death is not unaccompanied by painful sensations. But the following rant is simply silly:

On the peaks of rugged rocks, impaled and disembowelled, let
    him
Hang athwart, with gore and filth and blackened blood the rocks
    bedewing!

Not even the rocks themselves are more devoid of sensation than he would be who "hangs athwart," and on whom the curser fancies that he is invoking torment. Severe, indeed, were those curses, if the cursed could feel; but they are nothing at all, when there is no sensation. However, the acme of absurdity is this:

May he lack the tomb wherein his body should a haven find:
Where, when life hath ebbed, the body rests secure from human
  woe!

You see what a mass of error is involved with all this. He
fancies that there is a haven for the body; and that the dead
rest in the grave! Verily Pelops was greatly to blame for not
having his son properly instructed, and for not teaching him
the proper limits of human concern.

45. But why arraign the vain imaginations of individuals,
when we may sit in judgment upon the various errors of
whole peoples? The Egyptians, for instance, embalm their
dead, and keep them indoors; the Persians, again, encase
theirs in wax, when then bury them, that the bodies may
last as long as possible. The practice of the Magians is—not
to bury the dead of their order, unless they have previously
been torn by wild beasts. In Hyrcania the commonalty keep
public dogs for this purpose; the gentry, private. We know
what a famous breed of dogs that is; but in that country
everybody—according to his means—contributes towards
keeping a pack of them on purpose to be torn to pieces by
them. And this is considered to be the best form of disposing of the dead. Chrysippus, displaying his usual research
in all that appertains to history, has collected many other
facts relating to this subject; but so revolting are many of
them, that language positively shrinks from recording them.
The whole topic, however, is one which we can afford to
neglect altogether in our own case, though not perhaps in
the case of those who belong to us; with the limitation that
we, who are quick, are quite conscious of the fact that the
bodies of the dead are devoid of all consciousness. How far
the quick should defer to public opinion, is a question for
the quick themselves; it being always understood that nothing of this sort makes any difference whatever to the dead.

And now as regards the best time for meeting death with

the greatest equanimity. Surely it is when the sunset of life approaches, and can be cheered by a modicum of self-commendation. Nobody has lived too short a life, of whom it can be certified that he has discharged with consummate devotion the obligations of consummate manfulness (*virtutis*). I myself have had many opportune occasions for death: and would that I had met it! For I had not set my heart upon any particular object of ambition; the sum of life's duties had been accomplished; all that remained was a struggle with fortune. Wherefore, if sheer reason be unable to make one (me) think lightly of death, still, one's past life would render one conscious of having lived long enough, and more than enough. For, though consciousness departs, the dead are not without their due meed of praise and glory, inasmuch as glory, though it have in itself nothing for which we should desire it, attends virtue like its shadow.

46. The real truth is rather, that a correct verdict of the world—if ever there be such a thing—upon men of worth redounds to the public credit, than that they who have secured it are beatified thereby. Yet I cannot say that Solon and Lycurgus lack, in any acceptation of the term, the glory due to their legislation and constitutions; or Themistocles and Epaminondas that due to their military prowess. For sooner will Neptune bury Salamis itself than the memory of the victory at Salamis in oblivion; and Leuctra will be wiped off the face of Boeotia before the glory of the battle of Leuctra is effaced. Still slower will fame be to desert our Curius, our Fabricius, our Calatinus, our two Africani, our Maximus Fabius, Marcellus, Paullus, Cato, Laelius, and countless others; to whom whosoever hath caught but a touch of resemblance (not measuring that resemblance by the standard of popular estimation, but of the genuine praise bestowed by good men), will march forward—should

such be the course of events—in the spirit of confidence to death, wherein, as we have ascertained, there is either the chiefest blessing, or, at the very worst, no bane. Nay, it is at the height of his prosperity that he will yearn to die; for the flood of good fortune can never be so delightful as the ebb is distressing. And this seems to have been the idea at the bottom of that well-known saying of a certain Lacedaemonian, who—when Diagoras of Rhodes, a famous Olympian victor, had witnessed with his own eyes on one day the victories of two of his sons at Olympia—stepped up to the old man, and in congratulation said: "Now die, Diagoras; for thou wilt not ascend to heaven." The Greeks think, or rather did then think, a great deal—too much, perhaps—of such matters; and he who addressed such language to Diagoras—considering it to be a most extraordinary honour for three victors at Olympia to come from the same family—opined that to linger any longer in the world, exposed to the buffets of fortune, was a clear tempting of Providence.

Now, as regards yourself, I had answered your doubts satisfactorily in what appeared to me to be but a few words. For you had granted that the dead are not in evil case. Still I constrained myself to enlarge further, for the simple reason that in time of loss and sorrow that fact is our greatest consolation. For pain, which is all our own, and is felt on our own account, we are bound to take lightly, lest we should appear egotistical. The idea which tortures us with intolerable pain is the belief—if we have it—that they of whom we have been bereaved, are and are conscious of being in the midst of those evils to which the vulgar creed consigns them. This belief I was desirous of eradicating, at any rate from my own mind; and so, perhaps, I appeared somewhat tedious.

47. A. Tedious! Not to me, I assure you. For your earlier remarks made me feel quite desirous of dying; your later to

just feel no unwillingness, to just have no anxiety. And altogether your words have had the effect of preventing me
from counting death in the category of evils.

*M.* Well, then, do we still require the epilogue (peroration) after the fashion of the rhetoricians; or are we to
abandon their art altogether?

*A.* Oh! pray do not *you* abandon it, for you have always
done it grace, and very properly; for it—to tell the truth—
had first done *you* grace. But what is your epilogue to be?
Whatever it is, I long to hear it.

*M.* In the Schools they are wont to adduce decisions of
the immortal gods upon the subject of death; and not mere
fancies of their own either, but based upon the authority of
Herodotus and of many others. First and foremost is the
case of Cleobis and Bito, the two sons of a certain Argive
priestess. The story is well known. She had to drive in her
chariot to a temple, a long way off from the city of Argos,
to perform a solemn appointed service. The cattle did not
arrive in time. Then did these two young men, having laid
aside their garments, and anointed their bodies with oil,
place themselves beneath the yoke. Thus the priestess rode
to the temple in the chariot drawn by her two sons; and she
is said to have prayed the goddess to bestow upon them for
their piety the highest reward that could be bestowed on
man. After this, having supped, it is said, with their mother,
the young men lay down to rest, and in the morning they
were found dead. Trophonius and Agamedes are said to
have made a similar petition. They—having finished the
temple which they built to Apollo (at Delphi)—on going
to worship there, prayed of the god no insignificant recompense—it must be owned—for their toil and trouble;
namely, nothing definite but simply, "that which were best
for man." To whom Apollo signified that their prayer should
be granted on the third day from that time. When the day

dawned, they were found dead. A god—they argue—was the judge; and that god, moreover, to whom the other gods had conceded the spirit of divination beyond all the rest.

48. There is also another little story told, about Silenus, who had been captured by Midas, and is reported to have given him, by way of ransom, the following revelation: that the best thing for a man were not to be born, the next to die as soon as possible. Which sentiment Euripides has introduced into his *Cresphontes:*

> For 'twould beseem us—in full chorus all—
> To mourn the house wherein a babe is born,
> Bethinking us of all the ills of life:
> But him, whose woes have found an end in death,
> With shouts of joy to follow to the grave.

There is something similar in Crantor's *Consolation.* He says that a certain Elysius of Terina, being grievously afflicted at the death of his son, went to a divination-shop to inquire the cause of such a blow, and had delivered to him as a response the following three verses:

> Through witless minds in life we go astray:
> 'Twas Fate's decree Euthynöus took away;
> 'Tis best for him and thee, both now and aye!

On the strength of these and the like authorities, it is maintained that the question has been decided by the immortal gods, in a practical manner. Nay more, Alcidamas, a rhetorician of the old school, of the highest reputation, went so far as to write a panegyric on death, whereof the basis is an enumeration of human woes. And though he lacked those subtle arguments which have been more carefully grouped together by philosophers, he lacked not abundance of eloquence. Gallant deaths encountered in the cause of the fatherland are wont to be, in the eyes of rhetoricians, not only glorious but beatific. They go back as far as Erechtheus, whose very daughters were quite zealous to die for the people's sake; and Codrus who threw himself into the middle of the foe, in a slave's dress, lest he should be recognized if he wore his royal insignia; for an oracle had declared that, if her king were slain, Athens would be victorious. Nor is Menoeceus forgotten, who—also in consequence of an oracle—freely shed his blood for his country. Iphigenia, too, at Aulis, is urgent to be led to the slaughter, in order that the blood of the foe may be charmed forth by her own.

Thence a move is made to more recent dates. 49. Harmodius and Aristogeiton, Leonidas of Lacedaemon, Epaminondas of Thebes, still live between the lips. Our own heroes were not then known; whom it were quite a task to enumerate, so many are they by whom we observe that death accompanied by glory was regarded as a thing to be coveted. And yet—though so it be—we have, nevertheless, to employ great eloquence and speak on this subject as it were from the pulpit, to bring men in general either to show the first symptoms of coveting death, or at any rate to leave off fearing it. Yet what is more covetable, if the last day bring —not annihilation, but—simply a change of place? If, on the other hand, it entirely destroys and obliterates, what can be better than in the midst of life to fall asleep, and closing one's eyes be lulled to everlasting slumber? And, if this be the true state of the case; then the utterance of Ennius is better than that of Solon. For the former sings:

> Mourn not for me, no tearful tribute give,
> For on the lips of living men I live;

The latter, the man of wisdom, on the contrary:

> Let me not die unwept, but let the tear
> Of friends who mourn my loss fall on my bier!

As for ourselves, however, should anything happen of such a nature, that we seem to have received from the deity an order to depart this life—let us obey with joy and giving of thanks, and look upon ourselves as discharged from prison, and released from bonds; that either we may return to that home eternal which is our proper abode, or else be free from consciousness and cease from trouble. But if no such order come, let us be so minded as to think the awful day (as it is to others) a day of felicitation for us, and count nothing to be a bane which hath been appointed for us either by the immortal gods or by Nature the mother of all. For we are not born or created idly or fortuitously; but doubtless there is some power which takes thought for the race of men, and which was not likely to create and foster what—when it had accomplished all its toils—would sink into everlasting misery in death. Let us rather regard it as a haven and a refuge prepared for us: whither may we arrive with swelling sails! But if we be beaten back by adverse winds, still, sooner or later, we must bring up there. Besides, what is necessary for all, can that be a bane for any one?

So there you have your epilogue that you may not consider anything overlooked or neglected.

A. I have, indeed; and it has still further strengthened my convictions.

M. Good. And now let us make some allowance for health. But to-morrow—and every day that we remain at Tusculum—let us meet here, and discuss those questions especially which have a modifying effect upon sorrows, fears, and desires; for that is the most profitable out-come of all philosophy.

"To philosophize is to learn to die" is a principle followed to greater or less degree by all ethical philosophers, but the Romans seem to have been particularly obsessed by fear of death—because of terrifying Etruscan pictures of the future state, it has been suggested—and the inculcation of fortitude at the prospect of death was a major objective of Roman ethical teachers. Lucretius made the conquest of that fear one of his principal aims, Cicero deals with it here and elsewhere (for example, in On Old Age), and Seneca reverts to it repeatedly. But the fear of death is only one emotional factor that disturbs human happiness, and each of the remaining four books of the Tusculans deals with another. The second book teaches that pain must be despised: if it is an evil it is a slight one; virtue makes it insignificant, and death is a ready refuge. Book 3 declares that the causes of grief are due to our own mistaken opinion and hence voluntary; the sage is capable of freeing himself from the false opinions which cause grief. Book 4 similarly ascribes all other disconcerting emotions to false judgments, the error of which can be rooted out by philosophy. In the fifth book the teaching of the various schools is examined to show that virtue is of itself sufficient to secure a happy life; if Epicurus can think that the wise man is always happy then surely the philosophers who go back to Plato must think so.

# ON OLD AGE

On Old Age (*also called* Cato), *dedicated to his friend Atticus, is among the most personal as well as the most charming of Cicero's essays. It was written in 44 B.C., when Cicero's high hopes that the elimination of Julius Caesar would restore the republic were proven vain, when most of his friends had perished in the political turmoils and the survivors were threatened by Antony's ruthlessness, when his own laboriously constructed house of fame was in ruins. Cicero was 62, but in full possession of his powers; men who feel decrepit do not write about old age, and only a vigorous man's views of old age can interest other vigorous men. Aside from its literary qualities the essay reveals Cicero's essential stalwartness. Emerson alluded to it as "Cicero's famous essay, charming by its uniform rhetorical merit; heroic with stoical precepts; with a Roman eye to the claims of the state; happiest, perhaps, in his praise of life on the farm; and rising at the conclusion to a lofty strain."*

1.
And if, Titus, I somehow aid, your heart somehow relieve
Of the care that carps, the sting that rankles,
What my reward?

I may fitly address you, my dear Atticus, in the lines in which Flamininus was addressed by the man "poor in goods, rich in loyalty"—though I am very sure that you are not, as Flamininus was, "by day and by night ever anxious." I know how equable and well ordered your mind is, and am fully aware that you brought from Athens not only your surname but also Athenian culture and good sense. And yet I suspect that you are at times deeply moved by the same political circumstances that perturb me. Consolation on this head is of a profounder kind, and must be put off to another occasion. My present purpose is to dedicate to you an essay on old age. It is my desire to lighten the burden impending or at any rate advancing on us both; though in your case I am very sure that you support it and will support it with calm and philosophic temper. Upon resolving to write on this theme I thought of you as the proper recipient of a gift which might profit us both alike. To me, at any rate, the composition of this book has been so delightful that it has not only wiped away all the annoyance of old age but has rendered it easy and agreeable. Never can philosophy be sufficiently praised; the man who hearkens to its precepts is enabled to pass every season of life free from worry.

But on such topics I have said much and shall often say more; this book which I send you is on old age. I have put the whole discourse not, as Aristo of Ceos did, in the mouth of Tithonus—a mere fable would not carry conviction—but in that of Marcus Cato when he was an old man, to give it greater weight. I represent Laelius and Scipio at his house expressing surprise at his bearing his years so well, and Cato responding to them. If he shall appear to argue more learnedly than he himself was wont to do in his books, ascribe it to Greek literature, of which it is known that he became an eager student in his later years. But why need I say more? Cato's own conversation will unfold my sentiments on old age.

2. scipio. Time and again, in conversation with Laelius here, I have marveled, Cato, at the eminent, nay, perfect, wisdom displayed by you indeed at all points, but above all because I have observed that old age never seemed a burden to you, whereas most old men find it so irksome that they declare they support a load heavier than Etna. cato. It is no very difficult feat that arouses your admiration, Scipio and Laelius. Men who have no inner resources for a good and happy life find every age burdensome; those who look for all happiness from within can think nothing evil which the laws of nature entail. Old age is first in that category; all men wish to attain it, and yet grumble when they have done so—so inconsistent and perverse is folly. They say it steals upon them faster than they expected. In the first place, who compelled them to calculate wrong? Does old age steal upon youth more quickly than youth upon boyhood? Would old age be less irksome if they were in their 800th rather than in their 80th year? However long the past, when it had gone it could never solace or soothe a foolish old age. If then you are accustomed to admire my wisdom—and would it were worthy of your good opinion and of my surname Sapiens—I am wise in that I follow that good guide nature; it is not likely, when she has written the rest of the play well, that she should, like a lazy playwright, skimp the last act. There had to be an ending, just as fruits

and crops come in the course of time to a period of fall and decay. No wise man will resent this. What is warring against the gods, as the giants did, other than fighting against nature? LAELIUS. And yet, Cato, you will oblige us greatly (I venture to speak for Scipio as for myself) if, since we all hope or at least wish to become old men—you would allow us to learn from you in good time the principles by which we may most easily support the weight of increasing years. CATO. I shall certainly do so, Laelius, especially if, as you say, you both find it agreeable. LAELIUS. We do wish, Cato, if it is no trouble to you, to see what sort of place you have reached after the long journey upon which we too must embark.

3. CATO. I will do my best, Laelius. I have often listened to the complaints of old men—like consorts with like, as the old proverb has it—men like Gaius Salinator and Spurius Albinus, consulars and virtually my contemporaries, who lamented that they had lost the pleasures of the senses, without which life is a cipher, and that they were neglected by people who used to court them. Their blame seemed to me misdirected. If the fault were of old age, the same misfortunes would have befallen me and other older men; but I have known many who made no complaint, who were not grieved to be loosed from the thralldom of the passions and were not looked down upon by their friends. In all complaints of this kind, the fault is in the character of a man, not his age. Temperate old men who are neither testy nor ill-natured pass a very tolerable old age; discontent and ill-nature are irksome at any age. LAELIUS. It is as you say, Cato. But perhaps someone may suggest that it is your large means, wealth, and high position that make you think old age tolerable; very few enjoy such good fortune. CATO. There is something in what you say, Laelius, but by no means the whole story. For instance, the tale is told of The-

mistocles' answer when he was quarreling with a certain Seriphian, who asserted that Themistocles owed his brilliant position to his country's reputation and not his own. "If I had been a Seriphian," said he, "even I should never have been famous, nor would you if you had been an Athenian." The same may be said of old age. Not even to a philosopher could old age be easy in the depths of poverty, nor could a fool find it anything but burdensome even amid ample wealth. The arms best adapted to old age, Scipio and Laelius, are the attainment and practice of the virtues; if cultivated at every period of life these produce wonderful fruits when you reach old age, not only because they never fail—though that too is an important consideration—but also because the consciousness of a life well spent and the recollection of many virtuous deeds afford great satisfaction.

4. I was as fond of Quintus Fabius Maximus, who recovered Tarentum, as if he had been of my own age, though he was old and I was young. His dignity was seasoned by affability, nor had age altered his disposition. He was an elderly but not really an old man when I began to cultivate his acquaintance; his first consulship fell the year after I was born. When he was consul for the fourth time and I only a lad I served under him in the expedition to Capua, and five years later in that to Tarentum. Four years later, in the consulship of Tuditanus and Cethegus, I became quaestor; and he, now quite old, urged the passage of the Cincian law on fees and gifts. When he was quite old he conducted wars with the spirit of youth, and his perseverance checked Hannibal's youthful impetuosity. Well did my friend Ennius say of him:

> One man by delay restored our fortune;
> Safety he valued above the people's applause,
> Hence his glory brighter shines and will shine.

What vigilance, what prudence did he show in retaking Tarentum! It was in my hearing, indeed, that he made the famous retort to Salinator, who had retreated into the citadel after losing the town. "You recovered Tarentum by my instrumentality," Salinator boasted. "Unquestionably," Fabius said with a laugh, "for if you had not lost it I should never have recovered it." Nor was his civil career less eminent than his military. In his second consulship, unsupported by his colleague Carvilius, he resisted to the utmost of his power the efforts of the tribune Caius Flaminius to make allotments of the Picene and Gallic territory in defiance of the senate's will. As augur he dared to say that whatever was done in the interests of the state was done under the best auspices and that measures inimical to its interests were undertaken with adverse auspices. Much that was remarkable have I observed in that old man, but nothing more admirable than the way he bore the death of his son, an illustrious man who had held the consulship. When we read the eulogy, which is still in circulation, we feel that he surpassed the philosophers. Nor was he great only in public and in the eyes of the community; in private and domestic life he was even more outstanding. What conversation! What maxims! What broad knowledge of antiquity, and what expertness in augural lore! He was widely read, too, for a Roman, and knew by heart the history of all wars, domestic and foreign. I availed myself as eagerly of my opportunities of conversing with him as if I had already divined, what proved to be true, that when he should pass away I would have no one from whom to learn.

5. Why so much about Maximus? Because you must now see that it is monstrous to call such an old age miserable. Not everyone, it is true, can be a Scipio or a Maximus and have stormings of cities, battles by land and sea, general commands, and triumphs to recall. But there is also the

calm and serene old age of a life passed peacefully, simply, and gracefully. Such, we have heard, was Plato's, who died at his desk in his eighty-first year; such was Isocrates', who was ninety-four when he wrote his *Panathenaicus* and lived five years more. His teacher Gorgias of Leontini rounded out one hundred and seven years without suspending his diligence or his pursuits. When he was asked why he was willing to live so long, he replied, "I have no fault to find with old age"—a noble answer and worthy of a scholar. It is their own vices and faults that fools charge to old age; not so Ennius, whom I just now mentioned:

> As the gallant steed who oft in the last lap
> Conquered, and now foredone with age reposes.

His age he compares to that of a spirited and successful racehorse. You might well remember him, for the present consuls, Titus Flamininus and Manius Acilius, were elected nineteen years after his death, which took place in the consulship of Caepio and Philippus (the latter in his second term); I was sixty-five at the time, and was urging the Voconian law with a strong voice and sound lungs. At seventy—such was Ennius' span—he bore the two burdens which are esteemed the heaviest, poverty and old age, and almost seemed to take pleasure in them.

When I reflect on the subject, I find that the reasons why old age is regarded as unhappy are four: one, it withdraws us from active employments; another, it impairs physical vigor; the third, it deprives us of nearly all sensual pleasures; and four, it is the verge of death. Let us see, if you please, how much force and justice there is in these several reasons.

6. "Old age withdraws us from active employments." You mean, do you not, those that involve youth and vigor? Are there no old men's employments which are carried on by

the intellect even when the body is feeble? Was Maximus
not employed? Was Lucius Paulus, your father, Scipio, and
my excellent son's father-in-law, not employed? Were old
men like Fabricius, Curius, Coruncanius not employed
when their wisdom and influence were preserving the commonwealth? Appius was blind as well as old, and yet when
the inclinations of the senate favored peace and a treaty
with Pyrrhus he did not hesitate to utter what Ennius has
put into verse:

> Whither have your minds which used upright to stand
> In folly turned away?

And so on, in most impressive style. You know the poem,
and the actual speech of Appius is extant. He delivered
it seventeen years after his second consulship, though ten
years had intervened between his two consulships and he
had been censor before he was consul. This will show you
that at the time of the war with Pyrrhus he was a very old
man; yet this is the story handed down to us. There is nothing, then, in the argument that old age is devoid of useful
activity. To say that is like saying that a steersman sitting
quietly in the stern and holding the tiller contributes nothing to sailing the ship, for others climb the masts, run up
and down the gangways, man the pumps. He may not be
doing what younger men do, but what he does is better and
more important. Large affairs are not performed by muscle,
speed, nimbleness, but by reflection, character, judgment.
In age these qualities are not diminished but augmented.
Or perhaps you think that a military man like myself, who
fought in various wars as private, captain, general, com-
mander-in-chief, is now unemployed because he is not off
to the wars. But I direct the senate on what wars are to be
fought, and how; against Carthage, which has long been
plotting mischief, I have declared war far in advance. I

shall not cease to fear Carthage until I know it is utterly destroyed. That victory may the gods reserve for you, Scipio, so that you may complete the task begun by your grandfather. Thirty-two years have passed since his death, but all succeeding years will cherish his memory. He died the year before I was censor, nine years after my consulship; in my consulship he was elected consul for the second time. If he had lived to a hundred, would he ever have regretted old age? He would of course not have been practising running, jumping, spear hurling, sword play, but he would be using reflection, reason, judgment. Unless these faculties resided in old men, our ancestors would never have called their supreme council senate. In Sparta the highest magistrates are called, as they in fact are, elders. If you would turn to foreign history you will find that the mightiest states have been overthrown by the young and supported and restored by the old. In Naevius' *Wolf* there is a question: "How lost you, pray, your mighty state so soon?" There is a long answer, but the chief point is: "A crop of new advisers, silly striplings." Of course rashness belongs to blooming youth, prudence to old age.

7. But the memory is impaired. No doubt, unless you keep it in practice, or if you happen to be naturally dull. Themistocles had learned by heart the names of all the citizens of Athens; do you suppose he addressed Aristides as Lysimachus in his old age? I myself know not only living people but their fathers and grandfathers too; and in reading tombstones I am not afraid, as superstition has it, that I shall lose my memory, for their reading actually recalls the memory of the dead. I have never heard of any old man forgetting where he had hidden his money. The old remember everything that concerns them—appointments in court, who owes them money, to whom they owe money. What about lawyers, pontiffs, augurs, philosophers who are old?

What a multitude of things they remember! The old retain their intellectual powers provided their interest and inclination continue, and not only in the case of men in high and distinguished positions, but also in private and peaceful pursuits. Sophocles wrote tragedies up to extreme old age, and when this preoccupation was thought to impair his attention to business matters, his sons brought him to court to prove imbecility, on a law similar to ours which deprives a householder of the management of his property if he has proved incompetent. The old poet is then said to have read to the jury the *Oedipus at Colonus,* which he had lately written and was revising, and to have asked whether it seemed the work of an imbecile. After the reading he was acquitted. Did old age silence this man, or Homer, Hesiod, Simonides, Stesichorus, or Isocrates and Gorgias whom I have mentioned, or the founders of the philosophic schools, Pythagoras, Democritus, Plato, or Xenocrates, or, later, Zeno and Cleanthes, or the Stoic Diogenes, whom you lately saw at Rome? Did not the activity of each of these men terminate only with his life? To pass over these lofty pursuits, I can mention Roman farmers in the Sabine district, neighbors and acquaintances of mine, without whose presence scarcely any important farm work is done, whether sowing, harvesting, or storing produce. In field crops this is not so surprising, for no one is so old but that he expects to live another year; but they also bestow labor on what they know cannot affect them. "He plants trees to profit another age," as our own Caecilius Statius says in his *Comrades.* If you ask a farmer, however old, for whom he is planting, he will reply without hesitation, "For the immortal gods, who intended that I should not only receive these things from my ancestors, but also transmit them to my descendants."

8. Statius' lines on the old man making provision for a future generation are better than this other passage: "Ver-

ily, old age, if thou bringest with thee no other bane, this one is enough: by living long one sees much he likes not." And perhaps much he likes, and youth too encounters what it does not like. But the same Caecilius has something even more objectionable: "This I reckon old age's worst bane: old men feel they are tedious to the young." Agreeable rather than tedious! Just as intelligent old men take pleasure in young men of parts and find their old age ameliorated by the courteous attentions of the young, so do young men take pleasure in the maxims of their elders, by which they are drawn to the pursuit of excellence. I do not feel that my company is less agreeable to you than yours to me. But you see that so far from being listless and inert old age is always busy with work and plans, usually of the sort which occupied earlier years. Old men even learn new things; we find Solon boasting that he learned new things as he grew old. I myself have learned Greek as an old man, and grasped it as greedily as if I were trying to satisfy a long protracted thirst. That is how I learned the things you now see me use as illustrations. When I heard what Socrates had done about the lyre I should have liked for my part to have done that too, for the ancients used to learn the lyre; but at any rate I worked hard at literature.

9. Nor, again, do I now miss the bodily strength of a young man (for that was the second head in the disadvantages of old age) any more than as a young man I missed the strength of a bull or an elephant. What one has, that one ought to use; and whatever you do, you should do it with all your strength. Contemptible indeed was Milo of Croton's exclamation. When as an old man he was watching athletes exercising on the track he is said to have looked at his arms and to have remarked with tears, "But these are now dead." Not your arms, silly man, as much as yourself; it was not yourself that made you famous but your chest and biceps.

Sextus Aelius never uttered such a remark, nor Titus Coruncanius in the old days, nor Publius Crassus more recently.
All advised their fellow citizens in jurisprudence, and
their competence continued to their last breath. The orator,
I fear, does lose vigor by old age, for his craft involves not
the intellect alone but lungs and bodily strength. Yet as a
rule the musical ring in the voice somehow gains brilliance
with age; I have not lost it, and you see my years. It is the
subdued and unemotional style that best becomes an old
man, and the calm and mild discourse of a veteran often
wins itself a hearing. And if that cannot be managed, still
there are Scipios and Laeliuses to be taught! What is more
charming than an old age surrounded by the enthusiasm of
youth? Shall we not concede old age even strength to teach
the young, to train and equip them for the duties of life?
What can be nobler? For my part I used to consider Publius and Gnaeus Scipio and your two grandfathers, Lucius
Aemilius and Publius Africanus, fortunate men when I saw
them attended by a throng of noble youths. No teachers of
the liberal arts should be considered unhappy, however
much their physical vigor may have waned and failed. And
even that failure is more often chargeable to the follies of
youth than of age; a voluptuous and intemperate youth
bequeaths an exhausted body to old age. Xenophon's Cyrus,
for instance, speaking on his death bed in high old age, said
that he never felt his old age was feebler than his youth had
been. From my boyhood I remember Lucius Metellus, who
held the office of pontifex maximus for twenty-two years
after receiving it full four years after his second consulship;
to the end of his days he enjoyed such physical vigor that
he never felt the loss of youth. I need not speak of myself,
though that is an old man's habit and allowable at my age.

10. How frequently Nestor speaks of his own merits in
Homer! He was living through a third generation, and had

no fear that in speaking truth of himself he would appear impertinent or garrulous. As Homer says, "from his lips flowed discourse sweeter than honey"—for which he had no need of physical strength. And that famous general of the Greeks nowhere wishes he had ten men like Ajax, but like Nestor; if he had them he is sure Troy would quickly fall. But I return to my own case. I am eighty-three, and could wish I might make Cyrus' boast; but so much I can say: though I am not so strong as I was as a private in the Punic War, or as quaestor in the same war, or as consul in Spain, or as military tribune under Glabrio four years later, still, as you see, old age has not wholly unstrung my nerves or shattered me. Neither the senate, nor the rostrum, nor my friends, nor my clients, nor my guests miss the strength I have lost. I have never agreed to that hoary and much-lauded proverb that you must become an old man early if you wish to be one long. I would rather not be old so long than be old before my time. No one has wanted to meet me to whom I have denied myself on the plea of age. I have less strength than either of you, it is true, but neither do you have the strength of the centurion Titus Pontius; is he then the better man? Provided one husbands his strength and does not attempt to go beyond it, he will not be hampered by lack of requisite strength. At Olympia Milo is said to have walked the course with an ox on his shoulders: would you prefer such physical power or the mental power of Pythagoras? In a word, use your physical strength while you have it, and do not bewail it when it is gone—unless you believe that youth must bewail the loss of infancy or early manhood the passing of youth. Life has its fixed course, and nature one unvarying way; to each is allotted its appropriate quality, so that the fickleness of boyhood, the impetuosity of youth, the sobriety of middle life, and the ripeness of age all have something of nature's yield which

must be garnered in its own season. You must have heard,
Scipio, what your grandfather's foreign friend Masinissa
does to this very day, though he is ninety. When he begins
a journey on foot he will not mount, nor dismount if he
begins on horseback. No rain or chill can induce him to
cover his head. His sinewy body enables him to perform
the duties and functions of a king. Exercise and temperance
can preserve some of a man's vigor even in old age.

11. Is there no strength in old age? None is expected of
old age. Hence both by law and custom our time of life
is exempt from public services which require physical
strength. Not only are we not forced to do what we cannot
do; we are not even obliged to do what we can do. Yet, it
may be urged, so feeble are many old men that they can
perform none of life's duties or functions at all. But that
weakness is not peculiar to old age; it belongs also to ill
health. How feeble, Scipio, was your adoptive father
Publius Africanus! His health was so weak as to be non-
existent. But for this he would have shone forth as our
second great political luminary, for to his father's greatness
of spirit he added a richer culture. What wonder, then, that
the aged are sometimes weak when even young men cannot escape infirmity? My dear Laelius and Scipio, old age
must be resisted, and its deficiencies supplied by taking
pains; we must fight it as we do disease. Care must be bestowed upon health; moderate exercise should be taken;
food and drink should be sufficient to recruit, not over-
burden, our strength. And not the body alone must be
sustained, but the powers of the mind much more; unless
you supply them, as oil to a lamp, they too grow dim with
age. Whereas overexertion weighs the body down with fa-
tigue, exercise makes the mind buoyant. When Caecilius
speaks of "dotards of the comic stage" he means credality,
forgetfulness, languor, and these are faults not of old age

but of lazy, indolent, and drowsy old age. As wantonness and licentiousness are faults of the young rather than of the old, yet not of all young men but only of the depraved, so the senile folly called dotage is characteristic not of all old men but only of the frivolous. Four stout sons, five daughters, a large household, numerous dependents, did Appius manage, though both old and blind, for his mind was alert, like a bent bow, and did not succumb to old age by growing slack. He maintained not merely influence but absolute command over his large household. The slaves feared him, the children respected him, all held him dear; beneath his roof the usages and discipline of our forefathers were in the ascendant. Old age is respectable so long as it asserts itself, maintains its rights, is subservient to no one, and retains its sway to the last breath. I like a young man who has a touch of the old, and I like an old man who has a touch of the young. A man who cultivates this principle may be old in body, in mind never. I am now engaged on the seventh volume of my *Origines*. I am collecting all records of antiquity. I am just now revising the pleadings I delivered in famous cases. I am dealing with the augural, pontifical, and civil law. I read a good deal of Greek. Following the Pythagorean method, each evening I run over what I have heard and done during the day, for the sake of exercising my memory. These are my intellectual calisthenics, the running track of the mind, and when I sweat and strain at them I do not greatly miss bodily strength. I appear in court for my friends, I attend the senate frequently and introduce proposals I have pondered long and earnestly; these I support with intellectual, not physical, energy. If I were too feeble for these functions, my couch would afford me the entertainment of imagining the very operations which I was now unable to perform. But what makes me capable of doing this is my past life. For a man who is always living amid such studies and pursuits as mine is not aware of the stealthy approach of age. Life draws to its end by slow and imperceptible degrees; there is no sudden rupture but a gradual extinction.

12. The third charge against old age is that it lacks sensual pleasures. What a splendid boon if age takes from us youth's greatest blemish! Listen, my dear young friends, to what the great and eminent Archytas of Tarentum said in an ancient speech which was communicated to me when I was a young man serving with Quintus Maximus at Tarentum. "No more deadly curse," said he, "has nature inflicted on men than sensual pleasure. To gratify it our wanton appetites are roused beyond all prudence and restraint. It is a source of treason, revolution, clandestine commerce with the enemy. There is no crime, no wickedness, to which the lust for pleasure does not impel. Fornications and adulteries and every vice of that stripe are initiated by the enticements of pleasure and by that alone. Intellect is the best gift of nature or God; to this gift nothing is so hostile as pleasure. Where lust holds sway there is no place for temperance, nor where pleasure reigns can virtue find footing. To realize this more clearly, imagine a man aroused to the highest conceivable pitch of sensual pleasure. None will doubt that as long as he is in such a state that man cannot use intellect or reason or thought. Nothing is therefore so detestable and pernicious as pleasure, for if it is violent and enduring it darkens all the light of the soul." My Tarentine host Nearchus, who remained loyal to Rome, told me that he had heard from his elders that Archytas spoke these words to the Samnite Pontius, father of the man who defeated the consuls Spurius Postumius and Titus Veturius at the Caudine Forks. Plato is said to have been present at the conversation; I find that Plato did visit Tarentum in the consulship of Lucius Camillus and Appius Claudius. What

is the point of all this? To show you that if reason and wisdom did not enable us to reject pleasure, we should be very grateful to old age for depriving us of the desire to do what we ought not. Pleasure hinders thought, is a foe to reason, and, so to say, blinds the eyes of the mind. It has no dealings with virtue. I was reluctant to expel Lucius Flamininus, brother of the gallant Titus Flamininus, from the senate seven years after he had been consul; but I thought that his licentiousness must be stigmatized. When he was commanding in Gaul a courtesan prevailed on him at a banquet to behead a prisoner condemned on a capital charge. In the censorship of his brother Titus, my predecessor, he escaped; but so profligate and abandoned an act of lust Flaccus and I could never allow to pass, for it involved disgrace to the empire as well as personal infamy.

13. I have often been told by men older than myself, who said that they had heard it as boys from old men, that Gaius Fabricius was in the habit of expressing astonishment at having heard, when envoy at the headquarters of King Pyrrhus, from the Thessalian Cineas, that there was a man of Athens who professed to be a 'philosopher' and affirmed that all our actions were to be referred to pleasure. When he told this to Manius Curius and Publius Decius their remark was that they only wished that the Samnites and Pyrrhus himself would hold the same opinion; it would be easier to conquer them when they had given themselves up to pleasure. Manius Curius was intimate with Publius Decius, who, in his fourth consulship and five years before Curius held that office, had immolated himself for his country's salvation. Fabricius and Coruncanius had known Decius also, and from their experience and Decius' heroic deed they inferred that there does exist something intrinsically pure and noble which is sought for its own sake and is the

objective of all good men who spurn and despise pleasure. Why so much on pleasure? Because it is not only no reproach to old age but even its highest merit that it does not severely feel the loss of bodily pleasures. It must dispense with sumptuous feasts, loaded tables, oft-drained cups; it dispenses too with sottishness, indigestion, broken sleep. If some concession must be made to pleasure, its charms being so difficult to resist—Plato aptly calls it the bait of sin, for by it men are caught like fish—then old age, though it dispenses with immoderate feasting, can yet find pleasure in modest festivities. When I was a boy I often saw the venerable Caius Duilius, the first victor over the Carthaginians at sea, returning home from supper. He took particular pleasure in being escorted by torch and flute-player; though the privilege was unprecedented for a private citizen, his military glory allowed him the license. But why mention others? I return to my own case. In the first place, I have always had my club—it was in my quaestorship that the clubs were instituted, when the Idaean rites of the Great Mother were received in Rome. I used to dine with the brethren, moderately on the whole, yet with something of the joviality that belonged to my earlier years but which the progress of time gradually diminishes. I did not calculate the pleasure of those banquets by the pleasures of the body so much as by the gathering and conversation of friends. Our ancestors were quite right to style that presence of guests at dinner-table—seeing that it implies a community of enjoyment—a *convivium* or "living together." It is a better term than the Greek words which mean "a drinking together" or "an eating together." These seem to give the preference to what is really the least important aspect.

14. For my own part, owing to the pleasure I take in conversation, I enjoy even banquets that begin early in the

afternoon, and not only with my contemporaries, of whom few survive, but also with men of your age and with yourselves. I am heartily thankful to old age, which has increased my appetite for conversation and removed that for food and drink. But if anyone does enjoy these—let me not seem to have declared war on all pleasure, for some is justified by nature—I am not aware that old age does not appreciate them. I enjoy the ancestral custom of appointing a master of ceremonies, and the talk, which begins at the head of the table in the old-fashioned way, and small and dewy cups, like those in Xenophon's *Symposium*, and the cool breeze for the dining room in summer, and the sun or fire in winter. Even on my Sabine farm I keep up these customs, and daily fill my table with my neighbors, prolonging our varied talk to the latest possible hour.

But you may urge that there is not the same tingling sensation of pleasure in old men. No doubt; but neither do they miss it so much. Nothing for which you do not yearn troubles you. It was an excellent reply that Sophocles made to a certain man who asked him, when he was already old, if he still indulged in the delights of love. "Heaven forbid!" he said. "Indeed I have fled from them as from a harsh and cruel master." To men fond of such things it is perhaps disagreeable and irksome to be without them; but to those who are sated and cloyed with them it is more pleasant to be in want of them than to possess them; though indeed a man cannot "want" that for which he has no longing, and therefore I assert that the absence of longing is more pleasant.

But even granting that youth enjoys these pleasures with more zest; in the first place, they are insignificant things to enjoy, as I have said; and in the second place, such as age is not entirely without, if it does not possess them in profusion. Just as Ambivius Turpio gives greater delight to the spectators in the front row of the theater, and yet gives some delight even to those in the last row, so youth, looking on pleasures at close range, perhaps enjoys them more, while old age, on the other hand, finds delight enough in a more distant view. But what a blessing it is for the soul to be with itself, to live, as the phrase is, apart, discharged from the service of lust, ambition, strife, enmities, and all passions! If it has any scholarly interests stored up as it were provender, nothing can be more enjoyable than an old age of leisure. I used to see Gallus—your father's friend, Scipio—studiously charting heaven and earth. Dawn would overtake him when he had begun some problem at night, and night when he had begun in the early morning. How he enjoyed predicting eclipses of sun and moon far in advance! In studies less recondite but still requiring acuteness, what pleasure Naevius took in his *Punic War* and Plautus in his *Truculentus* and *Pseudolus!* I even saw old Livius Andronicus; he presented a play in the consulship of Cento and Tuditanus, six years before I was born, and lived on till I was almost a man. Why speak of Publius Licinius Crassus' devotion to pontifical and civil law, or of that of the contemporary Publius Scipio, who was lately made pontifex maximus? All these men I have named we have seen ardently engaged in their several departments in old age. Marcus Cethegus too, whom Ennius justly styled Persuasion's Marrow—what zeal I saw him display in his oratory even as an old man! How can the pleasures of feasting, games, and harlots be comparable to these? All of these involve learning, which, in wise and cultured men, increases with age. Creditable is the verse of Solon I have quoted, "I grow old learning many new things." There is no greater pleasure than the mind's.

15. I come now to the pleasures of agriculture, in which I find incredible delight. To these old age is no impediment,

and in them I think a man makes the nearest approach to the life of the sage. The farmer keeps an open account with the earth, which never refuses a draft, never returns a deposit without interest, sometimes, indeed, at a low rate, but generally at a high. Yet it is not the revenue which charms me, but the very nature and properties of the soil. When it has received the seed into its softened and prepared bosom it keeps it *buried* (whence our word *harrowing* is derived), and then by its pressure and the moisture it yields it cleaves the seed and draws from it the verdant shoot, which, sustained by its root fibres, grows till it stands erect on its jointed stalk, enclosed in a sheath as if to protect its downy youth, till, emerging, it yields the grain with its orderly arrangement in the ear, defended against predatory birds by its bearded rampart. Why should I tell of the planting, burgeoning, growth, of vines? Of this pleasure I can never have too much—to let you into the secret of what gives my old age repose and amusement. I pass over the inherent power of things generated from the earth, which, from so tiny a grape or fig seed, or from the minute seeds of other fruits and plants, produces such massive trunks and shoots, sprouts, cuttings, divisions, and layers enough to afford wonder and delight to any man? The vine, indeed, drooping by nature unless supported, is weighed down to the ground; but to raise itself it embraces with its hand-like tendrils whatever it can lay hold upon; and then, as it twines with intricate and wild profusion, the vine-dresser's art trims it close with the pruning knife, lest it run to wood and spread too far. So in early spring the joints of the branches that are left sprout buds from which the incipient grapes appear; these grow by the moisture of the earth and the heat of the sun, and though at first bitter to the taste, they sweeten as they ripen; its shelter of leaves allows it sufficient warmth, yet keeps off the intense heat of the sun.

What can be more delicious or more beautiful? It is not only the vine's utility, as I have remarked, that pleases me, but also the process of its cultivation and its very nature— the rows of stakes, the lateral supports, the tying up and training of the vines, the pruning of some of the twigs (as I have said) and the grafting of others. I need hardly mention irrigation, trenching, and frequent hoeing to increase fertility. Of the advantages of manuring I have spoken in my book on agriculture. The learned Hesiod, though he writes on agriculture, has nothing on this subject, though Homer, who preceded him, I think, by many generations, represents Laertes as relieving his longing for his son by cultivating and manuring his farm. Cornfields, meadows, vineyards, woodlands are not the only satisfactions of the rustic life; there are also orchards and gardens, grazing and bee-keeping, and the infinite variety of flowers. And besides planting there is also grafting—the most ingenious invention in agriculture.

16. I might continue my inventory of rustic pleasures, but I realize that I have been rather wordy. You must forgive me; I am carried away by my enthusiasm for country life, and old age is naturally prolix—I must not seem to exculpate it of every failing. Well, it was in this sort of life that Manius Curius, after he had triumphed over the Samnites, the Sabines, and Pyrrhus, spent his remaining years. When I look at his house (it is not far from mine) I cannot sufficiently admire the man's frugality and the strict standards of his age. When the Samnites brought him a large amount of gold as he sat by his fire he spurned the bribe; to possess gold was not so fine a thing, he thought, as to rule those who did possess it.

But not to wander from my subject, I return to the farmers. In those days senators (that is, "elders") lived on farms —if the story is true that Lucius Quinctius Cincinnatus was at the plough when he was notified of his election to that dictatorship in which, by his order, Gaius Servilius Ahala, his master of horse, seized Spurius Maelius and put him to death for attempting to usurp regal power. It was from the farmhouse that Curius and other old men were summoned to the senate, and from that circumstance those who summoned them were called *viatores* or "travelers." Was there any cause to pity the old age of these men who took such pleasure in the cultivation of the soil? In my opinion, scarcely any life can be happier, not only from the standpoint of duty performed, which benefits the entire human race, but also from the mere pleasure, to which I have already alluded, and from the rich abundance and provision of all things necessary for the food of man and the worship of the gods. Since these are objects of desire to some people, I thus make my peace with pleasure also. A thrifty and industrious farmer has a full wine-cellar, oil-cellar, larder, and his rich farm abounds in swine, kids, lambs, fowl, milk, cheese, honey. Then there is the garden, which the farmers themselves call their "second flitch." Zest is added by hunting and fowling in times of leisure. Why need I expatiate on the verdure of meadows, the rows of trees, the beauty of vineyard and olive orchard? In a word, nothing can be more bountiful for use or more decorative than a farm well cultivated. To such enjoyment old age so far from interposing hindrance, actually offers invitation and allurement. Where can old age find more genial warmth of sun or fire or, in proper season, more cooling shade or refreshing waters? Let the young keep their arms, horses, spears, clubs, balls, swimming matches, foot races, and out of so many sports leave us old fellows our dice and knuckle-bones. Or take away the dice-box too, if you will, for old age can be happy without it.

17. Xenophon's books are very useful for many purposes;

pray continue to read them attentively, as you have always
done. In what ample terms is agriculture lauded by him in
the book about husbanding one's property, called *Oecono-
micus!* But to show you that he thought nothing so worthy
of a prince as the taste for cultivating the soil, let me recall
the incident in that same book, related by Socrates in a
conversation with Critobulus. Cyrus the Younger, the
highly gifted and renowned king of Persia, was visited
at Sardis by the gallant Lacedaemonian Lysander, who
brought him presents from the allies. Among other courtesies to Lysander, Cyrus showed him an enclosed garden,
very carefully laid out. Lysander admired the stateliness of
the trees and the pattern of their arrangement, the clean
and well-cultivated soil, and the delicious odors breathing
from the flowers, and remarked that he marveled not only
at the industry but also at the skill of the man who planned
the park and laid it out. Cyrus answered: "I myself laid it
all out. The plan and arrangement is mine, and many of
those trees I planted with my own hands." Lysander looked
at his purple robe, his elegant grooming, his rich Persian
ornaments of gold and precious stones, and said: "Men are
right to call you happy, for in you fortune is joined to
merit." This fortune old men can enjoy; age does not pre-
clude our interest in other pursuits, but especially not in
agriculture, which may engage it to the end of life. Of Marcus Valerius Corvus we have heard that he continued to
live to a hundred; when his active life was over he stayed in
the country and tilled the land. Between his first and sixth
consulships there was an interval of forty-six years, so that
his official career covered the span which our ancestors
define as coming between birth and the onset of old age.
Moreover his old age was happier than middle life, because
his influence was greater and his labor less. Indeed, influence is the crowning glory of old age. How great was that

of Lucius Caecilius Metellus! How great that of Atilius
Calatinus, whose epitaph declared, "All nations agree
he was his country's foremost." The whole epigram is in-
scribed on his tomb and is well known. Deservedly weighty
was his influence if all were unanimous in his praise. What
a man did we lately see in Publius Crassus, the pontifex
maximus, and what a man in his successor Marcus Lepidus?
What shall I say of Paulus or Africanus or Maximus, if I
may name him again? Influence was inherent not only in
the speech of these men but in their very nod. So great is
the influence of old age, especially when it is distinguished
by office, that it outweighs all the pleasures of youth.

18. But in all I say remember I am praising an old age
whose foundations have been laid in youth. This implies
what I once said, with universal approval, that it was a
wretched old age which had to defend itself by speech.
White hair or wrinkles cannot usurp influence; this an early
life well spent reaps as the fruit of its age. Attentions which
seem trivial and conventional are marks of honor—the
morning call, being sought after, precedence, having people rise for you, being escorted to and from the forum, being consulted—courtesies carefully observed with us and in
other states so far as good manners prevail. The Spartan
Lysander, of whom I have just spoken, used to say that
Sparta is the best domicile of age, for nowhere else is age
so deferred to and respected. There is a story that when an
elderly man entered the theater at a festival in Athens
none of his countrymen in the large assembly gave place to
him, but when he approached the seats reserved for the
Lacedaemonians as ambassadors, all of them rose and invited the old man to sit down. When the whole assembly
greeted the act with repeated applause, one of the Spartans said, "The Athenians know what is right but will
not do it." There are many excellent rules in our augural

college, but especially is the one whereby each member has precedence in debate according to his age, and the oldest are preferred not only to those of higher official rank but even to functioning magistrates. What pleasures of the body can then be compared to the prerogatives of influence? Those who have employed it with distinction appear to me to have played the drama of life to its end, and not to have broken down in the last act like unpractised actors.

But old men are said to be peevish and fretful and irascible and disagreeable; they are miserly too, if we care to look for such. But these are faults of character, not of age. But peevishness and the rest may be extenuated if not justified. Old men imagine they are scorned, despised, mocked; and when the body is frail the slightest blow is irritating. But good habits and education can ameliorate these faults, as we can see in real life and in such a play as Terence's *Adelphi* with its two brothers. How grim one is, how genial the other! So it is: neither every wine nor every disposition sours with age. I approve of gravity in old age, but, as in all else, in moderation; of sourness not at all. The sense of avarice in an old man I cannot conceive; can anything be more absurd than to multiply luggage as one nears the journey's end?

19. There remains the fourth reason, which more than the others seems to make my time of life anxious and perturbed —the approach of death, which certainly cannot be far removed from old age. Wretched old man, not to have learned in a long life that death is to be despised! Death is wholly negligible if it extinguishes life altogether, and even desirable, if it conducts the soul where it will be immortal; surely no third possibility is imaginable. Why then should I fear death if I shall be not unhappy or else be happy? Even so, is anyone so foolish, however young he be, as to be sure he will live till evening? Youth has many more chances of

death than age. The young are more liable to disease, their sickness is more serious, their cure more difficult. Few reach old age; were it not so life would be better and wiser. Intelligence and reason and prudence reside in the old, and but for them there could be no community at all. But to return to the imminence of death—can it be urged as a charge against age when you see that it is shared by youth? The death of my own excellent son, and of your brothers, Scipio, men born to the highest expectations, taught me that death is common to every age. Yet a young man hopes to live long and an old man can entertain no such hope. The hope itself is foolish; what can be more stupid than to take things uncertain for certain, false for true? "An old man has nothing even to hope." There he is in better case than the young, for what the one hopes the other has attained; one wishes to live long, the other has lived long.

And can we, in heaven's name, call anything human long? Grant the very latest term of life; suppose we reach the age of the king of Tartessus—it is recorded that Arganthonius of Cadiz ruled eighty years and lived a hundred and twenty—still nothing that has an end is long. When the end comes what has passed has flowed away, and all that is left is what you have achieved by virtue and good deeds. Hours, days, months, years, glide by; the past never returns, and what is to come we cannot know. With whatever span is allotted us we should be content. There is no need for an actor to perform the whole play to give his audience satisfaction; enough to play his own role well. Nor need the wise man continue to the last curtain. A short span is long enough to live well and honorably; if you live on you have no more reason to mourn your advancing years than have farmers, when the sweetness of spring is past, to lament the coming of fall and winter. Spring typifies youth, and points to the fruits to come; the other seasons are appropriate for harvesting and storing the crop. The harvest of old age, as I have often said, is the memory and abundance of blessings previously acquired. Moreover, all that falls out according to nature must be reckoned good, and what accords better with nature than for old men to die? Nature struggles and rebels when the young die. When they die it is as if a violent fire is extinguished by a torrent, but the old die like a spent fire quenched of its own accord and without external effort. Unripe apples must be wrenched from the tree, but fall of their own accord when ripe and mellow; so from the young it is force that takes life, from the old, ripeness. So agreeable is this ripeness to me that as I approach death nearer I feel like a voyager at last in sight of land and on the point of reaching harbor after a long journey.

20. Old age has no fixed term, and one may fitly live in it so long as he can observe and discharge the duties of his station, and yet despise death. Fearless of death, old age may transcend youth in courage and fortitude. Such is the meaning of Solon's answer to the tyrant Pisistratus, who asked the grounds of his bold resistance; "old age" was Solon's reply. That end of life is best when, with mind and faculties unimpaired, Nature herself takes apart what she has put together. The builder of a ship or house is best able to tear it down, and so Nature who compacted man can best effect his dissolution. What is newly compacted is hard to tear apart, old fabrics come apart easily. It follows that old men should neither be avid of their brief remaining span nor desert it without cause. Pythagoras forbids us to desert our post and charge in life without the order of our commander, God. A couplet of the wise Solon expresses the wish that his death be attended by the grief and lamentation of his friends. He wants, I suppose, to be beloved by them. But I prefer Ennius' sentiment:

> Let none honor me with tears, nor at my funeral
> Make lamentation.

He holds that death followed by immortality is no cause for grief. There may be sensation in the article of death, but that is fleeting, especially in the old; after death there is either no sensation or a desirable one. Upon this we should reflect from youth up, so that we may be indifferent to death. Without such reflection none can be of tranquil mind. That we must die is certain; it may be this passing day. With death threatening every hour, how can a man who fears it retain composure? No extended argument seems called for when I recall—not Lucius Brutus, slain setting his country free; not the Decii, galloping to voluntary death; not Atilius Regulus, going to his torture to keep faith pledged to the foe; not the Scipios, who would block the enemy's march with their bodies; not your grandfather Paulus, who in the rout at Cannae atoned for his colleague's rashness by his death; not Marcellus, whom even a cruel enemy could not deny the honor of burial—but our own legions, often marching, as I have written in my *Origines,* with cheerful and unwavering courage to perils from which they thought they would never return. Should men neither young nor ignorant shrink from what rustics young and ignorant despise? In general, as it seems to me, weariness of pursuits produces weariness of life. Certain pursuits belong to boyhood; do young men long for them? Some belong to early youth; does settled middle-life desiderate them? That age in turn has its own, and these are not required in old age. Finally, there are the pursuits of old age. As the pursuits of the earlier periods fall away, so do those of old age, and when this happens weariness of life brings a season ripe for death.

21. I do not see why I should hesitate to tell you my own feelings about death, for I seem to have a clearer view of it

the nearer I approach it. I believe, dear Scipio and Laelius, that your excellent fathers and my very good friends are living, and that life too which alone deserves the name of life. As long as we are shut up in this bodily prison we are performing a heavy task laid upon us by necessity, for the soul, celestial by birth, is forced down from its exalted abode and plunged, as it were, to earth, a place uncongenial to its divine nature and its eternity. I believe that the immortal gods implanted souls in human bodies to provide overseers for the earth who would contemplate the heavenly order and imitate it in the moderation and constancy of their lives. To this belief I have been impelled not by reason and arguments alone, but by the distinguished authority of the greatest philosophers. I learned that Pythagoras and the Pythagoreans, virtually our countrymen and sometimes called Italian philosophers, never doubted that our souls were emanations of the universal divine intelligence. I was impressed also by the discourse on the immortality of the soul delivered on the last day of his life by Socrates, whom the oracle of Apollo had pronounced the wisest of men. I need say no more. This is my conviction, this my belief: Such is the rapid movement of souls, such their memory of the past and foresight of the future, so many are the arts, so profound the sciences, so numerous the inventions, that the nature which embraces these things cannot be mortal; and since the soul is always active and has no source of motion because it is self-moving, it can have no end of motion, for it will never abandon itself; and since the nature of the soul is uncompounded and has no admixture heterogeneous and unlike itself, it is indivisible and hence cannot perish. Furthermore, it is a strong proof of men knowing many things before birth that boys studying difficult subjects grasp innumerable points so quickly that they seem not to be receiving them for the first time but to be recalling and remembering them. This, in substance, is Plato's argument.

22. In Xenophon Cyrus on his deathbed speaks as follows: "Do not imagine, my beloved sons, that when I go from you I shall be nowhere or cease to be. While I was with you you did not see my soul, but inferred its existence from my actions. You must believe it is the same though you see nothing. The fame of illustrious men would not survive their death if their souls did nothing to perpetuate their memory. I could never be persuaded that souls which live while they are in mortal bodies die when they leave them, nor yet that the soul becomes unintelligent when it leaves the unintelligent body; only when it is freed from corporeal admixture and becomes pure and whole is it intelligent. When man's constitution is dissolved by death it is obvious what becomes of the other parts, for each goes whence it came; only the soul remains unseen, alike when present and when departing. Nothing in our experience so resembles death as sleep; and it is in sleep that souls manifest their divine nature, for being free and unfettered they foresee the future. This indicates what souls will be when they are entirely liberated from the shackles of the flesh. If these things are so, cherish me as a god; but if the soul will perish with the body, do you nevertheless, out of reverence for the gods who govern and guard this fair universe, preserve my memory with pious and inviolate regard."

23. Such were the sentiments of the dying Cyrus; let me now, if you will, give my own. No one will ever convince me, Scipio, that your father Paulus, or your two grandfathers Paulus and Africanus, or the latter's father and uncle, or other illustrious men whom I need not name, would have undertaken such noble enterprises which were to belong to the memory of posterity without a clear perception that posterity belonged to them. Or do you suppose, to take an

old man's privilege of boasting, that I would have undertaken such vast labors, day and night, at home and abroad, if I were going to limit my glory by the bounds of my life? Would it not have been better to pass a quiet and leisurely life, far from toil and strife? But my soul somehow always strained to look forward to posterity, as if it would really live only when it departed from life. Were it not that souls are immortal, men's souls would not strive for undying fame in proportion to their transcending merit. The fact that the wisest men die with perfect calmness and the foolish with great perturbation proves that souls with a keener and wider vision perceive that they are going to a better state, while those of duller vision cannot see beyond death. For my part, I am transported to see your fathers whom I revered and loved; and I long to meet not only those I have known, but also those of whom I have heard and read and myself written. When I have set out it will not be easy to draw me back or boil me into a new youth like a second Pelias. If some god should grant me reversion to childhood and let me bawl again in my cradle I would firmly refuse; when I have run my race I have no desire to be recalled from the goal to the start. What advantage does life have? What disadvantage does it not? Even granting that it has advantage, it also has satiety or an end. I have no desire to depreciate life, as many and even wise men have done; and I do not regret having lived, for I have so lived that I cannot think I was born in vain. I quit life as I would an inn, not a home, for nature has given us lodging for a sojourn, not for permanent residence.

O glorious day when I shall go to join that divine company and conclave of souls and depart from these turmoils and impurities! I shall join not only the men I have mentioned but also my son Cato, than whom no better man was ever born nor one who surpassed him in filial duty. It was I who lighted his pyre—though he should have lighted mine —but his spirit, never abandoning but looking back upon me, has certainly gone whither he saw that I too must come. I gave the appearance of bearing my calamity bravely, not because my heart was untroubled, but because I found solace in the thought that the parting and separation between us would not long endure.

For these reasons, Scipio, old age sits lightly on me—that is what you and Laelius wondered at—and I find it not irksome but actually agreeable. If I err in believing men's souls to be immortal, I err willingly, and as long as I live I do not wish an error which gives me such satisfaction to be wrested from me. If I shall have no sensation in death, as some paltry philosophers think, I have no fear that the dead philosophers will ridicule my error. But if we are not going to be immortal, it is desirable for a man to be erased in proper season; nature imposes a limit upon life as upon all else. Old age is the closing act of life, as of a drama, and we ought to leave when the play grows wearisome, especially if we have had our fill.

Such are my views on old age. I pray you attain it, so that you can verify what you have heard from me by experience.

# SCIPIO'S DREAM

AMONG the best of Cicero's writings, in form and content, is his On the Republic, begun in 54 and published in 51. This was his second large treatise after the On the Orator, and similarly deals with a subject in which Cicero himself possessed expert competence. But here too Cicero had the Stoic theorists to lean upon for content and Plato's Republic to suggest many details of treatment. Among these is the introduction of a mystical experience to conclude and summarize the book. Scipio's Dream at the end of Cicero's sixth book is a peculiarly appropriate Roman pendant to the Vision of Er at the end of Plato's tenth; where Plato envisages an endless ascent to the absolute ideal, the sufficient goal in Cicero is a pure and complete Roman patriotism. Until 1820, when about a third of the whole work was recovered from a palimpsest, Scipio's Dream was the only part of On the Republic extant. It had been preserved independently, with the commentary of Macrobius (about A.D. 400), in which form it was widely read in the Middle Ages and subsequently. Chaucer's account of his own dream in the Parlement of Foules starts from his reading of Scipio's Dream with the commentary of Macrobius.

I SERVED in Africa as military tribune of the Fourth Legion under Manius Manilius, as you know. When I arrived in that country my greatest desire was to meet King Masinissa, who had good reasons to be attached to my family. The old man embraced me tearfully when I called, and presently looked up to heaven and said, "I thank thee, sovereign sun, and ye lesser heavenly beings, that before I depart this life I behold in my realm and beneath my roof Publius Cornelius Scipio, whose very name refreshes my strength, so inseparable from my thought is the memory of that noble and invincible hero who first bore it." Then I questioned him about his kingdom, and he me about our commonwealth, and the day wore away with much conversation on both sides.

After I had been royally entertained we continued our conversation late into the night, the old man talking of nothing but Africanus and rehearsing his sayings as well as his deeds. When we parted to take our rest I fell into a deeper sleep than usual, for the hour was late and I was weary from travel. Because of our conversation, I suppose—our thoughts and utterances by day produce an effect in our sleep like that which Ennius speaks of with reference to Homer, of whom he used frequently to think and speak in his waking hours—Africanus appeared to me, in the shape that was familiar to me from his bust rather than from his own person. I shuddered when I recognized him, but he said: "Courage, Scipio, lay aside your dread and imprint my words on your memory. Do you see yonder city which I forced to submit to Rome but which is now stirring up the old hostilities and cannot remain at rest (from a lofty eminence bathed in brilliant starlight he pointed to Carthage), the city which you have come to attack, slightly more than a private? Within two years you shall be consul and overthrow it, and so win for yourself that which you now bear by inheritance. When you shall have destroyed Carthage, celebrated your triumph, been chosen censor, have traversed Egypt, Syria, Asia, and Greece as ambassador, you will be chosen consul a second time in your absence and will put an end to a great war by extirpating Numantia. But when you shall be borne into the capitol in your triumphal chariot, you shall find the government thrown into confusion by the machinations of my grandson; and here, Africanus, you must display to your country the lustre of your spirit, genius, and wisdom.

"But at this period I perceive that the path of your destiny is a doubtful one; for when your life has passed through seven times eight oblique journeys and returns of the sun; and when these two numbers (each of which is regarded as complete, one on one account and the other on another) shall, in their natural circuit, have brought you to the crisis of your fate, then will the whole state turn itself toward thee and thy glory; the senate, all virtuous men, our allies, and the Latins, shall look up to you. Upon your single person the preservation of your country will depend; and, in short, it is your part, as dictator, to settle the government, if you can but escape the impious hands of your kinsmen." —Here, when Laelius uttered an exclamation, and the rest groaned with great excitement, Scipio said, with a gentle smile, "I beg that you will not waken me out of my dream; listen a few moments and hear what followed.

"But that you may be more earnest in the defense of your country, know from me, that a certain place in heaven is assigned to all who have preserved, or assisted, or improved their country, where they are to enjoy an endless duration of happiness. For there is nothing which takes place on earth more acceptable to that Supreme Deity who governs all this world, than those councils and assemblies of men bound together by law, which are termed states; the governors and preservers of these go from hence, and hither do they return." Here, frightened as I was, not so much from the dread of death as of the treachery of my friends, I nevertheless asked him whether my father Paulus, and others, whom we thought to be dead, were yet alive? "To be sure they are alive (replied Africanus), for they have escaped from the fetters of the body as from a prison; that which is called life is really death. But behold your father Paulus approaching you."—No sooner did I see him than I poured forth a flood of tears; but he, embracing and kissing me, forbade me to weep. And when, having suppressed my tears, I regained the faculty of speech, I said: "Why, thou most sacred and excellent father, since this is life, as I hear Africanus affirm, why do I tarry on earth, and not hasten to come to you?"

"Not so, my son," he replied; "unless that God, whose temple is all this which you behold, shall free you from this imprisonment in the body, you can have no admission to this place; for men have been created under this condition, that they should keep that globe called earth which you see in the middle of this temple. And a soul has been supplied to them from those eternal fires which you call constellations and stars, and which, being globular and round, are animated with divine spirit, and complete their cycles and revolutions with amazing rapidity. Therefore you, my Publius, and all good men, must preserve your souls in the keeping of your bodies; nor are you, without the order of that Being who bestowed them upon you, to depart from mundane life, lest you seem to desert the duty assigned you by God. But, Scipio, like your grandfather here, like me who begot you, cherish justice and duty, a great obligation to parents and kin but greatest to your country. Such a life is the way to heaven and to this assembly of those who have already lived, and, released from the body, inhabit the place which you now see" (it was the circle of light which blazed most brightly among the other fires), "which you have learned from the Greeks to call the Milky Way." And as I looked on every side I saw other things transcendently glorious and wonderful. There were stars which we never see from the earth, and all were vast beyond what we have ever imagined. The least was that farthest from heaven and nearest the earth which shone with a borrowed light. The starry spheres were much larger than the earth; the earth itself looked so small as to make me ashamed of our empire, which was a mere point on its surface.

As I gazed more intently on earth, Africanus said: "How long will your mind be fixed on the ground? Do you not see what lofty regions you have entered? These are the nine circles, or rather spheres, by which all things are held together. One, the outermost, is the celestial; it contains all the rest and is itself the Supreme God, holding and embracing within itself the other spheres. In this are fixed those stars which ever roll in an unchanging course. Beneath it are seven other spheres which have a retrograde movement, opposite to that of the heavens. Of these, the globe which on earth you call Saturn, occupies one sphere. That shining body which you see next is called Jupiter, and is friendly and salutary to mankind. Next the lucid one, terrible to the earth, which you call Mars. The Sun holds the next place, almost under the middle region; he is the chief, the leader, and the director of the other luminaries; he is the soul and guide of the world, and of such immense bulk, that he illuminates and fills all other objects with his light. He is followed by the orbit of Venus, and that of Mercury, as attendants; and the Moon rolls in the lowest sphere, enlightened by the rays of the Sun. Below this there is nothing put what is mortal and transitory, excepting those souls which are given to the human race by the goodness of the gods. Whatever lies above the Moon is eternal. For the earth, which is the ninth sphere, and is placed in the center of the whole system, is immovable and below all the rest; and all bodies, by their natural gravitation, tend toward it."

When I had recovered from my amazement at these things I asked, "What is this sound so strong and sweet that fills my ears?" "This," he replied, "is the melody which, at intervals unequal, yet differing in exact proportions, is made by the impulse and motion of the spheres themselves, which, softening shriller by deeper tones, produce a diversity of regular harmonies. It is impossible that such prodigious movements should pass in silence; and nature teaches that the sounds which the spheres at one extremity utter must be sharp, and those on the other extremity must be grave; on which account that highest revolution of the star-studded heaven, whose motion is more rapid, is carried on with a sharp and quick sound; whereas this of the moon, which is situated the lowest and at the other extremity, moves with the gravest sound. For the earth, the ninth sphere, remaining motionless, abides invariably in the innermost position, occupying the central spot in the universe. But these eight revolutions, of which two, those of Mercury and Venus, are in unison, make seven distinct tones, with measured intervals between, and almost all things are arranged in sevens. Skilled men, copying this harmony with strings and voice, have opened for themselves a way back to this place, as have others who with excelling genius have cultivated divine sciences in human life. But the ears of men are deafened by being filled with this melody; you mortals have no duller sense than that of hearing. As where the Nile at the Falls of Catadupa pours down from lofty mountains, the people who live hard by lack the sense of hearing because of the cataract's roar, so this harmony of the whole universe in its intensely rapid movement is so loud that men's ears cannot take it in, even as you cannot look directly at the sun, your sense of sight being overwhelmed by its radiance." While I marveled at these things I was ever and anon turning my eyes back to earth, upon which Africanus resumed:

"I perceive that even now you are fixing your eyes on the habitation and abode of men, and if it seems to you diminutive, as it in fact is, keep your gaze fixed on these heavenly things and scorn the earthly. What fame can you obtain from the speech of men, what glory worth the seeking? You perceive that men dwell on but few and scanty portions of the earth, and that amid these spots, as it were, vast solitudes are interposed! As to those who inhabit the earth, not only are they so separated that no communication can circulate among them from the one to the other, but part lie upon one side, part upon another, and part are diametrically opposite to you, from whom you assuredly can expect no glory. You observe that the same earth is encircled and encompassed as it were by certain zones, of which the two that are most distant from one another and lie as it were toward the vortexes of the heavens in both directions, are rigid as you see with frost, while the middle and the largest zone is burned up with the heat of the sun. Two of these are habitable. The southern, whose inhabitants imprint their footsteps in an opposite direction to you, has no relation to your race. As to this other, lying toward the north, which you inhabit, observe what a small portion of it falls to your share; for all that part of the earth which is inhabited by you, which narrows toward the south and north but widens from east to west, is no other than a little island surrounded by that sea which on earth you call the Atlantic, sometimes the great sea, and sometimes the ocean; and yet with so grand a name, you see how diminutive it is! Now do you think it possible for your renown, or that of any one of us, to move from those cultivated and inhabited spots of ground, and pass beyond that Caucasus, or swim across yonder Ganges? What inhabitant of the other parts of the east, or of the extreme regions of the setting sun, of those tracts that run toward the south or toward the north, shall ever hear of your name? Now supposing them cut off, you see at once within what narrow limits your glory would fain expand itself. As to those who speak of you, how long will they speak?

"Let me even suppose that a future race of men shall be desirous of transmitting to their posterity your renown or mine, as they received it from their fathers; yet when we consider the convulsions and conflagrations that must necessarily happen at some definite period, we are unable to attain not only to an eternal, but even to a lasting fame. Now of what consequence is it to you to be talked of by those who are born after you, and not by those who were born before you, who certainly were as numerous and more virtuous; especially, as amongst the very men who are thus to celebrate our renown, not a single one can preserve the recollections of a single year? For mankind ordinarily measure their year by the revolution of the sun, that is of a single heavenly body. But when all the planets shall return to the same position which they once had, and bring back after a long rotation the same aspect of the entire heavens, then the year may be said to be truly completed; I do not venture to say how many ages of mankind will be contained within such a year. As of old the sun seemed to be eclipsed and blotted out when the soul of Romulus entered these regions, so when the sun shall be again eclipsed in the same part of his course and at the same period of the year and day, with all the constellations and stars recalled to the point from which they started on their revolutions, then count the year as brought to a close. But be assured that the twentieth part of such a year has not yet elapsed.

"Consequently, should you renounce hope of returning to this place where eminent and excellent men find their reward, of what worth is that human glory which can scarcely extend to a small part of a single year? If, then, you shall determine to look on high and contemplate this mansion and eternal abode, you will neither give yourself to the gossip of the vulgar nor place your hope of well-being on rewards that man can bestow. Virtue herself, by her own charms, should draw you to true honor. What others may say of you regard as their concern, not yours. They will doubtless talk about you, but what they say is limited to the narrow regions which you see; nor does talk of anyone last into eternity—it is buried with those who die, and lost in oblivion for those who come afterward."

When he had finished I said: "Truly, Africanus, if the path to heaven lies open to those who have deserved well of their country, though from my childhood I have ever trod in your and my father's footsteps without disgracing your glory, yet now, with so noble a prize set before me, I shall strive with much more diligence."

"Do so strive," replied he, "and do not consider yourself, but your body, to be mortal. For you are not the being which this corporeal figure evinces; but the soul of every man is the man, and not that form which may be delineated with a finger. Know also that you are a god, if a god is that which lives, perceives, remembers, foresees, and which rules, governs, and moves the body over which it is set, just as the Supreme God rules the universe. Just as the eternal God moves the universe, which is in part mortal, so does an everlasting soul move the corruptible body.

"That which is always in motion is eternal; but that which, while communicating motion to another, derives its own movement from some other source, must of necessity cease to live when this motion ends. Only what moves itself never ceases motion, for it is never deserted by itself; it is rather the source and first cause of motion in whatever else is moved. But the first cause has no beginning, for everything originates from the first cause; itself, from nothing. If it owed its origin to anything else, it would not be a first cause. If it has no beginning, it has no end. If a first cause is extinguished, it will neither be reborn from anything else, nor will it create anything else from itself, for everything must originate from a first cause. It follows that motion begins with that which is moved of itself, and that this can neither be born nor die—else the heavens must collapse and nature perish, possessing no force from which to receive the first impulse to motion.

"Since that which moves of itself is eternal, who can deny that the soul is endowed with this property? Whatever is moved by external impulse is soulless; whatever possesses soul is moved by an inner impulse of its own, for this is the peculiar nature and property of soul. And since soul is the only force that moves itself, it surely has no beginning and is immortal. Employ it, therefore, in the noblest of pursuits; the noblest are those undertaken for the safety of your country. If it is in these that your soul is diligently exercised, it will have a swifter flight to this, its proper home and permanent abode. Even swifter will be the flight if, while still imprisoned in the body, it shall peer forth, and, contemplating what lies beyond, detach itself as far as possible from the body. For the souls of those who have surrendered themselves to the pleasures of the body and have become their slaves, who are goaded to obedience by lust and violate the laws of gods and men—such souls, when they pass out of their bodies, hover close to earth, and do not return to this place till they have been tossed about for many ages."

He departed; I awoke from sleep.

# ON THE CHARACTER
# OF THE ORATOR

LIKE HIS *contemporaries and posterity Cicero properly regarded oratory as his highest function, and he entertained a deservedly high opinion* (To Atticus 13.19, To Friends 1.9) *of his On the Orator, which is a masterly treatment of the subject and itself, in effect, a consummate piece of oratory. On the Orator was written in 55 when Cicero was at the height of his artistic power but had been forced to withdraw from public life by the renewed coalition of Caesar and Pompey. The book is a serious effort by a responsible expert to put the fruit of his own experience on record for the benefit of future statesmen. He tells his brother Quintus, to whom the book is addressed, that it is intended to replace youthful essays on the subject, and points out the great difficulty, as well as the great usefulness of the orator's art. Cicero employs the customary dialogue form; the fictive date of the conversation is 91 B.C., and the important figures of that great age of oratory are made its interlocutors. The aim is to harmonize rhetoric with philosophy, to advance the craft to the status of a science. This is the substance of the first book, in which Crassus maintains the necessity of universal education for the orator and Antonius denies it. The range and versatility of interests displayed in the book is remarkable. The ease and grace of its style, its beautiful language and harmonious periods, its flashes of wit and drama, lull the reader into obliviousness to an essential weakness in the argument; with all his persuasive eloquence Cicero merely juxtaposes the craft and the science, but sets up no philosophical principle to establish a necessary connection between them.*

1. Whenever my thoughts and reminiscences take me back to the old days, my dear brother, I am always struck with the extreme felicity of those who, in the best days of our country's history, were distinguished both by official position and by their brilliant services to the state, and yet were able to maintain a life of such even tenor that they could as they pleased enjoy political activity without danger, or retirement without loss of honour. There was a time, indeed, when I thought that I too should be able to claim, with the almost universal consent of my fellow-countrymen, a moment for retiring and for turning my attention once more to those higher studies to which we are both of us devoted, if only some pause should come in the endless labours of public life and the engrossing occupations of a candidate for election, when my official career was closed and the prime of my life was past. This hope, which was present in all my thoughts and purposes, was disappointed by a combination of disastrous political events and various domestic misfortunes; for where I expected to find a most ample haven of rest and tranquillity, I was confronted by an overwhelming flood of vexation and a tempestuous storm of trouble, and as a matter of fact, much as I have wished and desired it, I have never been vouchsafed any enjoyment of leisure in which to prosecute and renew with you those studies to which from our boyhood we have been devoted. Thus my early years just coincided with the first collapse of old political principles, my consulship brought me into the very centre and heat of the political struggle, and all my energies between my consulship and the present time I have devoted to stemming the waves which were by my policy

173

diverted from overwhelming the country, only to recoil upon me and mine. However, even in spite of present hindrances, whether political difficulties or limitations of time, I will indulge the tastes which we share together, and what leisure is allowed me either by the evil designs of political enemies or the calls of friendship and public duty, I shall devote exclusively to literary work. Certainly to your command or your request, my dear brother, I cannot be indifferent; for there is no one whose authority or wishes can have more weight with me than yours.

2. I must therefore now try to recall to mind a story I heard some time ago. I have not a very distinct remembrance of it, but it will be sufficient, I think, for your purpose, and it will show you what has been the opinion of the greatest and most famous orators on the general theory of oratory. You have often expressed to me a wish that since the rude and imperfect work which fell from my pen in my boyhood or early manhood, the mere jottings from my notebooks, is scarcely worthy of my present years and the experience I have gained from the numerous and important cases in which I have pleaded, I should therefore publish something on the same subject more finished and complete. At the same time in our discussions together you occasionally differ from me on this question, arguing that whereas I hold that eloquence is inseparable from all the accomplishments of the profoundest erudition, you consider that it ought to be kept quite distinct from the higher learning, and made to rest on a certain combination of natural gifts and training. For my own part, when I contemplate the world's greatest and most gifted men, it has often seemed to me a question well worth the asking, why it is that more men have won distinction in all the other arts than in oratory; for, turn your thoughts and attention where you will, you will find that in any given branch of art (in those of the

highest importance, I may say, as well as in the less important) a very large number have attained excellence. No
one, I suppose, if he chooses to estimate the accomplishments of great men by the utility or by the grandeur of their
achievements, would hesitate to give the general precedence over the orator; but no one can doubt that military
leaders of consummate merit have been produced by this
single country in almost countless numbers, whereas of excellence in oratory we can only with difficulty cite a few
examples. Of men, too, able by their wisdom and counsel
to direct and guide the state, we have known many within
our own memory; still more were known within the memory of our fathers and even in the ages before them; whereas
for many centuries we find no good orators, barely indeed
one tolerable representative of the art for each generation. It
may, indeed, occur to an objector that oratory ought to be
compared with other pursuits such as deal with more abstruse subjects and imply a wide acquaintance with literature, rather than with the excellence of a general or the
practical wisdom of the good statesman; but let him only
turn to such other branches of study, and observe how
numerous are the distinguished names in each, and he will
very easily realise what a great paucity of orators there is,
and always has been.

3. You are no doubt well aware that of all the liberal arts
in high repute philosophy is considered by the learned to
be the mother, and 'the great original,' if I may borrow the
expression; yet in philosophy it is difficult to enumerate how
many men there have been of the greatest knowledge, of
many-sided interests and rich endowments, who have not
only done good work as specialists in some one department,
but have covered the whole range of knowledge possible to
them, either in their direct search after truth, or in their dia-
lectical discussions. We all know what obscure subjects are

handled in mathematics, how abstruse a science it is, how complicated, how exact, and yet so many have attained to perfection in it that no one, we may almost say, has given his serious attention to this science and not achieved success. Is there an instance of any one devoting himself to music, or the now fashionable study of language professed by the grammarians, as they are called, and failing to acquire a thorough knowledge of the almost unlimited range and subject-matter of those branches of learning? I think I may truly say that of the whole number of those who have engaged in the pursuit and acquirement of the liberal arts, the smallest contingent is that of first-rate poets and orators; and further, within this small contingent in which instances of real excellence are very rare, you will find by a careful selection of examples for comparison from the history both of Rome and Greece, that there have been far fewer good orators than good poets. And this must strike us as all the more surprising, because the subjects of all the other arts are drawn as a rule from remote and abstruse sources, whereas the whole province of oratory is within reach of every one, and finds its subject-matter in the practically universal experience of men and their ordinary manners and conversation; so that while in the other arts the highest excellence is found where there is the furthest remove from the intelligence and appreciation of the unlearned, in the orator, on the contrary, it is a fault of the very gravest character to be out of harmony with the language of every-day life, and the accepted usage of men of ordinary taste and intelligence.

4. And we cannot either (in explanation of this) maintain with any truth that more devote themselves to the other arts, or that those who do so are encouraged to master their subject by the greater pleasure of the work, or by higher hopes of success, or by more splendid prizes. In fact,

to say nothing of Greece, which has always claimed to be first in eloquence, and of that mother of all the arts, the city of Athens, where the art of rhetoric was invented and attained its highest development, in our own country, even, no study surely has ever had a more vigorous life than the study of oratory. For when after the establishment of our world-wide empire a lengthened peace secured to us the enjoyment of leisure, there was hardly a young man of any ambition who did not think that he ought to put forth all his energy to make himself an orator. At first, indeed, our countrymen in total ignorance of the theory, and believing neither in the virtue of training, nor in the existence of any particular rule of art, attained to what success they could by the help of native wit and invention; subsequently, after they had heard the Greek orators, studied Greek literature, and called in the aid of Greek teachers, they were fired with a really marvellous zeal for learning the art. They were encouraged by the importance, the variety, and the number of causes of every description, to supplement the learning, which they had severally gained from private study, by constant practice, and found this better than the instructions of all the professors. Further, to this pursuit then, as now, the highest prizes were offered whether in the way of popularity, or influence, or position. Finally, in respect of ability, as many indications lead us to conclude, our countrymen have always been far superior to any other nation in the world. All these considerations may surely justify some surprise at the fact that the history of all ages, periods, and communities presents us with so small a number of orators. The truth of the matter is, that this accomplishment is something greater than it is generally supposed to be, and is the combined result of many arts and many studies.

5. For when we consider the very large number of learners, the rich supply of teachers, the exceptional abilities of

the persons engaged, the infinite variety of causes, the splendour of the prizes which eloquence may win, where else can
we look for the explanation of the fact, except in the really
incredible greatness and difficulty of the subject? Eloquence, in fact, requires many things: a wide knowledge
of very many subjects (verbal fluency without this being
worthless and even ridiculous), a style, too, carefully formed
not merely by selection, but by arrangement of words, and
a thorough familiarity with all the feelings which nature has
given to man, because the whole force and art of the orator
must be put forth in allaying or exciting the emotions of his
audience. Further than this it requires a certain play of humour and wit, a liberal culture, a readiness and brevity in
reply and attack, combined with a nice delicacy and refinement of manner. It requires also an acquaintance with all
history, and a store of instances, nor can it dispense with a
knowledge of the statute-books and all civil law. I need
hardly add, I presume, any remarks on mere delivery. This
must be combined with appropriate movement of the body,
gestures, looks, and modulation and variety of tone. How
important this is in itself may be seen from the insignificant
art of the actor and the procedure of the stage; for though
all actors pay great attention to the due management of
their features, voice, and gestures, it is a matter of common
notoriety how few there are, or have been, whom we can
watch without discomfort. One word I must add on memory, the treasure-house of all knowledge. Unless the orator
calls in the aid of memory to retain the matter and the
words with which thought and study have furnished him,
all his other merits, however brilliant, we know will lose
their effect. We may therefore well cease to wonder why it
is that real orators are so few, seeing that eloquence depends on a combination of accomplishments, in each one of
which it is no slight matter to achieve success; let us rather

urge our children, and all others whose fame and reputation is dear to us, to realise the greatness of the task, and to believe that though they cannot attain to the goal of their ambition by the help of those rules, or teachers, or exercises which are in general use, there are certain others which will enable them to do so.

6. My own private opinion is, that no one can be a real orator in the full sense of the word unless he first acquires a knowledge of all the great subjects of human study; for a wide knowledge is needed to give a luxuriance and richness to language which, unless the speaker has thoroughly mastered his subject, suffers from what I may perhaps call a puerile vapidity of expression. Still I would not lay so great a burden on the orator, especially in our own country amid the urgent calls of the city-life of to-day, as to think that there is nothing of which they may enjoy the privilege of ignorance; although the very meaning of the word 'orator,' and the mere profession of eloquence, seems to imply a promise and undertaking to speak in good style, and with full knowledge, on any subject which may be proposed. This I am very sure most men would consider a task of incalculable and infinite difficulty. The Greeks also, I know, rich as they were not only in native wit and acquired learning, but also in leisure and enthusiasm for study, made a certain division of the arts, and did not devote their efforts individually to even one department as a whole, but separated from the other provinces of speech that particular subdivision which is concerned with the public discussions of the law-courts and deliberative assemblies, and assigned this only to the orator. For these reasons I shall not in this present treatise include more than what has been, after careful inquiry and much discussion, allotted to this division of the art by the all but unanimous judgment of the highest authorities; and I shall not go back to the 'beggarly elements

of the old-fashioned teaching which we received in our boyhood for any definite system of rules, but I will repeat to
you the substance of a conversation which I have been told
took place on a certain occasion between some of the greatest orators and leading statesmen of our own country. Pray
do not imagine that I would reject the rules which the Greek
professors of rhetoric have left to us, but as they are public
property, and within the reach of every one, and cannot in
any translation of mine be either set forth with better grace
or expressed in clearer language than they are, you will I
daresay, my dear brother, forgive me if I prefer to any
Greek professor the authority of those to whom the highest
place on the roll of orators has been conceded by the Roman
world.

7. We must go back to the time when the Consul Philippus was making a fierce attack on the policy of the leading
nobility, and when the tribunician power of Drusus, whose
object was to maintain the authority of the senate, was beginning to all appearance to lose its influence and stability.
At this juncture L. Crassus, I remember being told, retired
in the week of the Roman Games to his villa at Tusculum
to recruit his forces; he was joined there, I was told, by his
late wife's father, Quintus Mucius, and by Marcus Antonius,
who was connected with Crassus by ties of political sympathy and a strong personal friendship. There also left Rome
in attendance on Crassus two young men, who were at once
personal friends of Drusus, and of such a character that
their elder contemporaries at that time looked to them with
considerable confidence to uphold the dignity of the party;
these were Caius Cotta, who was standing for the tribuneship of the plebs at the time, and Publius Sulpicius, who
was thought a probable candidate for that office in succession to him. On the first day they had an earnest conversation, which was prolonged till the evening, on the political

crisis and the general situation of affairs,—this, in fact, being the motive of their visit. And in the course of their conversation, as Cotta used to tell me, these three ex-consuls
deeply deplored the signs of the times, and dwelt on them
with such prophetic insight, that no misfortune subsequently befell the state which they had not even at that time
seen to be impending; but, the conversation once finished,
so great was the geniality of Crassus, that after the company
had taken their bath and sat down to dinner all the gloom
of the preceding discussion was entirely removed, and such
was the fund of cheerfulness in the man, and so charming
his power of pleasantry, that though the day seemed to
have been spent in the atmosphere of the senate-house, the
dinner-party was truly worthy of the retirement of Tusculum. On the next day, after the older members of the party
were sufficiently rested, and they had all met on the terrace,
*Scævola,* when they had taken two or three turns, said 'Why
not do as Socrates does, Crassus, in the *Phædrus* of Plato?
The thought is suggested to me by your plane-tree here,
which, with its spreading branches, makes a no less perfect
shade for this spot than the tree whose shade Socrates
sought, which seems to me to have owed its luxuriant growth
not so much to the rivulet described in the dialogue, as to
Plato's pen; and surely what Socrates with his horny feet
did, threw himself, that is, on the grass, and so delivered
those divine utterances which the philosophers attribute to
him, this I with my softer feet may more fairly be allowed
to do.' *Crassus* rejoined, 'Nay, let us do so with an added
comfort,' and called for some cushions, and then they all sat
down on the benches beneath the plane-tree.

8. While they sat there, as Cotta used to tell the story, in
order to refresh the minds of the company after the conversation of the previous day, *Crassus* started a discussion on
oratory. He began by saying that Sulpicius and Cotta did

not, as it seemed, so much need encouragement from him as deserve his hearty commendation, in that they had already attained to such proficiency that they not only outstripped their contemporaries, but challenged comparison with their seniors; and, 'believe me,' he continued, 'nothing seems to me a nobler ambition than to be able to hold by your elo-quence the minds of men, to captivate their wills, to move them to and fro in whatever direction you please. This art of all others has ever found its fullest development in every free community, and more especially in states enjoying peace and tranquillity, and has ever exercised a dominant influence. What indeed is so truly wonderful as that out of an infinite number of men one man should stand forth able alone, or with few others, to use with effect what is really nature's gift to all? What pleasure is greater to mind or ear than a speech adorned with wise sentiments and weighty words and in perfect style? Can we imagine a more impos-ing display of individual power than that the passions of a people, the consciences of a jury, the grave deliberations of a senate, should be swayed by one man's utterance? What, again, is so royal an exercise of liberality and munificence as to bring help to the distressed, to raise the afflicted, to protect the rights of our fellow-citizens, to free them from danger, and save them from exile? What, moreover, is so practically useful as always to have in your grasp a weapon with which you can secure your own safety, attack the ene-mies of the state, or avenge yourself when provoked by them? Or once more, not to be always thinking of the fo-rum, its courts of justice, public meetings, and senate, what greater enjoyment can there be in times of leisure, what greater intellectual treat than the brilliant discourse of a per-fect scholar? It is in fact this one characteristic that gives us our chief superiority over the brute creation, the habit, I mean, of conversing with one another, and the power of expressing our feelings in words. This power, then, every one may well admire, and may well think that his best energies must be exerted to make himself superior to his fellow-men in that special gift which gives them their chief superiority over brute beasts. Finally, to come to what are the main advantages of speech, what other power could have gathered the scattered members of the human race into one place, or weaned them from a wild and savage life to the humane and civilised life of citizens, or, when their various communities were once established, could have defined for them their laws, their judicial procedure, and their rights? Its further advantages, which are well-nigh innumerable, I will not follow out in detail, but will comprise them in one brief sentence:—my deliberate opinion is, that the controlling influence and wisdom of the consummate orator is the main security, not merely for his own personal reputation, but for the safety of countless individuals, and the welfare of the country at large. For these reasons, my young friends, continue your present efforts, and devote yourselves to the pursuit which now engages you, that so you may be enabled to win distinction for yourselves, to benefit your friends, and to promote the best interests of your country.'

9. Then *Scævola*, with his habitual courtesy, said: 'In everything else I quite agree with Crassus, having no desire to depreciate either the accomplishments or the reputation of my father-in-law C. Lælius, or of my own son-in-law; but there are two statements of yours, Crassus, which I fear I cannot admit; the one, that orators were originally the founders and often the saviours of states; the other, that the orator, without limiting him to the various departments of public life, has attained perfection in every subject of discourse and polite learning. In the first place, who can agree with you either that originally mankind, when dispersed over the mountains and forests, were not forced by the wise

action of far-seeing spirits, but rather won by the persuasive words of the eloquent to fence themselves round in walled towns? Or again, that other useful dispositions, whether in the way of establishing or maintaining civilised communities, owed their origin to the eloquence of men of clever speech, rather than to the wisdom of men of resolute action? You surely cannot think that Romulus either collected his shepherds and refugees, or established inter-marriage with the Sabines, or checked the violence of neighbouring tribes by the power of eloquence, and not by the extraordinary wisdom of his policy. Look again at the history of Numa Pompilius, or Servius Tullius, and the other kings who notably did much towards the consolidation of the state; is it their eloquence of which we see the effects? Then again, after the expulsion of the kings—the actual expulsion of course was plainly the work of the brain, and not the tongue of Brutus; but the immediate sequel—does it not present a series of wise actions with a complete absence of mere words? Indeed, if I cared to quote from the history of our own country and others, I could instance more cases of loss inflicted upon communities by the agency of men of the greatest eloquence than of advantages owed to them; but omitting all others, I fancy the most eloquent men I have ever heard, with the exception of you and Antonius, were the two Gracchi, Tiberius and Caius, whose father, a man of sound sense and sterling character, but by no means eloquent, often did good service to his country, and especially in his censorship; he, you know, by no flood of elaborate eloquence, but by the mere expression of his will, transferred all freedmen into the city tribes, and but for this measure of his, what little of the old constitution still survives would long have ceased to exist. But those eloquent sons of his, ready speakers as they were, with all their advantages whether of nature or learning, born citizens of a

country to which their father's policy and their grandfather's arms had brought great prosperity, squandered the
resources of the state by the help of what, according to you,
is so excellent a director of the communities of men—the
power of eloquence.

10. Consider again our ancient laws and traditional usages, our auspices over which I, no less than you, Crassus,
preside for the preservation of our country; our religious
observances and ceremonies; the body of civil law which
has for generations been domesticated in my family, though
none of us has ever been famous as an orator; do these owe
anything in respect of origin, interpretation, or even general
treatment to the representatives of oratory? Indeed, if my
memory serves me, Servius Galba, a very gifted speaker,
M. Æmilius Porcina, and our friend Caius Carbo, the victim
of your youthful efforts, knew nothing of statute law, bog-
gled over traditional usage, and had little acquaintance with
civil law; and, with the exception of you, my friend, who
owe to your own enthusiasm more than to any special gift
peculiar to the orator the knowledge of civil law which you
have learnt from me, our own age is ignorant of law to an
extent that sometimes makes one blush for it. As to the as-
sumption which you made at the end of your remarks, with
all the assurance of an unquestioned title, that the orator
can be perfectly at home and is never at a loss in a discussion upon any topic, I should have scouted it at once, were
you not here lord of all you survey, and I should have instructed a host of litigants who would either contest your
claims by a prætor's injunction or challenge you to prove
your title by process of law, as having committed a rash and
violent seizure of the domains of others. For first of all the
Pythagoreans would go to law with you, and the Democri-
teans and all the other physicists would appear in court to
assert their claims, all of them accomplished and weighty

speakers, against whom you could not possibly make out a tenable case. Another heavy attack would come from the schools of the moral philosophers, beginning with Socrates, their first founder, proving that you had learnt nothing, made no inquiries, and knew nothing about the good and evil in human affairs, the emotions and the habits of men, or the true theory of life. Then, after they had made a combined attack upon you, each school would bring its separate action against you. The Academy would be upon you, forcing you to contradict with your own lips anything and everything you said; our friends the Stoics would hopelessly entrap you in the subtleties of their arguments and interrogations; while the Peripatetics would prove triumphantly that you must go to them for those very things which you believe to be the special requirements and ornaments of the orator, and would demonstrate that Aristotle and Theophrastus had written much better, and much more too, on these subjects than all the professed teachers of rhetoric. I say nothing of the mathematicians, grammarians, and musicians with whose arts your oratorical faculty has not even the most distant connection. For these reasons, Crassus, my opinion is that the large and comprehensive claims you make are quite beyond the mark. You must content yourself with this—and it is no slight thing—that you can guarantee that in the law-courts any case in which you plead will seem the stronger and more plausible, that in the national assembly and in the senate a speech from you will have most power to persuade; that you, in short, will produce an impression in professional men of the ability, in laymen of the truth, of your contention. If you succeed in doing more than this, the success I shall attribute not to the orator, but to some special gift attaching to the personality of the speaker.'

11. *Crassus:* 'I am fully aware, Scævola, that such are the

assertions made and the arguments habitually used by the Greeks; for I attended the lectures of their chief men when I stayed at Athens on my return from Macedonia, at a time, as I was told, of great prosperity with the Academy, when Charmadas, Clitomachus, and Æschines were its leading spirits. Metrodorus also was there, who, as well as they, had been a constant attendant at the lectures of the great Carneades, who was said to have been a speaker of exceptional vigour and the widest knowledge. Mnesarchus, also, a pupil of your hero Panætius, was in full activity, and Diodorus, a pupil of Critolaus the Peripatetic. Besides these there were many well-known lights of the philosophic world, all of whom I observed with almost one consent rejected the orator from the guidance of political affairs, debarred him from all learning and knowledge of more important subjects, and consigned and confined him to the law-courts and the hustings, as a slave to a pounding-mill. But I was not inclined to agree either with them or with the first and leading author of such discussions as the present, by far the most convincing and eloquent of all the philosophers, I mean Plato, whose *Gorgias* I read very carefully with Charmadas on this occasion at Athens; and indeed what struck me most in reading this dialogue was, that Plato, while satirising the orators, seemed himself to be the greatest orator of them all. The fact is, a mere verbal dispute has long been exercising the ingenuity of our friends the Greeks, who dearly love an argument and never mind the truth. For if we define the orator as the man who can speak with fluency only before the prætor, or before the bench, or in the popular assembly, or in the senate, still, even under these limitations there are many other qualifications which we must allow him; for he cannot deal even with such matters with due judgment and skill without close application to public affairs, without a knowledge of statutes, customs, and law, or without much insight into the nature and characters of men. Without these qualifications no one in any question he is dealing with can be quite safe even on the minor points of judgment and skill, and with them, surely, he cannot be wanting in knowledge on the most important subjects. If you will not allow any function to the orator, save that of expressing himself adequately in point of arrangement, style, and matter, then I ask how can he achieve even that without the further knowledge which you with others do not allow him? For the true virtue of rhetoric cannot have full play, unless the speaker has mastered the subject on which he intends to speak. Thus if the famous physicist Democritus expressed himself in admirable style (and on this point my own opinion coincides with the accepted tradition), while the subject-matter of his discourses is that of the physical philosopher, the style and language of them, we must believe, is that of the orator; and if Plato discoursed in most perfect language on subjects most remote from ordinary political questions; if likewise Aristotle, Theophrastus, and Carneades in their lectures proved themselves men of eloquence with all the charm of a polished style; the subjects of which they treat I readily admit belong to other branches of learning, but their language falls entirely within the one province which we are now discussing and investigating. Indeed we see that certain philosophers have treated of the same subjects in a meagre and jejune style, as, for instance, Chrysippus, who is spoken of for his extraordinary acuteness; but he did not therefore fail to satisfy the requirements of the philosopher, because he did not possess the gift of expression, which is the outcome of an entirely different branch of study.

12. What is it then that makes the difference, and how are we to distinguish the rich and copious diction of the philosophers I have named from the meagre diction of those

who have not the same variety and grace of language at their command? Surely the one differentia of these more eloquent philosophers we shall find to be that they bring to their work a style at once harmonious and eloquent, and distinguished by a certain note of artistic finish; and such a style, if not supported by a thorough knowledge of his subject on the part of the speaker, must either be conspicuous by its absence, or else provoke general derision. For nothing, surely, can be so idiotic as a mere jingle of words, be they as choice and perfect as you will, if there is no meaning or knowledge underlying them. Whatever then his subject may be, to whatever science it may belong and of whatever kind, the orator, if he has studied it as he would a brief, will speak on it with more skill and in better language than even the man who has made some original discovery or has technical skill in that special line. If I am met by the objection that there are certain trains of thought and questions appropriate to the orator, and a knowledge of certain subjects clearly defined by the limits of public life, I am quite ready to admit that it is with such subjects our profession as speakers is most constantly employed, but at the same time, even in connection with these, there is very much that does not fall within the teaching or apprehension of the ordinary professors of rhetoric. Thus, as every one knows, the virtue of oratory is most effectively displayed in arousing the anger, disgust, or indignation of an audience, or in turning them from such excitement of feeling to mercy and pity; and here no one but a man who has made himself thoroughly familiar with the characters of men, and the whole range of human feeling, and the motives whereby men's minds are excited or calmed, will ever be able to produce by his words the effect which he desires. This whole topic is of course generally considered to be the special province of the philosopher, nor will the orator with my sanction at all demur to this; but conceding to the philosophers the mere knowledge of such subjects, because they have chosen to concentrate all their efforts in that direction, he will further make himself responsible for the oratorical treatment of them, for which a knowledge of them is absolutely indispensable; for the special province of the orator is, as I have said already more than once, to express himself in a style at once impressive and artistic and conformable with the thoughts and feelings of human nature.

13. That Aristotle and Theophrastus have written on this subject, I admit; but does not this, Scævola, entirely confirm my contention? For where they and the orator are on common ground, I do not borrow from them; whereas they admit that their discourses on this subject belong to oratory, and therefore, while they give to their other treatises the title proper to their own profession, these they entitle "rhetorical," and refer to them under that name. Thus when, as very often happens, occasion arises in the course of a speech for the ordinary commonplaces, when the speaker has to enlarge upon the immortal gods, natural affection, kindly feeling, friendship, the common rights of humanity, justice, temperance, magnanimity, and all the other virtues, the cry will be raised, I suppose, by all the philosophical schools and sects that all this is their special province in which the orator has neither part nor parcel; but for my part, while I am ready to concede to them the right of discussing these subjects in the study by way of pastime, I shall still assign and allot to the orator the power of enlarging, with all the charm of impressive eloquence, on the same themes which they debate in the meagre and lifeless language of the parlour. This was the line of argument I adopted with the philosophers at Athens, being urged to do so by our friend Marcus Marcellus, who is now curule ædile, and would, I am sure, be here to take part in

our present discussion, if it were not for his official duties at the Games; indeed, even then, though a mere youth, he was an enthusiastic student of rhetoric. Again, when question arises about laws and contracts, about war and peace, about allies and tributaries, about the rights of the citizens, distinguished according to their different classes and ages, the Greeks are quite welcome to say, if they like, that Lycurgus and Solon (though, by the way, I am of opinion that they ought to be reckoned among the representatives of eloquence) had better knowledge than Hyperides or Demosthenes, two quite consummate masters of the most polished eloquence; or the Roman is welcome in this matter to prefer the decemvirs, who drew up the XII Tables and must therefore have been sagacious statesmen, to Servius Galba and your father-in-law Caius Lælius, who it is generally admitted were the leading orators of their day; for while I have no wish to deny that there are certain departments of the art special to those who have concentrated all their energies on the investigation and exposition of those departments, I do maintain that the complete and perfect orator is he who can speak on all subjects with fluency and variety.

14. Surely, it often happens that in cases which are admittedly the proper province of the orator, some topic arises for which the speaker has to draw, not on his practical experience of political life, which is all that you allow to the orator, but on the resources of some less familiar science, and he has to borrow from it. For instance, can a speech, I ask, either against or on behalf of a general, be made without some familiarity with military affairs, or, often, without some geographical knowledge of localities? Can a speech be made before the assembly either against or in support of a proposed law, or in the senate on any general question of state administration, without considerable knowledge both

theoretical and practical of state affairs? Can the power of
language be applied to the exciting or even allaying of the
emotions and feelings of an audience, which is a thing of
primary importance in an orator, without a most careful
study of all those theories which are put forth by philosophy on the different natures and characters of men? Lastly,
though I very much doubt whether I shall make my contention good to your satisfaction, I will not hesitate to assert
my sincere belief, that while questions of physics and mathematics, and all those others which you just now laid down
as special to the other branches of science, fall within the
knowledge of those who make such studies their business,
yet if any one wishes to elucidate such subjects rhetorically,
he must apply for aid to the oratorical faculty. For though
it is an admitted fact that the famous architect Philo, who
built the arsenal at Athens, explained his design to the assembly in a very able speech, we must not therefore suppose that the virtue of his speech was due to his skill as an
architect rather than to his skill as an orator. Nor, again, if
our friend Antonius here had had to speak for Hermodorus
on the design of his dockyard, would he, with previous
instructions from Hermodorus, have failed to speak in admirable style and with adequate knowledge on another's
handiwork. Nor, again, did Asclepiades, whom we knew
not only as a doctor, but as a friend, in so far as he used to
speak in admirable style, represent the medical so much as
the oratorical faculty. Indeed what Socrates used to say is
more tenable, though not true, that every one can be sufficiently eloquent on a subject which he knows; the real
truth being, that no one can either be eloquent on a subject
he does not know, or speak well on any particular subject
he does know, even if he has perfect knowledge of it, but
has no skill in the artistic composition of speeches.

15. Therefore, if what is desired is a comprehensive defi-

nition of the special faculty of the orator as a whole, the true orator, in my opinion, the man really worthy of this grand name, will be he who, whatever subject may arise for elucidation by language, will speak on this with judgment, in harmonious language, in perfect style, and with accuracy, all combined with a certain dignity of delivery. If the term I have used, "on any subject whatever," seems to any one too extravagant, he or any one else is welcome to trim and prune my definition in this direction as much as they like; but this I will hold to, that even if the orator has no knowledge of those matters which lie within the range of the other arts and branches of study, but only understands those which come within the debates and discussions of public life, still if he has to speak on such extraneous subjects, the orator, after instructions on the particular points involved in each case from those who do understand them, will speak far better than those who have special knowledge of them. Thus if Sulpicius should have occasion to speak on a military question, he will make inquiries of our connection, Caius Marius, and when he has received his answer, he will deliver himself in such a way as to give even Marius the impression that he knows his subject better than his informant. If he has to speak on a point of law, he will put himself in communication with you, Scævola, and thanks to his oratorical skill will surpass even so learned and experienced a lawyer as yourself in his treatment of those subjects on which he has been instructed by you. If, again, occasion should arise when he has to speak about human nature, the vices and desires of men, about moderation and temperance, about pain or death, he will perhaps, if it seem advisable— though the orator ought to be familiar with such subjects —consult with that learned philosopher Sextus Pompeius. One thing I am confident he will do, whatever the subject and whoever his informant, he will speak on it in far better

style than the man from whom he gained his information.
But if he will take my advice, as philosophy is divided into
three parts, the investigation of the secrets of nature, the
subtleties of dialectic, the study of life and morals, let us pass
by the first two as a concession to our indolence; but unless
we hold to the third, which has always been one of the orator's subjects, we shall leave the orator nothing in which he
can be really great. This topic, therefore, of life and morals,
must be thoroughly mastered by the orator; the other subjects, though he may not have studied them, he will be able,
if need be, to treat oratorically if he is put in possession of
the necessary material.

16. For if the learned world is agreed that Aratus, though
quite ignorant of astronomy, has composed a most eloquent
and artistic poem on the heavens and the stars, and that
Nicander of Colophon, though he never had anything to do
with agriculture, has written a noble poem on country life
by virtue of his poetical faculty and not from any knowledge of rustic lore, why should not the orator be able to
speak with the eloquence of a master on subjects which he
has only studied for a particular case and occasion? For the
poet is very near akin to the orator, being somewhat more
restricted in his rhythms, though freer in his choice of
words, but in many of his methods of ornament his fellow
and almost his equal; in this respect, at all events, nearly the
same, in so far as he recognises no limitations to his full and
perfect right of expatiating in whatever field he pleases with
the same mastery and freedom as the orator. For as to your
assertion that, were I not here lord of all I survey, you
would at once have scouted my remark that the orator
ought to be a perfect master in every subject of discourse
and every department of human culture, I assure you, Scævola, I should never have thought for a moment of making
the remark if I imagined that I had realised my own ideal.

But I do feel what Caius Lucilius used often to say—a man who was not on the best terms with you, and for that very reason not so intimate with me as he wished to be, but for all that we must admit his learning and great culture—that no one ought to be considered an orator who is not well trained in all those branches of learning which ought to be included in a liberal education; and though we make no immediate use of such subjects in a speech, still it becomes quite evident whether we are totally ignorant of them or have studied them. Just as with those who play at ball, though in their actual play they have no occasion for the exact dexterity of the gymnasium, still we may infer from their mere movements whether they have practised gymnastics or not; and similarly with sculptors, although at the moment they have no occasion for painting, still it is quite evident whether they know how to paint or not; so in our speeches delivered in the courts, or to the people, or in the senate, even though no direct use is made of the other arts, it is nevertheless plainly apparent whether the speaker has figured merely in the workshop of the ranter, or has prepared himself for his task by an education in all the liberal arts.'

17. *Scævola* then replied with a smile: 'I will not contest the point further with you, Crassus; for by some trick you have made good the particular point which you stated against me, first conceding to me that the orator does not possess certain qualifications which I held that he did not, and then by some legerdemain giving another colour to these qualifications, and allowing the orator a peculiar title to them. I remember that, when on my visit to Rhodes as Governor of Asia, I compared the lessons I had received from Panætius with the teachings of Apollonius, the famous professor of rhetoric in that city, he, in his usual way, expressed much scorn and contempt for philosophy, but his

remarks though witty were not very impressive. The tone of your remarks, however, has been very different; you have expressed no contempt for any art or branch of learning, but spoken of them all as the attendants and handmaids of oratory. Now if any one man could master all the arts, and at the same time combine with them your gift of consummate eloquence, I cannot but say that he would be a very remarkable and truly admirable specimen of humanity; but such a man—if there were, or ever had been, or ever could be such a man—would be you and no one else, of that I am sure, who, not only in my opinion, but in the opinion of every one, have monopolised—if my friends here will pardon the expression—the whole field of oratorical glory. But if there is no subject connected with civil and political life of which you lack the knowledge, and yet you have not mastered that further and comprehensive knowledge which you expect of the orator, it occurs to me that we may be attributing to him more than the actual facts of the case would warrant.' *Crassus:* 'Ah, you must remember I was not speaking of my own attainments, but of those of the ideal orator. Why, what have I learnt, or what could I know, my early introduction to active life having precluded all possibility of study? I was exhausted by my exertions in the forum, in elections, in politics, in the causes of my friends, before I could form any idea of such high subjects. But if you are pleased to find so much merit in one who, though not specially wanting, as you think, in natural ability, has been certainly wanting in learning and leisure, and I must admit too, in that keen desire to learn, what do you think? Supposing some one with even greater natural ability were to combine those qualifications which have been beyond my reach, to what perfection of oratory might not he attain!'

18. Here *Antonius* took up the argument. 'I quite agree,'

he said, 'with what you are saying, Crassus, and I have no doubt that if the orator understood the nature and theory of all arts and subjects of art, his speeches would gain greatly in richness of style. But in the first place such knowledge is difficult of attainment, especially amidst the many engagements of our modern life: and, in the second place, there is a real danger lest we should be tempted to give up the constant practice of speaking in the popular assembly and the law-courts. For it seems to me that we find quite a distinct kind of oratory in those men of whom you spoke just now, although I admit they express themselves with grace and dignity, whether their subject be the phenomena of nature or ethics. We find a character of elegance and luxuriance in their language, redolent rather of the polish of the schools than suited to the active excitement of our public life. I myself, I must tell you, though I had but a recent and superficial acquaintance with Greek literature, on arriving at Athens, on my way to Cilicia as proconsul, made a stay of several days there, really because the weather was not favourable for sailing; but as I was daily in the company of the leading philosophers, the same, speaking roughly, as you have just mentioned, and as somehow or other it had become known among them that I, like yourself, was constantly engaged in the most important causes, they each of them favoured me with such ideas as they could give me on the function and procedure of the orator. Among others your friend Mnesarchus also maintained that those whom we call orators were nothing but a set of journeymen speakers with ready and practised tongues; but that a real orator no one could be save "the philosopher," and eloquence itself, inasmuch as it was the knowledge of good speaking, was one of the virtues, and he who had one virtue had all virtues, and all the virtues were like and equal to one another; and therefore the eloquent man had all the virtues, and was, in fact, the philosopher. But the style of oratory he affected was crabbed and meagre, and very abhorrent to Roman taste. Charmadas, however, expressed himself with far more ease and fluency on the same subject, not by way of setting forth his own opinions, for the traditional custom of the Academy was always to oppose all comers in a discussion—but on this particular occasion what he gave us to understand was, that those who were called professors of rhetoric, and gave lessons in the art of speaking, knew absolutely nothing, and that no one could possibly acquire the power of speaking, except the man who had mastered the discoveries of philosophy.

19. The disputants on the other side were able speakers, citizens of Athens, who were conversant with politics and the law-courts. Among them was Menedemus, who was at Rome the other day as my guest; and when he argued that there was a special kind of wisdom which dealt with the investigation into the principles of the constitution and administration of states, Charmadas was up in arms in a moment, being, as he was, a ready man with all learning at his fingers' ends, and every variety of subject at his command to a degree quite inconceivable. He proceeded to prove that we must go to philosophy for all the constituent elements of that special kind of wisdom, nor were the regulations usually made in states about the worship of the gods, the education of youth, justice, endurance, temperance, moderation, and all such others, without which communities could not either exist or be in a sound condition, anywhere to be found in the treatises of the rhetoricians. If these great teachers of rhetoric included in their course this formidable array of really important subjects, why was it, he asked, that their text-books were full to overflowing with directions about exordiums, perorations, and rubbish of this kind—for so he dubbed them—whereas about the right

ordering of states, and the drawing up of laws, about equity, justice, and integrity, about the control of the passions, and the training of the characters of men not a single syllable could be found in all their writings. The actual directions they gave he would cover with ridicule, showing that they were not only quite innocent of the particular wisdom which they claimed for themselves, but did not even understand the scientific theory of oratory which they professed. The essence he supposed of oratory was, that on the one hand the speaker should appear to his audience in the character which he wished to assume; and this was a matter of personal ethics, on which these professors of rhetoric had given no guidance in their instructions; and on the other hand the audience should be affected as the speaker meant they should be; and this again could not possibly be the case unless the speaker had learnt in how many ways, and by what means, and by what style of oratory the feelings of men can be moved in one direction or another. All such knowledge was among the secrets of the most abstruse and most profound philosophy, which these rhetoricians had not touched even with the tips of their tongues. All this Menedemus tried to meet by quoting examples rather than by arguments; with his ready memory he quoted many splendid passages from the speeches of Demosthenes by way of proving that in swaying the feelings of judges or people as he would by the power of his words, he showed no ignorance of the means by which he could effect those objects which Charmadas maintained no one could master without a knowledge of philosophy.

20. Charmadas replied that he did not deny Demosthenes was a man of wonderful sagacity, and had a wonderful gift of speaking, but whether this was owing to his own native wit, or to his having been, as was well known, a constant attendant at the lectures of Plato, the question was not

what Demosthenes could do, but what the professors of rhetoric taught. On more than one occasion too he went so far as to maintain that there was no such thing as an art of rhetoric; and having proved this by argument, firstly, because we are so constituted by nature as to be able by winning words to blandish those of whom we have any request to make, and by angry words to intimidate an opponent; to set forth the facts of a case, and establish any charge we bring; to refute the statements of the opposite party; and finally, to appeal for mercy and commiseration,—this being the field in which the whole power of the orator finds its occupation;—and secondly, because habit and practice at once sharpen the powers of our understanding, and increase the readiness of our utterance; he would then quote a number of instances to support his contention. First, he asserted that no writer of a treatise on the art, one would almost think of set purpose, had ever been even moderately fluent, and he quoted instances beginning with Corax or some such name, and Tisias, who were admittedly the first inventors of the art; but instances of really eloquent speakers who had never studied such things, or even cared to know anything whatever about them, he quoted in really countless numbers: and among them, whether in joke or because he really thought so and had so been informed, he pointed to me as one who had not studied the subject, and yet as he was pleased to say, had achieved some success an an orator. To the former of these two statements, that I had not studied at all, I made no demur, but in the latter, I supposed he was either making fun of me, or was himself mistaken. But art, he said, there could be none, except where the subject-matter was known and thoroughly understood, had reference to one definite end, and was never uncertain; whereas all the subjects dealt with by the orator were contingent and uncertain; since on the one hand speeches on them were made by those who did not fully understand them all, and on the other were listened to by those in whom the speaker had to produce not scientific knowledge, but only a false, or at all events an indistinct opinion for the time being. Need I say more? By such arguments he seemed to me to prove that neither is there any systematic art of rhetoric, nor can any one, except a man who has mastered the teachings of the profoundest philosophy, be either an artistic or powerful speaker. And, while on this subject, Charmadas used to express a warm admiration for your abilities, Crassus; he had found me, he said, a very good listener, and you a very formidable debater.

21. It was with this belief that I was tempted to say in a little book which escaped from my desk without my knowledge and consent, and fell into the hands of the public, that I had known several good speakers, but up to that date not a single real orator, and I laid it down there that a good speaker was one who could speak with adequate acuteness and perspicacity before an ordinary audience from the point of view of what may be called the average intelligence, but a real orator was one who could add a charm and glamour of magnificence to the theme of his choice, and held within the compass of his own mind and memory all the springs of knowledge on all subjects which had any bearing on oratory. Granting that such attainment is difficult for us because we are overwhelmed by the calls of contested elections and public life before we have begun to learn, let us however assume it to be within the possibilities of the subject. Indeed, if I may venture on a prophecy, and judging from what I know of the abilities of our fellow-countrymen, I have good hope that we shall some day see some Roman, who, with a keener enthusiasm than we now have or ever have had, with more leisure and riper faculties for study, and with greater power of work and industry, will

after steady devotion to hearing, reading, and writing, prove the ideal of which we are now in search, and be qualified to claim the title, not merely of a good speaker, but of a real orator; though, after all, I am inclined to think that the man is here before us in the person of Crassus, or if, it may be, he is to be one of equal ability, who has heard, and read, and written somewhat more than our friend, it will not be much that he will add to his achievement.'

22. At this point *Sulpicius* exclaimed, 'It has been an un-expected, though by no means an unwelcome pleasure to Cotta and myself, that your conversation, Crassus, should have taken the turn it has. In coming here we thought it quite pleasure enough to look forward to, if we should have the chance of taking away with us something worth remem-bering from your conversation, supposing it had been on other subjects; but that you should fall into this discussion of all others, which has penetrated almost into the arcana of this pursuit, or art, or faculty, whichever it is, seemed to us a thing almost too good to hope for. For though from my earliest manhood I have been possessed with a warm admi-ration for both of you, with an affection, indeed, I may say, for Crassus which never allowed me to leave his side, I have never been able to draw a word from him on the virtue and method of oratory, though I have appealed to him again and again both personally and through the mediation of Drusus. And in this matter you, Antonius, I will frankly ad-mit, have never refused to answer my questions or solve my difficulties, and have very often told me the rules which it was your habit to observe in practice. On this occasion, now that you have, both of you, given us a glimpse into the se-cret of attaining to the exact object of our search, Crassus himself having begun the conversation, pray do us the kind-ness of following out your theories on the whole question of rhetoric in precise detail. If we can only prevail on you to

do this, I shall owe a deep debt of gratitude to your school and villa of Tusculum, and shall give a far higher place in my estimation to your suburban lecture-room than to the great Academy and Lyceum.' *Crassus:* 'My dear Sulpicius, let us ask Antonius, who not only can do what you want, but has been in the habit of doing it, as you told us just now. For myself, I admit that I have always fought shy of all such talk, and have again and again turned a deaf ear to your most urgent appeals, as you remarked a few moments ago. I did so not from any pride or want of courtesy, nor because I was unwilling to satisfy your very proper and most laudable curiosity, especially as I saw that nature had endowed you with quite exceptional and extraordinary qualifications for an orator; but I was deterred, I do assure you, by want of familiarity with such discussions, and want of skill in dealing with the traditional rules of the so-called art of rhetoric.' *Cotta:* 'Since we have succeeded in what we thought was the main difficulty, getting you to speak at all on this subject, Crassus, for what remains it will now be entirely our own fault if we let you go before you have fully answered all our questions.' *Crassus:* 'Only, I suppose, on those points on which, to employ the formula used in the taking up of inheritances, "I shall have the knowledge and the power."' *Cotta:* 'Why, do you think either of us is so conceited as to expect to have knowledge or power where you have neither the one nor the other?' *Crassus:* 'Come then, on these conditions, provided I am at liberty to say "I cannot," where I cannot, and "I do not know," where I do not, you may catechise me as you will.' *Sulpicius:* 'Nay, the only question we want to ask is, what do you think about the statement Antonius has just made? do you think that there is an art of rhetoric?' *Crassus:* 'Well, to be sure—do you take me now for one of your lazy talkative Greek friends, a learned man perhaps and well-read, and therefore

put before me some trifling question on which I am to hold
forth at pleasure? When do you suppose I have given any
thought or attention to such questions? Have I not always
rather laughed at the conceit of those persons, who, on taking their seat in a lecture-room, invite any member of a
crowded audience to speak if he has a question to ask? This
practice was started, we are told, by Gorgias of Leontini,
and he was thought to be undertaking an immense responsibility in giving notice that he was ready to speak on all
subjects on which any one wished to be instructed. Afterwards, however, the custom became general, and is so at
the present day, there being no subject, however important,
however unexpected, however novel, on which these people
do not profess that they will say everything that can be said.
If I had thought that you, Cotta, or you, Sulpicius, desired
to receive instruction on this subject, I would have brought
here with me some Greek professor to amuse us with such
discourse; indeed, it is not impossible to do so now, for my
young friend Marcus Piso, who is a devoted student of rhetoric, and a man of striking ability, and a great admirer of
mine, has staying with him a Peripatetic of the name of
Staseas, a gentleman with whom I am on the best of terms,
and who, I see, is recognised, by all who know, as the leader
of that particular school.'

23. *Scævola:* 'What is this nonsense about Staseas, and
the Peripatetics? You must humour our young friends, Crassus, who do not want to hear the every-day loquacity of
some Greek theorist, nor the stale prattle of the lecture-
room, but are anxious to learn the opinions of a man in
whose footsteps they desire to tread, the wisest and most
eloquent orator of the day, who has proved his pre-eminence, too, in wisdom and debate, not in rhetorical treatises,
but in the most important causes, and in Rome, the seat of
empire and the home of glory. For my part, though I have

always seen in you my ideal of an orator, yet I have never given you greater credit for eloquence than for courtesy; a courtesy which now more than at any time it becomes you to exercise, and not shirk a discussion to which you are invited by two young men of excellent parts.' *Crassus:* 'Well, well, I am very anxious to oblige your friends, and I will not refuse to state briefly, as I always do, what is my opinion on each point that has been raised. First of all—since I feel I should not be justified in slighting your claims upon my respect, Scævola—my answer is that I am of opinion that there is of rhetoric no art at all, or only a skeleton of one, the fact being that the whole controversy among the learned turns upon a verbal ambiguity. If we define an art according to the statement just made by Antonius as dealing only with subject-matter which is exactly known and thoroughly understood, removed from the sphere of mere arbitrary opinion, and grasped only by the scientific understanding, it seems to me there is no art of oratory; for all public speaking in its different branches deals with a variable subject-matter, and takes its colour from the ordinary opinions and feelings of mankind. If, however, the rules which have as a matter of fact and practice been followed by speakers have been observed and noted down by men of skill and experience, with a technical nomenclature and a scientific distribution into classes and subdivisions—a thing which I see may very possibly have been done—I perceive no reason why we should not admit an *art* of rhetoric, using the term, that is, not according to its strict definition, but in its ordinary acceptation. Still, whether there is an art of rhetoric or only the semblance of one, we cannot of course afford to despise it; though it must be understood that there are other and more important requirements for the attainment of eloquence.'

24. Here *Antonius* said that he heartily agreed with Cras-

sus, so far as he did not admit an art of rhetoric in the full sense usual with those who made oratory wholly and solely a question of art, nor on the other hand entirely repudiate such an art as most of the philosophers did. 'But,' he continued, 'I believe that an exposition from you of those requirements which you consider more helpful to oratory than any art will be very welcome to our friends.' *Crassus:* 'Well, I will say my say as I have begun, and will only beg of you not to let the public know of any "indiscretions" I may let fall. However, I shall keep a strict watch on myself, and avoiding all the airs of the master or professor, and speaking only as a simple Roman citizen who has had some experience of public life and a fair education, I shall endeavour to give the impression, not of having volunteered a discourse on my own initiative, but of having been accidentally drawn into a discussion started by you. Let me first remind you that when a candidate for office I used to ask Scævola to let me prosecute my canvass without his help, telling him that I now wished to be indiscreet, in other words, to make a successful canvass which could not possibly be done except at the cost of some indiscretion, and that he was the one man of all others in whose presence I was most reluctant to be guilty of such conduct. And now he, as fortune will have it, is here to see and witness my indiscretion; for surely it is the height of indiscretion to speak about speaking, seeing that any speaking can never be other than indiscreet except when it is necessary.' *Scævola:* 'Never mind that—only proceed, and I will take the responsibility of any blame you are afraid of.'

25. *Crassus:* 'Well then, my feeling about it is this:—In the first place, natural talents are a most important factor in oratory; those authors, for instance, of whom Antonius spoke just now, were not deficient in the theory and method of oratory, but in natural gifts. What is needed, is a certain

agility of thought and mind, so as to ensure readiness of invention, richness of expression and style, and strength and permanence of memory; and if any one supposes that these powers can be acquired by art—which is quite a mistake—indeed we ought to be well satisfied if they can be sharpened and stimulated by art, but that they should be put into us and given by art is quite impossible, being, as they all are, gifts of nature—what are we to say about those qualifications which are obviously part of a man's natural endowments, mobility of tongue, tone of voice, power of lung, physique, a certain conformation of feature and general pose of limb? I do not of course mean to imply that art cannot give a finish in some cases, for I know well enough that good natural gifts can be improved by teaching, and those which are not of the best may still in some manner be furbished up and corrected; but there are people so halting of speech, or with such unmusical voices, or so uncouth and awkward in look and carriage, that in spite of great abilities and skill they can never rank as orators; whereas some again are so gifted in these respects, so rich in natural endowments, that they seem not merely born orators but to have been created for that end by the Divine artist. A great burden of responsibility it is, surely, for a man to take upon himself, to profess that he and he alone is to be heard amidst universal silence on questions of the last importance in a great concourse of his fellow-men; for there is no one in such an audience who has not a keener and sharper ear to detect a fault in a speaker than a merit; and thus whatever there is that gives offence overshadows what calls for praise. Now I do not say this with the intention of deterring young men altogether from the study of oratory, if they happen to lack some natural gift, for, as we are all aware, my contemporary Caius Cælius won great distinction, though quite new to political life, by such moderate success as a speaker as he was able to achieve. Take another instance, Quintus Varius, who is more your contemporary; you all know that he, though a man of uncouth and repulsive exterior, has gained considerable influence in the state by the same sort of ability.

26. But as we are searching for the ideal orator, we must use our powers of oratory to portray a speaker free from all possible faults and endowed with every possible merit. For though it is undeniable that the large number of lawsuits, the great variety of public questions, the illiterate masses who make the audience of our public speakers, offer a field to even the most defective orators, we will not for that reason despair of finding what we want. On the same principle in those arts whose aim is not some immediately practical utility, but some less restricted intellectual enjoyment, how critically, with what a nice fastidiousness do we pass judgment! There are no lawsuits or points of contention which force us to tolerate bad actors on the stage in the same way as we tolerate indifferent speakers in the courts. The real orator, therefore, must use all care and diligence, not merely to satisfy those whom he is bound to satisfy, but also to win the admiration of those who are in a position to judge impartially. And if you want to know, as we are all friends together, I will frankly tell you what I feel—a secret I have hitherto always kept to myself on principle. My belief is, that even the best speakers, even those who have the best language always at their command, unless they rise to speak with some misgivings and feel some nervousness in the exordium of their speech are wanting, if I may say so, in proper modesty. I am assuming of course an impossible case, for the better the speaker the more painfully is he conscious of the difficulty of speaking, of the uncertainty of the effect of his speech, and of the expectations of an audience. A speaker on the other hand who can deliver nothing

worthy of the occasion, worthy of his profession, worthy of the attention of his fellow-men, he, however nervous he may be while speaking, also seems to me wanting in modesty. For it is not by feeling ashamed of ourselves, but by refusing to do what is unseemly, that we ought to avoid the reproach of immodesty. Any one who under such circumstances feels no shame—and such cases I see are very common—not only deserves blame, I think, but ought to be liable to some penalty. For my part, as I observe is the case with you, so in my own case I constantly experience this feeling; I turn pale at the beginning of a speech, my brain whirls, and I tremble in every limb; indeed once in my early manhood, when opening the case for the prosecution, I was so overcome that I owed a deep debt of gratitude to Quintus Maximus for adjourning the case the moment he saw that my alarm had quite unnerved and unmanned me.'

At this point all the company showed their assent by significant looks at one another and began to converse; for no one could deny that there was in Crassus a quite indescribable modesty, which, however, so far from being any drawback to his eloquence was really a help to it, as being a testimony to his sincerity.

27. Then *Antonius* resumed the conversation: 'Often as you say, Crassus, I have observed that you as well as all other first-rate speakers, though none has ever in my opinion been equal to you, are somewhat uneasy at the beginning of a speech; and when I tried to discover the reason of this—why it was that the more able a speaker was, the more nervous he was, I found the causes to be two. One was because those who had learnt from nature and experience were well aware that sometimes even with the best speakers the result of a speech did not turn out in full accordance with their wishes; therefore whenever they delivered a speech they not unnaturally were afraid that what might

occasionally happen would happen then. The other cause is this, and the unfairness of it often annoys me. In all the other professions, if tried and acknowledged exponents have on any occasion failed to give the complete satisfaction they generally do, they are supposed to have been out of the humour, or to have been prevented by ill-health from doing their best. Roscius, for instance we say, "was not in the humour for acting to-day," or "he was suffering from indigestion"; whereas, in a speaker, any fault that has been observed is attributed to stupidity, and stupidity admits of no excuse, because no one can be supposed to have been stupid either because he was dyspeptic or from deliberate choice. Thus we speakers have to face a more unsparing criticism, for whenever we deliver a speech, our reputation is on trial, and whereas one mistake in acting does not at once expose the actor to a suspicion that he does not know his business, in a speaker any fault that has provoked criticism creates an indelible, or at all events a very lasting, impression of incapacity.

28. Then again, what you said about there being very many qualifications which an orator must have from nature or else he would not get much help from any master, I heartily agree with; and in this respect more than in anything else I much admired Apollonius of Alabanda. Though he charged a fee for his lectures, he would not allow those who he thought could not become orators, to waste their time with him, but would dismiss them and urge them to devote themselves to that profession for which he thought them severally fitted. For in the acquirement of the other arts it is sufficient to have merely ordinary abilities and to be able to understand and remember the lessons given, or enforced, perhaps, if the pupil happens to be somewhat dull. There is no need for ease of utterance, for readiness of speech, or in short for those gifts which cannot be acquired

by training, gifts of feature, expression, and voice. In the orator, however, we require the subtlety of the logician, the thoughts of the philosopher, the language almost of the poet, the memory of the lawyer, the voice of the tragedian, the gestures I may add of the consummate actor. This is the reason why nothing in the world is so rare as a perfect orator; for merits, which win applause if found singly, even in a moderate degree, in the professors of the several arts, cannot command approval for the orator, unless they are all present in the highest perfection.' *Crassus*: 'Quite so, and yet observe how much more care is taken in what is but a trivial and insignificant profession than in ours which all admit to be of the greatest importance. Indeed I have often heard Roscius say that he has never yet been able to discover any pupil whom he could unreservedly commend; not that certain of them did not deserve commendation, but because, if there was any fault at all in them, it was absolutely intolerable to him; for nothing, we know, strikes us so forcibly or makes such an indelible impression on the memory as that which somehow offends our taste. Thus, to take our comparison with this actor as the standard of oratorical excellence, let me remind you how everything that he does is done in perfect style, everything with consummate grace, everything with unerring taste and in a way to touch and delight the hearts of all. The consequence is he has long been in this proud position, that any one who excels in any particular art is called a Roscius in his own profession. To require in the orator such absolute perfection, from which I am very far myself, is a somewhat shameless proceeding on my part; for while I am anxious to have allowance made for myself, I make none for others. Indeed any one who has not the ability, whose performance is short of perfection, any one, in fact, whom it does not become, he, I think, according to the recommendation of Apollonius, ought to be summarily dismissed to do that for which he has the ability.'

29. *Sulpicius:* 'Would you then recommend Cotta or myself to study law or military science? For who can possibly attain to that complete and absolute perfection on which you insist?' *Crassus:* 'Nay, it is just because I have observed in you quite rare and exceptional oratorical gifts, that I have said what I have; and I have chosen my language no less with a view to encouraging you who have the ability than to deterring those who have not. In both of you, indeed, I have perceived great natural gifts and much enthusiasm, but those qualifications which depend on externals, on which I have perhaps laid more stress than we are familiar with in the Greek professors, are present in you, Sulpicius, in a quite extraordinary measure. For no one, I think, have I ever listened to, whose gestures or mere manner and bearing were more appropriate, or whose voice was richer or more attractive; and those who have such natural gifts in a less degree may yet attain such measure of success as to use what gifts they have with propriety and skill, and to keep clear of all violations of taste. For this is the fault which must be most carefully avoided, and on this especially it is by no means easy to give any guidance, not only for me who am speaking on this subject as a layman, but even for so great an artist as Roscius, whom I have often heard say that "taste" was the main thing in art, but taste was the one thing on which no rules of art could possibly be given. But now let us change the subject, please; and after all this discussion converse together as ordinary citizens and have done with rhetoric.' *Cotta:* 'No! No! for we are now just at the point when we must really beg you, since you would keep us to the pursuit on which we are engaged and not dismiss us to some other profession, to let us into

the secret of your own oratorical power whatever estimate you may have of it. We would not be ambitious, you know; we are quite content with such moderate eloquence as you have attained; one question only we would ask you —for we have no idea of achieving more than the little you have already achieved in oratory—since according to you we are not strikingly deficient in those qualifications which are to be got only from nature, what more do you think we must acquire to supplement what we have?'

30. To this *Crassus* replied with a kindly smile: 'What do you suppose, except enthusiasm and a lover's devotion? which is really essential to anything worth doing in this world, and certainly without it no one will ever attain to that which is the goal of your ambition. Though, to be sure, you two, I see, need no exhortation in this direction, for as you will not leave even me in peace, I perceive that you are only too eager and ambitious. But, in all seriousness, no desire to arrive at any destination is of any avail unless a man knows the path which will guide and bring him to the end which he has in view; and, therefore, since the task you lay on me is but a light one and you ask me for information not on the art of oratory in the abstract, but on my own poor achievements as an orator, I will explain to you my method, though there is nothing in it very recondite, or very difficult, or very grand and imposing—the method which in early days I was in the habit of using when it was my privilege as a young man to devote myself to the pursuit you have adopted.' *Sulpicius:* 'O Cotta, what a happy moment is this for us! For what no prayers of mine, no watching nor waiting has ever succeeded in gaining for me, the privilege, that is, I will not say of seeing with my own eyes what Crassus did by way of practice and preparation for speaking, but of surmising it only from Diphilus,

his reader and secretary, I hope we have now secured, and that we shall now learn all we have long wanted to know, from his own lips.'

31. *Crassus:* 'Ay, but when you have heard all, Sulpicius, you will not, I expect, so much admire what I have told you as think there was not much reason for your original anxiety to hear me on this subject; for there will be nothing recondite in what I shall tell you, nothing that will come up to your expectations, nothing that you have not heard before or that is new to you. First and foremost, as would become any honest and well-bred gentleman, I will frankly admit that I learnt all the common and hackneyed rules which are familiar to you. First, that it is the orator's duty to speak in a way adapted to win the assent of his audience; secondly, that every speech must be either on some general abstract question without reference to special persons or circumstances, or on some subject with a definite setting of special persons and circumstances; but that in either case, whatever be the point at issue, the question usually arising in connection with it is either as to the fact or, if the fact be admitted, what is the nature of the act, or, may be, what name is to be given to it, or, as some add, whether it is justifiable or not; further, that disputes arise out of the interpretation of a document, in which there is some ambiguity of statement or some contradiction, or which is so worded that the strict letter of it is at variance with its spirit; and that to all these varieties there are attached appropriate methods of proof. Of questions, again, which are distinct from any general thesis, some are juridical, some deliberative; there is also a third class, as I was taught, which deals with panegyric and invective; and there are certain topics to be made use of in the law-courts where justice is the object of our efforts; others in deliberative speeches which are in all cases modified by the interests of those to whom

our advice is given; others, again, in panegyrics in which everything depends upon the personal dignity of the subject. I learned also that the whole activity and faculty of the orator falls under five heads:—that he must first think of what he is to say; secondly, not only tabulate his thoughts, but marshal and arrange them in order with due regard to their relative weight and importance; thirdly, clothe them in artistic language; fourthly, fix them firmly in his memory; fifthly, and lastly, deliver them with grace and dignity of gesture. I was further made to understand, that before we speak on the point at issue, we must begin by winning the favourable attention of our audience; then we must state the facts of the case, then determine the point at issue, then establish the charge we are bringing, then refute the arguments of our opponent; and finally in our peroration amplify and emphasise all that can be said on our side of the case, and weaken and invalidate the points which tell for the opposite side.

32. I had heard lectures also on the traditional rules for the embellishment of style; in connection with which the first requirement is pure and good Latin, the second, clearness and lucidity, the third, artistic finish, the fourth, suitability to the dignity of the subject and a certain elegance of form. I had also learnt special rules under each head. Besides this I had been made to understand that even those gifts which are exclusively natural may be artifically improved. On delivery, for instance, and the memory, I had been initiated into certain rules which, though short enough, involve much practice. For it is to the exposition of such rules as these that all the learning of our friends the professors is directed, and if I were to say that all this learning was of no use, I should say what is not true; for it is of some service, if only to remind the orator what should be his standard in each case and what he must keep before him

so as not to wander from the purpose which he may have set himself. But the real value of these rules I take to be this, not that orators by following them have attained to eloquence, but that certain people have noted down and collected the habitual and instinctive methods of the masters of eloquence; and thus eloquence is not produced by art, but the art has sprung from the practice of the eloquent. Still even so, as I have already said, I would not reject the art entirely, for though it may not be necessary for good speaking, the study of it may well find a place in a liberal education. A certain course also of practice is desirable for you—though to be sure *you* have long been on the right road—or at all events for those who are entering on their career and can even at this early stage learn and practise beforehand on a mimic arena what they will have to do on the real battle-field of the forum.' *Sulpicius:* 'It is just this course of practice we wish to know about; and yet we also wish to hear about the rules of the art which you have just briefly run over, though of course these are not unfamiliar to us. They, however, can wait; now we would ask what is your opinion on this matter of practice.'

33. *Crassus:* 'Well, for my part I quite approve of what you are in the habit of doing—of imagining some case similar to those which are brought into the courts and speaking on it in the manner as far as possible of real life; but most students in so doing exercise their voice only, and that not scientifically, and their strength, and affect rapidity of utterance, and delight in a great flow of words. But in this they are misled, because they have heard that men by speaking make themselves speakers. For, indeed, there is a saying equally true that by speaking badly men very easily acquire a bad style of speaking. For this reason, in the matter of these exercises, though the constant practice of speaking on the spur of the moment has its uses it is even more useful

to take time for reflection and to speak after preparation and careful study. The main thing however, which, to tell the truth, we very rarely do (for it involves considerable trouble and that most of us avoid), is to write as much as possible. The pen is the best and most effective artist and teacher of speech; and so it well may be, for if a sudden and extempore utterance is far inferior to the product of preparation and reflection, this latter again must certainly yield the palm to diligent and careful writing. For all the topics, suggested whether by art or the natural wit and sagacity of the speaker, which are inherent in the subject of our discourse, naturally and spontaneously occur to us, as we ponder and consider our subject with the unimpeded powers of the mind; and all the thoughts and words, which in their proper places add most brilliance to style, necessarily suggest themselves as we write, and flow to the point of our pen. The mere order, moreover, and arrangement of words is in the process of writing brought to perfection in a rhythm and cadence which may be called oratorical as distinct from poetical. It is these qualities which win for great orators shouts of admiration and applause; and these no one can hope to acquire unless he has written long, and written much, no matter how ardently he may have exercised himself in those unprepared deliveries to which I have referred. And the man who comes to speaking after a long practice of writing brings to the task this further advantage, that even if he speaks on·the spur of the moment, still his utterances have all the effect of a written speech; and more than this, if on any occasion in the course of a speech he introduces some written matter, when he lays aside his papers, the speech continues without any perceptible break. Just as when a boat is well underway, if the crew stop rowing for a moment, the boat still retains its motion and way even though the beat and stroke of the oars is interrupted, so in a continuous speech, when written notes fail, the speech still maintains an even tenor from its similarity to what was written and the momentum thereby acquired.

34. In my own daily exercises when a young man, I used to set myself by preference the same task which I knew that my old rival Caius Carbo had been in the habit of performing. I used to set myself some piece of poetry the most impressive I could find, or read some speech, as much of it as I could retain in my memory, and then deliver a speech on the same subject, choosing as far as I could other words. Afterwards I came to see that the practice had this defect; the words which were best suited to the subject in each case, were most eloquent; in fact, the best, had been already appropriated either by Ennius, if it was on his verses I was exercising myself, or by Gracchus, if I happened to select a speech of his as my task. If, therefore, I used the same words, I gained nothing; if others, I even lost, since I got into the habit of using inadequate language. After this I hit upon and employed in later years the following plan. I used to make a free translation of speeches by the leading orators of Greece, and by selecting them I gained this advantage; by translating into Latin what I had read in Greek, I not only used the best though familiar words, but I also coined others on the model of the Greek, which would be new to our language, provided always no exception could be taken to them. The management again of the voice and the breath, of the limbs and the tongue, and the different exercises connected with it are a matter not so much of art as of physical labour; and in this matter it is a very important consideration whom we should take as our model, whom we would wish to resemble. We must watch not only speakers but actors also, that we may not from defective training get into some ungainly or awkward mannerism. The memory, too, we must exercise by learning by rote as

many passages as we can both of our own authors and others; and by way of doing so I see no objection to the use, if such has been your habit, of that system of places and symbols which is traditional in the schools of rhetoric. The diction thus formed must then be brought out from the training-ground of the study and the cloister into the heat and dust and noise of the battle-ground and the conflicts of the forum; we must face the gaze of the world, we must put our intellectual strength to the test, and the meditations of the student must be exposed to the broad daylight of real life. We must also read the poets, study history, read and con over again and again all the teachers and authors in all the higher arts, and for the sake of the training to be got from it we must praise their merits, explain their meaning, criticise their faults, denounce their errors, and refute their mistakes. We must argue on every subject both for and against, and we must bring out every possible and plausible argument that is to be found in each case. We must learn civil law by heart, study the statute-book, know all antiquity, we must be familiar with the usages of the senate, the constitution of our country, the rights of our allies, all treaties, all conventions, and all imperial interests. We must extract also from every form of culture a power of graceful and refined pleasantry, to give flavour, if I may use the expression, and piquancy to our style. I have now freely given you all my opinions, and the same answer I daresay would have been given to your questions by any ordinary citizen you had pitched upon at any social gathering.'

35. After these remarks from Crassus, silence fell on the party; but though all present were quite satisfied that he had said enough for the purpose in hand, yet they all felt that he had come to the end of his remarks far sooner than they could have wished. At last *Scævola* asked: 'What is it, Cotta? Why are you and your friend silent? Does nothing

occur to you on which you would like a little more enlight-
enment from Crassus?' *Cotta:* 'Well, to tell you the truth,
that is just what I am pondering; for so great was the speed
of his words, and so rapid the flight of his eloquence, that
though I was fully aware of its vigour and force, I could
scarcely follow its track, and I felt as if I had been brought
into the richly furnished mansion of some millionaire, where
the hangings were not unfolded, nor the plate set out, nor
the pictures and statues arranged where they could be seen,
but all these numerous and costly treasures were huddled
up together and put away. So just now while Crassus was
speaking, I was aware of the riches and beauties of his mind
through curtains and coverings, so to speak; but though I
desired to examine them closely, I scarcely had a chance
of seeing them. Thus I can neither say that I am in complete
ignorance of the extent of his possessions, nor that I really
know and have actually seen them.' *Scævola:* 'Well then, why
not do as you would if you had been brought into some
town or country mansion full of treasures of art? If the
things were, as you say, all stowed away, being, as you
would be, very anxious to see them, you would not hesitate
to ask the owner to have them brought out for your inspection, especially if you were a personal friend of his. In the
same way now you will beg Crassus to bring out into the
light all his wealth of treasures of which we have had just
a hasty and passing glimpse, as at the wares in a shop-win-
dow, all piled together in one place, and you will ask him
to put everything in its proper light.' *Cotta:* 'Nay, I must
ask you to do that, Scævola, for modesty forbids my friend
and me to bother the most serious of men, who has always
thought scorn of such discussions, with questions which to
him perhaps seem but the first lessons of childhood. Pray
do us this kindness, Scævola; prevail on Crassus to amplify
and explain for our benefit what he has compressed into so

small and narrow a compass in the remarks he has just made.' *Scævola:* 'To tell you the truth, at first it was more for your sake than my own that I wished Crassus would do what you ask; for the desire I had to hear a discourse of this kind from Crassus is not equal to the pleasure I derive from his forensic speeches. But now, Crassus, on my own behalf also, I ask you, since we have a few hours of leisure such as it has not been our good fortune to enjoy for a long time, not to refuse to finish the good work you have begun; for the whole question, I perceive, is taking a wider and more interesting scope than I expected, and I am very glad it is.'

36. *Crassus:* 'Well, well, it passes my comprehension, Scævola, that even you should require of me a discussion on a subject which I do not understand so well as the professed teachers of it, and which is not of such a kind that, even if I understood it ever so well, it would be worthy of the attention of a philosopher like you.' *Scævola:* 'What is that you are saying? Supposing you do think that the common and hackneyed rules you have referred to are barely worthy of the attention of a man of my years, can we afford to despise those subjects which you said the orator must study, human character, morals, the different methods of stirring and soothing the minds of men, history, tradition, state administration, and, lastly, my own special subject of civil law? For that all this wealth of knowledge was possessed by a statesman like yourself I already knew, but I had not realised that such splendid wares formed part of the stock-in-trade of the orator.' *Crassus:* 'Can you then, if you will allow me to omit many other most important considerations and come at once to your specialty of civil law, can you regard as orators those gentlemen, who for many hours detained Publius Scævola when he was anxious to be off to the Campus Martius, half amused and half

angry, while Hypsæus, at the top of his voice, and at great length, was urging Marcus Crassus the prætor to allow his client to lose his case, and on the other side Cneius Octavius, an ex-consul (who ought to have known better) at equal length was protesting against his opponent losing his case, and his own client being relieved by the folly of his opponent from a degrading verdict of fraudulent guardianship and from all further annoyance?' *Scævola:* 'Nay, such men—and I remember hearing the story from Mucius—I cannot think fit to plead in the courts, much less to have the name of orators.' *Crassus:* 'And yet they did not lack eloquence as advocates, nor did they fail from want of theory or ability in speaking. What they lacked was knowledge of civil law. The one claimed more in a statutable action than was allowed by the law of the XII Tables—a claim which, if it had been allowed, would lose him his case; the other thought it unfair that he should be proceeded against for more than he was legally liable, and did not perceive that if the procedure were allowed, his opponent would be sure to lose his suit.

37. Take another instance—within the last few days, when I was sitting on the bench with my friend Quintus Pompeius, the city prætor, did we not have an advocate who is reckoned an able speaker, urging in favour of a client, from whom a debt was claimed, the old and familiar saving-clause "for which money payment is already due," which he did not see was devised for the benefit of the claimant; thus saving the claimant, in case the debtor who repudiated the obligation had proved to the judge that payment was demanded before it had begun to be due, from being non-suited in the event of a second action by the plea of previous litigation? Can there be anything more discreditable said or done, than that a man who has taken upon himself the role of defending the causes and interests of his friends,

of helping their difficulties, relieving their sufferings, and removing their oppressions, should prove such a broken reed even in the merest trivialities of the law, as to provoke in those who hear him feelings of mingled pity and contempt? Let me refer to an instance in my own family. Publius Crassus Dives was a man of many gifts and accomplishments, but I think his chief title to praise and commendation is this:—he used constantly to say to his brother, Publius Scævola, that as Scævola could not in civil law make his performance worthy of his profession unless he combined with it a command of language (as our friend, his son, my colleague in the consulship, has actually done), so he himself had not begun to conduct and plead the causes of his friends until he had mastered civil law. Or to take another instance, that of Marcus Cato. Was not he at once the greatest master of eloquence that could possibly have been produced in Rome at that date and in those times, and also the most learned lawyer of his day? It is with some diffidence that I have been speaking all this time on such a subject in the presence of one who holds the first rank as a speaker, the one orator who commands my special admiration, though it is true that he has always despised this subject of civil law. But since you have expressed a wish to have my thoughts and opinions communicated to you, I will make no reservations, but, so far as my ability serves, I will lay before you my sentiments in full detail.

38. Antonius owes it, I think, to his really wonderful and almost unrivalled and superhuman power of intellect, that, even though he is not fortified by a knowledge of civil law, he can easily hold his own and defend his position with the other weapons of sound practical sense. For this reason we may regard him as an exception; all others, however, I shall not hesitate to pronounce guilty of indolence in the first place, and of impudence in the second. For to bustle about

from court to court, to hang about the bench and tribunal of the prætors, to undertake private suits involving important issues, in which it often happens that the vital question is not one of fact, but of law and equity, to display great activity in the court of the centumviri which deals with rights of prescription, guardianship, kinship by clan or paternal descent, alluvial lands, islands formed in rivers, pledges, conveyances, rights with respect to party walls, lights and rain-drippings, the validity and invalidity of wills, and innumerable other matters, and all this when a man is absolutely ignorant of what constitutes private property, or of the distinction between a citizen and a foreigner, a slave or a freeman, is a proof of extraordinary impudence. Ridicule surely is the fitting reward of the conceit which confesses a want of skill with smaller craft, but professes to know how to steer quinqueremes or even larger vessels. You, who are bamboozled by the mere promise of an opponent in a private interview, and put the seal to a deed of your client's, in which deed there is a clause prejudicial to him, can I suppose that you are fit to be trusted in any case of importance? Sooner, in good sooth, could a man who has overset a pair-oar skiff in harbour, steer the ship of the Argonauts in the waters of the Euxine. Further, if they are not always trivial cases either, but frequently cases of great importance, which turn on a question of civil law, what effrontery must the advocate have who ventures to undertake such cases without any knowledge of the law? What case, for instance, can be of greater importance than the famous one of the soldier, a false report of whose death reached home from the camp, which his father believed, and in consequence changed his will, and made the person of his choice his heir, and subsequently died? Then when the soldier came home, and, as a son disinherited by will, instituted an action at law for the recovery of his paternal inheritance, the case came for trial before the centumviri. Surely in this case the point at issue was one of civil law, whether, that is, a son could be disinherited of his father's property, when the father had not in his will either named him as heir, or disinherited him by name.

39. Take another instance. In the litigation between the Marcelli and the patrician branch of the Claudian house, decided by the centumviri, the former contending that an inheritance reverted to them from the son of a freedman by title of family, the latter, that it reverted to them by title of clan—surely, in this case the counsel on either side had to argue on the whole law of family and gentile title. Here is another point which I have heard was contested in the same court. A man came to live in exile at Rome, having the right to do so under condition of attaching himself to some one who should stand in the relation of patron to him, and died intestate. In this case, surely, the whole law of "attachment," a subject about which there is much obscurity and ignorance, was explained and elucidated by counsel in. court. Again, not very long ago, I was pleading the cause of Caius Sergius Orata in a private suit, my friend here, Antonius, being counsel on the other side, and did not my defence turn entirely on a point of law? Marcus Marius Gratidianus had sold a house to Orata, and had not stated in the deed of sale that a certain portion of the house was subject to a servitude; and I maintained that any incumbrance on the property, if the vendor had known of it and not stated it, ought to be borne by the vendor. And so too our friend Marcus Buculeius, a man, who in my opinion, is no fool, and in his own, a great philosopher, and has no dislike for the study of the law, somehow or other lately made a blunder under similar circumstances. When selling a house to Lucius Fufius, in the act of conveyance he made a reservation as to all existing lights; but Fufius, as soon as some

building began in some quarter of the city, which could just be seen from the house, at once proceeded against Buculeius, because, as he thought, his rights were interfered with, whatever portion of the outlook was blocked, no matter how distant. Once more, look at that very famous lawsuit between Manius Curius and Marcus Coponius before the centumviri. How crowded the court was, how keen the interest taken in the pleadings! On the one side, Quintus Scævola, my contemporary and colleague, the most learned authority of his day on our system of civil law, a man of the keenest intellect and judgment, a master of the most refined and nervous eloquence, who in fact, as I often say, is the best orator of all our lawyers, and the best lawyer of all our orators, argued the rights of the case according to the letter of the will, maintaining that unless a posthumous son had been born and had also died before he attained his majority, the inheritance could not go to a man who had been named heir in the second place, in the event of the birth and decease of a posthumous child. On the other side, I argued that the intention of the testator had been, that if there were no son to attain his majority, Manius Curius should inherit. And did either of us cease for a moment in the course of the case to deal with opinions, precedents, testamentary technicalities, in other words, with fundamental questions of civil law?

40. I might quote several other instances of very important cases, of which there is an endless number; indeed our civic status even may often be involved in cases which turn on a point of law. Take the instance of Caius Mancinus, a man of the highest rank and of blameless character, who had held the consulship. The state envoy, according to the resolution of the senate, surrendered him up to the people of Numantia as the author of the unpopular treaty with that state, but on the refusal of the Numantines to accept

the surrender, Mancinus returned to Rome and without hesitation took his seat in the senate. Thereupon Publius Rutilius, son of Marcus, the tribune of the people, ordered him to be removed, alleging that he was not a Roman citizen, because it was the received tradition that any man who had been sold by his own father, or by the nation, or surrendered by a state envoy, had no right of recovery of citizenship. If this was possible, where can we find amid all the transactions of civil life a case involving a more important issue than one which concerned the rank, the citizenship, the freedom, the whole political existence of a man who had held the highest office in the state, and that, one which turned not on some criminal charge to which he might have pleaded not guilty, but on a technicality of the law? And under similar circumstances, in the case of a person of inferior rank, if a member of an allied community, having been a slave in Rome, had bought his freedom and then returned to his native town, it was a moot question with our ancestors whether he by law of *postliminium* had reverted to his own people and lost his Roman citizenship. Again, may not a case of disputed freedom, the most important issue that can possibly come up for decision, hang on a point of law? the question, for instance, whether a slave who has been entered in the censor's roll with the consent and will of his master is a free man at once, or not till the close of the lustrum? Once again, take a case that actually happened within the memory of our fathers. The head of a household returning from Spain to Rome left in the province a wife who was with child, and married a second wife at Rome without sending a bill of divorce to the former one; he subsequently died intestate, each wife having given birth to a son. Here surely a somewhat important issue was raised, the decision involving the political status of two citizens, that of the boy born of the second wife, and that

of his mother, who, if the verdict were that a divorce from
a former wife is only effected by a set form of words, and
not by the mere fact of a second marriage, would be in the
position of a woman taken into concubinage. Well then, that
a man who knows nothing of these and similar questions of
the law of his own country, should with a proud carriage
and head erect, with a keen and eager look on his face, turning his eyes this way and that, pervade the law courts with
a crowd at his heels, tendering and offering his protection
to clients, his assistance to friends, and the light of his genius and advice to society generally, this surely we cannot
but regard as a piece of scandalous impertinence.

41. Now that I have spoken of the impertinence of such
conduct, let me rebuke the indolence and laziness of men;
for even supposing the study of the law were difficult, still
its great utility ought to be sufficient to induce men to
undergo the labour of learning. But take my word for it, and
I should not venture to say this before Scævola were he not
in the habit of making the remark himself, there is no branch
of study which presents so little difficulty. Most people, I
know, think otherwise, and for well-defined reasons. In the
first place, the old masters of legal science, with a view to
maintain and increase their influence, refused to divulge the
secrets of their craft; and afterwards when the law was published and the different forms of procedure exposed by
Cneius Flavius, there was no one capable of arranging them
methodically and scientifically under different heads. Nothing of course can be reduced to a scientific system unless
he who is master of the particulars of which he desires to
establish an art, has the further knowledge necessary to
enable him to systematise materials which have not yet been
systematised. I am afraid that in my anxiety to state this
briefly, I have expressed myself somewhat obscurely. I will
try if I can make my meaning somewhat plainer.

42. All subjects which have now been brought under scientific treatment were once in a disconnected and chaotic condition; music, for instance, presented a chaos of rhythms, sounds, and tunes; geometry, of lines, figures, dimensions, and magnitudes; in astronomy there was the revolution of the heavens, the risings, settings, and movements of the heavenly bodies; in letters, the treatment of poetry, the study of history, the interpretation of words, their emphasis and accent; in rhetoric, finally, with which we are immediately interested, invention, expression, arrangement, memory, and delivery, were at one time considered by every one to be quite separate and wholly unconnected with one another. Thus the application of a certain science borrowed from quite a different sphere of knowledge, which the philosophers regard as their special province, was necessary to consolidate the separate and disconnected material, and unite it in a systematic whole. To apply this principle then to civil law, let us define its object thus:—the maintenance of equity as regulated by law and usage in all suits and causes between citizen and citizen. We must then distinguish between the different classes of case, and reduce them to a definite number, the smallest possible. Now a *class* is that which includes at least two sub-divisions which have a certain common qualification, but differ from one another in species. *Species* are those divisions which are included under the classes from which they are derived; and all names of classes or species must be accompanied with definitions to express their meaning. A definition, you know, is a concise and strictly exact statement of the qualities proper to that thing which we wish to define. I would quote instances to show what I mean, were I not fully alive to the nature of the audience I am addressing. As it is, I will state in one sentence the object I have in view. If I am allowed to carry out a long-cherished purpose, or if some one else forestalls me

owing to my many engagements, or completes the work in event of my death—if, I mean, he makes a digest, first of all, of the civil law according to the different classes of case (which are really very few), then distinguishes the different organic divisions, so to speak, of these classes, adding, finally, the definition significant of the exact nature of each class or division, then you will have a complete system of civil law, whose difficulty and obscurity will be nothing compared with the magnitude and wealth of its utility. And meanwhile, until all this scattered material is brought together, the student may, after all, by expatiating freely, and collecting information from every possible source, fill his mind with a very fair knowledge of civil law.

43. Here is an instance in point. Caius Aculeo who still lives with me as he always has, a member of the equestrian order, a man of singularly acute intellect, though with little general culture, has such a mastery of civil law that with the exception of our friend here, none of our most expert lawyers can be named before him. For really the whole subject lies at our very doors, is closely connected with our daily experience and our intercourse with our fellow-men in public life. It is not wrapped up in a great body of literature or in ponderous tomes; for the first publications, though by several authors, were really the same, and these with a few verbal changes have been rewritten again and again even by the same authors. Besides this, to add to the facility of understanding and mastering the subject, the study itself, though most people little think it, has a really wonderful charm and interest. For if a man is an admirer of the pursuits which Ælius has brought into fashion, he will find everywhere in the civil law, in the books of the pontiffs, and in the XII Tables, a complete picture of antiquity, in so far as the original forms of words may be studied there, and certain kinds of procedure illustrate the life and manners

of our ancestors. If he is a student of political science, which Scævola thinks is not the province of the orator but of some one belonging to another class in the world of learning, all such science he will find comprised in the XII Tables, with a description of all the different provisions and departments of state administration. If he is a follower of great and glorious philosophy, I will even venture to say that here, in the sources supplied by civil law and the statutes, he has the material for all his philosophical discussions. For it is from the laws that we not only perceive that personal merit is the one thing needful, since true worth and upright and honourable toil are decorated with titles, rewards, and glory, while the vices and crimes of men are punished by fines, degradation, bonds, stripes, banishment, and death; but we are also taught, not by endless polemical discussions, but by the authority and sanction of the law, to hold our appetites in check, to restrain all our passions, to protect what is our own, to keep our thoughts, eyes, and hands, from what belongs to others.

44. People may cry out as they will, but I will say what I think; I do verily believe that the single book of the XII Tables, if one has regard to the sources and origin of all laws, is superior to whole libraries of philosophy both in weight of authority and in richness of utility. And if, as is our bounden duty, we are touched by feelings of patriotism, a motive whose natural force is so great that the wisest of heroes preferred his dear home in Ithaca, perched as a nest among the ruggedest of rocks, to immortality, what ought our love, our enthusiasm, to be for such a country as our own, which is the chosen home, in all the world, of valour, empire, and all worthiness? And before all things we ought to be familiar with its spirit, its customs, and its constitution, partly because it is the parent of us all, partly because we cannot but believe that the wisdom which framed its laws

was as profound as that which has established its imperial greatness. From the study of law also you will reap another pleasure and delight. You will then realise more easily how vastly superior in statesmanship our ancestors were to the politicians of the other nations of the world, if you will compare the laws of Rome with the legislation of Lycurgus, Draco, and Solon in Greece. Indeed you would scarcely believe how crude, how absurd, I may say, all civil law is compared with the Roman system. This is a favourite topic of mine in ordinary conversation when I am insisting on the superiority of the statesmen of Rome over those of other nations, and Greece especially. These are the reasons, Scævola, why I said that for any who wished to make themselves perfect orators, a knowledge of civil law was absolutely indispensable.

45. Let me pass now to another point. How much honour, influence and dignity this knowledge brings to those who are its leading representatives, no one needs to be reminded. Consequently, whereas in Greece men of the lowest rank for a miserable fee act as assistants to the speakers in the courts, *pragmatikoi* (attorneys) as they are called, in our country on the other hand the service is performed by the most distinguished and honourable men, such as he was, for instance, who because of his knowledge of this subject was styled by our greatest poet "a man ful riche of excellence, Aelius Sextus war and wys," and many others who, having won respect by title of their ability, exercised an authority by title of their position as jurisconsults which was even more commanding than their ability. With a view moreover to relieving the solitude and dulness of old age, what more honourable resource can there be than the interpretation of the law? For my own part from my first entrance into manhood I have been careful to secure myself this support, not merely for the practical needs of the law courts, but also

as a grace and ornament for my declining years, that when my strength begins to fail me, a time which is now coming on apace, I may be spared the otherwise inevitable solitude of my home life. For surely it is a signal distinction for an old man who has served his country in the high offices of state to be able, and fully entitled, to say with the Pythian Apollo in the poem of Ennius, that he is the source whence his own countrymen, at all events, if not "nations and kings, seek counsel for themselves,"

> Uncertain of their weal; whom by my aid
> Assured and rich in rede I send away,
> Not blindly now to try a troublous task;

for we may without fear of contradiction describe the house of the jurisconsult as the oracular shrine of the whole city. Witness the door and entrance court of our friend here, Quintus Mucius, which in spite of his enfeebled health and advanced age is daily crowded with a vast concourse of citizens, including men of the highest rank and distinction.

46. It does not need many more words to show why I consider that the orator ought to be quite familiar with public law also, which specially concerns the state in its imperial capacity, as well as with the records of history and memorials of antiquity. For, as in cases and trials where private interests are concerned, the orator must often draw upon the civil law for his matter, and therefore, as I have already said, a knowledge of this branch of law is indispensable to him, so in public causes, whether in the courts of justice, the national assembly, or the senate, all these records of antiquity, the precedents of the public law, the principles and science of government ought to be at the command of the political speaker as material to draw upon. For the character we are endeavouring to portray in our present discussion is not some bawling ranter of an attorney, but the man

who, in the first place, is high-priest of an art for which we have by nature many qualifications, though the gift itself has been vouchsafed, as we believe, by Providence alone, in order that a power which is peculiar to man as man, might be regarded not as the acquisition of our own skill but as the result of direct inspiration; who, in the second place, can move with safety even among the weapons of the enemy, by virtue not of his official wand but of the simple name of orator; thirdly, who can by his eloquence expose the crimes and wickedness of the guilty to the hatred of their fellow-countrymen and bring them within the toils of punishment, who can by the buckler of his talents save innocence from the penalties of the law, who can rouse an indifferent and mistaken nation to a sense of honour or turn them from the path of error, who can kindle their indignation against treason or calm them when provoked with virtue, who, in short, whatever may be the state of feeling demanded by the circumstances of the case, can either arouse or soothe the hearts of his audience by his words. If any one imagines that a full account of such a power as this either has been given by the writers on the art of rhetoric, or can be given by me in so brief a space, he labours under a grievous mistake, and fails to appreciate not only the extent of my ignorance, but much more the real magnitude of the subject. For my part I have, since such was your desire, thought it my duty to point out to you the sources from which you may draw and the paths that lead to them, not with any intention of guiding you thither myself, which would be an endless and unnecessary labour, but merely to put you on the right track, like a man pointing out a spring to a wayfarer.'

47. *Scævola:* 'You seem to me to have done quite enough and to spare for the studies of our young friends, if they are really in earnest about the matter; for as we are told

Socrates used to say that his work was done if he had succeeded in rousing any one by his exhortations to a desire for
the knowledge and realisation of virtue, for that, when men
were once persuaded to set their hearts on nothing else but
the attainment of virtue, the rest of the lesson was easy
enough; in the same way, so far as I can see, if you will only
enter upon the task which Crassus has opened out before
you by his remarks, you will very easily attain the object of
your desire through "the door" which now lies open before
you.' *Sulpicius:* 'Yes, we are very grateful to you, Crassus,
for what you have said, and have been deeply interested.
But we still desire a little more information from you, and
especially on those points which you touched upon so very
briefly in connection with the special art of rhetoric, though
you admitted that you attached some importance to such
rules, and in fact had studied them yourself. If you will only
speak a little more fully on these, you will completely satisfy
the desire which we have so long and so eagerly entertained.
As it is, we have been told what we ought to aim at, which
in itself is, after all, no slight thing; but we still desire to
know the system and methods of the study.' *Crassus:* 'Supposing then, since I have already, in order to keep you with
me, consulted rather your wishes than my own habits and
natural inclinations, we ask Antonius to unfold to us the
secrets which he keeps to himself and has not yet given
to the world, of which he complained a while ago that one
little pamphlet had already slipped out of his possession,
and to reveal to us the mysteries of the orator's craft.' *Sulpicius:* 'Just as you please; for even if Antonius is the
speaker, we shall still perceive what you think of the matter.' *Crassus:* 'Well then, since the burden is laid on our
old shoulders, Antonius, by these enthusiastic young men,
I ask you to tell us what you think on this subject on which
you see they look to you for information.'

48. *Antonius:* 'It is painfully evident to me that I am caught in a trap, not only because I am expected to speak on a subject on which I have neither knowledge nor experience, but because our friends do not permit me to avoid on this occasion what I always fight very shy of in the law-courts, speaking, that is, immediately after you, Crassus. I will, however, attempt the task you lay upon me, with the more confidence because I hope my experience will be the same in this debate as it always is in public-speaking; no one, that is, will expect any flowers of rhetoric from me. For I have no intention of speaking about the art, which I have never studied, but only about my own prac-tice. And indeed those hints which I jotted down in my pamphlet, I may describe not as the outcome of any theo-retical teaching, but as having been tested by actual prac-tice in the courts. If my remarks do not command the ap-proval of your excellent learning, you must throw the blame on your own importunity who have asked me for a deliverance on a subject of which I have no knowledge, while you must commend my good-nature for having gra-ciously answered your questions against my own better judg-ment and to humour your desire.' *Crassus:* 'Pray proceed, Antonius; for there is no danger of your speaking otherwise than with such wisdom that none of us will feel any regret at having urged you to discourse on this subject.' *Antonius:* 'Well, I will begin with that which I hold ought to come first in all discussions, a clear statement of what is the subject of the discussion, that there may be no necessity for a speaker to digress and wander from his subject, as there must be if the disputants have not formed the same concep-tion of the point at issue between them. If we had happened to be discussing the art of generalship, I should have thought it necessary first of all to define the term *general;* and having defined the general as the man who is responsible for the

management of a war, we should then have proceeded to speak about forces, camps, marches, engagements, and sieges, about the commissariat, about ambuscades, how they are to be laid and how avoided, and everything else which forms an integral part of the conduct of a war. Those who in all these departments have the master's mind and knowledge I should have said were generals, and I should have referred to instances of men like Africanus or Maximus, naming also Epaminondas and Hannibal, and others of the same type. If again we had been discussing the character of the man who devotes all his experience, knowledge, and effort to the guidance of the state, I should have defined him as one who, understanding the means by which a country's interests are served and advanced, and employing these means, is worthy of being regarded as the helmsman of the state and the initiator of the national policy; and I should have cited as instances Publius Lentulus, the famous Princeps Senatus, Tiberius Gracchus, the elder, Quintus Metellus, Publius Africanus, Caius Lælius, and very many others, not only from Roman history, but from that of other countries. If again the question had been who was to be rightly called a jurisconsult, I should have said the man who is learned in the laws and unwritten usages observed by private citizens in their social relations, who can give an opinion to a client, instruct him in the conduct of a case, and protect his interests, and I should have mentioned Sextus Ælius, Manius Manilius, and Publius Mucius, as instances of men of this description.

49. And then, to come to the study of the lighter arts, if the musician, the grammarian, or the poet were to be in question, I could state in a similar way what each of them professes, and the utmost that is to be expected from each of them. Of the philosopher, finally, who in the pride of his peculiar wisdom professes little short of omniscience, we

may still give a sort of definition; we may apply the title to the man whose aim it is to know the meaning, nature, and causes of all things human and divine, and to understand and realise in practice the whole theory of morality. Now the orator, since it is he that we are considering, I do not define as Crassus did, who seemed to me to include under the single function and title of the orator all knowledge on all subjects and sciences. On the contrary, I conceive of him as the man who in all questions, such as commonly arise in public life, can command at once language to which it is pleasant to listen, and sentiments which are calculated to convince. This is the man I call an orator, and I expect him also to have a good voice and delivery and a certain gift of humour. Our friend Crassus, however, seemed to me to go near to defining the range of the orator's power, not by the proper limits of the art, but by the boundless capacities of his own genius. For he was in favour of putting into the hands of the orator the helm of civil government; and in this connection it did seem very strange to me, that you, Scævola, should acquiesce in such a claim, seeing that over and over again the senate has taken your advice on questions of the utmost importance, though you have spoken but briefly and quite simply. If that great expert in state affairs, Marcus Scaurus, who is in the neighbourhood, I am told, at his country residence, were to hear that the influence due only to a man of his high character and profound wisdom is claimed by you, Crassus (as is implied in your statement that this is the special province of the orator), he would come here, I expect, at once, and would terrify our loquacity into silence by a mere look of his eye; for though he is by no means contemptible as a speaker, he relies more on his sagacity in high matters of state than on any oratorical skill. And then again, given that a man has ability in both directions, it does not follow either that the leader in the councils of the nation and the good senator is simply for that reason an orator; or that the able and eloquent orator, if he is also an authority on state-administration, has acquired that knowledge by his ability as a speaker. There is really little in common between these two faculties; indeed they are quite distinct and separate one from the other; nor did Marcus Cato, Publius Africanus, Quintus Metellus, and Caius Lælius, who were all real orators, employ the same means to improve their own eloquence and to exalt the honour of their country.

50. There is nothing, you know, either in the nature of things, or in any law or tradition, to prevent any individual mastering more than one branch of knowledge. And for this reason it does not follow because Pericles was the greatest orator of his time at Athens, and at the same time the guiding spirit in the councils of the nation for many years, that we ought therefore to consider both these faculties to be characteristic of the same individual and the same branch of knowledge. Nor, again, because Publius Crassus was at once an orator and learned in the law, does it follow that a faculty of speaking implies also a knowledge of civil law. For if a combination, in any one man, of excellence in some special branch of knowledge or faculty with skill in some other branch, is to force us to the conclusion that the additional accomplishment is an essential element in that in which he shows his excellence, then we may on that principle assert that to play well at ball or backgammon is one of the characteristics of the lawyer, since Publius Mucius was an excellent hand at both these games. And by parity of reasoning we may say that those philosophers whom the Greeks call physicists were also poets, since Empedocles the physicist was the author of a noble poem. Why, not even the moral philosophers, who claim not only their special subject, but all others, as their own by title of possession,

go so far as to assert that geometry or music is part of the equipment of the philosopher because of the universal admission that Plato had exceptional attainments in both. And, surely, if we are still determined to credit the orator with all accomplishments, it is less objectionable to limit our statement of his merits thus:—since the faculty of speaking should not be arid or unadorned, but flavoured or relieved by a certain charm of variety and diversity, the ideal orator may be expected to have heard much, and to have seen much, to have expatiated freely in the region of thought and reflection and in the field of literature, though not to have harvested the fruits as his own possessions, but to have enjoyed them by the kindness of others. For I quite admit that in his profession he must show himself a man of parts, in no subject a mere novice or a fool; he must have made excursions into all subjects and be a stranger in none.

51. Nor, again, am I much disconcerted by what you said just now with a moving air of passion, such as we are familiar with in the philosophers, that no speaker can possibly excite the feelings of his audience or allay their excitement (this being the sphere in which the real force and greatness of the orator is most truly seen), except one who has a thorough understanding of all the laws of nature, the character and motives of men, and that this implies that a knowledge of philosophy is absolutely indispensable to the orator; a pursuit in which we know that men even of the highest abilities and most abundant leisure have spent their whole lives. Now I have no wish to make little of the wide learning of these men, or to depreciate the greatness of the subject; on the contrary, I have an immense admiration for both. But for us who take an active part in the politics of this great nation, it is enough to have such knowledge and use such language about the emotions as is not inconsistent with the ordinary ways of men. What great and powerful

speaker, if he wished to arouse the anger of the judge against an opponent, ever hesitated for a moment, simply because he did not know what anger was, whether it was a passion of the mind or a desire to avenge a wrong? Or who, when desirous of stirring and awaking the other emotions either in a jury or a popular audience, ever indulged in the commonplaces of the philosophers? some of whom maintain that the mind ought to be entirely free from passion, and that those who would arouse passion in the breasts of a jury are guilty of an abominable crime; while others, who affect a greater tolerance and a closer sympathy with the realities of life, maintain that such feelings ought to be very slight or rather mere passing moods. The language of the orator, however, is directed to exaggerating and intensifying the horror of those evils which in ordinary life are regarded as ills to be avoided, and in the same way to magnifying and enhancing the value of those good things which are popularly regarded as blessings to be desired. He does not wish to appear such a profound philosopher in a world of fools as that his audience will either think him a wretched pedant of a Greek, or else, even supposing they greatly applaud his ability, will, while they wonder at the speaker's learning, feel annoyed at being so ignorant themselves. But he is so familiar with all the by-ways of their minds; he touches so skilfully all the stops of human thought and feeling, that he has no need for the definitions of philosophy, or to waste words in discussing whether the *summum bonum* is a mental or physical good; whether it is to be defined in terms of virtue or of pleasure, or whether it may not consist in an union and combination of the two; or whether, again, as some have held, nothing can be known with certainty, nothing be absolutely understood and apprehended. On all such questions, I admit, great and varied learning has been expended, and there is a large number of conflicting and interesting theories; but it is something else, something very different, Crassus, of which we are in search. What we want is a man of clear intelligence, of good parts both natural and acquired, able to detect with unerring sagacity what are the thoughts, feelings, opinions, and expectations of his own fellow-citizens, or any audience of men whom he wishes to convince by the power of his words.

52. He must have his finger on the pulse of every class, age, and rank, and must divine the thoughts and feelings of those before whom he is going to speak, or is likely to have to do so. But the writings of the philosophers let him reserve for his delight against such a time of quiet retirement as we are now enjoying at Tusculum, that he may not be tempted to borrow from Plato, if at any time he has to speak on justice and honesty. For Plato, when he felt called upon to give expression to his theories on these subjects, portrayed in his pages a quite imaginary state; so utterly at variance with ordinary life and social manners was his conception of what ought to be said on the question of justice. Why, if his theories held good among nations and communities, who would have allowed a citizen of the highest repute and distinction, a leading statesmen like you, Crassus, to say what you did at a mass meeting of your fellow-countrymen?—"Deliver us from our miseries; deliver us from the jaws of those whose cruelty can be satiated only with our blood; suffer us not to be the slaves of any, save of you who form the nation, whose slaves we may and ought to be." I say nothing about the "miseries" in which, according to the philosophers, the true man cannot be involved; I say nothing about the "jaws" from which you desire to be "delivered" that your blood may not be sucked out of you by an unjust sentence, which they say cannot be passed upon the philosopher; but "slaves,"—that not only you, but the whole senate, whose cause you were then pleading, were slaves,

how durst you say that? Can virtue be a slave, Crassus, if we are to believe those whose teachings you include in the province of the orator—virtue which alone and always is free, and which, even though our bodies were taken prisoners in war or fettered in chains, must even so maintain its rights and its complete and untrammelled liberty of action? Your last words, however, that the senate not only "may" but "ought to be" the slaves of the nation, is there any philosophy, however easy-going and indifferent, however sensuous and hedonistic, that could possibly sanction the sentiment of the senate being the slaves of the nation—the senate to which the nation itself has intrusted the reins of government for its own better guidance and control?

53. Consequently, though I myself thought your speech was most admirable, Publius Rutilius Rufus, who is a most devoted student of philosophy, used to say it was not merely injudicious, but absolutely and scandalously immoral. He also used to find very grave fault with Servius Galba (whom he said he could very well remember) for having appealed to the feelings of the populace when Lucius Scribonius was moving for a criminal inquiry into his conduct, and Marcus Cato, his stern and implacable rival, had spoken of him in harsh and violent language before the national assembly. The actual speech Cato published afterwards in his *Origines*. Well, Rutilius found fault with Galba because he all but lifted on to his shoulders his ward Quintus, the son of his kinsman Caius Sulpicius Gallus, that the sight of him might move the populace to tears by awakening their recollections of the boy's illustrious father, and commended his own two little sons to the protection of the nation, and then, as if he were making his will on the eve of battle without the due formalities of law, declared that he named the Roman people as the guardians of their orphanhood. Thus, though Galba was at the time labouring

under a cloud of unpopularity and universal hatred, he won
a verdict of acquittal, Rutilius used to assert, by these moving tricks of tragedy; and I find it stated in Cato's book in
so many words, "that he would have been brought to justice
if it had not been for the children and the tears." Such proceedings Rutilius severely censured; and exile or death, he
used to say, was preferable to such abject humiliation. Nor
did he merely say so; it was his honest conviction and he
acted up to it. For though the man was, as you all know, a
model of innocence, and though there was not a more upright or a purer citizen in Rome, he not only refused to
appeal to the mercy of his judges, but would not even have
his cause pleaded with greater eloquence or at greater
length than the simple facts of the case allowed. A mere
fraction of his defence was intrusted to our friend Cotta,
though a most able young advocate, and own sister's son
of the accused. Some portion also of the case was conducted
by Quintus Mucius, after his manner, without any parade
of eloquence, in terse and perspicuous language. Whereas,
if you had spoken on the occasion, Crassus, you who were
just now saying that the orator must draw on the discussions of the philosophers to supply himself with matter for
his speeches, and if you had been allowed to plead for Rutilius, not in the style of the philosophers, but in your own,
why, then, however infamous his judges had been—and
infamous indeed they were, plague-spots on society and
worthy of condign punishment—yet even so, the force of
your eloquence would have plucked the spirit of cruelty
out of their very hearts' core. As it is, the country has lost
the services of this worthy man, because his cause was
pleaded on principles applicable to proceedings in Plato's
imaginary commonwealth. Not one of his supporters gave
vent to groan or exclamation, not one felt any grief, not one
protested, not one invoked the honour of the state, not one

asked for mercy; in a word, not one even stamped his foot in court, for fear, I suppose, of some one carrying tales to the Stoics.

54. Here, in a past consul of Rome, we have repeated the old story of Socrates, who, being the wisest of men, and having led a perfectly blameless life, adopted such a line of defence when on trial for his life, that he might well have been the instructor or master of his judges instead of a prisoner at the bar, dependent on their mercy. Besides this, when that most accomplished orator, Lysias, brought him a written speech to learn by heart, if he thought well, and deliver in his defence in court, he read it with some pleasure, and pronounced it a skilful composition, adding, however, "Just as if you had brought me a pair of Sicyonian shoes, I should not wear them, however comfortable they might be, or however good a fit, because they would be unmanly; so this speech of yours seems to me able enough and worthy of your art, but not manly and courageous." Thus he too was condemned; and that not only at the first voting when the court merely decided on the question of guilty or not guilty, but also at the second voting, which was required by law. At Athens, you know, on the prisoner being found guilty, if the charge was not a capital one, there followed a sort of assessment of the penalty; and when the judges were called upon to give their decision, the prisoner was asked what penalty at most he admitted that he deserved. When the question was put to Socrates, he answered that he deserved to receive the highest honours and rewards, and to have daily maintenance given him in the Prytaneum at the charges of the state, a distinction which the Greeks think is the greatest that can be conferred. This answer so exasperated his judges that they condemned the most innocent of men to death. If, indeed, he had been acquitted (which, though the matter does not concern us,

I heartily wish had been the case because of the marvellous genius of the man), we should have found the arrogance of the philosophers quite unbearable, for, even as it is, in spite of his condemnation for no other fault of his own except his deficient skill in speaking, they persist in saying that we must come to philosophy to learn the rules of oratory. I will not dispute with them which of the two pursuits is the superior or the more genuine; all I say is, that philosophy is one thing and oratory another, and that perfection in the latter can be attained without the aid of the former.

55. Now, I see what was your object, Crassus, in making so much of the study of civil law; in fact I saw it at the time. In the first place, it was by way of a compliment to Scævola, whom we are all bound to love, as he most richly deserves for his singular kindliness; you saw his muse was undowered and unadorned, and you enriched and embellished her with the dowry of your eloquence. Secondly, as you had spent a disproportionate amount of labour and industry on the subject, having always had a master at your elbow to encourage you in the study, you were afraid you might prove to have wasted your pains, if you did not magnify the science of your choice by combining it with eloquence. For my part I have no quarrel with this branch of knowledge any more than with philosophy. Let it have all the value you would give to it; for indeed it is, beyond all question, of great importance, has a wide range, affects numerous interests, has always been highly thought of, and the most distinguished men of our day, as at other times, are at the head of the legal profession. But are you not in danger, Crassus, of robbing and denuding the science of its own admitted and traditional distinction, in your anxiety to trick it out in a hitherto unheard-of and alien dress? If your assertion had been that the jurisconsult was an orator, and

similarly that the orator was also a jurisconsult, that would have been a recognition of two noble professions, parallel to one another and equally honourable. As it is, you admit that there can be, and indeed have been, numerous jurisconsults without that ideal eloquence which we are now discussing; but an orator, you assert, no one can be, unless he has also mastered the science of the law. Thus in your eyes the jurisconsult pure and simple is nothing but a sharp and wary attorney, a mere clerk of procedure, a man who has certain cant formulæ on his tongue, a master of verbal traps; but because the orator often appeals to the law in the exercise of his profession, you have therefore attached a knowledge of civil law to him as a sort of handmaid or lackey.

56. Then you expressed astonishment at the impertinence of those advocates who either in spite of their ignorance on small points of law made great professions, or ventured to deal in court with the most important questions of civil law, although they knew nothing about them and had never studied them. But in either case there is an easy and obvious justification. For neither is it any matter of surprise that a man, who does not know the exact form of words used in civil marriages, should be able to act as counsel for a woman who has been so married; nor, again, because the same kind of knowledge is required in steering a small as a large vessel, does it follow that the man who does not know the formulæ necessary in a demand for the division of an inheritance, is not qualified to conduct a suit for the division of an estate. So, too, as to the very important cases which you quoted, that come before the centumviri and depend on a point of law, which of all these, I should like to know, was such that it could not have been admirably conducted by an eloquent advocate without any knowledge of law? Indeed in all these cases, as, for instance, even in

that of Manius Curius, when you were counsel for the claimant, and in the suit of Caius Hostilius Mancinus, and in the
case of the son born of the second wife without the first having been formally divorced, the most learned lawyers were
absolutely disagreed on the question of law. I would ask,
therefore, what help to the speaker was a knowledge of law
in these cases where the victory was sure to be on the side
of the lawyer who had been supported not by his professional skill, but by borrowed aid; that is, not by legal knowledge but by eloquence? Here is a story I have often heard.
When Publius Crassus was standing for the ædileship, and
the elder Servius Galba, who had already filled the office
of consul, was accompanying him on his canvass (because
a marriage had been arranged between his son Caius and
the daughter of Crassus), a farmer in need of legal advice
accosted Crassus, and having taken him aside and laid his
difficulty before him, received an answer from him, very correct no doubt, but not equally favourable for his purpose.
Galba, seeing the man was disappointed, addressed him by
name, and asked him what was the difficulty he had put
to Crassus. When the man told him his trouble with evident
signs of distress, he exclaimed, "Oh! I see Crassus has answered you absently with his mind full of other things." He
then laid his hand on Crassus's shoulder and said to him,
"My dear friend, what possessed you to give the man this
answer?" Crassus, with all the confidence of the practised
lawyer, affirmed that the case was as he had advised, and
there could not be two opinions about it. Galba, however,
playfully quoted, with much variety of illustration, many
analogous cases, and enlarged on the matter from the point
of view of equity as opposed to the strict law, until at last
Crassus, we are told, being no match for his friend in argument—although he was admittedly an able speaker, but
by no means on the same level with Galba—took refuge in

authorities, substantiating his opinion by quotations from the work of his brother, Quintus Mucius, and the commentary of Ælius Sextus; in the end, however, he admitted that Galba's contention seemed to him plausible and possibly correct.

57. And after all, cases which are of such a nature that there can be no doubt about the legal aspect of them are not, as a rule, brought into court. Who, for instance, ever claimed a property under a will made by the head of a family before a son was born to him? No one of course, for it goes without saying that a will is cancelled by the subsequent birth of a son and heir; consequently there are no suits involving a legal issue of this kind. The orator, therefore, may safely ignore all this field of uncontested law, which, beyond all question, forms the largest portion of the subject. But when the law is a matter of dispute among the greatest authorities, it is very easy for the orator to find one of them in favour of the line of argument he may decide to adopt; and when he has got all his bolts in proper trim from him, he will be able to hurl them at his adversary with all the force and energy of the orator. Unless, of course—and I hope my very good friend here will not be offended by the remark—it was by help of the treatises of Scævola, or the maxims of your father-in-law, that you pleaded the cause of Manius Curius, and did not rather seize the opportunity of striking a blow for equity, and upholding the sanctity of wills and the last wishes of the dead. Indeed, in my opinion—and I often came into court to listen—you won the great majority of the votes by the polished brilliancy of your wit and by your sparkling humour, making fun of your opponent's excessive ingenuity and speaking with bated breath of the cleverness of Scævola, who had discovered that birth was a necessary preliminary to the grave, and producing instance after instance from laws, resolutions

of the senate, the ordinary conversation of society, selected
not only with skill, but with much humour and sense of the
ridiculous, where things would come to a deadlock if we
insisted on the letter to the neglect of the plain meaning.
The consequence was, the court was a scene of delight and
amusement; and what good all your training in civil law
did you, I fail to perceive—what won you the case was
a combination of striking eloquence with excellent pleasantry and charm of manner. Why, even Mucius himself,
as the champion of the legal profession, a position to which
he has succeeded as his father's son,—did he, as counsel for
the opposite party in that case, urge any plea derived
from the enactments of the civil law? Did he quote a single
statute? did he in the course of his speech explain anything that had hitherto been a mystery to the lay mind? His
whole speech, surely, was based on the contention that the
letter of a document ought to be of paramount weight. But
it is just questions of this kind that form the staple of our
school exercises, in which the pupils are taught, in similar
cases, sometimes to plead for the letter of the law, at
others for the equitable interpretation of it. In the case, too,
of the soldier, I suppose, if you had been counsel either for
the heir or the soldier, you would have trusted to the "Forms
of Legal Procedure" by Hostilius, and not to your own wits
and oratorical ability. I am sure, if you had appeared for the
party claiming by the will, you would have so handled the
case as to make us believe that the sacred rights of all wills
whatsoever were involved in that particular suit. If you had
been pleading for the soldier, you would, in your usual way,
have called his father from the grave; you would have set
him alive before our eyes; he would have embraced his son,
and with tears commended him to the mercy of the court;
you would, I dare aver, have wrung tears and lamentations
from the very stones, and have made the whole clause *Uti*

*lingua nuncupassit* (as the tongue has uttered, etc.) appear a mere quotation from a schoolmaster's text-book, instead of being as it is an enactment of the XII Tables, which you say that you prefer to all the libraries in the world.

58. Then, again, you find fault with the indolence of our young men for not learning your favourite science by heart; in the first place, because it is so easy. How easy it is, I will leave those to say who strut about in all the pride and confidence of their profession just as though it were very difficult; and you yourself, too, should have something to say on this point, who talk about the ease of mastering a science which you admit is not yet a science at all, but at some future day, if some one first learns some other science which will enable him to put this one on a scientific basis, may then become a science. Your second reason was because it is so interesting. As to this, all make you perfectly free of any pleasure you find in it, and are quite ready to forego it themselves; and there is not one of our young students who, if he should have to learn something by heart, would not select the Teucer of Pacuvius in preference to Manilius's "Formulæ for the Sale of Saleables." Another reason you give is, that motives of patriotism ought to induce us to make ourselves acquainted with the creations of our forefathers; but do you not see that our old laws either have become obsolete by sheer antiquity or have been removed by more recent legislation? As to your fancy that men are made good by the civil law, because by its enactments rewards are assigned to virtue and penalties to vice, I used to suppose that men were taught virtue—if, that is, virtue can be taught on any system—by instruction and persuasion, not by menaces and physical force, or the fear of them. One thing, at all events, we can find out without any study of law, and that is, the charm of avoiding evil. As for myself, the one man whom you admit to be capable of doing justice to a case

without a knowledge of law, my answer to you on this point, Crassus, is, that it is true I never studied the subject, but then I never felt the want of such knowledge, even in those causes which I found myself able to plead before the prætor; for it is one thing to be a master in some special branch of knowledge, and quite another to be wanting neither in appreciation nor in experience of the general usage of men in their ordinary life. Which of us, for instance, has much opportunity of visiting his estates or inspecting his farms, whether for business purposes or for pleasure? Yet none of us goes through life without using his eyes and wits enough to know something about seed-time and harvest, the pruning of vines and other trees, the proper seasons of the year for doing these things, and the proper methods. Supposing a man, then, has to inspect his estate, or give some instruction to his agent, or orders to his steward on the farming of his land, must he learn by heart the works of Mago the Carthaginian? May we not rather content ourselves with such common-sense as we all have on such matters? Why, then, may we not also in this matter of civil law, especially considering the wear and tear of our profession and the occupations of public life, be content with such equipment as will at any rate secure us from seeming to have merely a foreigner's acquaintance with our own country? And, if, after all, our services should be required for some unusually knotty case, it would not be very difficult, I imagine, to communicate with our friend Scævola here,— though the parties concerned, you must remember, put us in possession of all the legal opinions and the difficulties of their case. Granted that the necessities of our profession compel us to master intricate and often difficult problems, a question of evidence, perhaps, or of boundaries when we are engaged in a case of disputed ownership, or of mercantile accounts and receipts, is there really any danger that, if we have to make ourselves acquainted with the laws or professional opinions, we shall not be able to do so, unless we have studied civil law from our youth?

59. Is, then, a knowledge of law of no service to the orator? I would not venture to say that any branch of knowledge is of no service, especially to one whose eloquence ought to be equipped with a wealth of matter; but the accomplishments indispensable for the orator are so many, so great, and so difficult, that I am no advocate for dissipating his energies on more subjects than are necessary. No one would for a moment deny that in the matter of oratorical action and deportment the orator ought to have the gestures and grace of a Roscius. Yet no one would advise a young aspirant to oratorical fame to devote the pains that actors do to the study of action. Another absolute necessity for an orator is a good voice. But no student of oratory will, on my recommendation, give the same servile attention to his voice as the tragic actors of Greece, who not only practise sedentary declamation for several years, but as a daily exercise before playing in public, lie on a sofa and gradually raise the pitch of their voice, and then, after the performance is over, sit down, and drop their voice again from the highest to the lowest note by way of recruiting it. If we took it into our heads to do this, our clients would be condemned before we could recite our Pæan, or our hymn, the prescribed number of times. Well, then, if we are not in a position to devote special attention to action, which is of great assistance to an orator, and to the voice, which is the one thing above all others that sets off and supports a speaker's eloquence, but can only attain to a success in each commensurate with the leisure that is given us amid the round of our daily avocations, how much less should we be justified in diverting our energies to the task of learning civil law? Of this we can get a general notion without any special

study, and it also differs from the other things I have mentioned in this respect; that whereas voice and action are not things that can be picked up in a moment, or borrowed for the occasion, a workable knowledge of the law for any particular case can always be got at the shortest notice either from the lawyers or the law-books. And this is why those eminent speakers to whom you referred employ assistants in their cases who are learned in the law, being themselves totally ignorant of it—the persons who, as you just now observed, are called attorneys; though the Roman custom is far superior, whereby the statutes and laws are protected by the authority of our most illustrious citizens. Anyhow the Greeks, if they had considered it necessary, would not have failed to have the orator instructed in civil law, instead of attaching an attorney to him as assistant.

60. Again, you assert that old age is saved from solitude by a knowledge of civil law; but perhaps a man's balance at the bank may have a similar effect. At any rate, the question before us is not what is advantageous for ourselves, but what is necessary for the orator. Though, as we are taking so many points of comparison with the orator from one particular artist, I may remind you that Roscius again is in the habit of telling us that, as he gets older, he will make the flute-player use slower beats and lower notes. If he, bound as he is by a definite law of rhythm and metre, is seriously thinking of some relaxation in view of his failing faculties, how much more easily can we not merely lower our tones, but even alter them entirely? You, Crassus, must be well aware how many different styles of oratory there are—I may perhaps venture to say that you have set us the example in this matter, as you have for some time adopted a much calmer and less vehement style of speaking than you used to employ; nor does your present quiet and conversational, though very impressive, manner find less favour than your former vehemence and energy. There have

been many great speakers, such as, we are told, were Scipio
and Lælius, who delivered all their speeches in a tone only
a little raised above that of ordinary conversation, and
never with all that power of lung and strain of voice which
was characteristic of Servius Galba. But supposing you
come some day to have neither the power nor inclination
even for as much exertion as this, is there any danger, after
all your services as a man and a citizen, of your house being
deserted by the rest of the world, if it ceases to be the resort
of the litigious members of society? For my part, so far am
I from sharing in your feelings, that I not only do not think
that we must look to the number of those who will apply
to us for legal advice as the solace of our old age, but I even
look forward to the solitude which you dread as a haven of
refuge, my belief being that for our declining years no relief
is so delightful as rest. For the other aids to the orator, as I
admit them to be,—history, I mean, a knowledge of public
law, the records of antiquity, a mastery of precedents,—I
shall, if I have occasion for them, apply to my good friend
Congus, who has an encyclopædic knowledge of such
things. But I would not dissuade our friends from taking
your advice and reading and hearing all they can, and making themselves familiar with every recognised subject of
liberal culture; though, to speak the plain truth, I do not
think they will have so very much time for doing so, if, that
is, they mean to carry out in practice all your recommenda-
tions. Indeed it seemed to me that the conditions you im-
posed upon their young endeavours were almost too severe,
though no doubt almost necessary, if they are to attain the
goal of their ambition. For the extempore dissertations on
set subjects, the careful and studied essays, and the diligent
use of the pen which you very truly said is the one artist
and teacher of eloquence, all involve much hard work; and
the comparison of one's own efforts with the writings of
others, and the extempore criticism of the work of other

authors whether by way of praise or censure, of confirmation or refutation, requires no ordinary exertion either of memory to retain or of skill to imitate.

61. Your next demand was literally appalling, and I am much afraid it may act more powerfully as a deterrent than as an incentive. You expected each one of us to make himself a Roscius in his own profession, and you stated that the approval won by the merits of a speech was not comparable with the permanent disgust created by its defects; whereas my own belief is that our audiences are not nearly as fastidious as those of the actor. Thus we, I know, are often listened to with the utmost attention, even when we are hoarse, for the interest of the case is sufficient to hold the audience; whereas Æsopus, if he is a little out of voice, is hissed. For where we look for nothing but the pleasure of the ear, we take offence the moment anything interferes with that pleasure; but in a great speaker there is a variety of qualities to hold our attention, and if they are not all displayed in the highest though most of them in a high degree of perfection, those which are so displayed cannot fail of commanding our admiration. In conclusion, then, to return to the point from which we started, let us regard the orator, according to the definition given by Crassus, as the man who can speak in a manner adapted to win the assent of his audience; but let him limit himself to the ordinary social and public life of civilised communities, and putting all other subjects on one side, however exalted and noble they may be, let him devote laborious nights and days almost exclusively to this one pursuit. Let him follow the example of that great man who is unhesitatingly acknowledged by all to be the chief of orators, the Athenian Demosthenes, whose enthusiasm and perseverance, we are told, were so great that he first of all overcame his natural impediments by careful and unremitting diligence, and though he had such a lisp

that he could not pronounce the first letter of the very art which he was studying, succeeded by practice in winning the reputation of being the most distinct of speakers. Moreover, though he suffered much from shortness of breath, he effected such an improvement by holding in his breath while speaking, that in a single rhetorical period, as can be seen in his extant speeches, we find comprised two raisings and two lowerings of the voice. He also, according to the well-known story, used to put pebbles in his mouth and repeat long extracts from the poets at the top of his voice and in one breath; and that too, not standing still in one position, but while he was walking up and down, and even climbing a steep ascent. By such encouragements as these, Crassus, I heartily agree with you that our young friends should be stimulated to pursue their studies with diligence; but as for the other accomplishments of which you have made a collection from a great diversity of arts and sciences, though you have yourself mastered them all, I cannot but think they are quite distinct from the proper function and province of the orator.'

62. When Antonius had finished, Sulpicius and Cotta seemed to be much in doubt as to which of the two discourses came the nearer to the truth of the matter. Finally *Crassus* rejoined: 'You make the orator, we see, merely a sort of dull mechanic, but I am inclined to think you are not giving us your real opinion, but are merely indulging that wonderful trick of refutation in which you have no superior. It is indeed a gift, the exercise of which is a very proper one for the orator, but it is now almost confined to the practice of the philosophers, and more particularly of those who make a habit of arguing with the greatest fluency on either side of any question that may be proposed. I, on the contrary, did not suppose that I was called upon, before the present audience especially, merely to describe the pos-

sible attainments of the man who spends his days in the courts, and never expatiates beyond the necessary limits of the cause he undertakes; I contemplated a nobler ideal, when I gave it as my opinion that the orator, especially in such a state as ours, ought to lack nothing that can adorn his art. You, however, as you have circumscribed the "whole duty" of the orator within strict and narrow limits, will find it all the more easy to answer the questions that have been asked you on the functions of the orator and the rules he must observe. But we will leave that, I think, for to-morrow; we have talked quite enough for to-day. For the present, as Scævola has determined to go to his own villa here, he must rest a little till the heat of the day is overpast; and we too, considering the hour, may well consider our health.' To this all agreed, and then *Scævola* said: 'I only wish I had not made an appointment with L. Ælius to meet him at my villa to-day; I should much like to hear what Antonius has to say; for (he added with a smile as he rose) he did not so much annoy me by his strictures on my favourite subject, as amuse me by the frank confession of his ignorance of it.'

THE GENERAL *discussion of the orator's requirements in natural gifts and education is made more specific in the remaining two books, each representing the conversation of another day. Book 2 deals in some detail with techniques of rhetoric, and Book 3 with problems of style and delivery. The dialogue closes with a compliment to Hortensius.*

*In art as in ethics a discussion of principles is more philosophical than a catalogue of instances. But principles must receive embodiment, and cannot otherwise be fully apprehended. We turn now, therefore, to outstanding specimens of Cicero's actual oratorical practice.*

# FIRST ORATION
# AGAINST CATILINE

CICERO's *election to the consulship for 63 B.C. was the result of a coalition of right and center, as it were, to oppose clamant demands for greater participation in government and radical economic reforms. But discontent with the intransigence of the oligarchic group continued even after the election, and received some countenance from such respectable leaders of the* populares *as Caesar and Crassus. Under the leadership of the déclassé patrician Catiline the movement hardened into a conspiracy which looked to violent measures. When, near the close of the year, Catiline failed of election to the consulship for the year following, the conspirators settled upon a plan of campaign, the first act of which was to be the assassination of Cicero on the morning of November 6. Cicero was warned in time and took precautions. The following morning (November 7, 63) he delivered the First Catilinarian in the senate, with Catiline himself present.*

**1.** How much further, <u>Catilina,</u> will you carry your abuse of our forbearance? <u>How much longer will your reckless temper baffle our restraint?</u> What bounds will you set to this display of your uncontrolled audacity? Have you not been impressed by the nightly guards upon the Palatine, by the watching of the city by sentinels? <u>Are you not affected by the alarm of the people, by the rallying of all loyal citizens, by the convening of the senate in this safely-guarded spot,</u> by the looks and the expressions of all assembled here? Do you not perceive that your designs are exposed? Do <u>you not see that your conspiracy is even now fully known and detected by all who are here assembled?</u> What you did last night and the night before, where you were and whom you summoned, and what plans you laid, do you suppose that there is one of us here who does not know? Alas! what degenerate days are these! The senate is well aware of the facts, the consul can perceive them all; but the criminal still lives. Lives? Yes, lives; and even comes down to the senate, takes part in the public deliberations, and marks down with ominous glances every single one of us for massacre. And we,—such is our bravery,—think we are doing our duty to our country, if we merely keep ourselves out of the way of his reckless words and bloody deeds. <u>No, Catilina, long ere now you should yourself have been led by the consul's orders to execution; and on your own head should have been brought down the destruction which you are now devising for us.</u>

The most eminent P. Scipio, the chief pontiff, was not actually a magistrate when he executed Ti. Gracchus for attempting some not very revolutionary changes in the constitution of the state; and are we, the consuls now in office, to bear with Catilina, when he is thirsting to waste the whole earth with fire and sword? I do not refer to cases too remote in date, such as the execution by C. Servilius Ahala's own hand of Spurius Maelius when he was aiming at a revolution. But it was once, it was once deemed a virtue in this state for brave men to inflict more signal punishments on a destructive citizen than on the most hostile foreign enemy. We are already armed with a resolution of the senate against you, Catilina, in terms both forcible and weighty; we are not without the guidance of public deliberation and the decision of this noble order: we, we alone, I say it openly, we consuls are found wanting. 2. The senate once voted that the consul L. Opimius should provide for the protection of the state against harm: and before a single night had intervened, C. Gracchus, whose father, grandfather, and ancestors were all distinguished men, was executed on suspicion of certain treasonable aims; with him were put to death M. Fulvius, an ex-consul, and his two sons. A similar resolution of the senate committed the protection of the state to the consuls C. Marius and L. Valerius: and did L. Saturninus, tribune of the plebs, and C. Servilius, praetor, have to wait a single day after that vote, before they received the punishment prescribed by the state? Yet here are we waiting twenty days and allowing the senate's resolution to lose its edge. Yes, we have a formal resolution of the senate to this effect; but it remains an unpublished document, a sword still in the sheath, though it is a resolution, Catilina, which rightly understood required your immediate execution. Yet you live; and live not to abandon but to add strength to your effrontery. I desire, my lords, to be merciful; I desire at a moment so critical to the state not to appear careless; but I am even now convicting myself of conduct which is both remiss and wicked. Even in Italy a base of operations against the Roman people has been established among the hill-passes of Etruria; the number of our foes is increasing day by day; but the general who controls those operations and the leader who directs those foes we see within the walls of Rome, ay and even in the senate, plotting every day some fresh device for bringing internal ruin upon our state. If then at last, Catilina, I order your arrest or your execution, I shall presumably have more reason to fear that all loyal citizens will declare my action too tardy than that a single person will pronounce it too harsh. But this particular step, which ought to have been taken long ago, I have certain reasons for not being induced to take at present. You will perish in the end; but not till it is certain there will be no one in Rome so shameless, so desperate, so exactly the counterpart of yourself, as not to admit the justice of your execution. Just so long as there is a single man who dares to defend you, you will live: but you will live as you live now, held at bay by the staunch defenders whom I have stationed everywhere to prevent any possibility of your assailing the state. Many eyes and many ears, moreover, though you perceive them not, will be vigilant, as they have been vigilant heretofore, and will keep watch over all your actions.

3. And as a matter of fact, Catilina, for what are you waiting now, if the shades of night can no longer veil your abominable conferences, and if the walls of your private house can no longer contain the phrases used by your fellow-conspirators? What if everything is being exposed to the light and breaking out of concealment? Abandon your design even now; take my warning; forget your thoughts of fire and sword. You are hemmed in on all sides; clearer than daylight to us are all your plans; and you may proceed to review them with me. Do you remember that I said in the senate on the 21st of October, that an army would appear on a certain day, namely the 27th of October, under

the command of C. Manlius, acting as the paid agent and
manager of your audacious schemes? Was I not right then,
Catilina, not only as to the nature of the affair, abominable
and incredible as it was, but even, what is much more astonishing, as to the exact day? I said moreover in the senate that you had arranged for a massacre of the aristocratic
party on the 28th of October, I mean on that occasion when
many of our leading men departed hurriedly from Rome,
not so much to save themselves as to defeat your plots. Can
you deny that on that very day the guards with whom I
surrounded you, and the carefulness I showed, alone prevented a movement on your part against the government?
Can you deny that you said then that though the rest had
withdrawn, you were quite content to massacre those of us
who had stayed behind? Or again, when you were confident
that you would be able to capture Praeneste by a sudden
assault on the night of the 1st of November, did you not
find that at my orders that important colony-town had
been regularly garrisoned and furnished with sentries and
watches? There is no act, no scheme, no thought of yours,
which is not heard, nay, which is not seen and accurately
ascertained by me.

4. Review now with me the events of the night before last.
You will learn that my watchfulness to secure the safety of
the state is much more persevering than your efforts to ruin
it. I assert then that on the night before last you went to the
Scythemakers' Street,—nay, I will make no mystery of it,—
that you went to M. Laeca's house; and that there you met
several of your accomplices in this insane and criminal adventure. Do you dare to deny it? What is the meaning of
your silence? I will prove my assertions, if you deny them.
Yes, I see that there are here present in the senate certain of
those who met you there. Merciful heavens! Where are we?
In what country, in what city are we dwelling? What is

the government under which we live? There are here, here among our fellow-senators, my lords, in this deliberative assembly, the most august, the most important in the world, men who are meditating the destruction of us all, the total ruin of this city and in fact of the civilised world. These persons I see before me now, and I ask them their opinions on affairs of state; and I do not even wound by a single harsh expression men who ought to have been put to death by the sword. You were then, Catilina, at Laeca's house that night; you divided Italy into districts; you decided to what quarter you wished each of your friends to proceed; you chose whom you would leave at Rome and whom you would take with you; you assigned the different points at which the city was to be fired; you promised that you would soon leave Rome yourself; you said that you had still a reason for a brief delay, in the fact that I was not dead; two Roman knights volunteered to set your mind at rest on that point, and undertook to murder me in my bed that very night shortly before daybreak. I on my side ascertained all these facts almost before your conference broke up; I strengthened the defences of my house, I posted a garrison even more reliable; I shut out those whom you had sent to greet me in the morning, the persons who came being the very men whom I had previously indicated to many distinguished friends as likely to arrive at my house at that hour.

5. Under these circumstances, Catilina, I bid you pursue the course you have begun. Quit Rome at last and soon; the city gates are open; depart at once: your camp under Manlius's command has too long been awaiting with anxiety the arrival of its general. Take with you all your associates; or, at least, take as many as you can; free the city from the infection of their presence. You will relieve me from serious apprehension by putting the city wall between yourself and

me; you cannot possibly remain in our society any longer; I will not bear, I will not endure, I will not allow it. Our hearty thanks must be rendered to the immortal gods and especially to Jupiter the Stablisher, from the most ancient times the special protector of this city, for that we have now so often eluded this brutal man, this baneful and vindictive enemy of our country: but the supreme interests of the state must not be too frequently imperilled in the person of a single man. So long as you laid your treacherous plots against me, Catilina, when I was only consul-elect, I resorted for defence to my own private precautions, not to any public protection. When at the recent election to the consulship you intended to kill me, the presiding consul, in the Campus, and the other candidates, I baffled your abominable attempt by appealing to the protection and support of my friends, without any general summons to arms. In short, whenever you struck at me, I foiled you without public aid, although I was well aware that my destruction would necessarily have involved a great disaster to the state. At the present moment you are aiming an unconcealed blow at the whole government of Rome: on the temples of the immortal gods, on the buildings of the city, on the lives of all the citizens, on the whole of Italy, you are invoking destruction and devastation. So since I dare not yet take the most obvious course, and the course most truly consistent with my official powers and with the traditions of the past, I will take a line which is milder as regards severity, but more helpful with reference to the general safety. For if I order you to be executed, there will still remain the dregs of your conspiracy to trouble the state: but if you depart, as I have long been urging you to do, the city will be emptied of your dangerous associates, the political sewers will have been flushed. How now, Catilina? Do you hesitate to do at my command what you were intending to do of your own accord? Merely to depart from the city—this is the sole order given by the consul to a public enemy. Do I mean you, you ask me, to depart into exile? No, I do not order you; but, if you want my opinion, I do advise you to go.

6. What object indeed is there in this city, Catilina, in which you can feel any pleasure? There is not a man in Rome, outside your band of desperate conspirators, who does not fear you, not a man who does not hate you. Is there any form of personal immorality which has not stained your family life? Is there any scandal to be incurred by private conduct which has not attached itself to your reputation? Is there any evil passion which has not glared from your eyes, any evil deed which has not soiled your hands, any outrageous vice that has not left its mark upon your whole body? Is there any young man, once fascinated by your seductive wiles, whose violence you have not stimulated and whose lust you have not inflamed? What? Not long ago, after having by the death of your former wife created a vacancy in your house for a second match, did you not augment that crime by another too great to be credible? But this I pass over, and am content to leave it unnamed, lest it should be thought that in this community an outrage so brutal should either have been committed or have remained unpunished. I pass over the complete ruin of your financial position, which you will know to be inevitable on the Ides next ensuing. I turn now not to the personal infamy of your vicious life, not to your private embarrassments and iniquities, but to matters which affect the highest interests of the state and the lives and liberties of all of us. Can the light of the sun, Catilina, can the breath of heaven be pleasant to you, when you know that every member of this house knows well that on the 31st of December in the consulship of Lepidus and Tullus you had posted yourself in the Comitium

with a dagger in your hand? When they know that you had
got together a band to murder the consuls and the leading
men in Rome? When they know that your criminal and
reckless design was frustrated, not by any reflection or apprehension on your part, but only by the good fortune of
Rome? But I put those crimes aside: they are not unknown,
nor were they isolated crimes. How many attempts you
made to murder me when I was consul-elect, how many
when I was actually consul! How often have I avoided your
thrusts, so well aimed that it seemed impossible that they
should miss me, by the narrowest interval, by the veriest
hairsbreadth! Your efforts indeed are ineffective; yet you do
not abandon your attempts and intentions. How often your
dagger has been wrested from your grasp! How often has
some accident made you drop it and let it fall! Nor indeed
can I tell to what deity you have dedicated and consecrated
it, that you thus think it a sacred duty to plant it in a consul's heart.

7. But at the present moment what sort of life is yours?
I will address you in terms so mild that I shall be thought
to feel towards you, not the indignation which I ought to
feel, but a pity which you ought not to expect. A few moments ago you came into the senate-house. Did a single
person in this crowded assembly, did a single one of your
friends and relations here give you any welcome? If you
know that such a thing as this has never happened to any
one within human memory, are you waiting for positive insults, when you are already extinguished by that impressive
silence? What do you infer from the fact that your approach
emptied all the benches near where you are sitting, and that
all the ex-consuls, whom you have so often destined for
massacre, as soon as you sat down left the seats in that part
of the house absolutely empty and bare? In what spirit do
you intend to accept those intimations? Why, I protest, if

my own slaves feared me in the way in which all your fellow-citizens fear you, I should feel it high time to flee from my own house. Do you not feel any impulse to flee from the city? And if I saw myself exposed even unjustly to suspicions so grave, and giving such deep offence to my fellow-citizens, I should prefer to be deprived of the sight of those fellow-citizens to thus remaining the object of their hostile glances. And do you, when your guilty conscience forces you to recognise the universal indignation against you as justly felt and long deserved, do you hesitate to avoid the sight and presence of those whose thoughts and feelings you so bitterly offend? If your own parents were afraid of you and hated you, and you could not conciliate them by any expedients, you would probably withdraw to some place far from their sight. At the present moment your country, which is the common mother of us all, hates you and fears you and has long been convinced that your one thought is to work some murderous treason against her. Will you not then quail before her authority, will you not submit to her decision, will you not fear her power to punish? Your country, Catilina, pleads with you thus, and appeals with mute eloquence: "For several years now no crime has been committed without your help, no scandal has arisen in which you have not been implicated; you only have escaped scot-free and gone unpunished after killing many of my citizens, after persecuting and plundering my allies; you have been strong enough not only to despise my legal and judicial system, but even to destroy the one and disregard the other. Your earlier crimes, intolerable as they were, I tolerated as best I could: but now it is not tolerable that I should be in a perfect fever of alarm at you alone, that even the slightest sound should arouse my fear of Catilina, and that it should appear impossible for any design to be formed against me in which your evil mind is not concerned. Quit the scene then, and deliver me from these apprehensions. If they are well-founded, withdraw that I may not be utterly destroyed; if they are groundless, go that I may at last cease to be apprehensive."

8. If Rome, as I have said, should appeal to you in this fashion, ought she not to prevail with you, even if she cannot resort to force? Or again, what of your voluntary surrender of yourself to custody? What of your statement that for the sake of avoiding suspicion you were willing to live in M. Lepidus's house? Yes, and when he would not receive you, you actually dared to come to me, and you asked me to keep you safe at my own house! When you received the same answer from me, namely that I could not with safety be within the same four walls as you, since I found it sufficiently dangerous to be within the walls of the same town, you went to Q. Metellus the praetor. Rebuffed by him you tried to obtain lodgings with that worthy member of your guild, M. Marcellus, whom you naturally supposed would be of all men the most careful in watching you, the most wary in suspecting your movements, and the most strenuous in dealing with them! But what do you think should be the distance between the State Prison and the man who has actually pronounced himself to be deserving of confinement in a private house? Under these circumstances, Catilina, do you hesitate, if you cannot resign yourself to death, to depart to distant lands, and there spend in lonely exile the life which you have barely saved from many justly-deserved punishments?

"No," you say, "you must put the question to the senate." That is the demand you formulate; and you assert that, if this house formally resolves that it desires you to go into exile, you will obey its wishes. But I will not put this question to the senate; to do so would be foreign to my usual custom; I will however make you understand what the senators think of your position. Yes, Catilina, quit the city; deliver Rome from apprehension; go indeed into exile, if you are waiting for that word. What is it, Catilina? Do you not heed, do you not mark the silence of the house? Their silence denotes consent. Why do you wait for them to express their sanction in words, when you can see by their silence the nature of their wishes? If I had used this language to my excellent young friend P. Sestius, or to the gallant M. Marcellus, the senate would have been amply justified in laying violent hands upon me, consul as I am, here in this very temple. But in your case, Catilina, their calmness indicates their approval, their tolerance implies their deliberate assent, and their silence is equivalent to loud denunciation of you. Nor is it only these senators whose resolutions you of course regard with affection, though you hold their lives so cheap, who feel thus, but their feeling is shared by those honourable and virtuous Roman Knights and all the other gallant citizens who stand round about the senate, whose numbers you could observe, whose enthusiasm you could mark, and whose expressions you could hear not long ago. For long past I have hardly been able to keep back their hands and their swords from your person; and I can easily induce them when once you turn your back on all that you have long been intending to destroy, to escort you on your way even to the gates of Rome.

9. Yet why do I speak? Is it possible that anything can influence a man like you? Is it possible that a man like you will ever reform? That you will ever turn your thoughts to flight? That you will ever contemplate exile? Would indeed that heaven might inspire you with such a thought! Though I see clearly, if you are alarmed at my words and make up your mind to go into exile, what a storm of unpopularity it will bring down upon my head, if not at the present

moment while the memory of your crimes is still fresh, at any rate in future ages: but it is well worth while, if only the disastrous consequences are confined to my private fortunes, and do not involve results which are dangerous to the state. Still one ought not to demand that you, being such as you are, should be distressed by your own vices, that you should dread the penalties of the law, and sacrifice yourself to the interests of the state; no, Catilina, you are not the man ever to have been withheld from baseness by shame, from peril by alarm, or from recklessness by reason. Therefore, as I have often told you, leave this place; and if I am, as you proclaim, your personal enemy, and you wish to excite odium against me, proceed straightway into exile. I shall hardly be able to endure what men will say of me, if you take that step; I shall hardly be able to bear the crushing unpopularity which will descend upon the consul at whose command you will have gone into exile. If however you prefer to promote my honour and renown, leave the city attended by your savage gang, join Manlius, call to arms the disloyal among your fellow-countrymen, separate yourself from the loyal, declare war on your fatherland, and lead on in triumph your traitorous banditti; and you will make it clear that I did not throw you into the arms of strangers, but merely urged you to join your friends. And yet why should I urge you at all, when I know that you have already sent men forward to await you under arms at the Forum of Aurelius? When I know that you have a day settled and arranged with Manlius? When I know that you have even sent on in front the silver eagle, which I trust will be a bird of evil and deadly omen to you and all your friends, which was enshrined in your house in the secret chamber of your crimes? Have you sent it on that you may the longer be deprived of the idol which you always worshipped when you were bent on a murderous errand, on whose altar your unhallowed hand was often laid before it was directed against the lives of your fellow-citizens? 10. Yes, you will go at last to the place whither your unrestrained and rabid greed has long been dragging you: nor indeed does the step cause you any sorrow, but rather a sort of inconceivable gratification. For an adventure insane as this has nature produced you, your deliberate choice trained you, and fortune preserved you. Never have you fixed your affections on peace, nor even on any war that was not wholly abominable. You have obtained the aid of a disloyal gang composed of men desperate and altogether abandoned, not only by Fortune but even by Hope. Among them what raptures you will enjoy! What thrills of excitement you will feel! In what pleasures you will revel, when you know that in the whole number of your followers you will not hear or see a single honest man! To the promotion of your efficiency for a life like this have been devoted the laborious exertions, of which we are informed, your crouchings on the ground not only to be ready for filthy intrigues but even to perpetrate crimes, your watchings and lurkings not merely against sleeping husbands but also against the property of peaceable men. You have now a field for the display of your vaunted power to endure hunger, cold, and deprivation of all the means of life; but you will soon find yourself succumb. When I defeated your efforts to obtain the consulship, I effected this much: I obliged you to attack Rome from without as an exile rather than persecute her from within as consul: and I made your criminal schemes more correctly to be described as brigandage than as a civil war.

11. Now therefore, my lords, that I may solemnly purge myself of a certain not altogether unfair accusation which my country brings against me, give, I beg you, your earnest

attention to my words and commit them faithfully to your innermost hearts. If, in fact, my native land, which is much dearer to me than my life, if all Italy, if the whole state were to address me in these words: "M. Tullius, what do your actions mean? Do you intend in dealing with this man, whom you have ascertained to be a public enemy, whom you see will be the leader in the war, whom you know the enemy's forces are expecting as their general, who is the source of the crime, the head of the conspiracy, the author of the plan to raise the slaves and desperate citizens, do you intend to let this man quit the city, and so lead people to think that you have not so much set him free to quit the city as set him free to attack the city? Will you not rather issue orders for him to be thrown into chains, led at once to execution, punished with the utmost rigour of the law? What indeed is there to hinder such a course? The traditions of the past? But there have been very many instances in my history in which even private persons have inflicted the penalty of death on citizens of dangerous character. Or possibly the laws which have been enacted to regulate the infliction of punishment on Roman citizens? But never in this city have those who have forsworn their allegiance been held to retain the rights of citizens. Or are you afraid of the dislike of posterity? If so, you are displaying exemplary gratitude to the Roman people, who raised you, a man known only by your own career and not recommended by any ancestral distinctions, with such rapidity through all the stages of official rank to the highest magisterial power, if for fear of unpopularity or some personal risk you neglect to secure the safety of your fellow-citizens. But if you are afraid of unpopularity, is the unpopularity arising from a display of severity and courage more deeply to be feared than that which is earned by weakness and treachery? Or when Italy is being devastated by war, when cities are ravaged and houses burn, do you imagine that you will not then be exposed to a very furnace of unpopularity?"

12. To this most sacred appeal from my country and to the unexpressed thoughts of those individuals whose feelings are the same, I will give my answer briefly. For my part, if I judged it the best policy, my lords, to punish Catilina with death, I would not have allowed that ruffian the enjoyment of another hour of life. In fact, if men of the highest rank and reputation incurred no stain of guilt from the blood of Saturninus and the Gracchi and Flaccus and many more before them, nay, if they even ennobled themselves by shedding it, I certainly had no reason to fear that the execution of this murderous traitor would transmit any feeling of hatred against me to future ages: and even if I were imminently threatened with such odium, I was always inclined to regard the unpopularity which is the result of virtuous conduct as distinction and not unpopularity. Though it is true there were some persons even in this house, who either do not see the dangers which threaten us or else pretend not to see what they do in fact perceive; men who encouraged Catilina's aims by the feebleness of their sentiments, and strengthened the growing conspiracy by declining to believe in its existence: men under whose influence many persons, the inexperienced as well as the disaffected, if I had proceeded against the traitor, would have called my action cruel and despotic. Now however I am convinced that if the wretch finds his way to his intended destination, the camp of Manlius, no one will be so foolish as to be blind to the fact that a conspiracy has been formed, no one will be so disloyal as not to admit it. If however only this one man is executed, I am convinced that the plague can be stayed for a short time but not absolutely suppressed. But if he flings out of Rome and takes his associates with him, and if he can collect together his worn and wave-tossed

crew from all quarters, we shall then stamp out and utterly
destroy not only this fully-developed infection but also the
whole source and seed-bed of all our troubles.

13. Too long already, my lords, have we been environed
by the perils of this treasonable conspiracy; but it has
chanced that all these crimes, this ancient recklessness and
audacity has matured at last and burst in full force upon
the year of my consulship. If then out of the whole gang
this single villain only is removed, perhaps we shall think
ourselves for a brief period freed from care and alarm; but
the real danger will only have been driven under the surface, and will continue to infect the veins and vital organs
of the state. As men stricken with a dangerous disease, when
hot and tossing with fever, often seem at first to be relieved
by a draught of cold water, but afterwards are much more
gravely and severely afflicted; so this disease, which has
seized the state, may be temporarily relieved by the punishment of Catilina, but will return with greater severity if his
associates are allowed to survive. Let the disloyal then withdraw, let them separate themselves from the loyal, let them
herd together in one place, let there be a wall, as I have
often said, to sunder them from us. Let them cease to lay
plots to assassinate the consul in his own house, let them
cease to crowd menacingly round the City Praetor's judg-
ment-seat, let them cease to beleaguer the senate-house with
drawn swords and prepare their grenades and matches for
firing the city: in short, let the political principles of every
man be visibly written upon his forehead. I promise you
this, my lords, that in me and my colleague there shall be
found such energy, in you yourselves such resolution, in the
Roman knights such courage, in all loyal men such unanimity, that at Catilina's departure from Rome you shall see
everything that is evil exposed and brought to light, sternly
repressed and adequately punished.

With these ominous words of warning, Catilina, to the true preservation of the state, to the mischief and misfortune of yourself and to the destruction of those attached to you by every sort of crime and treason, get you gone to your unholy and abominable campaign. Then shalt thou, great Jupiter, who hast been established with the same rites as this city, whom we name rightly the Stablisher of this city and empire, keep this man and his associates far from thy fanes and from the other temples, far from the buildings and the walls of the city, far from the lives and fortunes of the citizens; and these men who hate the loyal, who make war on their country and pillage Italy like brigands, who are linked together by bonds of guilt and by complicity in abominable crimes, thou shalt grievously afflict in life and in death with punishments that shall never cease.

# FOURTH ORATION AGAINST CATILINE

DURING the night following the First Oration Catiline left for Etruria, and to quiet the general anxiety and deter the remaining conspirators Cicero delivered the Second Catilinarian to a mass meeting the following day. With his growing forces Catiline planned to strike on the day of the great slave-holiday, December 19. The conspirators were too numerous and influential to be arrested without strong evidence, and this was supplied, on December 2, by envoys of the Allobroges with whom they had intrigued. The Third Catilinarian, addressed to a mass meeting on December 3, reports the events which led up to the arrests. On December 5 the senate met in the Temple of Concord to determine the prisoners' fate. Earlier speakers proposed the death penalty, and Caesar urged leniency. The Fourth Catilinarian is Cicero's advocacy of the extreme penalty.

**1.** I perceive, my lords, that the faces and the eyes of all present are turned towards me: I perceive that you are anxious not only as to the danger to yourselves and the country, but even, supposing that danger to be averted, as to the personal danger to me. Pleasant indeed to me in the midst of misfortunes, and gratifying in the midst of sorrow, is this exhibition of your good-will; but, by the love of heaven, cast that good-will aside, forget my safety, and think only of yourselves and your children. I, having accepted the consulship, as I did, with the implied condition of bearing to the end all indignities, all forms of grief and anguish, will bear all not only bravely but even cheerfully, if only my labours may win honour and safety for you and for the people of Rome. Yes, I am the consul, my lords, for whom neither the Forum, in which all justice is centred, nor the Campus, which is hallowed by the auspices of the consular elections, nor the Senate-house, which is the asylum of the world, nor the home, which is the universal sanctuary, nor the bed which is dedicated to rest, no, nor even this honoured seat of office, has ever been free from peril of death and from secret treason. I have held my peace as to much, I have patiently endured much, I have conceded much, I have remedied much with a certain amount of suffering to myself, though the reason for alarm was yours. At the present moment, if it was the will of heaven that the crowning work of my consulship should be the preservation of you and the Roman people from a most cruel massacre, of your wives and children and the Vestal Virgins from a most grievous persecution, of the temples and shrines of the gods and this most fair fatherland of us all from the most

hideous flames, of the whole of Italy from war and devastation, let me even now confront whatever terrors fortune has
in store for me alone. Yes, if P. Lentulus was misled by sooth-
sayers to imagine that the name he bears was ordained by
fate to effect the ruin of the state, why am I not to rejoice
that my consulship has proved to be, as it were, ordained
by fate to preserve the safety of the Roman people? 2.
Therefore, my lords, take thought for yourselves, provide
for your fatherland, preserve yourselves, your wives, your
children, and your properties, defend the name and existence of the Roman people: cease to consider me or to think
of my interests. For in the first place I am bound to hope
that all the guardian deities of this city will reward me in
proportion to my merits: secondly, even if anything happens to me, I shall die contented and prepared; for no
form of death can be a disgrace to a brave man, a
premature end for one who has been consul, or a source of
grief to one who is wise. Yet am I not a man so iron-hearted
as not to be affected by the grief of my most dear and loving brother present here, nor by the tears of all these friends
whom you see seated around me. Nor can I prevent my
thoughts being often recalled to my own home by my de-
spondent wife and my terrified daughter and my infant son
(whom I think the state is cherishing as a sort of pledge
for my loyalty as consul), or by my son-in-law who stands
within my view awaiting anxiously the result of this day.
Yes, I am affected by all those thoughts; but my anxious
wish is that they all should be preserved with you, even if
any violence strikes me down, rather than that we and they
should perish together in the general ruin of our country.

Therefore, my lords, strain every nerve for the preservation of the state, look in every quarter for the storms,
which will burst upon you, if you do not see them in time.
It is no Ti. Gracchus, who is brought to bay before the tri-

bunal of your rigorous justice, for an attempt to be elected to a second tribunate, no C. Gracchus for an effort to rouse the land-party, no L. Saturninus for the murder of a C. Memmius. No, you have seized men who have remained behind at Rome to burn down the city, to massacre you all, and to welcome Catilina; you have seized their letters, their seals, their autographs: in short, you have the confessions of every one of them. They are appealing to the Allobroges, they are raising the slave population, they are sending for Catilina; in short they have formed the design that by the murder of us all no single man shall be left even to weep for the name of the Roman people and to lament the downfall of this great empire. 3. All these facts have been reported by the informers, confessed by the accused, adjudged true by you in many judicial decisions, in the first instance in that you thanked me in extraordinary terms and passed a resolution that the conspiracy of these abandoned men was detected by my energy and care, secondly in that you compelled P. Lentulus to resign the praetorship, thirdly in that you voted that he and the rest whom you adjudged implicated, should be committed to custody, and especially in that you passed a resolution for a public thanksgiving on my account, an honour never before conferred on a person acting in a civil capacity, and lastly in that only yesterday you rewarded munificently the envoys of the Allobroges and Titus Volturcius. All these facts tend to show, that the persons then committed to custody by name have been without any hesitation declared guilty by your verdict.

But I have determined to consult you, my lords, without reference to the past, as to your judgment on the facts and your decision as to the punishment. By way of preface, I will say no more than what I must say as consul. I saw long ago that great recklessness was rife in this state, that some new agitation was proceeding, and that some mischief was brewing; but I never imagined that Roman citizens were engaged in a conspiracy so vast and so destructive as this. At the present moment, whatever the matter is, in whatever direction your feelings and sentiments incline, you must come to a decision before sunset. You see how serious an affair has been brought to your notice; if you think that only a few men are implicated in it, you are gravely mistaken. The seeds of this evil have been carried further than you think; the contagion has not only spread through Italy, but it has crossed the Alps and has already infected many of the provinces in its insidious progress. It cannot possibly be stamped out by suspense of judgment and procrastination; however you decide to deal with it, you must take repressive measures without delay. 4. I see that as yet there are only two motions, one of that D. Silanus, who proposes that men who have tried to destroy so much, shall be punished by death, the other, that of C. Cæsar, who omits the punishment of death, but includes in his proposal the severities of all other forms of punishment. Both the proposers deal with the culprits with the utmost rigour, as their own high positions and the magnitude of the interests at stake demand. The former is of opinion that men who have attempted to deprive us all of life, to destroy this empire, and to blot out the name of the Roman people, ought not to enjoy for a single second the privilege of life and the breath which we all share; and he bears in mind that this particular punishment has often been resorted to at Rome in dealing with disloyal citizens. The latter understands that death has not been ordained by the immortal gods as a method of punishment, but is either an inevitable consequence of natural existence, or a peaceful release from labours and afflictions; thus the wise have never faced death with reluctance and the brave have often met it gladly; but imprisonment and especially perpetual imprisonment has certainly been devised as the exceptional penalty for abominable crimes. He therefore proposes to distribute them among the municipal towns for custody,—an arrangement which seems to involve some unfairness, if you mean to make it compulsory on the towns, and some difficulty, if you ask their consent: still let his resolution be passed, if you choose. I will give my attention to the matter; and I expect I shall discover people who will think themselves bound by their high position not to refuse to do what you determine to be best for the general safety. He adds a provision inflicting a severe penalty on the town, if any of the prisoners escape: by this he secures that their imprisonment shall be extremely close and such as these abandoned criminals deserve. He provides that no one shall be able by a vote of the senate or of the people to remit any part of the punishment of the condemned men: so he deprives them even of hope, generally a man's only consolation in affliction. Besides this he proposes the confiscation of their property; he leaves these abominable men nothing but their lives: if he had taken their lives, he would at one stroke have delivered them from many mental and physical pains, and in fact from all penalties for their crimes. Thus that there might be something to terrorise the wicked during their lives, our ancestors taught that there were ordained for the impious certain material punishments in the lower world, clearly because they understood that if these were abolished, death by itself need excite no apprehension.

5. At this moment, my lords, I see well which way my own interest lies. If you adopt the proposal of C. Cæsar, then since he has adopted that course in political life which is considered 'popular,' perhaps as he is the originator and advocate of the motion, I shall have less reason to fear an outburst of popular resentment. If you adopt the alternative proposal, possibly I shall bring upon myself a larger

amount of embarrassment. But in any case let the chances
of danger to me be entirely neglected in comparison with
the advantages to the state. We have then from Cæsar, as
his high position and the distinction of his family required,
a motion which is a sort of guarantee of the lasting nature
of his patriotism. He has realised the difference between the
irresponsibility of demagogues and a real devotion to the
true welfare of the people. I see that of those gentlemen
who are anxious to be considered 'popular,' a certain person is absent, afraid presumably of having to vote for the
capital punishment of Roman citizens. Yet the day before
yesterday this person helped to commit Roman citizens to
custody and voted a thanksgiving in my honour, and yesterday joined in bestowing the highest rewards on the informers. By this time no one can hesitate to pronounce
what opinion has been formed about the facts and merits
of the whole case by a man who voted for thus con-
fining the accused, congratulating the investigator, and re-
warding the informer. C. Cæsar, however, is aware that the
Sempronian law was enacted for the benefit of Roman citizens only; that a man who is an open enemy of the state,
cannot really be a citizen; in short, that the man who carried the Sempronian law was himself by the orders of the
people punished for treason to the state. Moreover he certainly does not think that this Lentulus, however extravagant in his bribes, having entertained so cruel and barbarous
a design for the ruin of the Roman people and the destruction of this city, can possibly be called a 'popular leader.'
Accordingly this mildest and most merciful of men does
not hesitate to consign P. Lentulus to perpetual chains and
darkness, and prohibits strictly any action in the future, by
which any one may advertise himself by remitting part of
the punishment and be hereafter 'popular' to the ruin of the
Roman people. He even adds to the penalties the confisca-

tion of the property of the accused, that every mental and physical pang may be aggravated by want and beggary.

6. Therefore, if you decide on this course, you will provide me when I address the people with a companion who is a popular favourite: if, on the contrary, you prefer to adopt the motion of Silanus, you will have no trouble in freeing me from the odious imputation of barbarity, and I shall maintain that it was by far the more lenient alternative. Although, my lords, in punishing a crime so inhuman, is there any possibility of barbarity? My opinion is determined by my own feelings: for I protest, as I hope to enjoy with you the benefits of the preservation of the state, that the sternness of my action in this case is not inspired by any harshness of temper,—who can be more merciful than I am? —no, but by a quite exceptionally humane and merciful state of mind. For I think I see before my eyes this city, the light of the world and the refuge of all nations, sinking into one sudden conflagration; my imagination pictures in a dead and buried city wretched heaps of unburied citizens; yes, I am always seeing the frenzied look of Cethegus as he revels in your slaughter! But when I contemplate the idea of Lentulus reigning as king, as he confessed that he had been led to hope by the oracles, when I imagine that Gabinius is acting as his grand-vizier, and that Catilina has arrived with his army, then I am dismayed by the lamentations of matrons, the hurried flight of girls and boys, and the persecution of the Vestal Virgins; and so, because such outrages seem to me grievously pitiable and to be pitied, I show myself severe and strenuous in dealing with those who intended to commit them. In fact, I ask whether a father, who finds his children killed by a slave, his wife murdered, and his house burnt, and does not wreak the bitterest vengeance on that slave, is considered mild and merciful rather than most unnatural and barbarous? I confess that

to me he would seem unfeeling and iron-hearted, in not assuaging his own pain and anguish by causing pain and anguish to the guilty person. So it is with us: if in dealing with these men who intended to butcher us and our wives and children, who tried to raze to the ground the homes of every single one of us and this city, which is the seat of all government, who worked with the object of establishing the tribe of the Allobroges on the ruins of this town and on the ashes of our demolished empire, if we act with the greatest severity, we shall still be accounted merciful; but if we choose to be too easy-going, then we must submit to be thought most utterly heartless in thus ignoring the ruin of our country and our fellow-citizens. Or perhaps some people thought the gallant and patriotic L. Cæsar too heartless the day before yesterday, when he said that his noble sister's husband, who was present and listening to his speech, ought to be deprived of his life, stating that his own grandfather was executed by the order of the then consul and his uncle, a mere lad, sent with a message by his father, was put to death in prison. And had they done anything like this? Had they entered into any plot to destroy the state? No! There was only a disposition to make some sort of distribution then prevalent at Rome, and a certain amount of competition between parties. And yet at that time the illustrious grandfather of this very Lentulus armed and pursued Gracchus! That Lentulus even received a severe wound on that occasion in his efforts to preserve from harm the highest interests of the state: this Lentulus calls in the Gauls to destroy the foundations of the Roman state, raises the slave population, summons Catilina, assigns the task of butchering us to Cethegus, and that of killing the rest of the citizens to Gabinius, the work of setting the city on fire to Cassius, and that of devastating and pillaging the whole of Italy to Catilina. You must be very much alarmed,

I should think, of being thought to have come to a decision too severe in dealing with a crime so brutal and abominable as this! No, there is much more reason to fear that the mitigation of the penalty will be considered a cruelty to our country, than that severity in punishing them will be taken as an excess of harshness towards these vindictive foes.

7. But, my lords, there are things coming to my ears which I cannot ignore. Expressions, which are brought to me, are being used recklessly by persons who seem to be afraid of my not having sufficient strength at my command to carry out the instructions upon which you may determine to-day. On the contrary, my lords, every precaution has been taken, every preparation and every arrangement made, not only with the utmost carefulness and diligence on my part, but also by the much more ardent desire of the Roman people to retain the supreme executive power unimpaired and to preserve the fortunes of all. All the members of all the privileged orders are present, all citizens, in short, of all ages: the Forum is full, the temples round the Forum are full, all the approaches of this temple and of this place are crowded. This is the only known instance since the foundation of the city of a cause in which all men are absolutely unanimous, excepting only those who, seeing that they were bound to perish, preferred to perish in the universal ruin rather than alone. These men indeed I willingly except and exclude from what I say; and I think that they should be classed not as bad citizens merely, but as vindictive foes. But all the rest, great heavens! in what crowds, with what enthusiasm, with what noble energy they unite in their desire to promote the general safety and honour! Why should I here mention specially the Roman knights? They concede to you indeed the chief place in rank and deliberative power, but they still claim to vie with you in patriotism. After an alienation of many years' standing from this noble

house they have been recalled to relations of union and harmony; and now the circumstances of this day and of this
affair, ally them closely to you. And if this alliance, cemented by the events of my consulship, is maintained by
us as a permanent political union, then I assure you that no
purely internal and civil mischief will ever hereafter affect
any department of our public life. I see that the gallant
order of the Tribuni Aerarii has come down animated by
equal ardour for the defence of the state: and similarly I see
that all the public clerks, though, as it happens, to-day
would have taken most of them to the Treasury, have been
diverted from their anticipations as to their assignments to
the far higher thought of the public welfare. The whole mass
of freeborn citizens is present, not excluding the poorest
classes: for who indeed is there to whom these temples, the
sight of the city, the possession of freedom, in short the
light of the sun and the soil of his fatherland, are not
more than dear, are not a source of joy and delight? 8. It
is worth while, my lords, to mark the enthusiasm even
of the freedmen, who having by their merits won the privilege of citizenship here, deem this their native land, which
certain men born therein, ay, and born in the highest positions, have deemed not their native land but a hostile city.
But why do I recount to you these individuals and classes,
who have been aroused to defend the safety of their country by the thought of their private properties, their common
political welfare, in short, their liberty, to all men the most
precious of possessions? There is no single slave, at least no
one serving under any endurable form of slavery, who does
not shudder at the violence of these citizens, who does not
desire this existing system to stand, who does not contribute
all the sympathy he dares and can bestow to support the
general safety. So if any of you chance to be disturbed by the
rumour which has been circulated, that one of Lentulus's

vile agents is running round among the small shopkeepers, and expecting that the support of the needy and inexperienced can be had at a price, it is true that the experiment has been begun and tried; but no persons have as yet been discovered so afflicted by fortune or ruined by their own bad habits, as not to desire the safety of the place of their workman's bench and their trade and daily livelihood, their sleeping-room and snug bed, the preservation in short of the peaceable routine of their lives. No! a very large majority of the shopkeepers,—I must rather say, the whole of the shopkeeping class,—is profoundly attached to peace and order. For every means of trade, every industry and source of profit, is supported by the presence of large numbers of citizens and is kept up by peace and order: and if the profit generally diminishes when the shops have to be shut, to what was it likely to fall, if they were burnt?

Under these circumstances, my lords, you will not be left without the open support of the Roman people; do you look to it that the Roman people may not think themselves left without yours. 9. You have a consul who has been preserved from very many perils and secret treacheries, yes, from the very jaws of death, not for the prolongation of his own life but for the promotion of your welfare. All the privileged orders are united in heart and mind and voice for the preservation of the commonwealth. The native land of all of us, beset by the firebrands and swords of an infamous conspiracy, extends to you her suppliant hands; to you she commits herself, to you the lives of all her citizens, to you the citadel and the Capitol, to you the altars of the Penates, to you the eternal fire of Vesta burning yonder, to you the temples and shrines of all the gods, to you the walls and buildings of the city. On the fate moreover of your own lives, of the souls of your wives and children, of the properties of all, of your homes and your hearths, you have yourselves to decide this very day. You have a leader who remembers you and has forgotten himself, an advantage you cannot always secure. You have all classes, all individuals, the whole people of Rome, to-day for the first time in a political question, absolutely unanimous. Reflect by what exertions this empire was established, by what energy our freedom was built up, by what special favour of heaven our fortunes have been augmented and accumulated, and how nearly a single night has destroyed all. To-day we must provide that hereafter no such design can ever be carried out, or even formed, by any Roman citizen; and all this I have said not to kindle your enthusiasm, which almost outstrips mine, but that my voice, which is bound to be the leading voice in the state, may not be thought to have wearied in the discharge of my duty as consul.

10. Now, however, before I turn to the question, I will say a few words about myself. I see that I personally have drawn upon myself the wrath of a host of enemies as great as the whole gang of these conspirators, and that you can see is large indeed; but I am of opinion that that band is discredited and weak and despicable. But if ever that gang is excited by the criminal recklessness of any individual till it is too strong for your authority and that of the state, still I shall never, my lords, repent of my actions and my policy. Death indeed, with which they perhaps threaten me, is the ultimate lot of all; but no one has yet obtained in life a position so honourable as that to which your resolutions have elevated me. In all former cases you have voted thanks for the good government, to me alone have you voted thanks for the preservation of the state. Let the great Scipio be ever famous, whose brave and wise policy compelled Hannibal to return to Africa and abandon Italy. Let the second Africanus, who destroyed the two cities most dangerous to this empire, Carthage and Numantia, be honoured with

extraordinary renown. Let the famous Paulus be deemed a man of mark, whose triumphal procession was made illustrious by the captive Perses, once the most powerful and most noble of kings. Let Marius have undying honour, who twice delivered Italy from invasion and from fear of slavery. Let Pompeius rank before them all, whose great deeds and merits are limited only by the same tracts and boundaries as those of the sun's course. Surely among these glorious memories our fame will find some place, unless perhaps it is greater to throw open provinces to our advance than to provide that even those who are absent may still have some home to which to return in triumph. However in one way the conquerors of external foes are in a better position than the conquerors of internal enemies, because foreign enemies are either crushed and reduced to slavery, or are made friends and think themselves bound to gratitude by the favour; but those members of the community who have been led astray by some insanity and once begun to be enemies of their country, you can never, after repelling their efforts to ruin the state, subjugate them by force or conciliate them by kindness. So I recognise that I have engaged myself in an endless war with abandoned citizens; but by the help of you and of all loyal men and by the remembrance of the past dangers (which I am sure will ever remain deeply rooted not only in this people which has been preserved from them, but even in the common talk and memory of all nations), I trust that that enmity can easily be averted from me and mine. Nor will there assuredly ever be found a force strong enough to break asunder and shatter the close alliance between you and the Roman knights and the perfect unanimity which exists among all loyal citizens.

11. Under these circumstances, my lords, in the place of the military command, the army, and the province, which I have given up, for the triumph and the other outward

signs of honour which I have spurned in order to act as
the guardian of the city's welfare and of yours, for the attachment of provinces to me as their patron and protector,
which nevertheless my work here in the city preserves as
indefatigably as it earns, for all these things, I say, and in
return for my extraordinary devotion to you, and for my
watchfulness for the preservation of the state, which is before your eyes, I demand nothing at your hands but that
you should remember this crisis and the whole of my consulship: so long as that remains rooted in your minds, I
shall regard myself securely fortified against all assaults.
But if my hopes are destined to be falsified and defeated by
disloyal violence, I commend to you my infant son, who
will surely find protection enough not only to secure his
safety but even to advance him to honour, if you but remember that he is the son of the man who has preserved all
that you hold dear, alone and at his own risk. Wherefore
come to a decision with care, as you have determined to do,
and with courage, as to the supreme welfare of yourselves
and of the Roman people, as to your wives and children, as
to your altars and hearths, your sanctuaries and temples,
the buildings and homes of the whole city, as to your sovereignty and your liberty, the safety of Italy, the whole
commonwealth of Rome. You have a consul who will not
hesitate to obey your instructions, and who is able to uphold your decisions as long as he lives and to take upon himself the entire responsibility.

# FOR CAELIUS

THE DEFENSE OF CAELIUS *is outstanding among Cicero's speeches for its malicious wit, its classic apology of wild-oat-sowing, and the historical interest of the personalities involved. The summation (of which the present speech is a revision for publication) must have been delivered on April 4, 56 B.C., on the first day of the festival of the Great Mother. The chief prosecutor Atratinus, who was only seventeen at the time, had a double motive for instituting proceedings: Caelius had not only accused his father, but had preceded himself in the affections of Clodia, "the Medea of the Palatine." Cicero doubtless undertook the defense to avenge himself on Clodia and her brother Publius Clodius, who had caused his exile. Clodia is the famous "Lesbia" of Catullus, who lost her to Caelius, if he is indeed the Rufus whom Catullus berates as a successful rival. The references to bathing and fourpenny pieces suggest that she entertained her lovers in the bath. Caelius himself is said to have called her "the fourpenny Clytemnestra," for she was rumored to have poisoned her husband Metellus Celer three years previously and the fourpenny piece was the regular admission to the baths. Another lover, Vattius, was said to have sent her a fourpenny piece when they severed relations. Caelius was acquitted, and Clodia appears to have gone into complete social and moral eclipse, as Catullus 58 suggests:*

> O Caelius, our Lesbia, that Lesbia
> That Lesbia, she whom Catullus only

Loved, more than his own soul or any other,
Now at the crossroads, in the narrow alleys,
Preys on the random sons of Father Remus.

*Caelius met no better fate. He joined Caesar at the out-*
*break of the civil war, but grew dissatisfied with his share*
*of the spoils and organized a revolt, in which he was killed*
*in 48 B.C.*

1. Gentlemen of the jury: Suppose that by some chance a stranger to our laws and law-courts and way of life were to come upon this scene and notice that this is the only court in session while the holidays and public games have caused all the other business in the forum to be suspended: doubtless he would wonder what atrocious crime was indicated in this case, and would surely conclude that the defendant was being accused of some deed of such enormity that the commonwealth would collapse if he were to go unapprehended. And suppose our stranger were told that the law in this case is one that takes no account of holidays, but absolutely required judicial investigation whenever seditious and criminal citizens have taken up arms and laid siege to the senate-house or offered violence to magistrates or attacked the republic: of such a law he could scarcely disapprove, but he would ask about the particular charge in this trial. And when he had heard that there is no question here of crime, no question of brazen insolence, no question of illegal violence, that rather a youth of distinguished talents, an industrious young man who commands many friends, is being prosecuted by the son of one whom he himself is now arraigning and has arraigned before in the past, that furthermore a certain lady of great influence but no reputation is the source of the attack, our hypothetical friend would say: "Atratinus is not to blame; he is doing what any good son would do. But may I suggest that you Romans would do well to keep female wantonness within bounds? And as for these jurymen, why, they are burdened beyond all sense and reason; everyone else is at leisure, but only they are allowed no leisure."

For if you are willing, gentlemen, to attend closely to the whole case and weigh everything objectively, you will conclude, first, that no one would have proceeded to make an accusation like this if he were acting as a free agent, and secondly, that he would have done so without hope, unless his hopes were founded on someone's ungovernable wantonness and over-bitter hatred. But I forgive my friend Atratinus; he is a cultivated young man and an excellent one; he can offer as excuse filial duty or compulsion or age. If he was willing to prosecute, well after all he is a son; if he did so under orders, he is not his own master; if he hoped for something, well, he is only a boy. But for the others, my motto is "No forgiveness, but resistance to the end."

2. Seeing that Marcus Caelius is still quite a young man, I think my best course is to begin this defense by replying to the prosecution's attempt to blacken his character and blast his reputation. They have used his father variously as a basis for detraction. They have said either that he lives too shabbily or that he has been badly treated by his son. Marcus Caelius the elder does not need any help from me in defending his dignity. For those who know him well and for the older people present he easily counters that charge without having to say a word. But as for some time now because of advancing age he has been less active among us in the forum, he may not be so well known to some of you. To them let me say that whatever respect may be consonant with the position of a Roman knight—and surely that can be a very great deal—such respect has always in the highest degree been accorded Marcus Caelius, and is so still by anyone with whom he has any dealings whatever. Is it a disgrace to be the son of a Roman knight? So says the prosecution—scarcely a view to commend itself to some of the jurors here, not to mention myself, the counsel for the defense. And as to what you

prosecutors have said about Caelius' treatment of his father, we may form what judgment we will, but the final
word must certainly come from the father himself. You
will hear what our opinion is from the character-witnesses;
but what the parents themselves feel is clear from this
mother here in tears and anguish, from this father here dissolved in grief and clothed in mourning. The prosecution further alleges that the young man had a bad name
with his fellow-townsmen. To that I need only point out
that the citizens of Interamnia never conferred any greater
honors on a resident than they gave to Marcus Caelius
after he moved away. Though he was a non-resident, they
made him a member of their highest governing body, and
without his requesting it gave him what many had sought
in vain. In addition they have sent a choice deputation of
senators and Roman knights to present to the court their
sincere and detailed commendation.

I flatter myself I have now laid the foundations of my
defense, resting as it does on the testimony of those bound
to the defendant by the closest of ties. For you might well
have looked with a cold eye on a man so young if he were
really an object of aversion not only to his worthy father
but to his distinguished and upright townsmen as well.
3. In fact, if I may be allowed to inject a personal note, I
myself rose to fame from such origins as these, and, whatever glory I have gained in the courts and the government,
the esteem of those closest to me has seconded it in no small
degree.

We come now to the charge of immorality. Here the
prosecution has been long on rumor and gossip, but lamen-
tably short on specific details. And nothing they have said
has upset my client enough to make him regret that he is
naturally handsome. That sort of talk is the usual lot of any
young man who happens to be good-looking. But gossip

is one thing, a criminal prosecution quite another. The latter calls for an exact presentation of the evidence, positive identification of the criminal, reasoned proof, and confirmation by witnesses; whereas slander has no aim or task except to spatter with infamy. If the job is done in ill-temper, we call it abuse, but if with grace, we call it wit. I was shocked and mortified to see that Atratinus had been assigned this part of the prosecution. This was unseemly. It was incongruous in view of his age, and you no doubt noticed that the modesty of a well-brought-up young man was a considerable embarrassment to him in treating of these matters. I would prefer for some of you more toughened veterans to have handled the role of slanderer, for then I would feel less compunction in speaking boldly and baldly in rebuttal. But I will treat you more gently, Atratinus, and will tone down my language out of consideration for your modesty and the friendly feeling I have for you and your father. But let me give you a bit of advice. First, if you want people to think of you as you really are, you had better keep your speech as free from immodesty as your conduct is. And second, I warn you not to ascribe to another something you would blush to hear if falsely retorted on yourself. Anyone, you know, can play at that game. Remember you are vulnerable too if someone in a fit of spleen cared to spread gossip about you. For even where there is no ground for suspicion, the mere fact of being a young man of some personal charm lends the charge a show of plausibility. But your assuming that role was the fault of those who compelled you to speak. All due credit then to your sense of modesty, since you obviously spoke unwillingly, and to your ingenuity, since you managed all so carefully and elegantly.

4. Still I can make short work of refuting what you had to say. The fact is, during the whole time that Caelius was

young enough to lend some credibility to the suspicion, he was protected not merely by his own modest nature but by his father's watchful eye and careful upbringing. I say nothing here of my own influence on him; that may be as you like; I simply say that as soon as the boy had assumed the toga of manhood I took him under my wing•at the father's request. So that all in all, while Caelius was passing through this dangerous age, no one ever saw him except occupied with the tasks of liberal education, and in the company of his father or myself or within the chaste walls of Marcus Crassus' home.

The prosecution has brought up Caelius' intimacy with Catiline. But that by no means substantiates the charge of immorality. You know when Caelius was still quite young Catiline and I were both campaigning for the consulship. And one must admit that a number of young men fell under the arch-villain's spell. But you are at liberty to suppose that Caelius really was too intimate with Catiline only if you can prove that he cultivated his acquaintance, or for that matter ever left my side at the time. "But," you say, "we know that subsequently Caelius was one of his friends. We saw it with our own eyes." Who denies that? But we are not concerned at the moment with that "subsequently." I am dealing with that period in my client's life that is weak in itself and particularly exposed to the lust of others. While I was praetor Caelius went with me everywhere; he did not even know Catiline, who at the time was propraetor in Africa. Next came the year when Catiline stood trial for extortion in his provincial administration. Caelius was still with me; in no way did he support him during the trial. It was the year afterward that I was a candidate for the consulship; Catiline was also in the running. At no time did Caelius join his faction; at no time did he leave my side. 5. Finally, after spending all these years in the public eye without being sullied by a shadow of suspicion or ill-repute, Caelius supported Catiline in his second campaign for consul.

Now just how long do you think tender youth ought to be protected? When I was a boy of that age, while we passed our probationary year, we had to refrain from all extravagant gestures when we wore the toga, and we had to exercise and play on the Campus Martius in our tunics. Or if we began our military service, straightway a similar system of discipline prevailed in the camp. And even under that regimen if a boy did not show himself earnest and upright, if he failed to add a sort of natural innocence to the instruction he had received at home, he could not escape infamy, and deserving it too, regardless of how closely he was watched. But if he kept himself pure and proof against temptation in those early stages, no one had a word to say against his reputation afterwards when he had matured and taken his place as a man among men. Be that as it may, after Caelius had been some years in public life already, he espoused the cause of Catiline. And so did many others of every rank and age. For Catiline had, you may recall, a great show of good qualities, not fully realized to be sure, but in outline. He numbered a pack of rascals among his friends, but also pretended to be devoted heart and soul to others, men of the best sort. A master at luring into vice, he could also inspire men to effort and exertion. The torch of debauchery burned brightly in him, yet he had everything needed for a good soldier. I don't suppose there was ever such another anomalous creature on earth, compounded of such contrary, diverse, and mutually conflicting inclinations and desires.

6. When the occasion demanded, was there ever another man more ingratiating to the decent elements of society,

or more intimate with the indecent? Was there ever another who at times yielded more fervent support to the constitutional party, only to show himself at other times the state's bitterest enemy? Was ever anyone more befouled by vice, more persevering in effort? In greed, who could have equaled him, or in liberality? The man was, in short, astoundingly accomplished, gentlemen: he had troops of friends, he danced attendance on them, he shared what he had with every comer, his purse was open to everybody, he was at your beck and call, would use his influence for you, wear himself out for you, go any lengths for you, even to committing a crime if you liked, he changed his nature to meet every emergency, twisted and turned hither and thither, puritan to the serious-minded, hail-fellow-well-met to the lax, model of decorum to the elderly, good companion to the young, virtuoso of cutthroats, nonpareil of debauchery. Thanks to this protean and shifting personality, when all the wretches and rascals of earth had flocked to his banner, it is not surprising that many worthy men too were taken in by his specious and pretended virtues. His heinous assault on the foundations of our state would never have been so successful if his monstrous bestiality had not been firmly based on a character of astounding perseverance and adaptability. And so we might as well throw out that line of thought, gentlemen; the charge of intimacy with Catiline simply will not stick. If you throw mud from that sty, there are too many good men who will get spattered. I myself—yes, I freely admit it—I myself at one time was almost deceived. He seemed to me a good citizen, a partisan of the best men, a firm and faithful friend. I had to see with my own eyes before I could bring myself to believe in his criminality. I had to have the proofs thrust into my own hands before I suspected the truth. So Caelius made one in that mob of friends? Then let him repent of his mistake as I have repented, but do not make him tremble at the charge, "This man was a friend of Catiline."

7. Next the prosecution, after trying to make their slanderous point about immorality, took up the invidious business of the conspiracy. Hesitantly and obliquely they sidled into the position that since this man was a friend of Catiline's he must have taken part in the plot against the state. At this juncture, not only did the charge not hold, but the argument of my inexperienced young friend hardly held together. Are you saying that Caelius is a lunatic? that his character or career bears any marks of such a weakness? When was the name of Caelius ever breathed in connection with such a suspicion? You waste my time making me answer such a thing. I will say only this. Caelius proved conclusively that he was not associated with the conspiracy, proved on the contrary that he was one of its most relentless opponents, when he made his debut in public life by prosecuting one of the conspirators. And since I am on the subject, I rather think the same reply could be made to those charges about illegal electioneering and campaign bribery. Would Caelius ever have been such a madman as to arraign another man for dirty politics if he had himself been spotted with the same filth? Would he have demanded someone else's suspicious conduct be investigated if he hoped to have a free hand forevermore to conduct himself similarly? If he had imagined he would ever even once have to undergo trial for illegal compaigning, would he have called a man to account on the same charge not once, but twice? Which he did not wisely, in my opinion, and much against my will. But still his eagerness was such that he seemed rather to be persecuting an innocent man than harboring any fears about himself.

Now about his debts. You chided his extravagance

and ordered him to produce his accounts. The demand is
easily disposed of, to wit: a man still by law under his father's jurisdiction keeps no accounts. Caelius has never
contracted one debt to pay off another. You base the charge
of extravagance on one thing, that he pays a high rent. You
put it at thirty thousand sesterces. I was nonplussed at first,
but then I saw the light. I am given to understand that
Publius Clodius has put up for sale the block of houses
where Caelius lives—paying I am told a rent of only ten
thousand. To gratify Clodius the prosecution has inflated
the truth a little so that he may make a better sale. Next
they blame Caelius because he moved away from his father's. Considering his age, there are no grounds for blame.
When he had emerged from his first law-case covered with
glory—much to my chagrin, I may say, but greatly to his
credit—and when it was time for him to enter politics, not
only did his father allow him to move, he even encouraged
him to do so. The family home was far from the forum, so
Caelius rented a place at a reasonable figure on the Palatine
Hill, to be near our houses and more accessible to his own
supporters.

8. At this point I might echo the quotation used by
my friend Marcus Crassus when he was lamenting King
Ptolemy's arrival in Rome: "Oh, would that never in the
Pelian grove—" Except for my purpose I might proceed
even further into the passage: "For never would my
lady then have strayed—" Nor ever would we have been
brought to this pass by that "Medea, soul-sick, struck with
savage love." For even so, gentlemen of the jury, you will
find, as I shall show when I come to it, that this Medea of the
Palatine and this setting out into the great world were the
occasions of all our young man's misfortunes, or rather of
all the gossip about him.

And so relying on your good sense, gentlemen, I have no

reason to fear the other feints and fictions of the prosecution. They say for instance that they are going to produce a senator to testify that he was assaulted by Caelius during the pontifical elections. If the senator does put in an appearance, I will ask him first why he did not institute legal action at once. And if he says that he preferred complaining about the offense to taking legal action, I will ask why instead of acting on his own he waits to be produced by you and why he has chosen so long afterwards to complain. And if he gives me sharp and clever answers, then I will force him to tell me who is behind him. If he is appearing on his own initiative I may be moved—I usually am by such accounts. But if he is a mere rill and rivulet flowing from the very fountainhead of the prosecution, then I will felicitate myself that only one senator can be found to gratify you, seeing that all your proceedings are backed by persons of such means and influence.

In any case, neither do I quail before that other class of eyewitnesses: I mean the night-owls. For the prosecutors have said that they will produce men who will swear that their wives were criminally attacked by Caelius on their way home from dining out. Very respectable fellows, I must say, who will have the cheek to say this under oath, thereby confessing that though sorely injured they did not try even to make a settlement out of court.

9. But you can see in advance, gentlemen, what their whole line of attack is likely to be. So you should be in position to repel it when it comes. The nominal accusers are not the ones who are really attacking Marcus Caelius. The weapons thrown at him openly are being brought up from far behind the lines. Don't misunderstand me; I am not saying that the open opposition is acting from base rather than creditable motives. They are doing their duty, defending their own, acting as good men usually act: wronged, they

are indignant; angered, they strike out; challenged, they fight. But just because my honorable opponents have good and sufficient reason for speaking against Caelius, you ought to have enough discrimination, jurymen, to see that this does not constitute good and sufficient reason for you to abandon your duty to your oath out of pity for someone else's wrongs. Take a glance around the forum. What a throng of men! what a variety of races and interests and types! Out of this multitude how many do you suppose would not hurry to offer their services to powerful, influential, clever men, even to the extent of appearing as witnesses if they thought they needed them. So if some of this kind appear in this trial, be shrewd enough to discount their interested zeal, gentlemen. Remember that not only are my client's career and your own honor at stake, but also involved is the question of what is to happen to any citizen beset by the rich and powerful. I want to put the matter on quite another footing than the testimony of witnesses. I will not allow the integrity of this court, which may by no means be tampered with, to be dependent on the witnesses' eagerness to please, than which nothing is easier to direct, deflect, and manipulate. I will base my contentions on proof and refute the charges with evidence clear as daylight. I shall fight point with point, reason with reason, inference with inference.

10. Therefore I am happy that Marcus Crassus has already dealt in detailed and convincing fashion with that part of the case that has to do with the riots at Naples, the manhandling of the Alexandrian envoys at Puteoli, and the property of Palla. I only wish he had also treated the affair of Dion. I hardly know what I am expected to say about it, since the man responsible for the crime is brazening it out, or rather openly confessing. I refer of course to King Ptolemy. And the man said to have been his instrument

and accomplice, Publius Asicius, won a complete acquittal.
What kind of charge is this? The man responsible does not
deny the deed, the man denying goes free, whereas a man
suspected of neither the deed nor complicity, is to stand in
jeopardy! The strength of Asicius' case prevailed over the
hostility that inspired his trial: are your slanders to harm
Caelius, who was never connected with the business by
either plausible suspicion or even idle rumor? But, you say,
Asicius got his freedom through a deal between prosecution
and defense. It would not be hard for me to answer that,
especially as I was the defense you refer to. At any rate,
Caelius thinks that Asicius had an excellent case, but that
excellent or not it had nothing to do with his own. And Titus
and Gaius Coponius agree wholeheartedly, young men of
the greatest learning and refinement, gently and strictly
reared young men, who had more cause than anyone else
to mourn Dion's death, since they were bound to him not
only by admiration for his culture and erudition, but by ties
of friendship as well. Dion used to live in Titus' home, as
you heard, and was well-acquainted with him in Alexandria. Titus' opinion of Caelius, and his brother's too, who
always makes such a splendid impression, you will hear
from their own lips if they are called on. So enough of these
quibbles. We come finally to the real underlying issues in
these proceedings.

11. I noticed, gentlemen, that you were very attentive to
my friend Lucius Herennius. For the most part he held you
by his cleverness and admirable style of declamation, but
at times listening I began to be nervous for fear the subject-
matter of his speech, so subtly arranged to lead to incrim-
ination, might win you over gradually and insensibly. He
had much to say about riotous living, sexual laxity, the
waywardness of youth, the morals of our times, and though
in his private life he is mild-mannered, cultured, pleasant,

and suave, just the type that almost everyone nowadays is delighted with, here he showed himself like a puritanical uncle or censor or schoolmaster. He dragged Caelius over the coals as no father ever dragged his son. He favored us with a long discourse on incontinence and intemperance.

What more could you ask, gentlemen? I can understand your listening so closely; my own flesh crawled when I heard that hard, harsh mode of speech. But the first part had less effect on me, the part where he said that Caelius had been on good terms with my friend Bestia, had dined with him, visited his home many times, and supported his campaign for praetor. These statements did not affect me much, since they were manifestly untrue. For he named as fellow-diners at Bestia's house several who either are not in court or have no choice but to stick to the prosecution's story. Nor do I care much for what he said about Caelius' being a fellow-member of the Luperci. Well, we all know that this pack of wolf-priests has a history that antedates law and civilization, but I never thought it was still such a rustic and countrified brotherhood that its members would not only denounce each other, but would actually mention their common membership in a prosecuting address, as though afraid someone might remain ignorant of the fact. But enough of this; I pass on to things that affected me more.

The sermon against loose living was long but milder, and being more argumentative than harsh was listened to all the more attentively. For when my dear friend Publius Clodius was making the heavens to resound with his virtuous and stringent denunciations, when in the flame of his righteousness he was putting to use his forceful vocabulary, his stentorian voice, I was moved to admire his power in speaking out so, but I was not very much frightened, for I remembered that several times before he had lost his case.

But let me answer Balbus first, though I do it with a prayer on my lips that it not be considered treason or blasphemy to defend a man who never refuses a dinner-invitation, sometimes goes to garden-parties, has been known to dab on a bit of perfume, and even puts in an appearance now and then at Baiae.

12. To tell the truth, I have seen and heard of a number of men in this republic who did not merely take a sip of this sort of life, dabble in it as we say with their fingertips, but who actually plunged their whole youth long into pleasure. Yet they finally came out with their heads above water as we say, regained their equilibrium and lived to work some good in the world and turn into worthy, upstanding men. By general consent we concede a young man a few wild oats. Nature herself showers adolescence with a veritable spate of desires. If the dam bursts without endangering anyone's life or breaking up anyone's home, we put up with it easily and cheerfully. But out of the bad things that are generally said about young men, you seemed to me to be fashioning some particular weapon aimed at Caelius alone. During all the time we were listening in respectful silence to your speech, though the defendant had been set up as a scapegoat, we were thinking in the silence of the sins of many. It is easy to denounce profligacy. The sun would set on me if I tried to exhaust what can be said on the topic. Seduction, adultery, impudence, extravagance—what fuel for speech is there! As long as you propose to talk not about the defendant but about vice in general, you have abundant means for playing the censor and the accuser. But, gentlemen of the jury, do not in your wisdom allow your view to be drawn away from the defendant, and when the prosecution has aroused you against the vices and degenerate morals of our day, do not discharge the sting of your censure upon a single man, and that man my client, who would

thereby have to suffer the venom excited not by his own
acts but by the fault of his age. So I don't dare to answer
your strictures as I ought. I had intended to bring out the
license we extend to youth and ask for indulgence on those
grounds. But now, as I said, I don't dare. I have to throw
away all those excuses that have to do with age; everyone
else may use them, but my client not. This only I ask.
Regardless of what indignation you may feel these days
about the debts, bad manners, and dissipations of the
young people—and I see you feel a great deal—still do not
let the misdeeds of others, the vices of his age and times,
be a detriment to Caelius here. And I for my part, granted
this, will not refuse to reply as carefully as I can to the
charges which properly apply.

13. There are two charges then, one about the gold and
one about the poison. And one and the same person is implicated in both. He got the gold from Clodia, he wanted
the poison to give to Clodia, they say. Nothing else is basis
for legal action; all else is simple slander, fitter for a quarrel
than a public inquiry. "You adulterer! You libertine! You
bribery-agent!" This is the language of abuse, not of legal
prosecution. There is no foundation for such accusations.
They are the rash insults of an irritated accuser acting without authority. But of the two aforenamed items I see the
author, I see the fountainhead, the fixed responsibility, the
prime mover. He needed gold; he got it from Clodia, got it
without a witness, kept it as long as he liked. A signal proof
this of a somewhat special intimacy! He wished to kill the
said Clodia; he secured poison, suborned her slaves, brewed
his broth, laid the scene for the crime, and brought the potion thither. Could it have been that when they fell out so
cruelly there was some consequent ill-feeling on her side?

Our whole concern in this case, jurors, is with Clodia, a
woman not only noble but even notorious. Of her I will say

no more than is necessary to refute the charges. And you too, Gnaeus Domitius, sensible man that you are, you understand that our whole business here is with her and her only. If she does not admit that she obliged Caelius with the loan of the gold, if she does not accuse him of preparing poison for her, then my behavior is ungentlemanly in dragging in a matron's name otherwise than the respect due to ladies requires. But if on the contrary aside from that woman their case against Caelius is deprived of all strength and foundation, what else can I do as an advocate but repel those who press the assault? Which I would do all the more vehemently if I did not have cause for ill-feeling toward that woman's lover—I am sorry; I meant to say "brother." I am always making that slip. But now I will handle her with moderation, and proceed no further than my honor and the case itself demand. I have never thought it right to take up arms against a lady, especially against one whose arms are so open to all.

14. First I would like to ask her: "Shall I deal with you severely and strictly and as they would have done in the good old days? Or would you prefer something more indulgent, bland, sophisticated?" If in that austere mode and manner, I shall have to call up someone from the dead, one of those old gentlemen bearded not with the modern style of fringe that so titillates her, but with one of those bristly bushes we see on antique statues and portrait-busts. And he will scold the woman and speak for me and keep her from getting angry with me as she might otherwise do. So let us call up some ancestor of hers, preferably old blind Appius Claudius himself. He will be the least likely to be grieved, since he won't have to look at her. Doubtless if he rose among us he would say something about like this:

"Woman, what business did you have with Caelius, a man scarce out of his teens, a man not your husband? Why were you so friendly with him as to lend him gold? Or how did you grow so unfriendly as to fear his poison? Did you never hear that your father, uncle, grandfather, great-grandfather, great-great-grandfather, and great-great-great-grandfather were consuls? Did you forget that only recently you were the wife of Quintus Metellus, a gentleman of the highest type, a distinguished patriot who had only to show his face to eclipse almost all other citizens in character, reputation, dignity? Born of a high-ranking family, married into a prominent family, how did it happen that you admitted Caelius to such familiarity? Was he a relative or friend of your husband? Not at all. What was it then but hot and headstrong passion? If the portraits of us male ancestors meant nothing to you, how could my granddaughter, Quinta Claudia, have failed to inspire you to emulate her domestic virtue and womanly glory? Or that vestal virgin of our name who kept her arms around her father throughout his triumph and foiled the tribune's attempt to drag him from his chariot? Why choose to imitate your brother's vices in preference to the good qualities of your father and grandfather and of men and women of our line on back to myself? Did I break the agreement with King Pyrrhus that you might every day enter into disgusting agreements with your paramours? Did I bring in the Appian Aqueduct that you might put its waters to your dirty uses? Did I build the Appian Way that you might ride up and down with other women's husbands?"

15. But perhaps it was a mistake for me to introduce such an august personage, gentlemen. He might suddenly turn on Caelius and make him feel the weight of his censorial powers. Though I will see to this later; I am convinced I can justify Marcus Caelius' behavior to the most captious of critics. But as for you, woman—I am not speaking to you now through the mouth of another—if you have in

mind to make good what you are doing, saying, pretending, plotting, and alleging, you had better do some explaining as well, and account for this extraordinarily intimate association. The prosecutors have been lavish with their tales of affairs, amours, adulteries, Baiae, beach-picnics, banquets, drinking-bouts, songfests, musical ensembles, and yachting-parties. And they indicate that they are describing all this with your full permission. Since for some rash, mad purpose you have been willing to have all these stories come out at a trial in the forum, you must either tone down their effect by showing they are groundless, or else admit that no one need believe your charges and your testimony.

But if you would rather I dealt with you more suavely, I will take this tack: I will whisk that old fellow off the scene, unfeeling rustic that he is, and will bring on someone of your own day, your younger brother, say, the most sophisticated of all that crew. He loves you dearly. When he was a young sprout he used to sleep with big sister because, I am told, he was subject to mysterious nervousness and fanciful fears at night. Suppose we let him talk to you: "Why are you making such a fuss, sister? Why are you behaving like an insane woman?

> Why, with shout and speech inflate
> A little thing into a great?

You saw a young man living nearby. He had a fresh complexion. He was tall. He was handsome. His eyes were attractive. You were much taken with all this. You wanted to see him more often. You met sometimes on the same suburban estates. A woman of means, you thought to bind the young man with fetters of gold, still dependent on a tight-fisted father. But you can't. He kicks, he spits, he bucks. He doesn't set much value on your presents. Well, go somewhere else. You have gardens on the Tiber. You deliberately chose them for their location, since they are at the very place where all the young men go in swimming. You can pick your bargains there any day. Why do you bother with this fellow who spurns you?"

16. I come now to you, Caelius. It is your turn now, and I must assume the authority and severity of a father. But I am in doubt as to what type of parent I ought to be. Shall I enact that choleric, flinty specimen in Caecilius:

> Now at length my soul is burning,
> Now my heart is heaped with wrath.

Or that other one:

> You wretch! You rascal!

Overbearing and past all bearing are fathers of that ilk:

> What shall I wish? What shall I say?
> You swine! your faults in every way
> Cause all I wish to go astray!

Such a father would say: "Why did you move to that whorish neighborhood? Why didn't you escape when you saw the snares?"

> Why did you flirt with another man's wife?
>     Scatter your pennies like peas?
> Well, in your hour of trouble and strife
>     Don't come to me if you please.
> I mean to hug for the rest of my life
>     Myself in my own bed of ease.

To such a disagreeable, blunt old curmudgeon Caelius might reply that it was not monetary considerations that made him stray. "What proof of that?" His lack of exorbitant expenses, lavish outlay, need to refinance debts. "But what about the stories?" How many people can escape gossip, especially in a town that dotes on it so? Do you wonder that the woman's neighbor was talked about when her own brother couldn't keep nasty people from spreading rumors?

Suppose I play the part of the kind and forgiving father, the one, you know, who says:

> So my son has demolished the door?
> We'll rebuild it once more.
> Has he ripped all his wardrobe to tatters?
> Well, not that that matters.

Then Caelius will have an easy time of it. For he will have no trouble defending all his conduct. I am not saying anything against that woman now; but if there were someone —not the same as her, you understand—some woman who made herself cheap and easy to approach, who always had some man or other hanging about openly acknowledged as her current interest, in whose gardens and home and place at Baiae anybody and everybody could arrange assignations with her permission, who even boarded young men and made up deficiencies in their allowances out of her own purse, if this person, being widowed, lived loosely, being forward, lived wantonly, being rich, lived extravagantly, being prurient, lived like a harlot, am I to think a man an adulterer if he does not address her exactly like a lady?

17. Someone will say, "Are these the lessons you taught him? Is this the way you educate young men? Was it for this that the father entrusted his boy to you? To waste his youth in love and sensual pleasure, and then bring you in to defend his conduct and his inclinations?" In answer I might say this, gentlemen: if there ever lived a man so upright and naturally virtuous and continent that he disdained all temptations of the flesh, sacrificed body and intellect to attain his ambitions, shut his ears to the call of rest and recreation and play and the distracting voices of his fellows, and thought nothing in life worth aiming at but what is con-

sonant with honor and dignity, such a man to my way of thinking was singularly blessed by heaven. I imagine that our Camilli, Fabricii, and Curii fell into that category, and all the heroes who did so much with so little.

But we look in vain for such paragons as things are today, and are hard put to find them even in books. The blueprints of that ancient austerity are crumbling with age. And not only in our own country, where this stern regimen was honored more in action than in words; the learned Greeks too, who used at least to be able to talk and write nobly even if they failed to live up to their teachings, have changed their code with the change in their fortunes. So some of them have taught that the wise make pleasure their universal criterion, a disgusting line of reasoning that even men of culture have dallied with. Others have opined that the life of honor ought to be combined with the life of pleasure, glibly yoking together a pair that are sure to kick each other out of the traces. While those who say, "No, the way to glory leads straight through the land of toil and self-sacrifice," hear their words resound in almost empty lecture-halls. For nature herself woos us with honeyed words, till virtue is lulled and can scarce hold up her eyelids, and then takes her by the hand and shows her those lubricious paths where she can hardly go or stay without disastrous trip or slip, and lastly indicates that wondrously enticing and richly varied world of pleasure and whispers, "Take it; it is yours." Is it any wonder that youth falls, when even seasoned climbers have been known to take the plunge? So if someone here and there is found to avert his eyes from the gorgeous surface of things, refuse to fall prey to the lures of scent and touch and taste, deaden his ears to all that sweet siren-song, I and a few others call him a darling of the gods, but the most of mankind will say he is a man of singularly morose disposition.

18. In consequence the path of rectitude lies deserted now. No one bothers to keep it open, and weed and thicket grow wild. Give youth some leeway then; allow our young men to stray a little; do not rein in every pleasure; let the ideal and forthright life suffer an occasional check; let reason give way now and then to appetite and desire. Provided that in all this some bounds are not overstepped. Let youth retain some measure of innocence; let it not corrupt another man's wife, throw away its patrimony, or whelm itself in debt; let it spare the homes and families of others, nor ruin the chaste nor wreck the righteous nor shame the good; let it abstain from violence, dangerous intrigue, and crime. So that at last when it has paid its respects to the demands of the flesh and allotted due time to boyish sport and the silly desires of the young and fervent blood, it may call a halt at last and face the claims of family, career, and country, and what reason in advance could not dissipate mere satiety may put away and experience despise.

We know many outstanding citizens, and our fathers and forefathers knew many more, gentlemen, whose youth blazed up in a holocaust of desire, only to leave in maturity a substantial residue of excellent qualities. I would rather not name names, but you can think of examples yourselves. I see no point in reviewing here the record of any illustrious life merely to smirch it by mention of some minor peccadillo. I could instance, if I liked, any number of famous men: this one as a youth chafed at the bit, that one squandered his substance on riotous living, a third was laid low by debt and extravagance, a fourth reveled in lust. But all these faults were palliated by the virtues that developed later, and anyone who cared might excuse them with the simple words, "Yes, but the man was young."

19. But the fact is, Marcus Caelius' case is different. I can

speak a little more confidently now about his more creditable activities, since I rely on your good common sense and boldly paint both sides of the picture. You will find no riotous living, no extravagance or debt in him, no ungovernable urge to go to carouses and dens of ill-repute. Not to mention the vice of gluttony, which in fact is not so characteristic of youth as of age. And the so-called delights of love, which are not generally bothersome to the more intelligent type of men when they mature—the desire flowers and withers early—never had so much power as to hold him completely enthralled. You heard him when he defended himself, you have heard him before in the role of prosecutor. (I say this not to boast of my pupil, but because his defense demands it.) And you have perception enough to understand what oratorical ability, what ease, what a wealth of words and sentiments he commands. And you saw that it was not merely a matter of natural talent, which often shines bright of itself when the light has not been nurtured by training, but rather that he had in him, unless my fondness deceives me, a systematic knowledge that could only be the product of education and practice, of toil and midnight oil.

Well, consider, gentlemen. Those vices that Caelius is charged with and these accomplishments I am discussing can hardly coexist in the same man. It is impossible for a mind enslaved to lust, love, longing, and desire, a mind distracted by either too much or too little of that sort of thing, to meet the standards of oratory, however low they may be set. A man of that kind could not deliver a good speech; he could not even prepare one. Or do you perhaps suppose there is some other reason why there are and always have been so few men who take the pains to speak well, although there are so many rewards in fame, satisfaction, influence, and honor to be gained by it? To reach the goal you have to keep recreation at a minimum, give up your hobbies, your sport, your moments of levity, your social life, and practically cut out seeing your friends. It is the labor involved that frightens men away, and not so much that their talents or early training are deficient. If my client had lived the life of pleasure, would he, while still a very young man, have haled an ex-consul into court? If he were a mere voluptuary afraid of work, would he engage every day in legal battles, making enemies, starting suits, exposing his own neck to the axe, and in general, for months on end, with the whole Roman people as audience, fighting the fight whose end is either glory or extinction?

20. "But," you say, "I get a whiff of something rotten when I think about his moving to that neighborhood and when I remember the gossip about him. And don't those trips to Baiae hint at something?" Not merely hint, they shout to heaven that a certain woman is so far gone in vice that, far from hunting for shadows and solitude to conceal her wantonness, she flaunts her outrageous conduct in broad day in the most frequented places. Anyone who thought young men ought to be forbidden to visit prostitutes would certainly be the virtuous of the virtuous, that I cannot deny. But he would be out of step not only with this easy-going age but also our ancestors, who customarily made youth that concession. Was there ever a time when this was not habitual practice, when it was censured and not permitted, in short when what is allowable was not allowed?

Here I will get to the root of the matter, without mentioning any woman's name: so much I leave to be inferred. Imagine a woman with no husband who turns her house into a house of assignation, openly behaves like a harlot, entertains at her table men who are perfect strangers, and does all this in town, in her suburban places, and in the crowded vacationland around Baiae; in fine, imagine that her walk, her way of dressing, the company she keeps, her burning glances, her free speech, to say nothing of her embraces and kisses or her capers at beach-parties and banquets and yachting-parties, are all so suggestive that she seems not merely a whore but a particularly shameless and forward specimen of the profession. Well, if a young man had some desultory relations with her, would you call him an adulterer, Lucius Herennius, or simply a lover? Would you say he was laying siege to her innocence, or simply gratifying her lust?

Clodia, I am not thinking now of the wrongs you have done me. I am putting to one side the memory of my humiliation. I pass over your cruel treatment of my family while I was away. Consider that nothing I have said has been said against you. But I would like to ask you a few questions, since the prosecutors say they have their evidence from you and are using you as their chief witness. If there were any such woman as I have just described, a woman unlike you, who lived and acted like a common prostitute, would you think it very disgraceful or dishonorable for a young man to have something to do with her? If you are not such a woman—and I hope indeed you are not—then what do you complain of in Caelius? But if they mean to say you are, then why are we to fear such an indictment, when you yourself snap your fingers at it? Answer, and establish the defense. Either be modest and admit that Marcus Caelius did nothing out of order, or flaunt your impudence and thereby give him and all the others an excellent wherewithal to defend themselves.

21. I think my speech has now escaped the reefs and crags, and the rest of the course is clear sailing. The two principal charges have to do with serious crimes, both involving the same woman. Caelius is alleged to have got from Clodia a sum in gold, and to have prepared poison for the purpose of killing the Clodia aforesaid. He got the gold,

they say, to give to Lucius Lucceius' slaves, to get them to murder Dion the Alexandrian, who was staying with Lucceius at the time. A serious charge, whether we think of it as plotting against a foreign ambassador or as suborning slaves to kill one of their master's guests. A design truly criminal in its audacity.

But first I would like to know, did Caelius tell Clodia what he wanted the money for, or not? If not, why did she give it? If he told her, then she was an accessory before the fact. Tell me, Clodia, did you dare to hand over the gold from your safe, to despoil that Venus of yours of her ornaments, as she had despoiled so many others, knowing all the while what a crime he wanted it for, knowing that it would be used to murder a legate and stain forever the name of that god-fearing, upright man, Lucius Lucceius? Your spirit ought not to have been privy to such a design, your popular home should not have been accessory to it, not your hospitable Venus made a confederate. Balbus foresaw this danger. He declared that Clodia knew nothing, that Caelius had got her to listen by saying that he wanted the gold for some shows he intended to give. If Caelius was as intimate with Clodia as you would picture him when you rave about his viciousness, then surely he must have told her what he wanted with it. But if he was not that intimate, I say she gave him nothing. And so, my dear lady, though I know you hate restraint, I must present you with a rather narrow choice. Either Caelius told you all, in which case you knowingly gave the gold for a criminal purpose, or he did not dare tell, in which case you did not give it at all.

22. Now need I bring forward any of the manifold reasons for disbelieving the charge? Need I point out that Marcus Caelius' character is utterly inconsistent with such a heinous crime? Is it conceivable that a man of his intelli-

gence would not have realized he ought not to trust another man's unknown slaves in an enterprise of such danger? And as I and all other lawyers do at times, I can ask
the prosecution to furnish additional information. Where
did Caelius meet with Lucceius' slaves? How did he
have access to them? If he approached them on his own, he
was incredibly rash. But if he used an intermediary, who
was it? I can discuss the thing step by step, I can flush every
suspicion from cover, but not a motive will I find, nor flaw
in the alibi, nor opportunity, nor accomplice nor hope
of carrying the deed through and keeping it hidden, nor
rational basis for action, nor clue such as a crime of that
magnitude would leave. But these are the stock in trade of
the advocate. And though they might have some result, I
could set them before you thanks not to any ingenuity of
mine but rather to my long practice and experience. Yet
since they would seem mere elaborations of my own, I will
leave them aside for brevity's sake.

Instead, gentlemen, I give you Lucius Lucceius himself,
the best of witnesses in this regard. He is a man of highest
integrity, and you will allow he is bound to be scrupulously loyal to his oath. If he had heard that Caelius had
tendered such an affront to his fame and fortunes, he would
never have overlooked it or borne it in silence. A man of
such culture, interested in philosophy and its techniques
and tenets, how could he have been indifferent to the danger of one whom he esteemed for attainment in that very
field? How could he have failed to guard against a crime
aimed at a friend in his own house, when he would be deeply
shocked to hear of such a plot against another's guest? He
would be indignant if told that such a thing had been done
by persons unknown. Would he be indulgent on learning
it had been attempted by his own slaves? He would censure
the deed if done in a field or a public square. Would he

shrug it off when tried in the city under his own roof? He would not ignore such a danger if offered to some country fellow or other. But with all his education would he think a plot against a great scholar's life ought to be cloaked in silence? But why keep you longer, gentlemen? Hear his own words given under oath. Attend carefully to the details of his testimony, and remember that you are listening to a man of scrupulous integrity.

Let the deposition of Lucius Lucceius be read. [*Deposition is read by clerk.*] What more would you have? Are you waiting for Truth herself to stand up and tell you the facts? This is the defense that innocence offers; these are the facts themselves speaking; this is the very voice of Truth. The charge is bolstered by no suspicious circumstance. No evidence has been presented. They say that a certain act was committed, but give not a scrap of proof as to expressed intention or place or time. They name no witness, no accomplice. Their whole case was concocted in a house that specializes in hatred, defamation, cruelty, lust, and crime Whereas the home where they say the vile deed was attempted is a place of honor, dignity, respect for duty and morality. You heard the words of the master of that household delivered under oath. Now you must squarely face the choice of which to believe. Did a headstrong, dissolute, angry woman manufacture this accusation? Or did a serious, wise, and temperate man give false testimony against all his scruples?

23. We have the business of the poison left to dispose of. And of that I cannot, in a very real sense, make head or tail. What motive had Caelius for poisoning the woman? To get out of paying back the gold? But she had not dunned him for it, had she? To get rid of an accomplice? No one had charged him with anything, had they? And most important, would this trial ever have taken place if Caelius himself had

not brought on someone else's trial? Why, it was even admitted that Lucius Herennius would never have had one word to say against Caelius if Caelius had not prosecuted his friend twice on the same account.

Are we to believe then that the attempt was unmotivated? Don't you see, gentlemen, that they have invented that whole story about Dion just to provide Caelius with a motive for poisoning Clodia? Well, who was trusted with the task? Who was his helper, confederate, accomplice? Who was to do the deed? Whose hands did he put his life into? The woman's slaves? so they say. You credit him with a little intelligence, gentlemen, even if you were to agree with the prosecution in not allowing him anything else. Well, was this intelligent man so insane as to trust all his fortunes to somebody else's slaves? And what sort of slaves? Certainly not the ordinary sort, but ones that he knew lived on pretty free and easy terms with their mistress. Who can fail to see, gentlemen, that slaves are not really slaves in a house where a Roman lady lives like a prostitute, where nothing is done that she can afford to have aired in public, and where the order of the day is not just your run-of-the mill type of orgy and debauchery, but enormities and vices undreamt of? In such a household the slaves would have to be trusted to carry out the orders, take part in the brawls, and keep things under cover. And no doubt they would get their share of their mistress's overflowing bounty. Do you suppose Caelius had not understood that? If he was as intimate with the woman as you would have him, he must have known that the slaves were equally intimate. But if he did not frequent the house as much as you insinuate, how could he have become so friendly with the help?

24. Again, what is the story about the poison itself? Where did it come from? How was it procured? Who was the go-between? How? Where? They allege that Caelius

had it in his house and tested its efficiency on a slave that he had brought in for the purpose. And that when the slave speedily turned up his heels, my client gave the potion his stamp of approval.—O gods above, why do you wink at the most monstrous crimes now and then, and take your time about punishing the sinner?

I was present, and saw with my own eyes, and drained the bitterest cup of my life, when Quintus Metellus was snatched away from the bosom of his fatherland. A fine man, never doubting that he had been born to serve his country well. I remember him a short time before he died. He was active in his public duties, came to the senate-house, spoke from the rostra. He was in the prime of life, had a rugged constitution, looked to be in the best of health. But three days later he was gone, an irreparable loss to the conservative party and the nation as a whole. I remember how he died. His mental faculties had begun to desert him, but his country was in his thoughts to the last. As I was weeping beside him, he looked at me, and, his words faltering, his voice failing, he warned me what a storm was threatening me, what a tempest was overhanging the state. And time and again he struck the wall that partitioned his room from the house next door where Quintus Catulus had lived, and called out, "Catulus! Catulus!" And then he would call my name. But more than anything he spoke of the republic. His chief mortification was not so much that he was dying, as that he would no longer be here to protect his country or me. This was the kind of man he was. When he was consul and his brother-in-law, being then in the first stages of his insanity, was bellowing out something or other, Metellus declared in the hearing of the senate that he would kill Clodius with his own hand. What wouldn't he have done when the lunacy was full-blown, if he had not suddenly, violently, and nefariously been whisked off the scene? And is it from his home that this woman dares to saunter forth and spread tales about swift-working poisons? One would suppose that she would be afraid the very house might speak, that she would shudder to behold those guilty walls or recall that night of gloom and travail. But let me get back to the charge. For even to mention that good man's name weighs my heart with grief and renders me scarce able to speak for tears.

25. Still there is nothing said about where the poison came from or how it was procured. They say it was given to Publius Licinius, a modest young man of good character, one of Caelius' friends. The slaves, they say, had instructions to go to the Senian baths. Licinius was to meet them there and hand over the poison in a little wooden box. I would like to know first why they agreed to meet at that particular place? Why didn't the slaves come to Caelius' house? If he was still on such excellent terms with Clodia, what would have been suspicious about one of her slaves being seen at his place? But on the other hand if they had had a quarrel and broken off, and no longer had anything to do with each other, in that case doubtless one might say: "Hence those tears!" Here one would have the explanation for all those crimes he is accused of.

"No, no! That isn't it at all," says my opponent. "When the slaves had revealed to their mistress the full extent of Caelius' wickedness, the clever lady told them to promise him anything, but, so as to catch Licinius in the very act of handing over the poison, she directed them to make a rendezvous at the Senian baths. And she was going to post friends there to lurk around in the shadows till Licinius had appeared and was handing the poison over, and then they were to jump out and lay hold of their man."

26. Well, gentlemen, the whole story takes very little re-futing. Why did she settle on a public bathhouse? That

hardly appears to me to afford a hiding-place for men in
their togas. If they had stayed in the vestibule of the building, they would have been in plain sight. But if they wanted
to go farther inside, they could not very comfortably have
done so with their boots and clothes on, and would probably not have been admitted. (Though they might have
been, of course, assuming that that lady of influence, a
member of the bathkeeper's guild herself, in a manner of
speaking, might have got them in by making a bargain with
the bathman to exchange services in kind.) Really I was
breathlessly waiting to learn who those worthy men were
who could testify to catching the malefactors in the act.
And waiting I am still, for not a name has been named. But
I don't doubt they are frightfully respectable, seeing that
they are bosom friends of this lady, and went forth on this
mission for her, and squeezed all together into some cranny
at the baths, which for all her power she would never have
gotten any but the most reputable and dignified of men to
do. But why do I bother about their dignity? Just consider
their diligence and valor. "They were shrouded in darkness
at the bathhouse." Fine eyewitnesses! "Then they jumped
out without a thought—." Wonderful examples of self-
restraint! For that is the story you tell. Licinius arrives. He
has the drug-container in his hand. He is about to hand it
over. He has not yet handed it over, when all of a sudden
out fly those witnesses of yours, who have such good repu-
tations but no names. Too late, however! Licinius, who already had his hand stretched out to give up the poison-box,
draws it back, and the sudden assault makes him take to his
heels. Great, oh great is the power of truth, that can easily
defend itself against the sly, ingenious, cleverly-contrived
plots of men!

27. For instance, how miserably the plot fails to work out

in the whole imaginary drama we have been viewing! How impossible for the lady-dramatist to provide a denouement, though an old hand at the trade with quite an extensive list of productions. I refer of course to the alleged fact that Licinius slipped right through the hands of so many men. For there would have had to be a good many to make sure of holding the culprit and to corroborate one another's testimony. Why did they let him escape? Was it any less feasible to catch him when he drew back and failed to hand over the container than if he had handed it over? They were stationed there to catch Licinius redhanded, and this could have been done regardless of whether he kept back the piece of evidence or had already surrendered it. This was the woman's whole plan of campaign, and this was what the men obliging her were assigned to do. And I fail to see why you say they jumped out thoughtlessly and prematurely. That was what they had been asked to do and put there to do; they were supposed to flush into the open the poison and the plot and the whole nasty business. What better time to pounce than when Licinius had arrived and was holding the box of poison in his hand? If the lady's friends had waited to make their sudden sally from the baths and seize their prey after the slaves had already received the poison, Licinius would protest his innocence and deny ever having laid a finger on the box. And how would they prove he was lying? By saying they saw him? In the first place they would invite prosecution on a very serious charge, and secondly they would claim to have seen something impossible to see from where they were posted. Consequently they came out on cue when Licinius had appeared and was taking out the box, stretching forth his hand, and delivering up the poison. Well, this is a closing-scene worthy of broad farce, not serious drama. When the author is at a loss how to work out his plot, he throws in a chase and somebody gives somebody the slip. Then clog-dance by the whole company, and curtain!

28. Licinius stumbles, turns this way and that, backs away, tries to flee. And yet that womanish handful of men come away empty-handed. Why? I would like to know. Why didn't they take him? Why didn't they nail down the charge by catching him with the goods before a crowd of witnesses and making him confess? Were they afraid so many strong, nimble fellows could not overpower one poor, weak, frightened youth? There is no proof in fact, no basis for suspicion as to motive, and the accusation leads no-where. Consequently their whole case rests on the reliabil-ity of their witnesses, since there is no question here of proof, inference, or evidence, all of which are the usual prerequisites for finding out the truth.

I am waiting for these witnesses, gentlemen. Far from being nervous about them, I rather hope to be entertained. I am simply agog to see them. First the young friends, fresh from the bath, of a lady rich and highly-born. And then the brave men the she-general stationed in ambuscade as guardians of the bath. I am anxious to know how they hid and where. Did they all crawl under a bathtub? Or was there a Trojan horse there to take in and conceal the host of invincible heroes waging their woman's war? I will make them answer me: Why did so many men, and such men too, fail to capture this lone weak boy you see here while he was still standing there? Or why didn't they overtake him when he ran? They will never worm their way out if I once get them into the witness-box. Granted they may be glib and witty at the dinner table and even eloquent now and then over wine. But the forum and a dining room are two very different places. The same appeal can't be made to a court-bench as to a banquet-couch. Jurors and tipplers see things through different eyes. And the sun sheds quite another sort of light than a ceiling-lamp. So I am prepared to parry all their foolish fun, if they appear. But I would like to say to them: "Listen to me. Do a favor if you like. Curry favor where you like. Show off otherwise as you please. Be as lovesome to that woman as your strength allows, outrival the others in spending, get as close to her as possible, stretch out prostrate, let her use you as she will. But do not, I beg of you, try to ruin an innocent man."

29. Moreover, acting on the advice of her prominent and aristocratic relatives, she freed those slaves we were talking about. At last we find her doing something out of regard for distinguished family. I would be curious to know what the act of freeing them means. Was it done to trump up a charge against Caelius? Or to keep them from being put to the question? Or was it necessary to reward the slaves, who had been privy to her multitudinous activities? "No, I did it because my relatives advised me to," she says. "Why wouldn't they advise you, since you told them you had discovered the affair yourself and no one else knew of it? I wonder if that dirty story going the rounds was a consequence of that imaginary box? Anything can happen to a woman like that. Everyone knows of it and talks of it. (You see, gentlemen, I have been talking for some time as I please, or rather as I don't please.) Well, if the tale is based on fact, certainly Caelius had nothing to do with the fact. Why should he have bothered? Probably some young sport who has more wit than modesty is to blame. But if fiction, it is indelicate, I grant, but a pretty telling anecdote. Would we all be whispering and believing it so delightedly if anything so filthy didn't, if I may say so, hit the fourpenny nail on the head?

My plea is spoken and done, gentlemen of the jury. Now you understand what matters of weighty import depend on your decision. You have been impaneled to judge a case of aggravated assault. The law involved is the one Quintus Catulus passed when the stage was almost on its last legs during armed civil conflict. It is a law vital to the sovereignty, majesty, and well-being of our country, a law that safeguards the lives and persons of all, a law under which the last smoking embers of conspiracy were extinguished after the main conflagration had been stamped out in my consulship. And this is the law now being invoked to put Caelius' young head on the block, to satisfy, not the exigencies of the nation, but the lust and caprice of one woman.

30. And yet at this point they even cite as precedents the condemnation of Marcus Camurtius and Gaius Caesernius. Foolishness! Or should I say astounding impudence? Do you dare, coming from that woman, to mention those names? Do you dare remind us of that nasty business, which time has glossed over but not blotted out quite? What was the crime they were convicted of? Nothing else but that they took vengeance for Vettius' outrageous conduct to placate this same woman's injured resentment. Did you drag Camurtius and Caesernius into the case just to bring in the Vettian affair and repeat the veteran story of the copper-piece? Of course they were not really liable to the law of aggravated assault, but they were so deeply implicated in the piece of mischief they did not deserve to escape the noose of justice.

But why is Marcus Caelius being haled into this court? Nothing he is charged with falls within the province of this judicial body, or even, the law aside, under the bane of your censure. His early youth was entirely devoted to training those skills that I myself use in forum and administration as a means to honor, prestige, and glory. His circle of friends includes such older men as he particularly wished

to imitate in industry and self-control, and such of the finest
and noblest of his contemporaries as were aiming like him
at careers in the government. When he had grown a little
older and steadier he went to Africa on the staff of the proconsul Quintus Pompeius, a man who lacks no virtue. His
father has property there, and we elders thought too that
he ought to get some experience in the provinces while he
was young. He left there with Pompeius' full commendation, as you will learn from his testimony. Then in accordance with the old custom, following the example of those
youngsters who afterwards became models of fame and
patriotism in the state, he set out to signalize himself in the
people's eyes by prosecuting some well-known man.

31. I wish his appetite for fame had led him in some other
direction, but then the occasion of our difference is gone
and forgotten. He accused Gaius Antonius, my colleague
in the consulship. Antonius unfortunately could not make
the memory of his signal services to his country outweigh
the impression produced by his alleged misdeeds. No one
else of his age ever after that outshone Caelius in the forum,
or outdid him in helping friends in business or in the courts,
and no one in those circles was more widely popular. Then,
at the turning-point of his career—you are all sensible, cultivated men of the world, and I have nothing to hide—as
our young man's car was rounding the bend of the race-
course, his reputation suffered a slight check. He was introduced to a new lady-friend, a new and unlucky neighborhood, a hitherto unsampled life of pleasure. Now desire,
when it has been repressed too long, dammed up and
hemmed in throughout early youth, sometimes suddenly
breaks the barrier and pours out in a flood. From this sort of
life—or rather from this alleged sort of life, since it was
never so bad as people made out, but be that as it may—he

emerged, completely and totally rescued himself. And he is so far from being on friendly terms with her today that it is her enmity and hatred he is busy repelling.

Then to put a stop to all the gossip about his being caught in the toils of sloth and dalliance, he prosecuted a friend of mine for illegal electioneering—much against my will, but still he did it, though I exerted all my influence. And when the man was acquitted, he called for a retrial. He pays no attention to any of us and is more vehement than I would like. But I am not talking about wisdom now, something not to be expected in one of his age; I am talking about the keenness of his mind, his desire to win or die, his consuming passion for glory. Such appetites in men of our age ought to be pruned down. But when they appear in youth, like green shoots they show what a harvest of virtue and industry there will be when the crop is ripe. Young men of parts always have to be reined in rather than spurred on to fame. More has to be clipped than sown at that age, if there is to be any blossoming at all of talent. So if he boils over now and then, if he seems excessively violent and fierce and stubborn in making enemies or carrying on feuds, if anyone is offended by trifles in him, his rich purple robe, his gangs of friends, his splendid, elegant appearance, reflect that those things will soon pass into thin air, that age and time and circumstance soon will have mellowed them all.

32. Do not then, gentlemen, rob the state of an accomplished citizen whose heart is, politically speaking, in the right place. I promise you and go surety to the republic that, if ever I myself have given her satisfactory service, this young man will follow the path where I have led the way. This I say not only on the basis of the friendship between us, but because he has already obligated himself in the strictest possible way by his own conduct. No one who has prosecuted an ex-consul for malfeasance in office can afford

to cause trouble to the state. No man who has not even ac-
quiesced in the acquittal of one he accused of illegal electioneering can ever afterwards get away with buying votes
himself. Marcus Caelius has given the state two prosecu-
tions, gentlemen, which may serve either as guarantees of
his good behavior or as hostages against his causing any
danger.

A few days ago Sextus Clodius was acquitted. For the
past two years he has been either helper or head man at
every riot. A wretch equally innocent of property, propriety, probity, prospects, or prosperity, foul-faced, foul-
tongued, foul-handed, foul everything, with his own hands
he set fire to one of our holy temples and consumed the
census lists and official records of the Roman people. He
defaced Catulus' monument, razed my residence, burned
my brother's, and on the Palatine Hill while the whole city
looked on aghast called on the slaves to rise and burn Rome
and slaughter the Romans. But he was acquitted. A woman's influence saved him. And in a state where a thing like
that could happen, will you offer up Marcus Caelius as a
sacrifice to the same woman's lust? Is she to think that she
and her unlawfully wedded brother can simultaneously rescue the vilest of bandits and ruin the finest of young men?

And when you consider Caelius' youth, consider too this
poor old man, who is wrapped up in his only son, who rests
all his hopes on him and trembles for his fate. He appeals
to your pity, puts himself entirely in your hands. And if he
is not prostrate at your feet it is because he relies on your
moral sensibilities. Remember your own parents, your delight in your own children, and lift him up. Here you may
make another's grief the occasion of indulging your own
family feeling and native goodness of heart. Gentlemen, the
elder Caelius is failing fast. Do not deal him such a blow as
to make him long for extinction before the time that nature

has ordained. And Caelius the younger, now in the green of youth, are you to lay him low as by a sudden storm? Do not rob father of son and son of father. Do not despise an old man now all but in despair. And this young man, so full of hope, who waits for your nurturing hand, will you smite and uproot instead? Give him back to us, to his loved ones, to his country, and you will bind him to serve you and your children all his natural life, and you yourselves will enjoy the rich and abundant fruit of all his labor and effort.

# THE SECOND
# PHILIPPIC

AFTER *Caesar had pardoned him for his adherence to Pompey in the civil war Cicero confined his oratory to speeches in support of the petitions of banished friends for rehabilitation. Upon Caesar's murder the hope that the republican constitution might be restored fired him to renewed activity, and it was under his leadership that the senate decreed amnesty for the murderers but confirmation for Caesar's acts. But Antony soon made his intention to succeed to Caesar's position plain, and war broke out in northern Italy. Cicero hoped that Antony could still be checked, but a conciliatory speech he delivered in the senate on September 2 so offended Antony that he delivered a furious attack upon Cicero on September 19. The Second Philippic, not delivered but published as a pamphlet, is Cicero's reply.*

1. To what strange fatality in my life, my lords, am I to ascribe the fact that no traitor has for these twenty years molested my country who has not immediately declared war upon me? I need not mention the names of individuals; you can recall them easily for yourselves. The rest for their violence towards me have suffered even more severely than I might wish; and as to you, Antonius, I marvel that while you imitate their conduct, you do not apprehend the same fate. Moreover the enmity shown towards me by some others was less surprising; none of my former foes assailed me of his own accord; I had myself provoked all those attacks in my efforts to serve my country. But you, though I have never uttered a single word which could have irritated you, to prove yourself more violent than Catilina and more reckless than Clodius, have chosen to provoke me by scurrilous language, imagining, I presume, that your estrangement from me will be your surest recommendation to the disloyal among our fellow-countrymen. What am I to think? that I myself am despicable? No, I cannot see anything in my private life, or in my influence, or in my political career, or in my abilities, moderate as they are, which can properly be despised by an Antonius. Or did the man believe that the senate would be the best audience before which to disparage me? No, this noble house in complimenting the most illustrious Romans has declared its recognition of good government in many cases, but to me alone has it rendered thanks for the preservation of order. Or is it possible that he wished to institute an oratorical contest between us? This is generosity indeed! Could any man have a richer, an ampler theme than I should enjoy if I had to speak for myself

339

and against Antonius? No, there was only that one reason; he did not see how to convince his party that he is the enemy of Rome, unless he made a demonstration of his hostility to me. So before I answer him on the other matters, I will say a few words about the breach of friendship of which he accuses me—to my mind a really serious accusation.

2. His complaint is that on some occasion not specified I appeared in a case against his interests. Was I, then, not free to appear against a stranger on behalf of an intimate personal friend? Was I not free to appear against one who had secured support not because he was a young man of moral promise, but because he had sold his good looks? Was I not free to appear against the unfair advantage which Antonius had maintained by the help of an unscrupulous interference and not by due course and administration of the law? No, Antonius, I imagine you have chosen to bring this case again into notoriety, as a method of recommending yourself to the lowest classes, though no one needs to be reminded that you married a freedman's daughter and that children begotten by you are the grandchildren of Q. Fadius, whose father was once a slave. Or again I am told that you had put yourself under my tuition—at least those were your own words; I am told that you had frequented my house. True it is that if you had indeed done that, you would have done more for your reputation for honesty and morality. But you never took such a step; nor, had you been anxious to come to my house, would your friend C. Curio have permitted you.

Another statement of yours is that you retired in my favour when we were standing for the augurship. How amazing is your impudence! how deserving of exposure your effrontery! The truth is that when Cn. Pompeius and Q. Hortensius nominated me for the augurship at the request of the whole board of augurs (not more than two nominators being permissible by law), you were actually insolvent, and were supposing you could not escape bankruptcy but in a general crash. Were you then really in a position to stand for the augurship, when C. Curio was absent from Italy? And on the later occasion, when you were elected augur, would you have been able to carry a single tribe without Curio's aid? As it was, some of his personal friends were convicted of riot, for having supported your claims with too much zeal.

3. Or again, I availed myself of your kind assistance. When was that? Though I am sure I have always acknowledged the particular service which you mention. I have preferred the imputation of being indebted to you to the risk of being thought ungrateful by persons of shallow judgment. But what was this 'kind assistance'? Do you refer to your kindness in not killing me at Brundisium? Were you really free to kill me, when the victorious general, who, as you yourself often boasted, had chosen you out of his gang to be captain, not only wished to see me safe but had even ordered me to proceed to Italy? Well, suppose you had been allowed. What, my lords, is the kindness of a brigand, unless it is the being able to state that he has granted the lives of those whose lives he has not taken away? Were this a kindness, then those who murdered the great man who had once spared their lives, those men whom you generally term illustrious heroes, would never have obtained such renown as they have. But what is the value of a kindness which consists in having kept yourself from an atrocious crime? In this matter it should be rightly not so much a cause for joy to me that I was not murdered by you as a humiliation that you would have been free to murder me with impunity. But supposing it to have been a kindness (and it is true that a brigand could not confer anything more worthy of the

name), in what particular can you charge me with ungrateful conduct? Was I bound to stifle my anguish at the death-
throes of Rome, for fear of being thought ungrateful to
you? Surely not; and yet when I expressed my anguish in
terms which were indeed sad and woeful but demanded by
the position in which the senate and people of Rome has
placed me, did I ever use any expression which implied an
insult? any expression that was immoderate? any that was
unfriendly? Nay, consider what forbearance it showed to
refrain from abusive language when I was deploring the
conduct of M. Antonius, and that at a time when you had
squandered the last penny of the public funds, after you
had instituted a degrading traffic at your house for the sale
of anything and everything, when laws which had never
even been published for inspection were being acknowledged by you as having been made by and for yourself
alone, after you had annulled the auspices as augur and
used your position as consul to annul the tribune's veto,
when you had committed the outrage of surrounding your
person with armed men, when you were daily in your im-
modest home engaged in every kind of indecency, though
yourself worn out by debauchery and drunkenness. Yet, as
if I were contending with M. Crassus, with whom I had in
the past many serious differences, and not with a single vile
cut-throat like this man, while I expressed my deep grief for
the state of Rome, I said no word about the individual; but
I will make him clearly understand to-day, what 'kindness'
he received from me then.

4. Again, the letter which Antonius said I sent him, was
read out to you by him with his usual want of breeding
and his usual ignorance of the decencies of society. Did any
man—any one at least even slightly acquainted with the
habits of gentlemen—ever produce and read in public a
letter sent him by a friend, because some difference had

subsequently arisen between them? To do this is to rob the
living of the possibility of social life, and to deprive us of
the means of communicating with our absent friends. Consider how many jocose remarks we make in letters, which
would seem silly, if they were to be published; consider
how many serious remarks there are, which are not however
intended for publication! But let us attribute this lapse to
your ill-bred habits; let me now call attention to the amazing stupidity of the accusation. With what evidence will you
confront me, my good sir, clever lawyer as you may be, in
the eyes of your Mustelas and Tiros? Nay, since your Mustela and your Tiro are standing here at this moment furnished with swords in the sight of the senate, I will indorse
their opinion of your legal ability, if you will show me how
you will defend them when they are tried for murderous
violence. But to resume, how would you meet a flat denial
on my part that I ever sent you that letter? By what evidence will you convict me of falsehood? By that of the
handwriting? Ah! I know you have a knowledge, not unprofitable, of handwritings. But how can you appeal to the
letter? It is written by a secretary. I cannot but envy your
master, who received the huge fee I shall mention presently
for his success in teaching you—to be a fool. Yes, how foolish it is, I will not say for a public speaker, but for any human being, to make an allegation against an opponent, the
flat denial of which pulls the accuser up short? Not that I
mean so to deny your statement about my letter; but I
prove that in making it you have shown not only ill-breed-
ing but downright foolishness. For is there a single word in
that letter which does not breathe of good-breeding, proper
feeling, and generosity? The only possible charge is that I
do not express an unfavourable opinion of you in the said
letter, that I write as to a fellow-citizen, as to an honest
man, and not as to a scoundrel and a brigand. However, I

will not retaliate by producing your letter, though I should be justified by the provocation you have given me; you ask me in that letter to consent to your recalling a certain person from exile, and you protest that you will not do it against my wishes. Your request I of course granted; what reason was there in my trying to oppose your violence, since it could not be controlled by the expressed wishes of this house, by the public opinion of Rome, or by the law of the land? But after all, what need was there for you to make an appeal to me, if your protégé had already been recalled by Caesar's law? The presumption is of course that he wished to secure the credit for me—in a case where there could have been none for himself, as the law was already passed!

5. But since I am obliged, my lords, to say something in my own praise and not a little to the disparagement of M. Antonius, I ask you to hear graciously what I have to say for myself, and for the other topic I will myself ensure your close attention to what I have to say against him. And herewith I make this further request: that, if you have not been unconscious of the moderate and modest character of my whole career and more especially of my public utterances, you will not think me inconsistent to-day, in answering this villain according to the provocation he has given me. I shall not treat him as consul; he has not treated me as an ex-consul. Though I must say that he is not in any respect really a consul, whether you regard his life or his administration or the manner of his appointment; while no one can deny that I have actually held the consulship. To inform you, therefore, of his own view as to the duties of his office of consul, he made my tenure of the consulship one of his charges against me. That high office was nominally mine, my lords; but virtually it was undertaken by the senate. Every arrangement of mine was made, every act of mine was done, at the advice and on the authority and with the

express consent of this honourable house. This was the policy which you, with a wisdom as remarkable as your eloquence, have dared to vilipend before those by whose advice and wisdom it was carried out. Who indeed besides you and Publius Clodius ever dared to come forward and vilify my tenure of the consulship? But for you, as for C. Curio, is Clodius's doom reserved, since there is that by your hearth, which brought an evil doom on both your predecessors. M. Antonius, it appears, disapproves of my consulship. Yet it was approved by P. Servilius, whom I name first of the ex-consuls of that time as the one most recently deceased. It was approved by Q. Catulus, whose high influence will ever be felt at Rome; it was approved by the two Luculli, by M. Crassus, Q. Hortensius, C. Curio, C. Piso, M'. Glabrio, M'. Lepidus, L. Volcatius, and C. Figulus, by D. Silanus and L. Murena, who were then the consuls-elect for the ensuing year; the same policy that found favour with the ex-consuls was approved by M. Cato, who in voluntarily quitting life acted wisely in many respects, and especially in avoiding the sight of your elevation to the consulship. And above all, my consulship was specially approved by Cn. Pompeius; for he, as soon as he met me on his return from Syria, complimented me affectionately with the phrase that to me he owed his chance of seeing his country again. But why do I repeat the testimony of individuals? This noble house at a very crowded sitting approved so warmly of what I had done as consul that there was no one present who did not thank me as a father, no one who did not credit me with the preservation of his life and fortunes, his children and his country.

6. But since Rome has long been bereft of all those great men, whose names I have recalled, let us turn to those who survive; among whom there are two of the ex-consuls left. L. Cotta, whose good sense was as supreme as his ability,

for the political proceedings which you are now censuring, proposed a public thanksgiving in the most complimentary terms, and the other ex-consuls, whose names I have just given you, with the whole senate, assented to his motion: and this was an honour which had never since the foundation of Rome been conferred on any one acting in a civil capacity before my case. The other was L. Cæsar, your own uncle; remember the intrepidity and dignity with which he spoke and voted against his sister's husband, your step-father. Yet you, Antonius, though you should rightly have taken him as the guide and director of your whole life and of every thought, you preferred to resemble your stepfather rather than your uncle. I was not related to him, and yet I availed myself of his advice when I was consul; you are his sister's son, but have you ever referred any political question to him? Ah! to whom does Antonius refer his policy? Great heavens! to those to be sure, of the dates of whose birthdays he takes care to remind even us! To-day Antonius has not come down to the house. What detains him? A birthday-fête in his pleasure-grounds! In whose honour? I will not mention names; you can suppose he is fêting a Phormio one day, a Gnatho the next, and a Ballio the next! Oh! what outrageous indecency! What intolerable impudence and wickedness and licence! Is it possible that you, having a leading senator, an eminent citizen, so nearly related to you, should never refer political questions to him, but refer them to the penniless sycophants whose policy is to drain your purse? No wonder your consulship is beneficial and mine disastrous.

7. But have you really lost your sense of propriety as well as your purity so completely, as to have dared to make this statement here, in this temple in which I used to consult the noble senators of my time, once the prosperous rulers of the world, while your chief performance has been to station

there your desperadoes armed with swords? Yes, you have even dared—is there anything beyond your daring?—to state that when I was consul the slope of the Capitol was crowded with armed slaves. To force those atrocious resolutions of mine on the house, I presume, I was ready to use violence towards the senators? Miserable man, if you do not know the facts—you know nothing good—or if you know them, miserable indeed to speak with such impudence before this noble house! Every Roman knight, every young man of noble family in Rome but you, every single member of any class who remembered that he was a Roman citizen, was assembled on the slope of the Capitol, when the senate was meeting in this temple. Every name was offered for enrolment; though there were not enough clerks to take them, nor were their writing-boards large enough for the lists of our defenders. For when such atrocious villains were admitting their murderous treason, when they had been forced by the information lodged by their accomplices, by their own handwritings, and by the accusing voices, so to speak, of their own letters, to admit that they had conspired to fire the city, massacre their countrymen, devastate Italy, and blot out the name of Rome, who would there have been not impelled irresistibly to join in the defence of society? especially as the senate and people of Rome had then a leader such that, if any like him were our leader now, he would have meted out to you the same fate that befell those vile men. But he says I did not give up his stepfather's corpse for interment. This is a charge that was never made even by P. Clodius: and, since I was amply justified in my hostility to him, I am sorry to find you even more proficient in every sort of vice. But why did it occur to you to constrain us to recollect that you were brought up in the house of P. Lentulus? Were you afraid we should not think you possessed natural capacity sufficient to produce so much wickedness, unless it had been strengthened by the education you received there? 8. Were you really so senseless as to use at every point of your speech arguments which tell against yourself, as to say things not merely inconsistent, but altogether contradictory and incompatible, till you make your contest throughout not with me but with yourself? You admitted that your stepfather was implicated in that conspiracy, but you complained of his having suffered punishment: you commended our action as far as I was personally responsible for it, but what was done entirely by the senate, you preferred to censure. The arrest of the guilty persons was by my authority; the treatment they received was determined by the senate. He is so clever that he does not see that he is praising the opponent against whom he is speaking, and abusing the audience in whose presence the speech is made! And observe what audacity it indicates—no, I will not say audacity, since he is anxious to gain a reputation for that—but what folly (the quality he least covets), what unsurpassable folly it indicates to allude to the slope of the Capitol, when armed men are posted here among our benches! when even within the sacred fane of Concord, ye immortal gods! where when I was consul those patriotic speeches and votes were given which have preserved our lives to this day, men have now been stationed and stand with their swords in their hands! But shower your accusations on the senate; on the knights, who were then as a class in close alliance with the senate; on all the privileged classes, on all the citizens, provided that you do not deny that at this very moment this noble house is beleaguered by your Iturean guards. Yet it is not to your audacity that I attribute the impudence of your statements, so much as to the fact that you do not perceive the gross contradictions they involve. Clearly you have no sense at all. What can more surely indicate insanity than to resort to arms yourself in a manner destructive of the state, and then taunt an opponent with employing them for beneficial purposes? And besides all this in a certain part of your speech you intended to be witty. Great heavens! how unbecoming your attempt was! and for this failure some blame attaches to yourself; you might have borrowed some piece of humour from the actress who performs your wife. 'Let the sword give way to the gown,' you quoted. Well? did it not give way on that occasion? though true it is that since then the gown has had to give way to your weapons. Let us inquire whether it was better the weapons of desperate men should give way before the liberties of the Roman people, or that your armed followers should bear down our liberties thus. However I will give you no further answer as to my verses: I will only say briefly that you know no more about them than you do about any other form of literature; that I, without having ever failed my country or my friends, have by my published works of every description made the results of my midnight studies of some use to the rising generation and of some credit to the name of Rome. But no more of my poems; let us turn to more important topics.

9. You have alleged that the murder of P. Clodius was instigated by me. Why, what would be the popular belief on that subject, if Clodius had been killed on the occasion when you pursued him with a drawn sword through the forum in the sight of all Rome, and would have settled the business there and then, if he had not taken refuge in the staircase of a bookshop, and by barricading himself there baffled your impetuous onslaught? I do not mean to deny that I looked with approval on your performance; but even you do not assert that I advised it. In Milo's case however I was not able even to wish him success; for he had carried the affair through before any one suspected that he was likely to take it in hand. But possibly I advised him? It

is of course notorious that Milo's courage was so faint that he could not serve his country without some one's advice! Or possibly I rejoiced at Clodius's death? What if I did? Ought I, and I alone, to have shown grief when the whole of Rome was rejoicing? But after all, there was a commission to inquire into the circumstances of Clodius's death. It was not indeed a well-arranged inquiry: for what point was there in holding an inquiry into a single case of homicide under a specially enacted law, when there was a court appointed by statute to try such cases? Still an inquiry was held. No one made any charge of this kind against me during the investigation; has it been left for you to make this monstrous accusation after so many years?

But as to the allegation you have dared to make, and at some length too, that I was the author of the estrangement of Pompeius from Cæsar, and that I must therefore be considered responsible for the outbreak of the civil war, you will find that on that subject you have made mistakes, not indeed in your general statement, but in what is most important, the dates. 10. I admit that when our eminent countryman, M. Bibulus, was consul, I left no effort untried, no stone unturned, to win Pompeius away from his coalition with Cæsar. Cæsar however was more successful in his efforts; and he detached Pompeius from his intimacy with me. But when Pompeius had once surrendered himself body and soul to Cæsar, what sense would there have been in my trying to disentangle him? It would have been mere folly to hope for, sheer impudence to counsel such a course. But before things went so far, there were two occasions, on which I certainly did advise Pompeius to take some step against Cæsar. You may censure my action at those points, if you can. The first crisis was when I advised Pompeius not to allow the prolongation of Cæsar's government for another five years: the second when I urged him not to permit the motion to be made that Cæsar's claims should be considered in his absence. If I had succeeded in my efforts on either of these points, we should never have been plunged into this series of calamities. But I took the opposite line when Pompeius had intrusted all his resources and all the resources of the Roman people to Cæsar, and was beginning too late to perceive what I had long foreseen, and when I saw that an unholy war was being waged against Rome; ah! then I never ceased to advocate peace, harmony, compromise; and the sentence ever on my lips is known to many: 'Ah! Pompeius would that your compact with Cæsar had either never been made or else never been broken. In refusing to make it you would have shown your sound principle, in refusing to break it your common-sense.' These, M. Antonius, were ever my counsels for the good of Pompeius and for the good of Rome; and if they had prevailed, Rome would still be standing, while you would long ago have been brought low by your crimes, your beggary, and your evil reputation.

11. But all these are old accusations; I turn to the more modern charge. You allege that I instigated the murder of Cæsar. And here, I am afraid, my lords, that you will think me guilty of the disgraceful trick of having put up some one to act in collusion with me as prosecutor, and to praise me not only for my own, but also for other people's performances. As a matter of fact, has my name ever been mentioned in the list of those who shared that glorious deed? and was the name of any member of the party concealed? Concealed indeed! was there any name which was not published abroad at once? I should be more inclined to say that some persons had boasted in order to be thought members of the band when they had not been, than that any one who had been in it was anxious to conceal the fact. Besides, what probability is there that among a number of men half of whom were not known and the other half comparatively

young and not likely to conceal any one's name, my name would have been able to escape publicity? If, in fact, men were wanted to show others how to free their country, was I the man to stimulate the Bruti, when both of them see daily in their halls the effigy of L. Brutus, and one of them that of Ahala as well? Would the descendants of such ancestors be likely to turn to strangers for instructions rather than to their own kin, or to go outside their own homes for counsel? Or again, is it likely that C. Cassius, the scion of a house which could never endure despotic power, or even any man's improper ascendency, was in need of instructions from me? that C. Cassius who without the aid of his illustrious friends would long ago have settled this affair in Cilicia at the mouth of the Cydnus, if Cæsar had brought his fleet up to the bank at which he had arranged to anchor, and not to the opposite side of the river! Was Cn. Domitius stirred up to vindicate the cause of freedom by my influence, and not by the slaughter of his illustrious father, the death of his uncle, and the loss of his official rank? Did C. Trebonius need my persuasion? I should never have dared even to offer him my advice: and therein Rome owes him the greater gratitude, because he was a man who valued the freedom of her people more than private friendship, and chose to destroy the tyrant rather than to share his throne. Or did L. Tillius Cimber act under my instructions? In his case my surprise that he did the deed has been far stronger than any reason I had to suppose that he would do it,— surprise that the remembrance of his duty to his country could make him forget the benefits he had received from Cæsar. What of the two Servilii?—are they Cascas, or can they be Ahalas? Do you imagine that they too were roused by my influence rather than by their affection for Rome? It were tedious to repeat all the names: but the length of the list is an honour to Rome and a source of fame to the individuals.

12. But I must ask you, my lords, to recall the exact form in which this sagacious person convicted me. 'When Cæsar had been despatched,' such is his story, 'Brutus at once brandished aloft the reeking dagger, and calling on Cicero by name, bade him rejoice with them at the restoration of liberty.' But why on me? Was it because I knew already? What if the reason he appealed to me was that after a deed resembling that which I myself had accomplished, he wished me specially to observe that he had emulated my famous achievement! But you, most foolish of men, do you not comprehend that if the having desired Cæsar's death, which you impute to me, is criminal, to have shown joy at it is no less to be accounted a crime? What difference is there between advice to do the deed and approval of it when done? What difference does it make whether I have desired his murder or am rejoiced at its perpetration? And is there any living man, excepting those who rejoiced to see him establishing a despotism, who desired him not to be killed, or who disapproved of the deed when done? You must then blame all or none; in fact, every good citizen was, as far as he could be, an accomplice in Cæsar's murder. Some had not the skill to contrive, others lacked the courage to strike, and others again the opportunity; but no one lacked the will. Yet observe the stupidity of the man—or should I say, of the brute beast? His actual statement was this. 'Brutus, whom I mention with all respect, held up the bloody dagger and shouted aloud the name of Cicero; from this it ought to be understood that Cicero was privy to the plot.' So then I am termed a vile criminal by you, merely because you have a suspicion that I suspected something; the man who brandished the reeking dagger, he is 'mentioned with all re-

spect'? Let it be so; let us agree that there is in your words this gross stupidity: is there not more, far more, in the way you acted and voted? Force yourself to determine definitely, sir Consul, what judgment you pass on the Bruti, on C. Cassius, Cn. Domitius, C. Trebonius, and the rest: sleep off your drunken lethargy, I say, let the fumes of wine evaporate; or must one bring flaring lights to awake the man who is snoring over a question like this? Will you never comprehend that you must decide in your own mind whether the doers of that deed are murderers or the avengers of freedom?

13. No, give me a brief attention, and for a single moment try to follow a sober line of thought. I, Cicero, being by my own admission the friend, and, on your showing, the accomplice of the conspirators, I say that you must apply one of two terms to their conduct. If they are not the liberators of the Roman people and the saviours of Rome, I do not deny that they are worse than assassins, worse than murderers, worse than parricides, since it is more atrocious to kill the father of one's country than one's own parent. Now by what name do you, most wise and well advised of men, call them? If they are parricides, why have you always addressed them 'with all respect' before this noble house and also before the assembly of the Roman people? Why was M. Brutus at your motion exempted from the statutory obligation not to be absent from Rome more than ten days? Why at the celebration of the games of Apollo was such extraordinary respect shown to M. Brutus? Why were provinces assigned to Brutus and to Cassius? Why were they granted additional quaestors? Why were the numbers of their lieutenant-governors raised? Yet all this was certainly effected by your agency: you cannot therefore think them murderers. It follows then that in your opinion they are liberators, since there can be no third alternative. What is the matter? am I

confusing your mind? Possibly you do not understand an argument in the form of a dilemma. However that may be, the substance of my argument is this: since you have declared them free from guilt, you have inferentially pronounced them deserving of the most distinguished rewards. Accordingly I may now retract my argument on this point. I will write to them that, if they are asked by any one whether the charge you made against me is true or not, they are not to deny it: in fact I am afraid that the having kept me in the dark may be considered dishonourable in them, or the having declined their invitation extremely discreditable to me! For in truth, by Jupiter most holy, was there ever an achievement greater than that deed in Rome, nay, in the whole world? Was there ever a deed more glorious? more sure of immortal remembrance? Do you, Antonius, mean to include me, Cicero, in this league and compact, among the chieftains hidden in this modern Horse of Troy? I do not refuse the honour. I can even thank you, whatever may be your object; for the result is so great that I cannot consider the unpopularity which you wish to excite against me as comparable with any ordinary commendation. For can anything be more blest than the lot of those men whom you boast that you have exiled and driven into banishment? Is there likely to be any spot so uninhabited or so uncivilised as not to welcome them with open arms the moment they approach it? Are there any men so savage as not to feel that the sight of them is the greatest boon that human life can receive? Will any generation yet to come ever be so forgetful or any period of literature ever so ungrateful as not to cherish their fame in eternal remembrance? By all means include me in such a list.

14. But there is one point on which I apprehend your disapproval: if I had been one of them, I should have freed Rome not merely from the despot, but from despotism; and

had my dagger collaborated with theirs, if I may use the expression, I should have put the finishing touches not only to a single act but to the whole of this tragedy. And yet, if it is criminal to have desired Cæsar's death, let me ask you to reflect, Antonius, what will happen to you, who most notoriously contemplated an attempt on his life with Trebonius at Narbo, and on account of your complicity then were, as we saw, called aside by Trebonius at Cæsar's assassination. For my part—observe how far removed from unfriendliness is the way I treat you—I commend you for having once had good intentions; I thank you for having held your tongue; I even pardon you for not having taken an active part; an affair like that demanded a man. But if any one summons you to stand your trial for the murder and employs the famous Cassian interrogatory and asks, 'Who profited by the crime?' take care that you do not find yourself implicated! Although Cæsar's death was, as you said at least, a gain to all who did not wish to be slaves, yet to you who are now more likely to be a tyrant than to be a slave, it is a special gain; a special gain to you, I say, who have extricated yourself from an enormous mass of debts by your visit to the Temple of Plenty; who by means of the same accounts have dispersed an amazing amount of money; to whom so many articles have been conveyed from Cæsar's house; whose house is a manufactory—and a very paying one—for forged papers and signatures, and a market in which territories, towns, taxes, and exemptions from tribute, are scandalously bought and sold. In fact, what was there but Cæsar's death which could possibly have relieved your penury and paid your debts? But you seem to be somewhat disturbed. Are you secretly afraid of being included in the list of the accused? I can dispel your fears; no one will ever credit the charge: it is not in your nature to render any service to your country. Rome can rely on the illustrious men who were responsible for that most glorious deed: I say no more than that you are pleased, I do not charge you with having done it. I have answered the most serious charges: I must now reply to the rest.

15. You have taunted me with my presence in Pompeius's camp, and with the whole of that period: but if, as I have said, my advice and influence had prevailed at that period, you would to-day be a beggar, and we should be free men; Rome would not have lost so many Roman generals and so many Roman armies. I confess that I, foreseeing that what did happen, would happen, was plunged into dejection as deep as all the rest of the best citizens would have felt, if they had foreseen what I did. I did lament, my lords, I did indeed lament, that Rome, once preserved by your policy and mine, would so soon perish: but yet I was not so ignorant and inexperienced as to be reduced to despair by clinging to a life which would only torture me if preserved, while the losing it would deliver me from all my troubles. I did indeed desire that the lives of those eminent men, those bright ornaments of their country, should be preserved, that so many men of consular and praetorian rank, so many honourable senators, the very flower of the youthful aristocracy, whole armies of the best and bravest of our countrymen, should survive: if they still lived, on terms of peace however unfair—to my mind peace at any price between fellow-citizens seemed more advantageous than civil war—we should today retain constitutional government. And if my voice had prevailed, if those for whose lives I was anxious had not been the first to withstand me in the excitement of anticipated victory, then, to say the least, you, Antonius, would never have kept your place in this house, no indeed, nor even in this city. The fact was, you say, that the tone of my language estranged Cn. Pompeius from me. But was there any one for whom he showed more affection? was there any

one with whom he conversed or took counsel more frequently? and it was no slight matter that, though we differed on the most important political questions, we remained on the same terms of intimate private friendship. I saw plainly his feelings and principles and he saw mine. I wished to secure the safety of our fellow-citizens, that we might afterwards take thought for their honour; he preferred to take thought for their honour at once. The fact that both of us had alike a definite end in view, made our difference of opinion more endurable. But the feelings of that exceptional and superhuman man towards me are well known to those who followed him in his flight from Pharsalus to Paphos: he never alluded to me except in complimentary terms, in language full of the most affectionate regret, acknowledging that I had 'foreseen the future more correctly,' though he had 'entertained the more sanguine hopes.' And do you, sir, dare then to reproach me in the name of the man whom you admit to have been my friend, while you are only the dealer in his confiscated property? 16. But let us pass over that war, in which you were far too fortunate. I will not reply even to your taunts about the jokes which you said I made in Pompeius's camp. That camp was indeed a place of much anxiety; but men even in the midst of trouble, still, if they are human, sometimes relax. And as he blames me for my dejection in one sentence and for my jokes in the next, it may be fairly inferred that neither my dejection nor my levity were excessive.

Further, you have stated that no legacies were ever left to me. I should indeed rejoice if this count in your indictment were true: for then more of my friends, and of my intimates, would still be living. But how has this idea ever entered into your head? The truth is that my receipts under the head of legacies amount to more than twenty million sesterces. However I admit that you have been more fortunate in this way. No one not a personal friend ever made me his heir; so that whatever profit I have derived from inheritances, was attended by a certain amount of regret. You I know were the heir of L. Rubrius of Casinum, a man whom you never even saw. Yes, just think how attached to you he was, though you don't know whether he was light or dark! He passed over his nephew; the son of Q. Fufius, an honourable Roman knight, who was on excellent terms with him, whom he had always publicly designated his heir, he does not even name in his will. He made you his heir, you whom he had never seen, or at any rate never spoken to. Tell me if you can, unless I am troubling you too much, what L. Turselius was like, how tall he was, what town he came from, and in what tribe he voted. 'I can only tell you,' you will say, 'what estates he possessed.' That no doubt is why he disinherited his brother and made you his heir! There are many other cases in which our friend forcibly ejected the rightful heirs, and seized large sums of money left by utter strangers, as if he was their natural successor. However, what has astonished me most is your effrontery in alluding to inheritances, when you never took up your succession to your father's estate.

17. Was this all the material you could collect, you demented man, after so many days spent in practising rhetoric in a country house not your own? Although what your friends say is probably true, I mean, that you practise declamation not to sharpen your wits, but to rouse yourself after a debauch. But perhaps it is only for a jest that you employ as your master a man who may be a professor of rhetoric in the opinion of yourself and your boon-companions, whom you permitted to say what he liked in abuse of you, and who is I dare say witty enough all round, though it is easy to find witticisms at the expense of you and your friends. But mark the difference between your grand-

father and yourself; he was cautious in saying even what would help his case; you are hasty in saying what is damaging to yourself. But what a huge fee was paid to the professor! Listen, my lords, listen; and learn the atrocities inflicted on our country. Two thousand acres in the Leontine Plain were bestowed on your rhetoric professor, Sextus Clodius, and those tax-free; this was the fee the Roman people had to pay to have you taught to be a fool. Did you find this also, you villain, among Cæsar's papers? But I will speak elsewhere about the Leontine Plain, and about the Campanian too, both of which domains he wrested from the state and defiled for ever with settlers of the most degraded character.

And now, since I have sufficiently answered his charges against me, I must say a few words about the critic himself, the censor of my career. But I will not discharge everything at once; and then, if I have to cope with him oftener, as I shall, I shall always have new material. And I shall find material enough and to spare in the abundance of his vices and crimes.

18. Shall we then survey together your manner of life from your boyhood? I think we will: and let us begin from the beginning. Do you retain any memory of the fact that you were bankrupt in your teens? 'Well,' you will say, 'but that was my father's fault.' You may say so; your plea is one distinguished by filial affection. Your subsequent conduct was distinguished by effrontery of your own, I mean, your taking a seat in the fourteen rows, though the Roscian Law assigned a special place to bankrupt knights, even if their bankruptcy was due to misfortune and not to their own fault. You came of age; and on your shoulders the toga of a man soon became that of a certain kind of woman. At first you plied for hire; your prices were fixed, and anything but low; but soon Curio appeared on the scene, removed you

from the open market, and made you, so to speak, an honest lad by something similar to a legally contracted union. No slave purchased to be the victim of lust was ever so completely in his master's power as you in Curio's. How often did his father eject you from his house? How often did he have the house watched to prevent your crossing the threshold? Though you under cover of night, impelled by passion and greedy for your fee, contrived to crawl down over the tiles, till the family could not endure the scandal any longer. Are you aware that I am speaking of matters with which I am intimately acquainted? Carry your mind back to that occasion when the elder Curio lay weeping on his bed; when his son was throwing himself at my feet in tears and commending you to my protection; when he was imploring me to defend him from his father's anger, if he asked for a sum of six million sesterces; he had, he said, given security for you to that amount. In his passion for you he protested that he could not bear the pangs of being torn from your arms, and that he would follow you into exile. On that occasion remember how I mitigated or rather entirely averted a great disaster which threatened a prosperous house. I persuaded the father to pay his son's debt; to redeem a young man of the highest spirit and intellectual promise by well-timed pecuniary assistance, and to debar him by the whole weight of paternal authority from any sort of intimacy or even association with you. Remembering my share in these transactions, would you have had the audacity to rouse me by your insults, if you did not rely wholly on the swords we see round about us? 19. But let us turn from his indecencies and immoralities; there are some things which a gentleman cannot mention; you may count yourself the less encumbered in having stained yourself with crimes which cannot be alleged against you by an opponent who feels any sense of decency. But mark, my lords, the rest of his early career;

and even that I will survey rapidly; for I am anxious to hurry on to the crimes which he perpetrated in the civil war, amid the dire calamities of his country, and to the crimes that he is committing every day: and as to these, though many of them are better known to yourselves than to me, I beg you to continue the attention which you are giving me now. In such matters your anger ought to be excited not only by your actual knowledge of the events but even by the remembrance of them: though I think we must be brief over the middle of his career that we may have plenty of time when we come to the most recent stages of it.

Very intimate with Clodius, when he was tribune, was this man who now recites the favours he then conferred on me: he fired the train in every disturbance Clodius created, and even within Clodius's own house he had a little plan of his own for a disturbance. He is fully aware of the subject of my allusion. The next thing was his expedition to Alexandria, made in defiance of the senate's resolution, of the authority of the government, of the religious difficulty: but I know Gabinius was his chief in this, and anything he did with Gabinius would be quite right! What were the circumstances, what was the character of his next step, his return from Egypt? On his way back from Egypt he went to the other end of Gaul before he returned home. And what was his home? Every man had his own home then; so you of course had none. Home indeed! Had you any place of your own on which to rest your weary feet except a single farm at Misenum, which you shared with a joint-stock company like the mines at Sisapo? 20. You arrived from Gaul to stand for the quaestorship. Dare, if you can, to say that you went then to your mother's house before you came to mine! I had received a letter from Cæsar, asking me to receive your apologies; and so I did not allow you even to mention reconciliation. After this I was courted by you, and you were greatly assisted by me when you stood for the quaestorship. This was the occasion on which you attempted to kill P. Clodius in the open forum amid the applause of the people; and though the attempt was entirely your own affair and not in any way prompted by me, you publicly announced that it was your conviction that to kill him was the only amends you could make to me for the injuries you had inflicted upon me. And herein I am surprised that you should charge me with having instigated Milo to kill Clodius, knowing as you well do, that I never encouraged you when you were voluntarily offering me the same service. However, if you had been meaning to persevere, I was anxious that the deed should redound to your credit rather than be taken as a debt of gratitude to me. You were elected quaestor: at once without any decree of the senate, without waiting to have your province assigned to you by lot or bill, you hurried off to Cæsar. You thought of course that he was the only refuge in the wide world for you, for an impecunious and evil-minded debtor who had wandered far from respectability. When you had gorged yourself there with his donations and your own extortions —if one can use the term of what is disgorged the next minute—you flew back to Rome with empty pockets to take the tribuneship, and show yourself in that office, if you could, a worthy helpmeet for your old protector.

21. Now, my lords, let me relate to you, not the want of decency and self-restraint with which he has disgraced himself and the honour of his family, but the outrages and the unhallowed violence with which he has assailed us and our property, that is, the whole commonwealth of Rome. You will find in his wickedness the prime source of all our woes. For when in the consulship of L. Lentulus and C. Marcellus, on the first of January, you were anxious to up-

hold the constitution, already tottering to its fall, and were ready to act with consideration towards C. Cæsar, if he showed any sanity, then this wretch used the tribunician powers, which he had sold and delivered into another man's hand, to thwart your policy, and thereby deserved the axe which has descended on many tribunes for smaller crimes than his. Yes, M. Antonius, by a formal resolution of the senate, and that senate an undiminished body, not yet deprived of its most brilliant members, the measures were voted against you which by long established custom are voted against enemies who are of Roman blood. Have you, you, dared to speak against me before these noble lords, though by them I was solemnly declared the saviour and you the enemy of this state? They may have long delayed to remind you of your crime, but they have not forgotten it. While the human race exists, while the name of Rome remains,—and that will be for all eternity, if you suffer it to continue,—your baneful exercise of the veto will be known and named. Was any partiality, was any rashness shown by the senate, when you, young as you were, by your single voice, not only once, but several times, prevented a whole order of the state from passing a resolution to preserve their country, when you did not allow the claims of the senate's resolution to be urged upon you? Nor was anything urged but that you should not choose Rome to be utterly destroyed and ruined, at that crisis, I say, when neither the entreaties of the leading men in Rome nor the warnings of your elders nor the arguments of a crowded house could make you remove a veto that had been bought and sold. Then after many attempts had been made, it was absolutely necessary to inflict on you the extreme sentence, inflicted on but few before you, none of whom had escaped with their lives; then this house ordered the consuls and the other higher magistrates and officials to take up arms against you;

and you would never have escaped, if you had not taken refuge with Cæsar's army. 22. You, you I say, M. Antonius, are the first of those who when C. Cæsar was anxious to bring about revolution furnished him with a pretext for making war upon his country. Did he ever allege any other cause? Did he ever give any reason for his insane policy and action, beyond the disregard of the veto, the violation of the tribune's legal powers, the senate's interference with Antonius? I pass over the falseness, the levity of such excuses, seeing that no one can have any valid reason whatsoever for making war on his country. But I will say nothing about Cæsar; you assuredly cannot deny that the cause of that fatal war was the part you played on that occasion. Miserable must you be if you comprehend this, still more miserable if you do not comprehend, that it is securely recorded in history, that it is handed down to posterity, that our descendants to the remotest ages will never forget, that the consuls were driven from Italy and with them Cn. Pompeius, the light and glory of the Roman empire, that all the ex-consuls whose health allowed them to effect that disastrous retreat, the praetors, the ex-praetors, the tribunes of the plebs, a large proportion of the senators, the whole of the rising generation,—that, in a word, the whole commonwealth was ejected and evicted from its proper habitation by you. And as truly as the seed is the cause of trees and plants, you were the cause of this most lamentable war. My lords, you mourn for three Roman armies slain in the war; they were slain by Antonius. You weep for the loss of the most illustrious of our fellow-citizens; they were torn from us by Antonius. The authority of this house has been trampled on; it was trampled upon by Antonius. Everything that we have seen since—and what calamity have we not seen? —if we reckon accurately, we shall find part of our debt to one man, to Antonius. As Helen to the Trojans, so has he been to Rome, the cause of war, the cause of destruction and desolation. The remaining months of his tribunate were like the first: he carried out every measure which the senate had succeeded in preventing while the government of Rome was still untouched.

23. But mark the vile inconsistency of his villainy. He was reinstating many persons who had been ruined and banished; among these there is no mention of his uncle. If he wished to act with severity, why was he not severe to all alike? if he wished to show his clemency, why did he have no mercy for his own relations? I will only take one instance. Licinius Denticula, who had been convicted for gambling, and who had gambled with him, he restored to his former status, as if he felt it illegal to game with a convicted person; but he restored him only on condition of his accepting inclusion in the bill in lieu of the sums he had lost to him. What reason did you give the Roman people for the propriety of his restoration? You alleged, I suppose, that he had been prosecuted in his absence? that he had been tried without any opportunity of defending himself? that gambling was not punishable by law? that he was crushed by armed violence? or possibly, as was said about your uncle, that he was convicted by a bribed jury? No, nothing of the sort. It is possible that he was an excellent man and a deserving citizen. That of course is not material; still, since a mere conviction counts for nothing, I would excuse you if he really were so: but as it is, by rehabilitating an abandoned man who would not hesitate to gamble even in the forum, and who was convicted by the law under which gambling is a legal offence, does not our friend here give us a clear revelation of his own tastes? And again, during his same tribunate, when Cæsar on his departure for Spain had left Italy under his heel, remember the progresses he made on the roads, remember his peregrinations

round the country towns! I know that I am dealing with
subjects which have long been on every one's lips, and that
what I am saying and about to say is better known to all
who were, than to me myself who was not, in Italy; but I
will just mention the details, though of course you will find
my remarks inadequate in comparison with your own recollections. In fact has any one ever heard anywhere of behaviour so openly scandalous as his? of conduct so notoriously
disgraceful? 24. The tribune of the plebs was driving in a
carriage; he was preceded by lictors wreathed with the laurel; and in their midst was borne, in an uncurtained litter,
an actress whom the honest burghers of the country towns,
who were obliged to meet him on his progress, had to address not by her well-known stage-sobriquet but by the
name of Volumnia. Next came a coach-load of pandars, a
wicked crew; his mother was left to follow in the train of
her profligate son's mistress as if attending on a daughter-
in-law. Miserable indeed the mother whose offspring has
been so deadly a curse to his country! On every borough
and country town and colony, on every part of Italy, he has
left the mark of these outrageous insults.

To criticise the rest of his performances, my lords, is a difficult and hazardous task. He took part in the war; he drank
the blood of Roman citizens very different from himself; he
was fortunate, if fortune can be the consequence of crime.
But since we wish not to injure the veterans, though it is
true there is little resemblance between your position and
that of the soldiers—they only followed, you hunted about
for a leader—still, for fear you should make mischief between them and me, I will say nothing about the general
character of the war. You returned victorious from Thessaly to Brundisium in charge of the legions. There you re-
frained from murdering me. Stupendous generosity! I admit
you had the power. And yet there was not a man among

your then companions who did not feel that my life ought
to be spared. For so strong is the sentiment of patriotism,
that my life was held sacred even by your legionaries, because they remembered my preservation of our country.
But let us assume that it was a piece of generosity to leave
me what you did not take away, and that I hold my life as
a gift from you, because you did not rob me of it; did your
insults allow me to be as grateful for the boon as I wished
to be, especially as you saw that I should answer you thus?
25. But you came to Brundisium, you came to the warm embraces of your play-actress? How now? Am I accusing you
falsely? How miserable it is not to be able to deny what it
is a degradation to admit! If you felt no shame before the
burghers, did you feel none even before the veteran legionaries? And was there a single soldier in the army who did
not see her at Brundisium? was there any one ignorant of
the fact that she had taken a journey of so many days to
welcome you? was there any one who did not lament that
he had not known till too late what a wicked man he had
followed? You were whirled back through Italy, the play-
actress with you as before. Your soldiers were billeted on
various towns in a humiliating and oppressive manner. In
Rome, gold, plate, and wines, particularly the last, were bru-
tally taken from the owners. The next step, Cæsar being at
Alexandria and so unaware of the proceedings, was, that
Antonius was made master of the horse by the kind services of the dictator's friends. Then he thought that as *master
of the horse* he might justifiably live with a man named
*Hippias,* and that he might intrust to Sergius the actor the
horses received as tribute from the provinces: at that time
he had selected not the house which he now occupies,
though on a precarious tenure, but M. Piso's as his headquarters. Need I recount to you his decrees, his robberies,
his grants of inheritances, and his plunder of heirs? He was

urged on by his impecuniosity; he had nothing else to turn to. He had not yet secured the huge estates left him by L. Rubrius and L. Turselius; he had not yet started up as the unexpected heir of Cn. Pompeius and of many persons absent from Italy. He was obliged to live like a brigand, and to subsist on just what he might have got by plundering others.

But let us turn from these manifestations of a sturdier side of his wickedness: let us rather speak of frivolities of an especally infamous description. Look at the huge throat, the massive sides, and the whole frame as well knit as a prize-fighter's! Yet you drank so much wine at dinner at Hippias's marriage, that you could not help being sick in the sight of the Roman people next day! What a filthy performance, as filthy to describe as to witness! If it had happened at the dinner-table in the midst of your bestial potations, any one would have thought it a disgrace to you. But this was at an assembly of the Roman people, and it was the master of the horse, in charge of public business, who, though it would be disgraceful for him even to hiccough, was actually sick, and covered his clothes and the whole platform with scraps of solid food reeking with wine. But this incident he admits to be among his less brilliant achievements; let us proceed at once to the more glorious deeds.

26. Cæsar returned from Alexandria, the favourite of Fortune, as he seemed in his own eyes, though to my mind no one who is the enemy of his country can be accounted fortunate. The spear was set up and a public auction was held before the temple of Jupiter the Stablisher, and the goods of Cn. Pompeius—alas! I have spent my tears, but the thought will never cease to cause me anguish—the goods, I say, of Cn. Pompeius Magnus were put up and sold by the unsympathetic voice of the public auctioneer. For that

one moment Rome forgot her bonds and groaned aloud, and though all minds were enslaved by the all-pervading fear, still the Roman people was free as yet—to groan. And while all were waiting and wondering who would be so profane, so mad, so hateful to heaven and earth, as to dare to take part as purchaser in that abominable confiscation and sale, no one could be found but Antonius, and that though the place was crowded with men who had audacity enough for anything short of such a deed: Antonius was the one man who could be found with daring enough to do what the audacity of all the others had recoiled from with horror. Was the fatuity, or I should more truly call it, the frenzy which possessed you such as to make you forget that as a man of family dealing in confiscated property, and as the dealer in the confiscated property of Cn. Pompeius, you would be cursed and abhorred by the people of Rome, and the object now and ever of the hatred of heaven and earth? But with what insolence did his greedy mouth close at once on the property of the great man whose valour had made the Roman people more dreaded by foreign nations, and whose justice had made it more beloved? 27. Having then gorged himself in a moment with that great man's vast possessions, he strutted with joy like a character in a farce, Out-at-elbows one day and *nouveau riche* the next. But as some poet says, 'Ill-got's ill-spent.' It is incredible, it is portentous to relate, by what methods and in how few months, nay in how few days, he dissipated those vast accumulations. There was an immense stock of wine, a large quantity of the best plate, costly tapestry, much handsome and splendid furniture in several places, all the property of a really affluent though not an extravagant man: of all this in a few days there was nothing left. Was a Charybdis as voracious as this? Charybdis indeed! If Charybdis existed, she was only a single creature. No, I protest, I think that the Ocean

itself could hardly have engulfed so instantaneously property so scattered and deposited in such distant localities!
Nothing was secured, nothing was sealed up, nothing was
inventoried. The wine-cellars were abandoned to the raids
of the vilest criminals; here actors and there actresses were
looting the house; the rooms were crammed with gamblers
and choked with drunken men; the potations lasted whole
days and went on in many places at once. The loss caused
by this waste was frequently augmented by his gambling
debts—he is not always lucky; you might have seen the
beds in the slaves' bedrooms covered with Cn. Pompeius's
rich purple draperies. You may cease then to wonder that
this property was so rapidly squandered: not merely a single estate however large—and that estate was large indeed
—but even whole towns and kingdoms could have been
swallowed up by such iniquitous excesses. In spite of this
he also seized upon Pompeius's house and gardens. What
brutal effrontery! Did you dare even to enter Pompeius's
house? Did you dare to cross that hallowed threshold? Did
you dare to intrude your lust-stained features into the presence of the gods of that hearth and house? Once no one
could behold or pass by that house without tears; and are
you not ashamed of occupying rooms in that house so long?
However dull you are, still you cannot find any pleasure in
such a home. 28. Or when you see the memorials of Pompeius's naval victories in the fore court, do you imagine
that you are entering your own house? No, it is impossible.
For though you may be without intelligence and without
feeling, as indeed you are, still you have some acquaintance
with yourself and your belongings and your kin. Nor do I
believe that you can ever have any ease of mind whether
awake or asleep; for though you be, as indeed you are, passionate and violent, you could not fail, if you saw in your
dreams the form of that illustrious man, to start from your

sleep in panic, and to rave of the vision even when awake. I pity indeed the walls and fabric of that house. In Pompeius's time it had never seen anything that was not modest, anything that was not the outcome of the highest character and the most pious training. That great man was, as you know, my lords, not more illustrious in public than admirable in private life, and he deserved as much praise for his domestic habits as for his behaviour in society. And in his house the bedrooms have become brothels, and the living-apartments tap-rooms! Oh! but he denies all this now; pray don't refer to the past! He has turned over a new leaf; he has sent his female friend about her business; he has taken the keys from her in the form prescribed by the Twelve Tables, and turned her out of doors. Besides, what a reputable, what a respected member of society he is! Why, in his whole life his most decent act has been this divorcing of his play-actress!

But how often he repeats his phrase, that he is 'a consul and an Antonius': he might as well say 'a consul and the most profligate,' or 'a consul and the most iniquitous of men.' What else is now the connotation of the name Antonius? If any honourable quality were implied by the name, your grandfather would have said on some occasion, I suppose, that he was 'a consul and an Antonius'; which he never did. Even my colleague, your uncle, would have used the phrase, unless you are the only Antonius genuine. But I pass over the faults not particularly appropriate to the characters under which you have persecuted your country: I return to your own special *rôle,* I mean to the civil war, which was conceived and worked up and fostered by you and you alone; though indeed in the war not only your timidity but your sensuality kept you from playing a prominent part. 29. You had tasted, or rather you had drunk deep of Roman blood; you had commanded a wing at the battle of Pharsalus; you had slaughtered the illustrious and highborn L. Domitius; and many besides him, who had escaped from the field, whom Cæsar would perhaps have spared, as he spared not a few, had been savagely hunted down and butchered by you. And after all these great and glorious deeds, what reason had you for not following Cæsar to Africa, especially as so large a part of the war still remained unfinished? Tell me, too, what place you occupied in consequence in Cæsar's favour after his return from Africa? Of what account were you held by him? When he was governor you had been his quaestor, when he was dictator his master of the horse; you had been the prime cause of the war, the instigator of his barbarities, the sharer of the spoil; you were according to your own account adopted as his son by his will; yet you were dunned by him for the money still owing for the house, the gardens, and the confiscated property you had bought up. At first you replied with a display of temper and (I don't wish to be too hostile to you) your statements were almost fair and equitable. 'To think that C. Cæsar should demand payment from me! Why he from me rather than I from him? Did he win his victories without me? No, nor was he ever strong enough. I gave him the pretext for the civil war; I proposed the disastrous measures; I declared war against the consuls and generals of Rome, against the senate and the people of Rome, against the gods of Rome and their altars and hearths, against my native country. Is it to profit himself alone that he has been victorious? Why should not the spoils be shared by those who have shared the adventure?' Your claim was valid; but what did that matter? He was the stronger. And so he turned a deaf ear to your phrases and sent soldiers both to you and to your sureties; and then you suddenly published that wonderful catalogue! What ridicule it excited! Such a long catalogue of numerous and miscellaneous pieces of property, out of which except his share in the estate at Misenum there was absolutely nothing which the vendor could call his own! And when the auction took place, how lamentable was the sight! Pompeius's tapestry, not much of it, and what there was dirty; a few battered silver cups once his, and a few shabby slaves; till we felt sorry that there were any relics of his property left for us to see. And even this sale was stopped by L. Rubrius's heirs under an order from Cæsar. The scoundrel was in a fix; he knew not where to turn; besides, at that very moment an assassin sent by him was said to have been arrested with a dagger on his person at Cæsar's house, and Cæsar complained of this attempt before the senate and made an undisguised attack on you.

Cæsar left Rome for Spain, having given you a few days' grace on account of your impecuniosity; even then you did not follow him. Rather early, surely, for a distinguished champion like yourself to retire upon his laurels? Need any one then be afraid of a man who showed so much timidity in supporting his party, that is to say, in pushing his own fortunes? 30. At last he actually did start for Spain; but he could not, as he says, reach that country in safety. Then how did Dolabella reach that country? Either you should not have attached yourself to that cause, Antonius, or, having joined it, you should have supported it to the last extremity. Cæsar fought three decisive battles against Roman citizens, in Thessaly, in Africa, and in Spain; Dolabella fought by his side in all these battles; in that in Spain he was actually wounded. If you ask my opinion, I had rather he had not been there; but still, though I must reprehend his original decision, I must commend his brave consistency: were you either right or consistent? Cn. Pompeius's sons were then making an effort primarily to recover their native country—very well; let us say that their efforts affected your whole party equally—but they were in addition trying to recover their ancestral gods, their household altars and hearths, the tutelary deity of their family, of all of which you had taken possession. And when those who were legally entitled to these things were in arms to reclaim them, then—though what equity can there be in a resistance so inequitable?—still who ought in equity to have headed the resistance to the sons of Cn. Pompeius? Who indeed but you, the dealer in the confiscated property? Or while you were occupied at Narbo in being sick at the dinner-tables of your hosts, was Dolabella to be doing the fighting for you in Spain?

But what was the mode of his return from Narbo? He actually asked me why I returned so suddenly and interrupted my journey. I laid before you, my lords, not long ago the reason of my return. I wished, if possible, to be at my country's service even before the first of January. So to your question as to the mode of my return I will only reply, first, that I arrived by day and not in the dark; secondly, that I wore ordinary shoes and the toga, not Gaulish slippers of any sort or a heavy cloak. But even now you regard me fixedly and, as it seems, with anger. Ah! you would assuredly seek a reconciliation with me, if you knew what bitter shame I feel for your infamy, though you feel none yourself. Of all the disgraceful acts I have ever seen or heard of this is the most outrageous. Though you thought you had been master of the horse, and were standing for, or rather begging for, the consulship of the following year, you dashed along through the boroughs and colonial towns of Gaul—towns from which, when men stood and did not beg for consulships, we used to ask support—attired in a heavy travelling cloak and Gaulish slippers. 31. But mark the man's frivolity! On reaching the Red Stones about the middle of the afternoon, he dived into a low inn and lurked there boozing in secret till nightfall; then he hurried on to Rome in a light gig, and arrived at his house with his cloak over his head. 'Who goes there?' says the porter. 'A letter-carrier from Marcus.' He was at once conducted to the lady he had come to see and handed her his letter. When she was reading it with tears—it was a very affectionate composition; the main point of the letter was that he would have nothing more to do with the actress, that he had recalled all his affection from her and transferred it to his wife—but when she began to weep copiously, the tender-hearted husband could not bear the sight; he uncovered his head and fell upon her neck. You infamous man! what else can I call you? There is no term I can more properly employ. So it was simply that your wife might unexpectedly behold a Ganymede like you on your sudden exhibition of yourself to her, that you disturbed Rome by a midnight alarm, and Italy by a panic which lasted many days? Yes, you had one pretext at your own house, your marital affection; outside it an even less creditable reason, your wish to prevent L. Plancius from estreating the bail given by your sureties. But when you were brought forward at a public meeting by a tribune of the people and said in answer to a question that you had come to Rome on private business, you forced even the populace to be witty at your expense. But this is more than enough about such trifles: let us turn to more serious matters.

32. When C. Cæsar was returning from Spain, you went a considerable distance to meet him; you went and you returned with some rapidity, to show him that, if not as brave as you might be, you were nevertheless energetic; so somehow or other you became intimate with him again. This was quite in Cæsar's manner: any one who was utterly impecunious and overwhelmed with debt, if he knew him to possess also real wickedness and audacity, he readily ad-

mitted into his favoured circle. You had these recommenda-
tions in an eminent degree; and orders were issued that you
should be declared duly elected consul, and as his own colleague. I am not complaining of the way in which Dolabella was induced to stand, led on, and finally thrown over.
Every one knows what treachery you both showed towards
Dolabella in this matter. Cæsar intercepted and transferred
to himself the office which had been promised and guaran-
teed to Dolabella: you aided and abetted his breach of
faith. The first of January arrives; we are summoned to the
senate: Dolabella attacked the treachery in an invective far
more eloquent and elaborate than my present speech. Antonius however flew into a passion; and I still shudder at the
thought of his language. First, though Cæsar had made
public that before his departure he would give orders that
Dolabella should be consul—and yet they say he was not
a despot, when he was always doing and saying something
of this sort!—however, though Cæsar had actually said so
much, then this admirable augur said that he had been intrusted with those religious powers that he might at will
interrupt or annul the election by use of the auspices, and
he vowed that he would actually do so. And in this performance I ask you to observe first the amazing fatuity of
the man. What do you say? This act, which you said was
in your power by virtue of your priestly functions, would
you have been unable to do it if you had been consul instead of being augur? Surely you would have had even less
difficulty. We augurs have only the power of reporting on
the auspices when consulted; the consuls and the other
higher magistrates have the right of observing them for
themselves. Very well; let us suppose it was your ignorance
of the rules: one cannot demand the jurisprudence of the
auspices from a man who is never sober. But mark his impudence. Many months before the event, he said in the sen-

ate that he would either stop Dolabella's election by means of the auspices, or would do what he actually did. Now is it possible for any man to guess beforehand what defect there is going to be in the auspices, unless he has made up his mind to watch the heavens for something inauspicious? But it is illegal to do this at an election; and further, any one who has observed the heavens, is bound to report the result, not when the election is being held, but before it begins. But his ignorance and impudence are inextricably interwoven: he does not know what an augur should know, nor does he do what a decent man should do. And so recall to yourselves the character of his consulship from that day up to the Ides (15th) of March. Was ever any footman so humble, so grovelling? He could do nothing by himself; he asked for everything; he used to poke his head in at the back of the litter and ask his colleague for places which he might retail. 33. The day for Dolabella's election arrives. The lots are drawn for the first place in voting: he makes no sign. The result is reported: he holds his tongue. The first class is called and its vote reported; next, in the usual course, the knights give their votes; then the second class is called: and all this took less time than I have taken in describing it. When the whole business was completed, this admirable augur—a second C. Lælius, you might call him— said curtly that the election was 'postponed.' What extraordinary insolence! What had you seen, or felt, or heard? You did not then and do not now assert that you had really observed the heavens. The impediment was therefore that defect in the auspices, the occurrence of which you had foreseen on the first of January, and announced so long before the time. Thus then, I protest, to your own grievous injury, as I hope, rather than to the injury of Rome, you falsified the auspices; you hampered the action of the Roman people by a religious difficulty; you, as augur, reported so as to impede a brother augur, and a consul so as to thwart the other consul. I will say no more, that I may not be thought to be cavilling at Dolabella's acts as consul, which must some day be referred to our board. But mark, my lords, the presumption and arrogance of the man. So long as you choose, Dolabella's consulship is invalid: on the contrary, when you so please, Dolabella's election was no violation of the auspices. If it is immaterial when an augur reports in the terms in which you reported on that occasion, you must admit that, when you declared the election 'postponed,' you were drunk: but if there is any meaning in those terms, I demand as one augur of another to know what that meaning is.

But for fear my speech should pass without comment over the most brilliant of his many exploits, let us now turn to the Feast of the Luperci. 34. He cannot conceal his alarm, my lords; he is visibly agitated; he perspires, he grows pale. Well, let him do anything but be sick in public, as he was in the Portico of Minucius. But what defence can he make for an act so disgraceful? I am anxious to hear his reply, that I may see if it bears any trace of the huge fee his rhetoric-master received, that is, of the grant in the Leontine Plain. Your colleague was seated on the rostra, draped in a purple toga, sitting in a chair of gold, wearing a wreath of laurel. You ascend the rostra, you approach his chair, and—I know you were one of the Luperci, but you ought not to have forgotten that you were the consul—you exhibit a royal crown. A loud groan ran through the forum. Where had you got the crown? You had not picked it up in the street; no, you had brought it with you from your own house; the crime was premeditated and planned. You tried to place the crown on his head and amid uproar from the people; he continued to reject it amid applause. You then, you accursed villain, were the only man in existence, who having paved the way for a despotism, were anxious to have as your master the man who was your own colleague: you were the only man base enough to try experiments on the patience and endurance of the Roman people. But you even tried to appeal to his compassion; you threw yourself humbly at his feet. What was your petition? to become his slave? that boon should have been sought for yourself alone, who from early boyhood had lived as one ready to submit to anything, ready to become a slave: from us and from the Roman people you certainly had no such commission. How high-flown was your eloquence, when you addressed the people without your clothes! Could anything be more disgraceful or indecent? more deserving of any kind of punishment? Are you waiting till we goad your dull senses into action? No, if you have any vestige of feeling, these words of mine must surely torture you and cut you to the heart. I do not wish to impair the renown of our illustrious liberators; but my anguish compels me to say this. Is it not most monstrous that the man who proffered the crown should survive, when all allow that the man who spurned it has been rightly put to death? He even gave orders that a note should be made in the Calendar against the Lupercalia, to the effect that C. Cæsar, perpetual dictator, had been offered despotic power by M. Antonius, consul, at the command of the people, and that Cæsar had refused to accept it. I am not astonished now that you are disquieted by peace and order; that you hate not only the sight of Rome but the light of day; that you live with your robber-band not only extravagantly but even without thought for the morrow. It is only natural: where will you be in time of peace? How will you stand with regard to the laws or the regular courts of Rome, all of which you, as far as you could, superseded by a despotism under the style of monarchy? Was it for this that L. Tarquinius was expelled, Sp. Cassius, Sp. Mælius, and M. Manlius slain, that many centuries afterwards M. Antonius should perpetrate the unhallowed act of establishing a king of Rome?

35. But let us return to the auspices, the question on which Cæsar was intending to raise a discussion in the senate on the Ides of March. Let me put this point to you: what line would you have taken on that occasion? I was informed that you had come down carefully prepared, because you thought that I was likely to say something about the auspices, which you had falsified, but which had of course to be obeyed. The fortune of Rome prevented that debate from taking place. Has the death of Cæsar also prevented you from forming an opinion as to those auspices? But the incident which I have mentioned must take precedence of the matters which I had begun to discuss. How fast you ran, how alarmed you were on that glorious day! How soon your guilty conscience made you despair of your life! Yet after your first flight you were allowed, by the mercy of those who did not wish you to be harmed if you behaved sensibly, to retire secretly to your house. Alas! my forecasts of the future have ever been true, yes, too true, in vain! I assured our great liberators in the Capitol, when they desired me to go to you and urge you to join in the defence of Rome, that, as long as you were frightened, you would promise anything; as soon as you ceased to be afraid, you would be your old self again. So when the rest of the ex-consuls were going to and fro, my opinion remained unaltered. I did not see you either that day or the next, nor did I believe that there were any terms on which a secure compact could be made by honest citizens with a most cruel foe. Two days later I came to the Temple of Earth, unwillingly enough, since every approach was occupied by armed men. Was not that a great day for you, Antonius? Although you have suddenly broken out into open hostility

against me, still I am sorry for you for having been so much your own enemy!

36. Great heavens! what a man, what a great man you would have been, if you could have preserved the attitude of that day! We should still be enjoying the peace which was secured by your giving as a hostage that young aristocrat, M. Bambalio's grandson. But though on that day fear, never for long the motor force of duty, made you act rightly, yet your audacity, which never leaves you when fear is absent, soon made you wicked again. Though even then, when in spite of my opposition they all held you to be quite honest, you presided in the most criminal manner at the tyrant's funeral, if funeral it can be called. You are responsible for the delivery of that fine panegyric, for that pathetic, that inflammatory address. You, you I say, kindled those flames, the flames of the fire which half-charred his corpse, and the flames which utterly consumed the house of L. Bellienus. You sent those desperate ruffians, mostly slaves, whom we only routed by hand-to-hand fighting, to attack our houses. But you very soon washed off the grime and smoke, and passed the remaining days in the Capitol making those glorious decrees of the senate, that no lists of indemnities or of special privileges for individuals should be posted after the Ides of March. You remember what you said about the exiles, you know what you said about an indemnity for them. But the finest decree of all was the one in which you abolished for ever the title of dictator; and by making this you showed that you felt such hatred for despotism, that you abolished every possible name for it on account of your fear of the last dictator. Others thought that constitutional government was restored, but I did not, since with you at the helm I feared every sort of disaster. Was I wrong? Could he have maintained his disguise any longer? You saw for yourselves lists posted in every part of the Capitol, and immuni-

ties of various kinds were for sale not only to individuals but to whole communities; the franchise was granted not to individuals by name but to entire provinces. So if these grants remain valid, as they cannot if Rome is to continue to exist, you have lost, my lords, whole provinces; and not merely the revenues, but the whole sovereignty of the Roman people has been frittered away over the counter at Antonius's house. 37. Where are the seven hundred millions of sesterces, the sum total in the accounts which are kept at the Temple of Plenty? His was a blood-stained hoard, but still, if it was not to be given to those to whom it really belonged, it might save us from the property-tax. And the forty millions of sesterces which you owed on the Ides of March, how was it you had ceased to owe them on the first of April? The purchases which were being made from your gang, not without your knowledge, were countless; but there was one really remarkable decree, that affecting King Deiotarus, a firm friend of Rome, posted up in the Capitol. And when that decree was published no one could refrain from laughter even in his indignation. Who ever hated another man more than Cæsar hated Deiotarus? He hated him as much as he hated the senate, the knights, the people of Massilia, as he hated all whom he knew to retain any affection for the Roman constitution. So although King Deiotarus never secured any equity either in person or by his ambassadors from Cæsar while he lived, he has become a favourite with him since his death. When Cæsar visited him, he had sent for his host, he had named a sum, he had obtained the money, he had established one of his Greek retinue in Deiotarus's tetrarchate, he had deprived him of Armenia, which had been given him by the senate. All that he took from him while he lived, his dead hand has restored. But what were his expressions? One moment he said it seemed to him 'fair,' another 'not unfair.' What a wonderful collocation of terms! Cæsar himself—I always appeared to plead before him for the absent Deiotarus—Cæsar never said that any of our demands for him 'seemed to him fair.' A bond for ten millions of sesterces was agreed to by his envoys, men honest but timid and inexperienced, without my advice or that of the king's other friends in Rome, in Antonius's wife's rooms, a place where many things have been and are being sold. But I advise you to consider what action you will take on this bond; for Deiotarus of his own motion and without the help of any of Cæsar's papers, as soon as he heard of Cæsar's death, recovered his own proper possessions with his own sword. He was a sensible man, and knew that it has always been legitimate that things seized by tyrants should be recovered by their proper owners, after the tyrants are killed. So no lawyer, not even the man who is a lawyer in your eyes only and who is acting for you in this affair, will say that anything is due to you on that bond for what was recovered by him before the bond was given. Deiotarus did not buy from you; he was actually in possession, before you could sell him his own property. He was a man: we are contemptible creatures, hating that man and upholding the acts for which he was responsible.

38. But why need I speak of those interminable notes, of his assortment of autograph papers? There is a retail trade in them now, and men hawk them about openly like the programmes of the gladiatorial shows. And thus such heaps of money are being accumulated in Antonius's house, that the amounts are now estimated by weight and not by tale. But how blind cupidity is! A notice was recently posted to the effect that the richest communities in Crete are exempted from the tribute, and it is provided that after the governorship of M. Brutus Crete is to cease to be a province. Are you really sane? Ought you to be at large? Could it have been a decree of Cæsar's which makes Crete auton-

omous 'after the expiration of M. Brutus's term of office,' when Crete had no connexion with Brutus before Cæsar's death? But by the sale of this decree—don't think it has been wholly ineffective, my lords—you have lost the province of Crete. There has never been any one wanting to purchase anything who has not found Antonius willing to sell it. The bill relating to the exiles too, which you posted, did Cæsar move that? I do not wish to persecute any ruined man: I am only complaining, in the first place of the slur cast on the recall of those whose cases Cæsar decided to distinguish; in the second place I know not why you do not bestow the same boon on the rest of the exiles. As it is, there are not more than three or four persons left; they are in the same evil plight, and why do they not equally enjoy your clemency? Why do you treat them like your uncle? You declined to move for his recall, when you moved for that of the rest: you afterwards induced him to stand for the censorship, and you promoted his candidature in a way which left men both amused and indignant. But why did you not hold the election? was it because a tribune of the plebs reported an ominous flash of lightning on the left? When your own interests are involved, the auspices do not count: when it is only your relations who suffer, you become very scrupulous. Did you not throw over your uncle in the matter of the Commission of Seven? Some one turned up, whom I suppose you could not refuse without personal risk. In short, you have loaded him with every kind of insult, though you ought to have treated him as a second father, if you had any natural affection. You have divorced his daughter, your first cousin, having procured and previously arranged another alliance. Nor is that enough: you have brought a foul charge against a most virtuous woman. Is there any aggravation that can be added? Yes, you have not been content with this. In a very full house on the first of January, your

uncle being present, you dared to assert that your reason for hating Dolabella was that you had ascertained
him to have had criminal connexion with your cousin and
wife. Who can decide which was the most prominent feature
of his conduct, impudence in saying this in the senate, un-
scrupulousness in saying it against Dolabella, indecency in
saying it before his uncle, or cruelty in saying it against his
poor wife with such ribaldry and unfeelingness?

39. But let us revert to the autograph papers. How did
you conduct your investigations? Cæsar's acts were ratified
by the senate to secure peace; but the senate ratified only
Cæsar's own acts, and not everything that was stated to be
Cæsar's act by Antonius. Whence have all these documents
of yours been launched upon us? Who guarantees them on
production? If they are false, why are they being accepted?
If they are genuine, why are they being sold? But the terms
of the decision were that you, the consuls, should proceed
to investigate Cæsar's acts on the first of June with a committee. What was the committee? whom did you ever summon to a meeting? What did you understand by the first of
June? was it that first of June on which you returned surrounded with a bodyguard from your inspection of the set-
tlements of the veterans?

What a magnificent progress you made in April and May,
I mean on that occasion when you tried to plant a settlement even at Capua! We know how you quitted Capua, or
rather how you all but could not quit Capua; now you are
again threatening that town. Would that you would try the
experiment again, that the 'all but' might be omitted this
time! But how renowned is that visit of inspection! Need
I describe your sumptuous dinners, your frantic intoxica-
tion? In all those proceedings you injured yourself; the injury you did us is different. When the Campanian Land
was being removed from the list of taxable lands, to supply

allotments for distribution to the soldiers, we still thought it a serious loss to the state; you went a step further, dividing it among the companions who shared your gluttony and gambling: I mean, my lords, the low actors and actresses who were settled on the Campanian Lands. If I say anything more about the Leontine Lands, it is because these tracts of arable land in the Campanian and Leontine districts were once reckoned very fertile and productive portions of the inheritance of the Roman people. Your doctor got three thousand acres; what would he have got, if he had cured you? Your rhetoric master two thousand; how many more, if he could have made you an able speaker? But let us return to your journey and to Italy. 40. You planted a settlement at Casilinum, where Cæsar had previously founded one. You consulted me by letter, about Capua it is true, but I should have given the same answer about Casilinum. You asked whether it was legally in your power to plant a new settlement in a place where there was one already. I said that no new settlement could legally be planted in an old settlement which had been founded with the proper ceremonies, without impairing its rights: to your letter I replied that new settlers might be added to the list of citizens. You however were so carried away by arrogance that you disregarded all the legal and ceremonial rights of the case and planted a new settlement at Casilinum, where one had been founded only a few years before; you went so far as to hoist the flag and mark out the site with the plough as usual. Yes, and with that ploughshare you almost grazed the gate of Capua, thus encroaching on the demesne of a flourishing settlement. Fresh from this high-handed disregard of religious regulations, you pounced on the estate at Casinum of the upright and pious M. Varro. What right, what excuse did you allege? 'The same,' you will say, 'which I had to the landed property of the heirs of

L. Rubrius and the heirs of L. Turselius, and to the rest of
my innumerable estates.' Well, if they were sold to you by
auction, let the confiscation and sale hold good, let the accounts be accepted; but let them be Cæsar's and not your
own compilations, let them be the accounts in which you
are debited with the purchase-money and not those by
which you wiped off the debt. But who says that Varro's
estate at Casinum was for sale? who saw the auction held
to sell it? who heard the auctioneer put it up? You say you
sent to Alexandria to buy it from Cæsar. Of course it was
too much trouble to wait for his presence! But I say who
ever heard—and yet no one ever had more persons interested in his fortunes—that Varro's property had been affected in any way? If on the contrary Cæsar really wrote to
you to restore his estates, how can we adequately describe
your impudence? Withdraw for a short time the swords we
see around us. You will soon learn that Cæsar's confiscations
are one thing, and your audacity and presumption quite
another matter: not only the lawful owner, but any acquaintance, neighbour, family-friend, or agent of his will
soon eject you from that house.

41. Ah! how many days you indulged in disgraceful rev-
elry and riot in Varro's house! from an early hour of the
morning you and your friends were drinking, dicing, and
being sick. I grieve for those unhappy halls, 'passed to a
lord how strange!' Though how can Antonius be called
their lord? still by how strange a tenant were they inhabited! Varro intended that house to be a place for his own
studies, not a public haunt of passions. Ah! remember the
words and thoughts, remember the literary pursuits for
which that house was once famed! The laws of Rome, the
records of past ages, every branch of learning and every
school of philosophy. But when you were the tenant—I
will not say the owner—every part of the house echoed

with drunken yells, the floors were swimming and the walls dripping with wine; boys of noble birth were mixed up with men of infamous life, and common prostitutes with noble dames. People came to visit him from Casinum, Aquinum, and Interamna; no one was let in; and a good thing too, since by this disgusting man the insignia of his high office were being dragged through the dirt. When on his way from Casinum to Rome he approached Aquinum, a large crowd—the borough being a populous one—came out to meet him. But the boor was carried through the town in a closed litter, like a corpse. It was a foolish act on the part of the Aquinates: still their town was on his route. What did Anagnia do? Though the town lay off the main road, still the inhabitants came down to pay him respect exactly as if he were consul. It is an incredible story; but it was only too notorious at the time that no notice was taken of the attention, although Antonius had with him two natives of Anagnia, Mustela and Laco, one of whom has charge of his armoury and the other of his plate-chest. Need I repeat to you the threats and insults with which he abused the natives of Sidicinum and persecuted those of Puteoli, because they had put themselves under the patronage of C. Cassius and the two Bruti? They had done this with great enthusiasm, judiciousness, kindness, and affection; they had not chosen them under compulsion and force of arms as you and Basilus were chosen and others like you, men whom no one would care to have as clients, still less to be clients to them.

42. Meanwhile in your absence, what a glorious day that was for your colleague, when he threw down the monument in the forum to which you used to pay reverence! When you heard the news, you fainted, as was agreed by all who were with you. What happened afterwards I know not—I suppose the fear of your soldiers was sufficient; it is certain you brought your colleague down from his pinnacle

and made him—well, not even now like you, but at least quite unlike his former self. But think of your return thence to Rome! think of the panic which pervaded the city! We remembered the usurpation of Cinna, the subsequent tyranny of Sulla, we had just witnessed the despotism of Cæsar. Cæsar perhaps had swords at his command, but they were concealed and at any rate not very numerous; but your despotism, how un-Roman it all is! Your armed mercenaries follow you in close order; we see litters full of shields borne along. And it is no new thing, my lords; we have become hardened by the frequent recurrence of the spectacle. On the first of June when we wished to attend the senate according to arrangement, we were forced to disperse suddenly in great alarm. But Antonius, having no need for a senate, did not regret any one's absence, but was delighted at our withdrawal and at once carried out his astounding schemes. Though he had maintained the genuineness of Cæsar's manuscript notes for his own personal profit, he annulled Cæsar's published laws, and good laws too, in order to damage his country. He extended the term of years for provincial governments: and simultaneously, though he ought to have been a firm supporter of Cæsar's acts, he rescinded Cæsar's acts both in public and in private matters. In public affairs there is nothing more secure than a law: in private matters the most binding thing is a will. Some of Cæsar's laws Antonius swept away without even publishing the text of his own measures; others he abolished by means of such publication. Cæsar's will he invalidated, though the validity of wills has always been maintained for even the humblest citizens. The statues and pictures which Cæsar left to the public with his pleasure-grounds, he conveyed away partly to Pompeius's gardens and partly to Scipio's country-house.

43. And you are the man who cherishes Cæsar's memory!

You love your dead master! Had he obtained any honour greater than the assignment of a sacred couch, an image, a gable on his house, and a priest? Has the deified Julius then a priest, as Jupiter, Mars, and Quirinus have theirs, in the person of M. Antonius? Then why are you delaying? Why do you not get yourself installed by an augur? Choose your day, look for some one to install you: we are colleagues as augurs; no one will refuse to act. Oh you execrable wretch! whether you are Cæsar's priest or the priest of any dead man? My next question is whether you are ignorant what day to-day is? Do you not know that yesterday was the fourth day of the Roman Games held in the Circus? Do you not know that you yourself proposed a bill to the popular assembly that there should be a fifth day added in honour of Cæsar? Why are we not in our purple robes? Why do we allow the honour conferred on Cæsar by your law to be un-observed? Or did you permit the public thanksgivings to be desecrated by the addition of the extra day, but refuse to abide such a desecration of the ceremonial banquet? Either ride rough-shod over the ordinary religious scruples in all points, or respect them in every particular. You ask me whether I approve of the grant of the sacred couch, the gable on his house, and the priest. Personally I disapprove of all. But you, who uphold Cæsar's acts, what excuse can you give for insisting on some of these honours and taking no interest in others? Your reason, perhaps, is in your wish to indicate that you estimate everything by your own ad-vantage and not by the honour accruing to him? But what is your reply to all this? I am anxious to get a specimen of your eloquence. I know your grandfather to have been a very able speaker, but your style in speaking is even more intelligible and open: your grandfather never addressed a meeting without his clothes: we have seen his grandson's honest breast bared to public view. But will you reply to this? or will you dare to open your mouth at all? Will you find any point in my long speech, on which you can trust yourself to answer me?

But let us dismiss the past. Take this single day, this single day, I say, which is now passing, this moment of time in which I speak, and find a defence for it, if you can. Why is the senate surrounded by a ring of armed men? Why do your henchmen listen with their hands on their swords? Why are the great doors of the Temple of Concord not open? Why have you brought down to the forum these bowmen from Ituræa, the most uncivilised country in the world? He says it is to protect his personal safety. Is it not better, then, to die a thousand deaths, than not to be able to remain alive in one's own country without the protection of armed men? There is no protection there, believe me: you ought to be entrenched in the affection and good-will of your fellow-citizens, not behind your armèd men. The Roman people will wrest and wring your weapons from you; and may we survive to see it! but however you deal with us, you cannot, believe me, while you retain your present designs, be long untouched. In fact your wife, though she is far from niggardly—the term is not disrespectful— has too long been in arrears with the third instalment of what she owes to the Roman people. Rome has those to whom she can intrust the helm; and in whatever part of the world they are, there will be found the complete defence of the state, or rather Rome herself, who has as yet only avenged her wrongs but has not regained her strength. Rome has assuredly her young men of the highest rank prepared to defend her: let them retire as studiously as they like in the interests of peace, they will be recalled by the voice of their country. The name of peace is dear, and the work of peace is truly beneficial; but there is a vast difference between peace and slavery. Peace is the tranquil enjoyment of freedom; slavery is the last and worst of evils, and must be resisted by war, resisted even by death. And even if our great liberators have withdrawn themselves from our gaze, they have left us the example of their great achievement. They did what no one had done before them. Brutus declared war on Tarquinius, who was king at a time when a king might exist at Rome. Sp. Cassius, Sp. Mælius, M. Manlius were killed on suspicion of aiming at regal power. Our friends have been the first to attack and slay not one who was aiming at but one who was in possession of a throne. The deed they did is in itself a glorious and super-human act, and it is moreover set before us for imitation; and the more so that they have won by that act a fame which towers even to heaven. And though the conscious-ness of having performed a most illustrious deed is its own best reward, still, I think, no mortal should despise the guer-don of immortal glory.

45. Recall therefore, M. Antonius, that memorable day on which you declared the dictatorship abolished; call up vividly to your eyes the joy of the senate and the people of Rome; contrast it with this awful trafficking of yourself and your friends: and then you will see what a gulf there is fixed between gain and glory. But no doubt, as some men are prevented by a diseased or torpid condition of the palate from enjoying the taste of food, so the vicious, the grasp-ing, and the criminal have no relish for true glory. Yet if glory cannot allure you to right courses, has fear no power to deter you from the foulest deeds? You do not dread the arm of the law. If you rely on your innocence, I praise you; but if on the violence at your command, will you never un-derstand what the man, who does not fear the law for such reasons as yours, must necessarily apprehend? But if you do not fear brave men and eminent citizens, because your person is secured against them by your armed followers,

your own friends, believe me, will not much longer bear with you. And what sort of existence is it for a man to fear his own friends day and night? Yet you cannot pretend that they are bound to you by greater obligations than those by which your master had secured certain of those who slew him, or that you are worthy in any respect to be compared with him. He possessed genius, method, memory, culture, a mind painstaking, thoughtful, and industrious; his wars, though ruinous to our constitution, were still imposing. For many years he had set his mind on regal power, and after much labour and many perils he had accomplished his design; by shows and public buildings, by bounties and banquets, he had conciliated the thoughtless masses; he had secured his adherents by substantial benefits, and his opponents by a show of clemency. In a word, he had at last brought a community of free men, partly terrorised and partly acquiescent, to tolerate a slavery grown familiar. 46. I can compare you with him in your appetite for despotism, but in no other respect are you in any way worthy to be compared. Still, among all the evils of which he left the indelible mark on our unhappy country, there is this much good, that the Roman people has learnt at last how much to trust this man or that, on whom to rely, of whom to beware. Have you not laid this to heart? Do you not comprehend that brave men require only to have learnt the lesson, how essentially noble, how deserving of gratitude, how sure of renown, is the act of tyrannicide? Or do you think that when men did not endure him, they will bear with you? There will soon, believe me, be competition for this task; and the moment to strike, if it is long in coming, will be anticipated!

Reflect, I pray you, and be wise in time; remember your ancestors and not your associates. Treat me as you will; but be reconciled to your country. However you will take your own course; I will state my position plainly. I defended my country when I was a young man; I will not desert her in my old age. I defied Catilina's swords; I shall never quail before yours. Nay, I would willingly bare my breast to them, if the freedom of this country could be secured at once by my death, that the anguish of Rome might at last effect the deliverance with which it has been so long in travail. Yes, if twenty years ago in this very temple I said that a man who had lived to be consul could not complain of an early death, how much more truly shall I say the same of a man who is advanced in years? To me, indeed, my lords, death is now actually desirable, since I have discharged all the duties that have been committed to me and all that I have undertaken. I have but two desires now, the one that my dying eyes may see the Roman people still in the enjoyment of freedom—no greater boon can be granted me by heaven; the other, that every man may receive that recompense, which his own conduct towards his country deserves.

AFTER *such invective there could be no reconciliation. Cicero's remaining Philippics (there are fourteen in all) were futile against the realistic energy of the opposition. Octavian, whom Cicero and the senatorial party had sought to use as a counterpoise to Antony, joined Antony (and Lepidus) in a triumvirate. When they drew up their proscription list of 2000 equestrians and 300 senators, Octavian yielded Cicero to Antony's vengeance. He was hunted down and beheaded on December 7, 43 B.C.*

# LETTERS

WHETHER for the political history of the period, or its intellectual texture, or its social structure, or for the character of Cicero himself, no better source can be imagined than the corpus of 900 personal letters, mostly Cicero's own, some addressed to him, which has come down to us. A selection made from any of these points of view would in itself constitute a substantive treatise on its subject. The extent and range of the correspondence makes selection difficult; the specimens here offered have been chosen to illustrate various aspects of the collection.

## To Atticus 1.1

THE letters to Atticus are the most numerous, comprising nearly a half of the whole collection. To read them is as tantalizing as to overhear one end of a telephone conversation, but we do know a good deal, both from the letters and from other sources, about Atticus. The friendship began when both were students, but whereas Cicero entered law and politics, Atticus avoided public life and removed to Athens, where he was unaffected by the dangerous political vicissitudes of the capital and devoted himself to a cultured life of Epicurean ease and to moneymaking. The present letter, except for a few unimportant ones belonging to the three preceding years, is the earliest we possess. It is almost en-

*tirely taken up with Cicero's prospects of election to the
consulship.*

*To Atticus* (AT ATHENS)
*Rome, July, 65 B.C.*

You are eager to know how my candidacy is coming on.
As far as I can make out, the situation is this: The only one
as yet to come out openly is Publius Galba. He gets an out-
right, old-fashioned *no*. Gossip has it that his premature
announcement has made capital for me. For most persons
in denying him declare themselves as my supporters; and
so my expectations are aroused somewhat as the rumor gets
around that my friends are in the majority. I shall probably start my canvass at the election for tribune, July seven-
teenth. My competitors who seem most certain of running
are Galba, Antonius, and Cornificius. At this news, no
doubt, you have either smiled or groaned. It will be enough
to make you tear your hair to hear that in some quarters
Cæsonius is regarded as likely to run. Aquilius will hardly
be a candidate, for he has issued a denial in which he pleads
as excuses ill health and his position in the courts. Catiline
is sure to compete unless in his coming trial for embezzle-
ment the jury shall decide that the sun does not shine at
midday. As for Aufidius and Palicanus, I fancy you will
hardly wait for me to write.

Of the candidates for this year's election, Cæsar (Mark
Antony's uncle) seems sure of winning. According to report, the race for the other seat will be between Thermus
and Silanus. They have so few friends and are so little
known that I imagine that Curius could be brought in as a
dark horse. No one, however, thinks so but me. It seems to
suit my interest best that Thermus should be elected, for
since he has gained some prominence as commissioner for
the repair of the Flaminian Way, there is none of the pres-

ent candidates who if left over till next year would be a more formidable rival. Such in brief is about the way I am able to size up the political situation thus far.

## To His Friends 5.12

EVEN *in antiquity, which made no cult of coy self-deprecia-tion, Cicero's self-esteem and appetite for applause were notorious. The following request for immortalization in a literary work is disarming in its frankness. The canon for imaginative writing (not chronicles or fiction) here set forth is that of the schools: a narrative must be essentially true, its elaborations must have verisimilitude, and the whole must be edifying.*

To Lucceius
Antium, June, 56 B.C.

A certain sense of shame has often halted me when I have been minded to take up with you face to face the topic which I now will set forth more boldly in your absence; for a letter does not blush. I burn with a longing incredible but yet not reprehensible, as I believe, to have my name honored and celebrated in your writings. Although you have often signified your intention of doing so, yet I would have you pardon my impatience; for although I always had the keenest expectations as to your work in hand, yet what I have already seen has so far surpassed my anticipations that I long to have my consulship written up by you as soon as possible. Not only am I seized with a hope of immortality in the praises of the ages to come, but I long while still alive to enjoy—if it so be—the authoritative expression of your judgment on my exploits, the proof of your kindly feeling toward me, or at least the charm of your native ability. I am, of course, not unaware how presuming I am not only in imposing on you the task of narrating my deeds—for you might make the excuse of being too busy—but also in demanding that you sound my praises. "What," some one might suggest, "if you should not deem my exploits worthy of commendation?" Still it becomes him who has over-stepped the bounds of modesty to be wholly and thoroughly brazen; hence I ask you again and again to embellish that episode more than your opinion might warrant and in the process to put aside the rules of historical composition and grant a little more to your love for me than the truth might allow.

If I should induce you to undertake this task, you will find in it, I feel sure, a topic worthy of your eloquence and your powers; for covering the period from the beginning of the conspiracy to my exile, there can be got together, no doubt, a fair body of material which will allow you to display your well-known knowledge of the civil commotions either in explaining the causes of civic troubles or in setting forth their remedies. All the while, you will find fault with what should be blamed and will approve of what stands the test of reason, and if you should think that you should be as frank as you usually are, you will put the brand of infamy on many for their treachery toward me.

Also in your task my career with its variety of vicissitudes will furnish a certain pleasure which with you as author will intensely interest the reader; for nothing is more likely to please than diversity of events and change of fortune. Although these were not to be desired as matters of experience, they will be pleasing as subjects for reading; for there is pleasure when one in safety recalls past sorrow; and those who have never had any trouble upon beholding the misery of others take some pleasure in pity itself.

Mere chronicles furnish a degree of interest as do the data of an almanac; but the varying fortunes of a prominent man produce wonder, apprehension, joy, annoyance, expectation, and fear. Moreover, if the whole be summed up in a notable conclusion, the mind takes the greatest delight in the reading.

I do not fear that I may seem to be a flatterer in fishing, as it were, for your favor when I show myself as being very eager to be praised by you; you are not the one to be ignorant of your own worth nor, on the other hand, am I so foolish as to be willing to risk my reputation to one who would not himself gain honor in praising me. Therefore it will redound to my joy of soul and to the magnifying of my memory if you of all writers will put me into your pages; because I shall have the advantage not only of your intellect, just as Themistocles had of Herodotus', but also of the authoritative judgment of a gentleman most eminent in society, well versed in politics, and thoroughly approved of among his fellows; so that I shall seem to have had the advantage not merely of a trumpeter, as Alexander said was the case of Homer and Achilles, but also of the unimpeachable testimony of a great and famous man. I approve, to be sure, of the sentiment of Hector in a play of Nævius' when he said that he rejoiced not so much at being praised as at being praised by a praiseworthy man.

If I should fail to obtain this request of mine, I shall be compelled to do that which is often criticized—namely, write about myself. Although I have, to be sure, the example of many famous men as a warrant for my undertaking, yet the objections to an autobiography cannot escape you. One must write more modestly about one's self if there is anything to be praised, and one must pass by whatever is to be criticized. Furthermore, there is less of authority and credence in autobiographies. This awkwardness of situation we desire to avoid, and if you will take up our case, we shall be successful; hence I make this appeal to you.

If you wonder why I urge my request so at length although you have repeatedly assured me of your intention of writing a full and complete history of the critical events of my career, know you that I am fired, as I said in the beginning, with a feeling of impatience that, while I am still alive, I may be known to others through your books and that I myself may have a little pleasure in my own glory. Please let me know, if you are not too busy, what you will do about this matter. If you will undertake the case, I will furnish you with a compilation of my notes. If you put me off to another time, I shall talk with you face to face. In the meantime you will put the finishing touches on your present task and will keep on loving me.

## To His Friends 5.2

Upon laying down his consulship Cicero was prevented from making the customary farewell address by the tribune Quintus Metellus Nepos (an agent of Pompey), who interposed his veto on the ground that Cicero had put Roman citizens to death without trial. Cicero retorted in an oration, which evoked a remonstrance from Nepos' brother Celer, then proconsul in Gaul. The following letter is a reply to this remonstrance.

To Quintus Metellus Celer (in Gaul)
Rome, January or February, 62 B.C.

You write that in consideration of our mutual affection you had never expected to be made fun of by me. What the import of this remark may be I cannot well make out, but

I surmise that a report has reached you of what I said in the senate when I was maintaining that there were a great many who took it ill because it was I that had saved the state. In the course of my remarks I said that in deference to your brother you kept quiet and did not carry out your intention of speaking in my praise before the senate. During my speech when I set forth how eagerly I had been looking for your laudation and how I had been deceived, my hearers saw the joke and raised a bit of laugh—not at you but at my mistake and at the naïve and frank way I confessed my eagerness to be praised by you. Surely on the occasion of my glorious triumph I could do you no disrespect by expressing a wish to have a word of testimony from you.

As to your phrase "in consideration of our mutual affection," I am at a loss to know what you mean by "mutual." I myself view it as a giving and receiving of like good will. If I should say that it was for your sake that I forwent having a province, no doubt you would call my excuse piffle, for my plan of life excluded foreign service. But I do say this, that as soon as I had publicly announced my intention of not taking a province, I straightway began to plan how I might turn it over to you. I say nothing about the allotting of the province. I would merely have you suspect that my colleague did nothing in that matter without my cognizance. You remember the rest: how immediately upon the finishing of the allotment I called a session of the Senate, how in your behalf I delivered a speech which you yourself characterized as being not only commendatory of yourself but also as derogatory of your rivals. Furthermore, the very preamble to the decree which made the appointment, as long as it is extant, will testify to my services in your behalf. When you have compared all these acts of mine, you may judge whether your recent demonstration of force near the city is an example of being "mutually minded one toward the other."

As to your writing that I ought not to have attacked your brother because of a phrase he had uttered, when I found that he was making it the chief endeavor of his tribuneship to bring about my downfall, I pleaded with your wife Claudia (the famous Clodia) and your sister Mucia (Pompey's wife) to dissuade him from his design. But as you know full well, on the last day of the year he treated me, the consul, savior of my country, as no one has ever treated the most disloyal citizen, holder of a most trivial magistracy; he refused to let me address the people as I laid down my office. His insult, however, brought me great honor; for when he allowed me to do nothing except to take the oath, in a loud voice I swore a most true and beautiful oath; the people with a great shout answered that I had sworn truly. Though I had been insulted so signally, yet on that very day I sent common friends to beg him to desist from his purpose. He replied that he was no longer free to act, calling attention to his recent address in which he had said that he who had put others to death unheard should himself be denied a hearing. Accordingly I resisted him to his face.

Notwithstanding all this, mark you my gentleness of nature. In whatever measures were taken against your brother I cast no vote against him. I even add this, that owing to his being your brother I did my best to help him.

Hence, you see, I did not attack your brother; I merely withstood him and so far was I from showing myself fickle toward you as you write, that, though abandoned by you, I persisted in my affection for you. At this time also when you write what is practically a letter of threat, I make you this reply: I not only forgive you for your spirit of vexation but I also give it high praise; for my own feelings advise me how great is the power of brotherly love. I beg you, however, to make yourself an impartial judge of my own distress. If I have been attacked by a member of your family bitterly, monstrously, and unreasonably, you will conclude not only that I should not yield to you but that I should even have your help and that of your army in a cause of such a kind. I have always wished you to be my friend; I have striven to have you feel that I was a friend of yours. I abide by this wish of mine, and I shall do so just as long as you will allow, and out of my love for you I shall be more quick to cease hating your brother, than out of hatred for him to diminish aught of my affection for you.

## To His Friends 5.7

BY THE *end of 63 Pompey had completed his subjugation of the East and announced his successes to the senate. The senate's rebuff to his reasonable political expectations was to turn him to the coalition with Caesar and Crassus, and perhaps the incipient strain made him cooler to Cicero's own achievements of 63 than Cicero expected. Cicero's disappointment is expressed in the following letter.*

*To Pompey* (IN ASIA)
*Rome, June, 62 B.C.*

From your official dispatches all of us have taken keen delight; for you have given such promise of peace as, relying on my trust in you, I have always been wont to prophesy.

Your letter to me, although it gave scant indication of your regard for me, afforded me pleasure; for I am in the habit of rejoicing in nothing so much as in the consciousness of having served my friends. If I do not meet with reciprocity in this matter, I readily acquiesce in having the balance in my favor. I do not doubt that if my support of your interests has failed fully to bring about a union between us, at least the interests of the state will do so.

That you may not be ignorant of what I failed to find in your letter, I'll be frank in what I say, just as my nature and our relationship demand. Our friendship and the public weal had led me to expect in your letter some recognition of what I had done in my consulship. This was passed over by you, I fancy, because you feared to hurt somebody's feelings. But be assured that what I did for the public welfare meets the approval of the whole world. When you come, you will find out that I have acted with so much wisdom and spirit that though you are greater than Africanus and I a bit less, perhaps, than Lælius, you will readily admit of our being close political and personal friends.

## To Atticus 1.16

In December 62 *the patrician Clodius, dressed in woman's clothing, made his way into the solemn and exclusively feminine festival of the Good Goddess being celebrated at the house of Caesar. ("Caesar's wife must be above suspicion.") Clodius was tried, and acquitted over Cicero's opposition.*

To Atticus (in epirus)
Rome, July, 61 B.C.

You ask me what happened that the trial (Clodius') turned out so contrary to expectation and why I fought less vigorously than is my wont. I shall reply in Homeric fashion to the last question first.

As long as there was any need of championing the dignity of the Senate I contended so sharply and energetically that I gathered around me a great crowd and aroused mighty bursts of applause. If you ever felt that I displayed vigor in the cause of the state, you would have admired me then. When Clodius as a last resort began to harangue the rabble, and—great guns!—tried to bring discredit upon my name—what a bloody fight did I not put up! Ye gods! I missed you not only as an advisor in my counsels but also as a witness to my marvelous battles.

But after Hortensius thought out the scheme to let Fufius bring in a bill that differed not a whit from the consular bill except in the way in which the jury was to be chosen —the crucial point, however—and after he actually supported the new bill convinced, as he was, that no matter what the jury was, Clodius would be convicted, seeing the poverty of the panel I took in my sails, testifying to nothing but what was perfectly well known, (namely, that Cicero had seen Clodius within three hours of the time the latter had sworn he was eighty miles away).

To return to your first question, if you wish to learn the reason of the acquittal, know you that it was the poverty and the shamelessness of the jury. This was the fault of Hortensius who for fear of Fufius' interposing a veto to the consular bill, not seeing that it was better for Clodius not to be brought to trial at all rather than to risk a shaky and untrustworthy panel, allowed the tribune (Fufius) to bring in the indictment. Then when the challenging of the talesmen began, amid a mighty uproar, the prosecutor, like an upright censor threw out all of the most worthless names, and the defendant like a merciful buyer of slaves for the gladiatorial games, eliminated all the more respectable. As soon as the jury sat, the *Optimates* began to be dubious about the issue; for never did a worse crew assemble in a low-down music hall. There were censored senators, bank-rupt knights, treasury clerks—not so much tellers of sums but told for a sum. There were a few honest men whom Clodius couldn't get rid of by challenging. Sad of counte-nance, they grieved to sit in their strange surroundings, and were greatly distressed for fear of contamination.

At this point as the several matters came up in the pre-liminary proceedings, there was an austerity unbelievable, entire unanimity; the defendant obtained no favor; the prosecutor got more than he asked. Hortensius was greatly elated that he had been so prescient. There was not a soul but supposed that Clodius was as good as convicted a thou-sand times. When the claquers of Clodius began to hoot upon my coming forward as a witness, no doubt you have heard how the jury arose and rallied around me to expose their throats to P. Clodius for my life. The next day as large a crowd welcomed me as that which escorted me home the day I laid down my ensigns of office. The jury, most worthy protectors of the law, exclaimed they would not sit unless protected by a guard. The question was referred to the sen-ate. It passed a decree couched in most dignified terms. It praised the jury and turned the request over to the magis-trates. Nobody supposed Clodius would appear to stand trial.

"Tell me Muses, how first—" You know that bald-headed eulogist (Crassus) of my exploits, about whose fine words in my behalf I wrote you. In two days with the help of a miserable slave from the gladiatorial training school, he smashed the whole case. Some of the jurymen he summoned to himself personally, others he tampered with through emissaries, making promises and distributing bribes. And, O ye gods! some, too, accepted assignations with prominent women as an additional bribe. Accordingly, although the

*Optimates* absented themselves and the Forum was blocked with slaves, twenty-five jurymen were brave enough in the face of danger to risk their lives for the safety of their country; thirty-one with whom famine prevailed over fame. When Catulus saw one of the latter, he said: "Why did you ask a guard of us? Was it to safe-guard your money bags?" You have in as few words as possible an account of the trial and the reason for the acquittal.

Next you ask what is the political situation and my standing with reference to it. That fine state of politics which you consider due to me, but I to the gods—that state which the prestige of my consulship seemed to have founded and set on a coalition of all the better elements of society, unless some god takes pity on us, know you, has slipped from our hands by reason of this one verdict. Yet I as ever —I do not feel that I am boasting too much when I talk with you about myself, especially in a letter which I do not wish to be read by others—I, I say, revived the downcast spirits of the *Optimates*. By attacking the bribe-bought jurymen and nagging at them, I took all the edge off their elation and humbled Clodius himself. On the Ides of May when the Senate had assembled, the foppish youth (Clodius) arose and threw it up to me that I had been at Baiæ. A falsehood, but what of it? "It is," I replied, "as if you should say that I had been caught disguised as a woman." "How long," said he, "shall we endure the insolence of this *rex?*" "Do you talk about *rexes*," said I, "when your brother-in-law, Quintus Rex, did not mention you in his will?" Clodius had already spent what he had expected to get from Rex. "You have bought a house," he said. "From your tone one would suppose," answered I, "you were charging me with having purchased a jury." "They did not trust you on oath," sneered he. "Twenty-five," said I, "trusted my testimony;

thirty-one trusted you so little that they insisted upon having their money first." Overwhelmed by uproarious hooting he broke down and shut up.

## To His Friends 14.4

CLODIUS *never forgave Cicero, and to obtain vengeance had himself adopted into a plebeian family, so that he might become tribune and as such drive Cicero into exile. The humiliation reduced the mercurial Cicero to utter despair, as the following letter shows. A dozen years later he divorced Terentia, but his affection for Tullia continued the principal family tie of his life.*

To his family in Rome
Brundisium, 29 April, 58 B.C.

I write you less often than I might because when I am reading your letters or writing you, I am so completely overcome with tears that I cannot bear up. Would that I had not been so eager to live! I should have seen little or no sorrow in my life. If fortune has saved me in the hope that some day I may rehabilitate my estate, I made no mistake (in not committing suicide); but if my troubles are past mending, I long to see you and to die in your embrace, since neither the gods whom you have cherished so piously nor men whom I have served so continually have proved grateful.

I am setting out from Brundisium to-day. I am making for Cyzicus. O how wretched I am! How cast down! Why should I ask you to come to me, you a woman sick, weak of body and of mind? Shall I not ask you? Yes, I shall adopt the following policy: if there is any chance for my recall,

you by staying will help things along; but if, as I fear, everything is all over, see that you exhaust every means of coming
to me. Know this one thing; if I shall have you with me, I
shall not appear as being utterly undone. But what will
become of little Tullia? You will have to look out for her
prospects, for all judgment fails me. In every possible way
we must maintain the poor girl's standing with her husband
and in society. Again, what will my son do? I would have
him always in my embrace. I can write no more; grief pre-
vents. How you have fared I know not; whether you have
anything left or whether you have been entirely despoiled.

You urge me to be of good cheer and to hope for a recall.
I wish there were grounds for such optimism. Now alas,
when shall I receive any more of your letters? Who will
bring them? For the future, Terentia, bear up as best you
may; I have lived; I have had my day; I have been without
fault except that I did not put an end to my life when my
downfall came. Take the greatest possible care of your
health and be persuaded that I am more distressed over
your situation than I am over mine. My Terentia, my most
faithful and excellent wife, and my dearest little daughter,
and the stay of my life, my son, farewell.

## To His Friends 7.1

FROM *the period of Cicero's first political eclipse we have a
number of non-political letters dealing with the ordinary
topics of social intercourse. The following is an account of
the public games presented by Pompey in honor of his east-
ern victories, addressed to a friend who did not attend
but asked Cicero for a report.*

*To Marcus Marius* (AT CUMAE)
*Rome, Fall, 55 B.C.*

If it was ill health that kept you from the games, I congratulate you on your good fortune; but if it was your dislike for such diversions that detained you I rejoice doubly: that you are well and that you are sane enough in mind to scorn the silly admirations of the people. I say this, however, on the supposition that during the days of the games you were putting in your time profitably. You would withdraw, no doubt, to that den of yours, which looks out over the Bay of Naples, and in the seclusion of your charming retreat you would spend the morning hours in cursory reading; whereas we, who left you for the show were going to sleep over the performance; the rest of the day you were passing according to your fancy; whereas we had to put up with what could pass the Board of Censors.

In fact, the offerings were most elaborate but, to judge your taste by mine, not at all to your liking; for first, to do honor to the occasion those actors returned to the stage from which they had retired to do honor to themselves. Why, the voice of your particular favorite, Æsop, failed him in an especially impressive passage.

Why should I say more? Being familiar with such programs, you know what events came next. These did not have the charm even of ordinary shows, for the elaborateness of the spectacle took away all delight. I am sure you missed the display with perfect equanimity. How could one be pleased with six hundred mules in the *Clytemnestra*, or three thousand punch bowls in the *Trojan Horse*, or varied paraphernalia of cavalry and infantry in some battle scene! These spectacles won popular approval, but they would have pleased you not at all. If during the days of the games you had heard your slave Protogenes read anything whatsoever except my orations, you would have had more delight than any one of us.

As to the Greek and the Oscan shows, I am sure you did not miss them; for you can see the Oscans show off any day in your town council, and as for Greeks, you take to them so little that you will not take the Greek highway to your villa. Why should I suppose that you missed the athletic games when I know that you scorn gladiators? In these performances even Pompey acknowledges that he wasted his money and his pains. The final event consisted of hunting shows, two of them, continuing through five days, magnificent, to be sure; but what pleasure can a gentleman take in seeing a puny man torn to pieces by a monstrous beast or a beautiful animal pierced by a spear? The last was the day of the elephant-baiting, which brought the crowd much wonder, but little pleasure. Nay rather the beasts aroused some sense of pity as if there were some community of feeling between them and man (so that the crowd rose up and cursed Pompey).

I have written you a longer letter than usual out of an abundance, not of leisure, but of affection, because in a certain letter, if you but remember, you gave me a half-way invitation to write you something that would console you for having missed the games. If I have attained my object, I rejoice; if not, I comfort myself with the reflection that hereafter you will come to the show and visit me and not stake your hope of enjoyment on a letter from me.

## To His Friends 3.6

IN 51/50 B.C. Cicero was governor of Cilicia, much against his will. The following letter tells us something of Cicero's

*provincial administration, of his feeling of injured preroga-*
*tive, and of his courtesy to the brother of a man who had*
*injured him deeply.*

> To Appius Claudius (AT TARSUS)
> *Headquarters, 29 August, 51 B.C.*

When I compare my course with yours, although in
preserving our friendship I am less partial to you than to
myself, yet I am much more satisfied with myself than with
you.

(As you know from my letters, I took especial pains to
suit your convenience in my plans for taking over the province, even going so far as to change the course of my journey several times so as to be sure to meet you.) For this reason I am exceedingly well pleased with myself, for in no
other way could I have shown more affection.

Consider now in turn how you have acted. You not only
did not do me the courtesy of meeting me upon my arrival
in the province, but you even removed yourself to a place
where I could not be expected to reach you within the thirty
days allowed you by law for leaving the province. In fact,
to those who are ignorant of how good friends we are, you
appear to be acting like a stranger—to put a most favorable
construction upon your action; but I, like a most intimate
and loving friend. Meanwhile malevolent men—the world
is full of such creatures—basing their gossip on plausible
grounds, ignorant of my steadfast nature, tried to turn me
against you. They said that you were holding court at Tar-
sus, settling matters, making decisions, passing judgments
—though you had good reason to suppose that your successor was on the ground. You exercised, they said, all these
functions although the usual practice is for governors to
intermit them when about to be superseded.

By such talk I was not at all disturbed. Nay even—I

would have you believe me—whatsoever of my duties you performed, by just that much I felt I was relieved and I rejoiced that my twelve months' term, which seemed long, was already reduced almost to eleven if in my absence the work of one month was subtracted.

But there is one thing that does disturb me: out of my two legions, which are very much depleted, the three best manned cohorts are gone and where they are I know not. Consequently, I am sending to you Decimus Antonius to take over the troops, if it is agreeable to you, that, while the season permits, I may do some campaigning. In this business our friendship and your letter had led me to hope that I might have the benefit of your advice. Not even yet am I utterly discouraged; but frankly, if you don't write, I haven't the least idea when or where I shall see you.

I shall take great pains to let friend and foe know that I am entirely your friend. You have given our enemies some occasion for drawing an opposite conclusion in regard to your attitude; if you will correct this impression, you will do me a great favor. That you may know where you may meet me—thereby observing the provisions of the law— here is my itinerary: I entered the province on the last day of July; I am passing through Cappadocia into Cilicia; I am moving camp from Iconium on the last day of August. Now that you have the data, if you think we should meet, you will appoint the place and day that suit you best.

## To Atticus 9.10

CAESAR's crossing of the Rubicon in January 49 was the first overt act in the civil war between him and Pompey. Pompey's coolness to him and the inefficiency of senatorial

*measures for resistance at first caused Cicero to waver. In the
following letter he expresses his determination, despite his
disappointments and misgivings, to join the cause he considered just.*

To Atticus ( AT ROME )
Formiae, 18 March, 49 B.C.

I seem to have been mad from the beginning, and I am
tormented because in every vicissitude I did not, like a common private, follow Pompey as he was slipping, or rather
rushing to destruction. January 17 I saw him in a panic. On
that day I felt what he would do. Never after that did
he please me, never cease making now one mistake, now
another. Meanwhile not a line to me, not a thought except
flight!

Why then should I go to him? As in the case of lovers
traits of inelegance, insipidity, and indecency alienate the
affections, so with me the unseemly spectacle of Pompey's
flight and sloth estranged my love; for nothing that he did
was such as to make me accompany him in his flight. Now
my love emerges; now I cannot bear the separation; now
my books, my literary pursuits, my learning avail me
nought. And so day and night, like the halcyon looking out
on the sea, I long to fly away.

## To Atticus 13.52

AFTER *his victory over Pompey Caesar permitted Cicero
to return to Rome, where he lived quietly, and delivered
speeches only on behalf of the restoration of banished
friends. Caesar even accepted Cicero's hospitality at a dinner party at Puteoli; the account of the party follows.*

*To Atticus* (AT ROME)
*Puteoli, 19 December, 45 B.C.*

What a fearsome guest! and yet I do not regret his visit, for it was very delightful. On the second day of the winter holidays he put up at the villa of Octavius' stepfather, Philippus. The company so packed the establishment that there was hardly a place left for Cæsar to dine in; two thousand men there were. You may be sure I was disturbed as to the morrow; but Barba Cassius came to my relief; he posted guards, made camp in the fields, and protected my villa.

Cæsar stayed with Philippus until noon of the next day; nobody was admitted to his presence; no doubt, he was going over his accounts with Balbus. Then (coming to Cicero's villa) he took a walk on the seashore; at one o'clock a bath. Then word was brought him concerning Mamurra; he did not move a muscle of his face. He next took a rub down in oil, after which he dined. Since he was undergoing a course of emetics, he ate and drank without fear and with pleasure. The dinner was well got up, and not only that but it was well cooked and well seasoned; the conversation was delightful; and, to take it all in all, everything went off agreeably.

Besides, in three rooms Cæsar's suite was entertained very bountifully. The ordinary attendants and the slaves had all they wanted; the more fashionable guests were served right elegantly. In fact, I showed off as a good provider.

As for my guest, he is not one to whom one would say: "Pray, my good fellow, on your way back stop off again with me." Once is enough. The talk avoided politics but fell much on literary topics. In short, he was in a charming and agreeable mood. He was to spend one day at Puteoli and another at Baiæ. There you have an account of his visit, or shall I say his billeting, which, though it brought me some trouble, as I have said, occasioned me little annoyance.

## To His Friends 6.15

CICERO *had no part in the conspiracy of the Ides of March of 44, but he applauded the deed, as the following shows.*

To Basilus
Rome, Ides of March, 44 B.C.

Congratulations for you! Felicitations for myself! My dear fellow, I am entirely at your service. I would have you love me and keep me informed of what you are doing and what is going on.

## To Atticus 16,1a

HOPES *for restoration of the republic recalled Cicero to political activity, but he was still concerned for and consulted about matters of style. Here is a criticism of a speech of Brutus*.

To Atticus (AT ROME)
Sinuessa, 18 May, 44 B.C.

Brutus has sent me his speech that he delivered before the assembly on the Capitol. He wants me to correct it frankly before he publishes it. He has composed it with all possible good taste in thought and expression. If, however, I had had such a case to handle, I should have displayed more fire. You note what the theme is and understand the character of the speaker; therefore I cannot do his bidding, for as regards the style of oratory that Brutus wishes to follow, in this oration he has attained his ideal to the utmost. I have set before myself another ideal; whether rightly or wrongly I know not.

I should like you to read the speech, unless you have already done so, and to let me know what you think of it. Possibly in submitting it to you I run some risk of your siding against me, for under the spell of your name you may be biased in favor of the Attic School, which Brutus affects. Still, if you will call to mind how Demosthenes could fulminate, you will understand how one can speak in the most powerful manner and yet be thoroughly Attic. But more on this subject when we meet.

## To His Friends 16.21

AT THIS *same period Cicero's son Marcus (for whom Cicero was writing* On Moral Duties) *was at the university of Athens and making bad use of his prodigal allowance. Pressure was brought to bear by various correspondents of Cicero in Athens, and the young man found it prudent to show signs of reform. The following entertaining letter is addressed not to Cicero himself but to his trusted secretary Tiro, who could be relied upon to carry the news.*

*Cicero Junior to Tiro*
*Athens, 44 B.C.*

I had been looking for a letter when one finally came, forty-six days out. Its arrival brought me the keenest joy; for in addition to the pleasure I got from the kind words of my father your most delightful letter filled my cup of joy to overflowing. Accordingly, I was not sorry that there had been a break in our correspondence, but rather was I glad; for I profit greatly by your writing after my long silence. Therefore I rejoice exceedingly that you have accepted my excuses.

I don't doubt, my dearest Tiro, that you are deeply gratified over the rumors that are reaching your ears, and I will guarantee and strive that with the passing days this nascent good report may be increased two-fold. You may, therefore, keep your promise of being a trumpeter of my good repute, for the errors of my youth have brought me such pain and sorrow that not only does my soul recoil at the acts themselves but my ear shrinks from the very mention of them. I know full well that you shared in the anixety and worry of this experience.

Since I then brought you sorrow, I'll warrant that now I will bring you joy in double measure. Let me tell you that I am associated with Cratippus not as a disciple but as a son, for not only do I listen to his lectures with pleasure but also I am greatly privileged to enjoy him in person. I am with him all day and very often a part of the night since by much pleading I often succeed in getting him to dine with me. Now that he has got used to this habit, he often drops in on me at dinner time and, laying aside the severe demeanor of a college professor, he jokes with me like a human. See to it, therefore, that you embrace the earliest opportunity of meeting the eminent gentleman, of finding out what he is like, and of becoming acquainted with his merry disposition.

What now shall I say of Professor Bruttius? I keep him with me all the time. He is a regular stoic in his habits of life but a jolly good fellow withal, for he is very much of a wit both in his lectures and in his discussions. I have hired lodgings for him next door, and, as best I may, out of my slender purse I relieve him in his slender circumstances.

Besides, I am studying public speaking in Greek with

Cassius. I am planning to do the same with Bruttius in Latin. On Cratippus' recommendation I am on very intimate terms with certain learned gentlemen whom he brought with him from Mytilene. I also spend a good deal of time with Epicrates, the chief Athenian, Dean Leonidas, and other men of that sort. So much for what I am doing. (Of course, I followed your suggestion as to getting rid of Gorgias, though to tell the truth he was a great help in my daily exercises.) Still I laid aside all considerations if only I might obey my father who had sent me unequivocal orders to dismiss him instanter.

I am deeply grateful to you for looking out for my commissions; please send me as soon as possible a secretary, by all means one who knows Greek; he will save me much labor in copying out my notes. Of all things, be sure to take care of yourself that we may be able to pursue our studies together. I commend you to Anterus (the postman).

## To Brutus 1.9

CICERO *had sought solace for the death of his beloved Tullia by writing the (lost) Consolation. Now Brutus had suffered a similar loss in the death of his Portia, and Cicero addresses a letter of consolation to him to his headquarters in Macedonia, where he was presently to fight the disastrous battle of Philippi which doomed republican hopes.*

To Brutus (IN MACEDONIA)
Rome, 8 June, 43 B.C.

I would do as you did in my grief (over the death of Tullia) and write you a letter of consolation (for the loss of Portia) if I did not know that in your case you had no need of those remedies with which you alleviated my sorrow; may you heal yourself now more easily than you did me then; it is not in keeping for a man of your character not to be able to carry out for himself the advice he has given to another. In my own grief not only the reasons you got together but also your authority restrained me from too extravagant sorrow; for, when you thought I was bearing my loss more effeminately than becomes a man, especially one who is wont to console others, you upbraided me more severely than was your custom.

Accordingly, holding your judgment in high esteem and reverence, I gathered myself together and by the addition of your authority gave all the more weight to what I had learned, read, and approved. In my case it was a matter merely of paying due regard to natural feelings; whereas in yours it is a case of what the public will say of the part, so to speak, that you must play; for, since the eyes not only of your army but also of every citizen and almost every nation have been cast on you, it is not at all becoming that he to whom the rest of us owe our courage should show weakness of character. You have suffered a loss, to be sure, for you have been bereaved of that which had no rival on earth and in such severe sorrow you should grieve; or else to be without any ability to feel sorrow will make you more miserable than the affliction itself. Still, as it is helpful for others, so it is useful for you to grieve in moderation. I should write further if, seeing that it is you whom I am addressing, I had not already said more than enough.

We are awaiting you and your army; otherwise we can hardly hope to secure our freedom even though all else turn out to our liking.